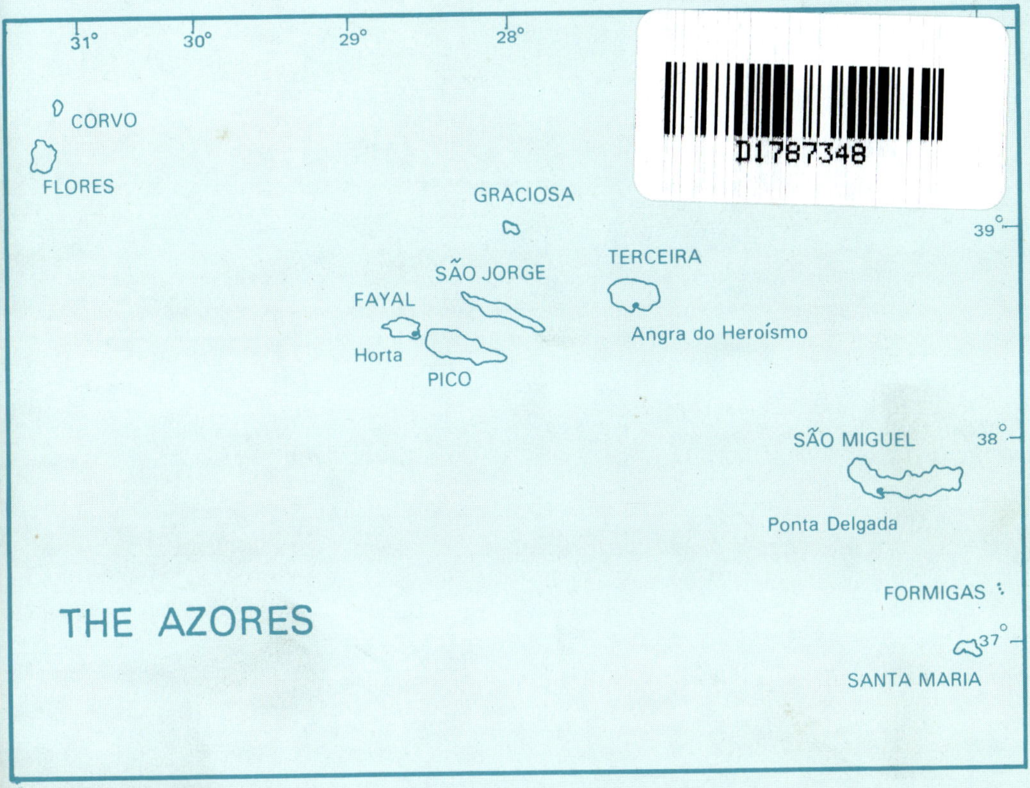
31°
30°
29°
28°
39°
38°
37°
CORVO
FLORES
GRACIOSA
TERCEIRA
SÃO JORGE
FAYAL
Horta
PICO
Angra do Heroísmo
SÃO MIGUEL
Ponta Delgada
FORMIGAS
SANTA MARIA
THE AZORES

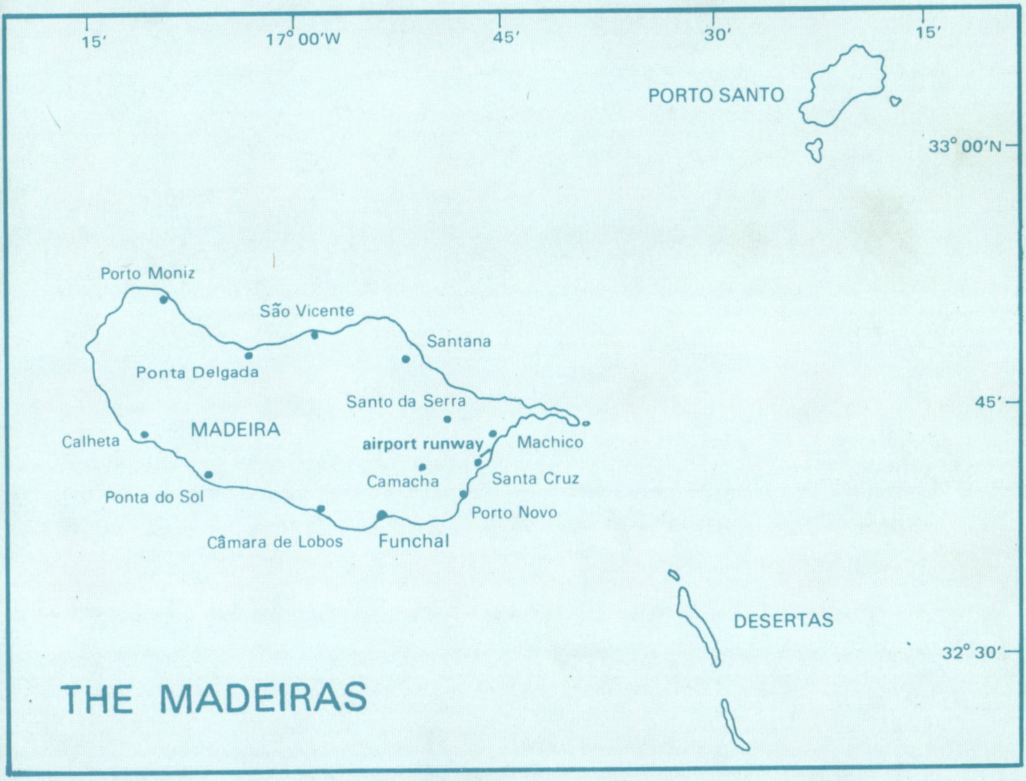
15′
17° 00′W
45′
30′
15′
PORTO SANTO
33° 00′N
Porto Moniz
São Vicente
Santana
Ponta Delgada
Santo da Serra
45′
MADEIRA
Calheta
airport runway
Machico
Camacha
Santa Cruz
Ponta do Sol
Porto Novo
Câmara de Lobos
Funchal
DESERTAS
32° 30′
THE MADEIRAS

ATLANTIC ISLANDERS OF THE AZORES AND MADEIRAS

Books by Francis M. Rogers

Higher Education in the United States
A Summary View

The Obedience of a King of Portugal

The Travels of the Infante Dom Pedro of Portugal

The University of San Marcos in Lima, Peru

The Quest for Eastern Christians
Travels and Rumor in the Age of Discovery

Europe Informed
An Exhibition of Early Books
Which Acquainted Europe With the East

Precision Astrolabe
Portuguese Navigators and Transoceanic Aviation

Americans of Portuguese Descent
A Lesson in Differentiation

The Portuguese Heritage of John Dos Passos

Atlantic Islanders of the Azores and Madeiras

U.S.S. *Dyer* anchored off Ponta Delgada, São Miguel. (The destroyer on which Franklin Delano Roosevelt went to Europe in 1918 as Assistant Secretary of the Navy. Painting by Charles Edwin Ruttan in the Franklin D. Roosevelt Library, Hyde Park, New York.)

ATLANTIC ISLANDERS OF THE AZORES AND MADEIRAS

By

FRANCIS M. ROGERS
Harvard University

> To the States or any one of them, or any city of the States,
> *Resist much, obey little*,
> Once unquestioning obedience, once fully enslaved,
> Once fully enslaved, no nation, state, city of this earth,
> ever afterward resumes its liberty.
> Walt Whitman

THE CHRISTOPHER PUBLISHING HOUSE
NORTH QUINCY, MASSACHUSETTS

COPYRIGHT © 1979
BY FRANCIS MILLET ROGERS
Library of Congress Catalog Card Number 78-72837
ISBN: 0–8158–0373–7
First Edition

The publication of this book was subsidized in part by the Solomon Lincoln Fund of the Department of Romance Languages and Literatures, Harvard University.

The Christopher Publishing House
North Quincy, Massachusetts
02171
PRINTED IN
THE UNITED STATES OF AMERICA

To my Wife

ELSIE

*Companion in the Azores and Madeiras
and also in Continental Portugal
and the Cape Verde Islands*

CONTENTS

Introduction: A Choice of Destinies 11

Part I

THE LIVES OF AZOREANS AND MADEIRANS

1. Peaks Out of the Ocean 23
2. Settlers Out of Continental Europe 39
3. Supervision From Distant Lisbon 57
4. The Bones of Peter and Michael 73
5. The New Politics 87
6. Sex and Class 105
7. Sailing Ships and Steamers 125
8. Boston Brahmins in the Azores 145
9. Dots, Dashes, and Submerged Wires 175
10. Flying Boats and Wheeled Planes 191
11. Voices From Deep Down and High Up 209
12. Farming in Sight of the Sea 231
13. Tourism and Transplantation by Sea and Air 257

Part II

THEIR VALUES

14. The "State" and the "Church" 279
15. Parish Church and *Festas* 295
16. Cousins and Godparents 309
17. Relatives in America 325
18. Atlantic Brand of Language 333
19. Schooling and Brain Drain 343

20.	Doctors and Midwives	365
21.	High Culture	391
22.	Folk Culture	405
	The Heritage of Islanders	419
	A Selection of Sources	427
	Index	449

ILLUSTRATIONS

Frontispiece

U.S.S. *Dyer* anchored off Ponta Delgada, São Miguel. (The destroyer on which Franklin Delano Roosevelt went to Europe in 1918 as Assistant Secretary of the Navy. Painting by Charles Edwin Ruttan in the Franklin D. Roosevelt Library, Hyde Park, New York.)

Photographs—by the author

Amphitheatrical setting of Funchal, Madeira	12
Western tip of Fayal in 1939	31
Western tip of Fayal in 1974	32
Earthquake damage, Velas, São Jorge, in 1964	34
Horta, Fayal—Joint Cable Station (left), Trinity House (right)	38
A *levada* above and behind Funchal	47
Hauling agar, Porto Judeu, Terceira, July 1977	49
South coast of Madeira from seaward ... top	66
Interior of Madeira—Curral das Freiras ... bottom	66
Milk distribution, north side of Pico, Spring 1964	83
Superposition of graffiti on a Funchal wall, June 1975	92
Vila do Porto, Santa Maria—Teófilo Braga Street	104
"Portugal used to be a man's world" — country scene on Fayal	109
Three social classes on a Funchal street in 1964	122
Lawn of Hotel de São Pedro, Ponta Delgada, São Miguel	124
Horta—transatlantic yachts and view of Pico	128
Hickling home near Rosto de Cão, São Miguel	144
Yankee Hall, Furnas, São Miguel	147
The Cedars, Horta home of John Pomeroy Dabney	174
Entrance to Horta's *liceu*, with Fredonia in background, 1974	182
Horta's hospitable Bagatelle	197

Angra do Heroísmo, Terceira—noon on Easter Saturday
    1972 202
Airport's single runway, Porto Santo, June 1978 208
Tourist-heavy Madeira—spectacular terrain and products 214
Straw hut (*palheiro*) on Madeira employed to house cows 236
Landing tuna at Santa Cruz, Madeira, June 1964 241
Loading cattle off Santa Cruz, Flores, June 1964 247
Procession of the Infirm, Furnas (first Sunday after Easter) 256
The large and splendid beach of Porto Santo, June 1978 259
Elongated São Jorge from the north side of Pico 265
Basking in the early-morning sunshine on Corvo 267
Traditional cultivation of Terceira's land, 1974 280
"No choice but to conform"—São Sebastião, Terceira, 1964 ... 304
Doing laundry in a running Madeiran brook, January 1973 317
Bride from Terceira arriving off Praia, Graciosa 318
Horta, Fayal, Azores—"European city closest to Boston" 326
Funchal's Industrial and Commercial School 349
An entrance for each sex, Vila do Porto, Santa Maria, 1970 352
Berquó Palace, Ponta Delgada 364
TAP regional flight with ambulance capability, Porto Santo 371
Michaelese Theater, Ponta Delgada 390
Gulbenkian Foundation bookmobile, north side of Terceira 393
Cultivation of grape vines on Madeiran hillside 395
Easter bread with hard-boiled eggs, Angra do Heroísmo,
    1972 415
Noon sight—12:54 GMT, June 9, 1964, course 045°: 35°
    18′ N 421

Maps—drawn by Patricia N. McCobb

Atlantic Ocean .... left endpapers
Azores .... top, right endpapers
Madeiras .... bottom, right endpapers
Selected Submarine Telegraph Cables 1929 176
Selected Transatlantic Flights 1919-1949 194
Atlantic Interairport Distances 205
Selected Submarine Telephone Cables 1977 213
Selected Communications Satellite and Earth Stations 1977 217

INTRODUCTION
A CHOICE OF DESTINIES

> Preferably to die as free men
> than to live in peace subjugated.
> *(A proposed motto for the new Azores)*

The country known as Portugal consists primarily of CONTINENTAL PORTUGAL in the southwestern portion of the Iberian Peninsula. The place-name also connotes INSULAR PORTUGAL, two flower-bedecked semitropical offshore archipelagoes strategically located in the North Atlantic Ocean.

The nine Azores islands lie due west of Portugal's capital city of Lisbon. The nearest, Santa Maria, is 758.0 nautical miles away by great-circle course and the farthest, Flores, is 1,026.7 nautical miles distant (a nautical mile being one and one-eighth statute miles).

The two inhabited islands of the Madeiran archipelago, the island of Madeira itself and the island of Porto Santo, are situated southwest of Lisbon and southeast of the Azores. Porto Santo is distant 483.5 n mi. from Lisbon and 488.4 from the Azorean Santa Maria. The two archipelagoes and the mainland territory thus form a Portuguese Atlantic triangle; France, the NATO nations, the Soviet Union, and the African countries are well aware of that fact.

To affirm, however, that the three corners of the triangle form a homogeneous and harmonious whole is to go beyond the evidence of the centuries. Although astride shipping and air lanes and used in days of old as submarine telegraph relay stations, the Azores and the Madeiras together with their inhabitants have survived in a state of isolation. Excepting the residents of the city of Funchal, amphitheatrically set on the southern slopes of Madeira, protected from the chills and rains brought by the northeast trade winds, Continental Portuguese hardly knew the islanders, to whom they referred as *ilhéus* "oceanic hicks." In fact, they really did not care about them. In 450 years of Portuguese monarchy, from roughly 1460, when Portuguese and a few foreigners first peopled the hitherto unknown and uninhabited islands, to 1910, when the monarchy fell and the Portuguese Republic was established, a royal couple sailed out from Lisbon purposely to visit them only once—in 1901.

Amphitheatrical setting of Funchal, Madeira

Azoreans and Madeirans have been dominated by Lisbon and exploited by Lisbon, dominated via a series of clumsy administrative arrangements and exploited by the simple devices of taxation and obligatory military service. Yet Azoreans and Madeirans have ever been loyal Portuguese, although they have also wanted a voice in running their own affairs. They have long aspired to autonomy, to forming two autonomous regions within Greater Portugal.

An alternative to autonomy is of course independence, a subject discussed even in the nineteenth century, at least in the Azores. But independence was hardly viable in those days when Britannia ruled the waves and no one ruled the skies. Independence inevitably meant seeking the protection of a great power, and that power could only have been the United States of America. Indeed, a very literate daughter of Charles William Dabney (1794-1871), U.S. consul in the Azores from 1826 to 1869, has written that her father "always predicted that the Sandwich Islands (as Hawaii was then called) would be annexed to the United States, and some day or other very probably the Azores, also."

That was in the nineteenth century, in the days of kings and queens. With the advent of the Republic, it looked briefly as if the situation would change. The first (provisional) President of the Republic and, following him, the first elected President were both Azoreans. But in 1926, a military coup toppled democracy and introduced an authoritarian right-wing regime which lasted until April 25, 1974. Lisbon dominated Azoreans and Madeirans to a greater extent than ever, sending Continentals to the islands to serve as bishops, civil governors, military governors, and port captains, and to serve in just about every other important capacity.

With independence and real autonomy (and naturally annexation by a friendly foreign power) ruled out in the nineteenth and most of the twentieth century, those of the Azorean and Madeiran masses who combined discontent with guts moved out. They emigrated.

Most Azoreans and many Madeirans emigrated to the United States, to Southeastern New England, California, and Hawaii. These Portuguese and others from the Continent and Cape Verde Islands continue to enter the United States. In the fifteen months ending September 30, 1976, of all European emigrant groups who departed home and entered the United States, the Portuguese constituted the second largest, almost as large as the group from the United Kingdom. More Portuguese entered than Greeks and than Italians, more even than Canadians. Of these Portuguese of 1975-1976, the most recent on whom I have statistics, the majority came from Insular Portugal, the "Adjacent Islands," as Lisbon terms them; and the overwhelming percentage of the islanders came from the Azores. Of the Portuguese entering the United States in that period, exactly twice as many entered Massachusetts as entered California or New Jersey. The states of Rhode Island, Connecticut, and New York followed in that order in welcoming Portuguese immigrants.

Emigration was a solution to a problem, and the moving and

melting of Azoreans and Madeirans and the pressures on them in America constitute another story. The islanders who remained behind, including the elitist upper class, pondered other solutions. In the early 1930's, some of them even attempted revolt—unsuccessfully. With the Revolution of April 25, 1974, new possibilities suddenly presented themselves.

Lisbon terminated its three colonial wars in Africa and witnessed the independence of virtually all its colonies, including the Cape Verde Islands. A series of provisional governments ruled unevenly and at times, from the point of view of the economist, chaotically. These governments tended to the left; one which dominated most of 1975 was definitely of the left. From the moment of the Revolution onward, leaders in Insular Portugal assumed a more conservative stance. Renewed demands for autonomy were made. Talk of "separatism," that is, independence, filled the air, especially in the Azores, most specifically on the Azorean island of São Miguel (St. Michael's) with one third the area and over half the population of the entire archipelago. That talk reached the ears of the Portuguese immigrants in the United States and their descendants, above all of the Overseas Azoreans who were being looked to for financial and other types of aid.

A new Azorean flag, of the "liberation" front, came to be displayed widely. It was conservatively blue and white in memory of the monarchical flag of old which gave way to the familiar green and red in 1910. In its center was a golden hawk, an *açor* in the Portuguese language, for the Açores are said to be the Islands of Hawks, although, to paraphrase a Russian wit's comment on conservative William F. Buckley, Jr.'s 1975 visit to the Azores, they are today rather dovish than hawkish. Beneath the bird a graceful curve of nine golden stars symbolize the nine inhabited islands of the archipelago.

The foreigner visiting Insular Portugal in the summer of 1977 encountered no difficulty in purchasing the Azorean flag. On Madeira, however, it was another story. Madeirans seemed more attached to the notion of autonomy than of independence. Their less active independence movement appeared clandestine and illegal, and the liberation front's flag proved impossible to buy. Curiously, the new Madeiran flag carried a note of nostalgia for Mother Portugal. Of broad blue and gold stripes, it displayed in its center the five shields of the original—medieval—coat of arms of the kings of Portugal.

Introduction: A Choice of Destinies

In April 1975, the Portuguese people elected deputies to a Constituent Assembly. Socialists captured the largest number of seats but not quite a majority. Of the twelve deputies from Insular Portugal, however, only two were Socialists. The ten were Social Democrats, next to the right. Insular Portugal was thus, if not at loggerheads, at least in opposition to the dominant Socialists.

The Constituent Assembly drew up a new Constitution of the Portuguese Republic, one which committed the country to transformation into a classless society. The document went into effect in April 1976 and made of the Azores and the Madeiras two Autonomous Regions, each with its own Regional Assembly and its own Regional Government. Both, however, were still very much under Lisbon's thumb.

On the day the new Constitution went into effect, the Portuguese people elected Deputies to the new and definitive Assembly of the Republic. The same pattern occurred again. The Socialists held more seats than any other party, but not the majority of them. Of the twelve Deputies from Insular Portugal, this time three were Socialists, eight Social Democrats, and one an even more conservative Center Democrat.

Then, on June 27, 1976, the Portuguese people went to the polls for the third time in almost half a century and freely elected a President of the Republic, the Insular Portuguese on that day electing Deputies to their Regional Assemblies. In the Azores, 27 of 43 seats were captured by the Social Democrats, only 14 by the Socialists. In the Madeiras, of 41 seats 29 were taken by the Social Democrats and 8 by the Socialists.

Azoreans and Madeirans thus showed their colors yet another time. Then the politically neutral President of the Republic named as Prime Minister the Socialist leader Mário Soares, who had earlier written that his mother had been viscerally anticlerical, that he himself had never been a Catholic. When Soares, in turn, formed a largely Socialist Government in Lisbon, the breach between the capital and the quite Catholic Adjacent Islands, if it did not widen, certainly did not narrow.

Island leaders sensed that they had the distant—and theoretically irrelevant—backing of conservative supporters in the United States, immigrants in the New World who were becoming ever more insulated from the surrounding society by a series of forces which had become increasingly operative in recent years. The Insular leaders therefore continued in partial if not total opposition to the Socialist Government in Lisbon. They recognized that Soares had to have support from other than his own party to get anything done. Would he eventually form a coalition with the Communists, pitting 143 left-wing Deputies against 114 of the right? If he had done so, many Azoreans, especially of St. Michael's, and some Madeirans might have attempted some sort of independence. He did not do so, however.

Increasingly powerless, on December 8, 1977, the Feast of the Immaculate Conception, to whose Virgin Portugal is dedicated, Soares lost a vote of confidence in the Assembly of the Republic. The Communists failed to vote with the Socialists, and the First Constitutional Government of the new Republic fell.

On January 26, 1978, Soares formed a Second Constitutional Government based on the combined support of the Socialists and, yes, the Center Democrats, with the Social Democrats as well as the Communists still in the opposition. This Government consisted of fifteen regular ministers (ten Socialists, three Center Democrats, and two Independents). On July 24, 1978, the three Center Democrats resigned, and on July 27 the President of the Republic dismissed the Prime Minister.

☆ ☆ ☆

It is with Soares's second fall from power that this book about the Azoreans and Madeirans in their archipelagoes ends. It is not suffused with politics. Rather, it is a background book. It aims constructively to acquaint English-language readers with beautiful islands, two lovable and loving peoples, and the background of their many present-day problems. The stress is on depth of humanistic understanding.

Hopefully, the book provides materials for observers abroad, including even political leaders in Lisbon and other capitals, to draw their own economic and political conclusions about the hitherto isolated Insular Portuguese. Hopefully, also, its major message will be obvious: the need for social reform—not political or economic but social reform—in Portugal in general and Insular Portugal in particular. The only predictions which it makes relate to this social problem. Unless the upper class becomes aware of its responsibilities and acts responsibly in the late-twentieth century's meaning of the terms, all reforms will prove to no avail. In other words, the Portuguese Revolution of 1974 must be successful in a

Introduction: A Choice of Destinies

social sense. It must be a real Revolution. It must not be frustrated, above all by misguided or misinformed or even uninformed outsiders. If the Revolution is successful, the lot of the masses of Azoreans and Madeirans will improve, and dramatically, within the next few years; and the islanders will be able to assume their proper place proudly and optimistically on the North Atlantic stage amid three major continents.

In other words, this is a subjective book. It is also very personal, for five of my seven grandparents were born in the Azores. One acquires additional grandparents when real ones marry twice, and all three of my Azorean-born real grandparents did just that.

My maternal grandfather, born in the city of Horta on the island of Fayal, first married a lady from Flamengos ("Flemings") in the interior of that island. They met in Boston's South End about the time of the Great Fire (1872), married, lived there, and had a daughter, my mother's half sister. The mother became ill, and all three went to Fayal, where she died. Father and daughter returned, this time to New Bedford, Massachusetts. My aunt continued to live there until her death in 1973 at the age of 97. Blue-eyed, she conveyed to me my Flemish heritage, for surely her mother was a descendant of the Flemings who went out to Fayal in the fifteenth century.

The widowed father then married, in New Bedford, a lady from the island of Pico just east of Fayal. As she always spoke to me of Queen Maria Pia in adulatory tones, I gather that she immigrated after King Luís's marriage, which took place in 1862. This couple had my mother (1888-1975), but my grandfather died before I was born. From him, indirectly, I received a Horta heritage. From my grandmother, who died in 1932, I received my Pico heritage, my predilection for graceful volcanic peaks rising from the sea to a height of several thousand feet.

This real grandmother remarried in New Bedford. My stepgrandfather was one of several suave and handsome Massachusetts brothers who had come from Santa Maria, the southeasternmost Azores island. I knew him and his stories well, for he died only in 1944. From him I received my Santa Maria heritage.

A genealogical complication enters the picture: my half aunt, she who died in 1973, in her youth married a brother of this Santa Maria stepgrandfather of mine. She became a widow very young, and I never knew her husband. From him via her, however, my Santa Maria heritage was reinforced.

My Horta heritage was likewise reinforced, and in a major way. My paternal grandfather was born in that city on February 2, 1837. On August 10, 1852, he clandestinely slipped aboard the bark *United States* (Captain Thomas Wilcox, of Stonington, Connecticut). In May 1853, after helping acquire 1,500 barrels of whale oil, he stepped ashore in the Connecticut port. A U.S. official asked him his name. "João da Rosa," he replied. The official's Portuguese was less than perfect, so he wrote down "John Rogers," my grandfather's name until his death in New Bedford on July 25, 1907, seven years before I was born.

John Rogers remained in the whaling service for exactly forty years: boat-steerer in 1855, third mate in 1857, second mate in 1865, first mate in 1870, master (of the bark *Mary and Susan*) in 1884. He first married a lady from Taunton, Massachusetts, of Irish birth. After her death, he married a second time, my grandmother, who was born in Ireland in 1846 (the year of the potato famine) and two years later immigrated to North Easton, Massachusetts, where she identified more with the humble "Polanders" than with exalted Ames's. In my youth I spent many happy vacations with relatives in North Easton, admiring at a distance the Richardson monuments and absorbing a sense of responsibility for the downtrodden in opposition to the ruling elite. This Irish grandmother remained a fire-eater until her death in 1937, ever the enemy of the class and religious bigotry and the xenophobia which she had experienced. I knew her well, for she lived with us for eighteen years. Indeed, it can truthfully be affirmed that I was brought up Irish Catholic.

John Rogers's mother back in Horta lived until a ripe old age, and he and my Irish grandmother visited her on occasion. On at least one trip they continued on to Madeira, Continental Portugal, Spain, France, and Great Britain, embarking for home in Glasgow. Although so near, my Irish grandmother never wished to see her native land. Rather, she fell in love with Fayal, which she saw through the rose-colored glasses of a whaling master's wife liberally supplied with dollars. It was she who interested me in the Azores, and in Portugal in general. Her tales and postcard album convinced me to switch, when in graduate school, from French Studies to Portuguese Studies. Irish, she amplified the Horta heritage of my grandfathers, which in turn was supplemented by the Pico and Santa Maria heritages already alluded to. In fine, I claim a pan-Azorean heritage combined with a solid Irish background.

Introduction: A Choice of Destinies

Prominent among our neighbors as I grew up in New Bedford was a very friendly Yankee family related by marriage to another New England family with close Fayal associations. At an early age and in a nonethnic setting I used to hear of the Azores, their beauty, and their products (especially crivo). That neighborhood connection, remote as it was, kindled a scholarly spark, as my Irish grandmother's influence nurtured a sentimental streak. Even in the 1920's, I was interested in my Insular roots.

Intended for general reading, this resulting book contains no notes, bibliography, or other scholarly paraphernalia, although at its end I do include a few indispensable references. As for acknowledgments of indebtedness to the many individuals who have helped me with this book over the eight years of specific composition and the forty years of general accumulation, they are simply too numerous to list. Above all, I am grateful to Harvard colleagues and to the Harvard and Radcliffe undergraduate, Harvard graduate, and University Extension students who have provided and checked facts and been a fruitful source of ideas as well as inspiration and encouragement. They have represented the grand university tradition at its best, for scholarship does not result only from the single professor's efforts but from the total give and take within the university community of masters and students. I must mention one individual, however, who has been so helpful over so long a period that to omit his name would constitute a grave injustice: Mr. George E. Ryan of the staff of *The Pilot*, the weekly newspaper of the Archdiocese of Boston. Finally, I wish to express my thanks to the Calouste Gulbenkian Foundation of Lisbon for many favors over many years and, specifically, for travel grants which enabled me to go around the Portuguese world in 1962 and visit the Azores and Madeiras in the 1970's.

F. M. R.
Nancy Clark Smith Professor of
the Language and Literature
of Portugal

August 16, 1978

PART I

THE LIVES OF AZOREANS AND MADEIRANS

> No man is an Island, entire of itself, every man
> is a piece of the Continent, a part of the main.
>
> *John Donne*

1
PEAKS OUT OF THE OCEAN

The voyages to the moon which began in July 1969 were preceded by fictional voyages, including even a seventeenth-century attempt by means of a space chariot to which more than a score of geese were hitched as propellants. Just so, actual voyages from Europe out into the ocean sea to south and west, journeys which were made possible only when naval architecture, cartography, and celestial navigation had evolved sufficiently, were preceded by legendary voyages. These latter led to legendary discoveries of legendary islands and to considerable controversy among scholars in our day.

By the end of the first quarter of the fifteenth century, a series of European maps were in existence which depicted graphically and artistically a host of Atlantic islands. Among them were St. Brendan's, the island of Brazil, a group which included Corvi Marini and S. Zorzi, the famed island of Antilia which gave us our word Antilles, and another group which included Legname. The maps on which these legendary islands were drawn hardly constituted navigational charts, and no sober navigator could have attained the islands by means of them. Rather, they were works of graphic art. They reflected great works of medieval European literature and were designed to grace walls or libraries of the cultured elite living the good life.

Apart from the classic island waypoints of the Norsemen—Faeroes, Iceland, Greenland, and Helluland-Markland-Vinland (Newfoundland-Nova Scotia-New England?)—one Atlantic archipelago depicted on early maps did correspond to reality, namely, the Canary Islands. They were earlier known as the Fortunate Islands. One of the group, Canaria, was named not for canary but dog (Latin *canis*). The island of Tenerife is unique among all Atlantic islands for possessing the tallest peak, Pico de Teyde, rising to 12,198 feet above sea level. Moreover, its broad Valle de la Orotava, a valley opening out on the north side of the island and concluding with the charming resort town of Puerto de la Cruz, is one of the scenic wonders of the world.

The Latin writer Pliny the Elder described the Fortunate Islands, although not with one hundred percent accuracy. The Alexandrian geographer and astronomer Claudius Ptolemy, of the second century A.D., inherited this knowledge and did something clever with the Canarian archipelago. He recognized it as the westernmost land of all Eurasia and for his famous world map used it as the basis of a prime meridian. The known world of his day and for many a day thereafter extended from that zero longitude line eastward for 180° all the way to East Asia. The westernmost island is today, in Spanish, called Hierro, earlier known as Ferro (Iron). The Ferro meridian was used by many modern nations down to 1884, when the International Meridian Conference held in Washington, D.C., adopted the Greenwich Meridian. Unfortunately for navigators, longitude has been measured 180° to east and west of these more recent prime meridians instead of 360° in a single direction.

Mainlanders were well-acquainted with the Fortunate Islands in the later Middle Ages. The twelfth-century Arab geographer al-Idrisi, while resident in Sicily, told of an expedition of the Adventurers out into the Atlantic which clearly reached the Canaries. In 1341, a Genoese expedition likewise visited the Canaries, with the cooperation among others of the King of Portugal. In 1344, the pope awarded overlordship over the islands to a Spaniard, thus beginning papal intervention in island discovery and occupation. In 1401, title to part of them passed to two Normans, one named Bettencourt. The fact that the Canaries had a native population meant that, in effect, Europeans conquered and subjugated Canarians. In reality, Europeans well-nigh annihilated the Guanches, as the natives were known, and some Guanche bones may be seen in the museum of Las Palmas on Gran Canaria. That there is today in the archipelago a movement aimed at independence from Spain is understandable and not unreasonable, for in both area and population the Canaries are larger than Azores, Madeiras, and Cape Verde Islands put together. Few full-blooded Guanches, however, are around to lead the movement.

By the beginning of the fifteenth century, then, real knowledge of real Canaries, which are in fact visible on a clear day from the African coast, fifty-seven nautical miles away, lent credibility to the notion that other islands existed farther out in the misty sea—

islands also depicted on maps. But today there is no historical evidence that knowledge of such islands existed at that time.

The sudden emergence of an oceanic island from out of the mist or from under a cloud is for a sailor at sea a most dramatic event. It is one not to be overlooked by fisherman or whaleman or other seafarer but rather to be reported at once to higher authority, who would then dispatch a follow-up expedition. Aware from legends, then, of the possibility of coming upon such islands, the Portuguese in 1415 initiated their overseas expansion.

In that year, they captured Ceuta in Morocco on mainland Africa, next to the southern Pillar of Hercules and opposite Gibraltar. Ceuta, which lies just east of the spectacular mountain named Sidi Mousa, so familiar to ship passengers traversing the Strait of Gibraltar, today represents the first non-European place captured by Europeans which is still in European hands. It passed to Spain in 1580 and is yet Spanish, although its municipal coat of arms continues to be that of Portugal.

Prince Henry the Navigator (1394-1460) played an active role in the conquest of Ceuta, along with his father the king and his two older brothers. As a result of this pioneer among Marine amphibious operations, he and others in Portugal became bitten by the overseas-exploration-and-conquest bug. At a later date, he set up some sort of headquarters at Sagres next to Cape St. Vincent in the southwest corner of Portugal from which he supervised maritime expeditions proceeding ever farther south along the West African coast. Exploration in this direction had been proving easy for the Portuguese because of the northeast trade winds and south-setting Canary Current. (Winds are traditionally designated by the direction from which they blow, currents by the direction toward which they set.) In 1434, a Portuguese team had rounded Cape Bojador south of the Canaries, dreaded because of rumors of marine monsters and other hazards beyond it. By Henry's death the Portuguese had progressed as far as Sierra Leone.

The problem was the return to Portugal against wind and current, even from so nearby a locality as the Moroccan coast below the Strait. The only feasible method was to head out to sea west and northwest, tacking. Hence the need for specially designed lateen-rigged caravels which could beat to windward close-hauled. When at the latitude of the home port in Portugal, at first Lagos in the southern province known as the Algarve and later Lisbon, the intrepid Portuguese navigators would head east and run their latitude down. Hence the need for at least a crude method of celestial navigation in order to be able to determine latitude on the high seas.

Returning to Portugal in 1418 or thereabouts, a group of Portuguese mariners were blown a considerable distance out to sea. Suddenly they came upon majestic, low-lying, and barren Porto Santo (Holy Haven) flanked by two islets. On the next fairly clear day they caught sight of rugged Madeira twenty-two nautical miles to the southwest, and eventually they spotted the three Desertas more or less due south of Porto Santo. The following year the Portuguese revisited the archipelago, which lies 225 nautical miles north of the Canaries and 344 from the African coast. Their purpose was to "discover" (that is, uncover or explore) Madeira, named for the common noun for wood because it was heavily wooded in its lower regions.

At some later date the Portuguese came upon a tiny group of dots in the sea two-thirds of the way from Madeiras to Canaries. These Selvagens (Salvage Islands), ever uninhabited, still belong to Portugal and are administratively part of the Madeiras. Selvagem Grande (Great Salvage Island) rises to a height of 499 feet and Selvagem Pequena (Great Piton Island) reaches to upwards of 150 feet. They show no lights but are reported to be good radar targets.

In a return from the African coast in the 1420's or 1430's, Portuguese mariners sailed still farther west and north before turning to run before the prevailing westerlies toward Portugal. They encountered the beginning of the Azores, the tiny and still uninhabited islets known as the Formigas (Ants). To their southwest on August 15 (Our Lady's Day) they came upon the island which they named Santa Maria. From St. Mary's on the next clear day they discovered a large island lying on the northern horizon and named it São Miguel. From this St. Michael's they reached the third island and called it Terceira (Third), also known in early days as the island of Jesus Christ. From Terceira the gracious island named Graciosa to northwest was seen and, to southwest, the islands of São Jorge (St. George) and Pico (Peak). The latter is possessed of a beautifully symmetrical volcanic cone rising to 7,615 feet, "a quarter of a mile higher than Mt. Washington," reported a New England traveler in 1856. It is the Atlantic's third highest peak and Portugal's highest. From these two islands, Fayal becomes visible. By 1439, seven Azores were thus known to the Portuguese.

In the Portuguese language the ending *-al* means "a grove of." Fayal was a grove of *faias* or beech shrubs, just as Funchal, the city on Madeira, was at one time a grove or garden of *funcho*, fennel, what the Italians enjoy as *finocchio*, what the pre-Linnaean classification system knew as "Foeniculum sylvestre" and listed just after "Foeniculum dulce Azoricum amplà umbellâ." Today Fayal is better known for its magnificent blue hydrangeas, often used not only to mark the edges of roads but also to delimit farm plots. These hydrangeas exist in two varieties, "single" and "doubled." In Portuguese they are called *hortênsias*, a word which it is tempting to conclude derives from the name of Fayal's port city, Horta, although it probably is based on *horta* "vegetable garden."

Only much later, in 1452, did Flores (Flowers), well over a hundred nautical miles northwest of Fayal, and adjacent Corvo (Crow or Raven) become known to the Portuguese. They lie, with respect to Terceira and Fayal, in the general direction of Newfoundland and Labrador.

About the time Flores and Corvo were found and explored, the Portuguese, by now well down the African coast, came upon their third archipelago in yet another sweep out to sea. These islands lie off the green cape which marks the westernmost point of Africa. The Portuguese had named this promontory Cabo Verde; we in English normally call it Cape Verde. When the newcomers found the offlying islands, they naturally called them the Cape Verde Islands. Known poetically as the Hesperides, they form a graceful semicircle open to the west. The most impressive is Fogo (Fire), a volcanic cone which rises to 9,281 feet and represents the Atlantic's second highest peak. It dwarfs tiny Brava lying to its lee.

The reader cannot have failed to notice a correspondence between two pairs of names, between the obviously Italian Corvi Marini (Cormorants or Marine Ravens) and S. Zorzi (northern Italian dialect for St. George) on the one hand and Corvo and São Jorge on the other. If he knows his Italian and Portuguese, he realizes that both Legname and Madeira stand for wood. It is easy, but I believe erroneous, for him to assume that the Azores and Madeiras were known to Europeans and named by them before the Portuguese came upon them in the fifteenth century. The reverse appears to be the truth. The Portuguese under Prince Henry's interested eyes found the islands. Knowing the legends, they very naturally applied legendary names to real islands.

Nor should the reader be surprised that names for birds and words connoting trees, shrubs, and flowers were applied to islands unknown to man. Birds from nearby and even distant continents have the capability of alighting and nesting on islands. Birds, as well as wind and waves, carry the seeds which give rise to island flora.

In the case of the Azores, a mid-Atlantic archipelago, and the Madeiras, from a strictly geographic but not from a human point of view an African archipelago, the matter of prior knowledge has little political implication. The islands have been indisputably Portuguese ever since they were first discovered and peopled by the Portuguese. This is fact, however much their present-day inhabitants may wish true autonomy in the manner of the Elizabeth Islands, Martha's Vineyard, and Nantucket vis-à-vis Boston—if not true independence like that of the Cape Verde Islands. One may, therefore, without political repercussions, identify Plato's Lost Continent of Atlantis with the Azores and Madeiras and believe that the Irish monk St. Brendan visited the former.

One may even accept the suggestion that Phoenicians came upon the Azores in 590 B.C. and also crossed the South Atlantic to Brazil. A stone statue of a man on horseback and Carthaginian coins are said to have been found on Corvo, and the Corvo statue has entered Brazilian literature via a late-eighteenth-century epic poem written by a nonnautical Augustinian monk. This author has a South American native, Guaçu, receive the sacrament of baptism at the hands of a Christian transported miraculously by an angel to Brazil. After death Guaçu's body, transformed into a statue, is somehow conveyed to and placed on a high point on Corvo, thenceforth to indicate to Portuguese mariners the course to that Brazil which they revealed to Europe in 1500. The course is doubtful. Transatlantic sailing vessels normally pass the Azores eastbound, not westbound.

Seven Iberian bishops may have fled to São Miguel after the Arabicized Moors from Morocco invaded the Iberian Peninsula in 711. On São Miguel these seven may have founded seven cities (that is, the sees of seven dioceses) still commemorated today in the magnificent double crater lake at the western end of the island, the Sete Cidades (Seven Cities). The water in the southern half appears emerald green and that of the northern half azure blue due to reflections respectively of vegetation and sky. During the years of its transatlantic flying boat service to Europe via the Azores, beginning in mid-1939, Pan American maintained a mooring buoy there, to be used in the event of a grave emergency. If a clipper had alighted there, it would have had to be dismantled and brought out by muleback.

Theories concerning nonhistorical maritime journeys abound, and a crew of young men have recently crossed the Atlantic in an oxhide-hulled currach to prove that St. Brendan and fellow monks could have done it in the sixth century. They may have proved that it could have been done. They did not prove that it was done. That the early Portuguese who visited Corvo thought they saw an equestrian statue is very possible. The imaginative can see almost anything on mountains, on clouds, on the surface of the moon. But I have yet to see the Carthaginian coins on Corvo, in spite of three journeys by ship to that island and visits to every museum in the archipelago.

No more can I accept the notion that Celts came to North America long before the Christian era, partly because I do not believe that they had the navigational capability. This notion has been amplified to suggest that the Celts came from the ancient Roman province of Lusitania. Duly promulgated in the daily press and in popular books—e.g., *America B. C.*—it naturally attracts the attention of the Portuguese in the United States, for Lusitania embraced what in A.D. 1140 and following years became Portugal.

One legend concerning Madeira is purely literary, but it does possess a topographical overtone. A pair of lovers named Robert Machin and Anne d'Arfet around 1340 fled from disapproving parents in England and were driven ashore at the southeastern end of the island. There they lived all too briefly and died overlooking the beautiful bay of the town subsequently named Machico, just east of the airport and Hotel Atlantis (ex-Holiday Inn).

The geographer al-Idrisi reenters our story in connection with the name Azores. As already noted, the word supposedly means hawks, that is, goshawks, but the famous ornithologist who authored four beautifully illustrated volumes on the *Birds of the Atlantic Islands* affirms that there never were any in the archipelago. One theory holds that the Sicily-based geographer used the word Raca, bird of prey, to designate an Atlantic island and that the

Portuguese translated and pluralized the word to designate their new archipelago. If Raca and Corvo both designate the same bird, then Raca, to follow the logic of a recent writer, is Corvo. He discusses "Raca Island or Corvo, famous for its large figs, of which a shipload was sent to either Charlemagne or Capet of France"!

☆ ☆ ☆

Teyde, Fogo, and Pico are nothing more nor less than volcanoes rising up from the bed of the ocean, and the archipelagoes as a whole are the result of seismic activity of ages past. The exact nature of Azores, Madeiras, Selvagens, Canaries, Cape de Verdes (as Melville calls them in *Moby Dick*), and, to the west, Bermudas in relation to the entire Atlantic can be perceived most clearly on the National Geographic Society's fascinating map of that ocean minus the water.

The depths of water alongside these mountain islands are incredible. At one point in the St. George Channel, between São Jorge and Pico, navigators encounter a depth of 864 fathoms, 5,184 feet. Six miles south of the eastern tip of Pico are 950 fathoms of water. And eleven miles off the western tip of São Miguel are 1,751 fathoms. (Multiply fathoms by six to obtain feet.)

Volcanic activity has continued over the years in the Azores. In the town of Ribeira Grande on the north side of São Miguel one may still observe the effects of an eruption in 1565. On Fayal an important eruption occurred in 1672. Lava overflowed in two areas at the western end of the island, Praia do Norte and Capelo, to create what are known locally as *mistérios* (mysteries), vast, creepy-looking, mysterious wastelands. On February 22, 1718, the last eruption occurred on Pico. It was responsible for four *mistérios* only today being brought under cultivation.

Finally, on September 27, 1957, a tremendous submarine volcanic eruption took place off the western tip (Ponta Comprida) of Fayal at a place called Capelinhos Islets. More activity continued over the ensuing months through October 21, 1958, and caused considerable destruction in the same area of the island. As a result of these events, Fayal acquired a land extension westward, and the then civil governor of the administrative district of Horta has wittily remarked: "I am the only Governor since the Age of Maritime Discovery who has made an addition to sovereign Portuguese territory."

Western tip of Fayal in 1939

The old Capelinhos Lighthouse was no longer on the point but inland from the south coast, and a new Vale Formoso Lighthouse had to be erected. Later, a modest vulcanological museum was opened nearby to inform visitors of what had happened. It is not as elaborate nor as gruesome as the famous Mont Pelée Museum on Martinique because the Fayal disaster did not take the toll in lives of the 1902 Caribbean eruption. Much later, in 1968, the Regional Tourism Commission of the District of Horta published an informative book with maps and photographs (some in color) which covers Fayal's total volcanic activity over the years 1957-1967. In the meantime, the population of Fayal, especially of its western portion, was terrified and created a huge refugee problem on the island. Azoreans everywhere felt compassion, and the

Western tip of Fayal in 1974

congressional representatives of those in Southeastern New England acted promptly.

Smoke still appears at the peak of Pico, and hot springs bubble in Furnas in east-central São Miguel. A *furna* is a hole or cavern. The place-name Furnas connotes the openings from which hot steam and mud exude, with the strong odor of sulphur, to create an eerie atmosphere well known to nineteenth-century European and American seekers after health spas. Still today a modern and well-equipped bathing establishment caters to those who like to take their waters. For modern youth who prefer swimming and diving, there is, in the magnificent Park behind the Terra Nostra Hotel, a huge outdoor pool of brownish, warm, sulphuric water, in which I have exercised in mid-March.

Throughout the Azores a very visible effect of volcanic activity consists of the many craters, called *caldeiras*, the Portuguese word for a boiler in a steamship. São Miguel's Sete Cidades and Furnas Valley are gigantic *caldeiras*. The most symmetrical is Fayal's, where the circular crater attracts all visitors to the island. It measures 6,560 feet in diameter and 1,312 feet deep. Its bottom is 1,640 feet above sea level.

Earthquakes also have a long history in the Azores. One on October 22, 1522, completely destroyed the first capital of São Miguel, Vila Franca do Campo. Thereafter Ponta Delgada served as chief place. The year 1926 was a bad one for Horta. At 9:15 P.M. on April 5 the city experienced a severe shock which badly damaged the parish church of Our Lady of the Immaculate Conception located at its northern end. At 8:35 A.M. on August 31 a worse blow struck. It lasted some twelve to fifteen seconds, finished off the church, and rendered three quarters of the houses in town uninhabitable, or at least forced extensive repairs upon them. The concrete work on the new submarine telegraph cable station and power house, being built by Boston's electrical engineering firm of Stone & Webster, Inc., escaped all damage—the foundation of the cable station with the first floor having been completed. The houses which Stone & Webster were building for Western Union staff use, two of which were practically roofed over, suffered only a few minor cracks. Refurbished, they still stand majestically as the Hotel Fayal.

A disastrous earthquake struck São Jorge on February 18 and 21, 1964, in the form of a destructive series of earth tremors. On the following May 30, I went ashore at Velas, São Jorge, to survey the extensive damage. I was extremely moved, as I noted in my diary, by the family solidarity of the Azoreans in the face of adversity and utterly disgusted at the slow pace of reconstruction.

As recently as 12:30 P.M. on November 23, 1973, an earthquake of force eight on the Wood-Newman scale rocked Pico. Press accounts stated that it wrecked eighty percent of the homes on the island, rendering 1,824 persons totally homeless. Most damage was done in the northwest portion of the island, although considerable damage was also done to the north end of Horta. In July 1974 the destruction on both islands was still very visible. Discreet inquiries concerning the whereabouts of the financial aid sent with alacrity by relatives and friends in the United States resulted only in raised eyebrows, shrugged shoulders, and the intelligence that the money was tied up in a bank account due to the intervening change in form of government. In July 1977, however, repairs and reconstruction were everywhere in evidence and, of all things, an airport in the Pico area was nearly completed.

Earthquake damage, Velas, São Jorge, in 1964

On April 21, 1975, a quake of force four on the same scale was felt on the eastern end of São Miguel: its epicenter was in the sea some thirty-five miles west of the island. And on May 26 of the same year a strong quake—force 7.5 on the Richter scale—was felt in the Madeiras, but fortunately its center was out to sea some two hundred miles to the northwest.

It appears to be a fact that man has succeeded in dominating in varying degrees all the forces of nature except what the Portuguese call "telluric" activity. He can track hurricanes and thereby avoid them. He can produce rain. He can build breakwaters, as in Horta, Ponta Delgada, and Funchal. He cannot as yet prevent an earthquake or an eruption, although he can predict them to some extent. People who live on volcanic islands therefore constitute a special breed: they are fatalists. This quality in the character of Azoreans is definitely included within the meaning of the word *açorianidade*, Azoreanity.

High mountains rising out of the sea are inevitably striking and all the islands of Insular Portugal are extremely beautiful, especially when bathed in sunshine. The Insular Portuguese, until the

1974 Revolution, were accustomed to beauty from birth—and to cleanliness and orderliness. The color contrast between the Azorean and Madeiran green on the one hand and the blue sky and blue or green sea on the other is remarkable. The form of the islands, especially of Pico, is spectacular. The neatness of the houses and their spick-and-span condition—even of those belonging to very poor farmers—is most noteworthy, as was the lack of clutter in city squares and country roads. And there is no more impressive view anywhere than that from a ship passing along the south coast of Fayal, the Blue Island, when the fields are flooded with sunlight and the rows of pale blue hydrangeas are plainly visible.

The Insular Portuguese in general were not accustomed to sordidness. Their aesthetic sensibilities were cultivated to a high degree without their even realizing it. With the Revolution came posters plastered on almost every wall and signs painted not only on walls but even on public buses. Combined with the ever-increasing pollution from motor vehicles—particularly noticeable along the jacaranda-lined and gorgeous Avenue of Prince Henry in Funchal—the graffiti have changed the nature of Insular Portuguese cities and towns, above all of Ponta Delgada and, of course, of lovely Lisbon. The visitor from abroad blames the mess on political immaturity engendered by forty-eight years of authoritarian rule.

Telluric activity and the force of wind and wave have provided Insular Portugal with but a single natural port. Taken advantage of by world shipping from the seventeenth century onwards, Horta lies on the east side of Fayal facing Pico and is protected by sizeable promontories to north and south. The other cities have no real ports. Angra on Terceira, Ponta Delgada, and Funchal, however, are all located on a south coast and are relatively protected from prevailing winds. The huge breakwaters in Ponta Delgada and Funchal today provide great artificial ports for the respective islands. Praia, near the Air Force base at Lajes, is being developed to render a similar service to Terceira.

The telluric activity which originally created the islands and the surrounding ocean floor now interests large numbers of scientists of several nations. Indeed, oceanography today attracts many students aware of the future role of the sea in supplying the needs of Planet Earth as well as in furnishing a zone for belligerency. A well-publicized research project was FAMOUS (French-American

Mid-Ocean Underseas Study), which also involved Canadians and British. It was particularly active in the summer of 1974. Three small deep-diving submarines, together with their tenders, were based on Ponta Delgada in order to study a particular section of the Mid-Atlantic Rift located some four hundred miles to the southwest.

Telluric activity is not the only physical influence on the Portuguese Atlantic archipelagoes. Submarine convulsions may have thrown the islands up in the first place, but erosion due to rainwater and, also, in the cases of the Madeiran Porto Santo and Desertas, the very lack of rainwater, have had their marked effects.

The Azores, also known as the Western Islands, are green and gently undulating. The large island of Madeira, singularly free of eruptions and earthquakes in recent centuries, is very accidented, with precipitous drops on all sides. The most impressive of these drops is Cabo Girão, on the south coast just west of Funchal, a rocky wall which rises to a height of 1,903 feet and was depicted on a 1972 Portuguese postage stamp. To use a word of which Madeirans are fond, the island's problem is orographic. Madeira is so mountainous that any visitor subject to acrophobia had best forego automobile or bus drives around the island on narrow roads hewn out of the sides of cliffs. It is so irregular that the only available airport—a 5,249-foot runway labeled 06 or 24 and likewise cut out of the side of a cliff—is barely capable of filling the new American-type hotels plus the Savoy and the elegant older Reid's. Concerned engineers are struggling with the challenge of providing a longer runway somewhere.

Each archipelago of Insular Portugal, then, has its distinguishing physical features. The island of Madeira possesses water; it lacks usable land to such an extent that many cows are obliged to spend their entire lives in little straw huts called *palheiros* (from *palha* "straw") poised on terraces up the sides of mountains. If these animals were let out, they would either tumble down the mountainsides or else eat the vegetables being grown on the terraces for human consumption. Madeira is also afflicted by a cruel wind from Africa known on the island as the *Leste* (east wind). Very dry, it hits Madeira from the Sahara every few years, coming in at high altitude, bringing red dust like a plague, and drying out and cracking wooden furniture. The Azores, by way of contrast, have everything, but not so the Azoreans.

Madeirans can ascribe the origin of their many problems to

physical causes. Azoreans, prior to April 25, 1974, had only the human race to blame, specifically the local landed gentry and the absentee rulers located in Lisbon and elsewhere. Under dictators António de Oliveira Salazar (ruled 1928-1968) and Marcello Caetano (ruled 1968-1974) one did not publicly blame such gentry and such rulers and, consequently, the plight of the Azores went relatively unnoticed.

Times, however, have changed.

Horta, Fayal—Joint Cable Station (left), Trinity House (right)

2
SETTLERS OUT OF CONTINENTAL EUROPE

Absentee rulers and local landed gentry are nothing new in either Azores or Madeiras. In fact, they were there from the beginning. They constituted the multisecular system which faced change with the 25th of April, 1974.

When the Portuguese navigators came upon Atlantic islands in the fifteenth century and reported their relatively precise location and exact nature back home, the Crown claimed the new property. The kings of that period, however, instead of making grants of the newfound lands to specific individuals to develop them *in situ*, made donations of them to intermediaries, members of the royal family. These *donatários* or recipients of the king's largesse (donataries or lords proprietor) in effect enjoyed, in Continental Portugal, the income derived from Insular Portugal, and—gingerly affirms a recently written history of Azorean society and culture—"History never registered the coming of any donatary on any visit to the Azores."

The first donatary was—who else?—Prince Henry the Navigator. In 1433, his brother Duarte, just turned king, granted him the Madeiras "with all of the rights and income from them which we by right have, and should have, with the civil and criminal jurisdiction except in cases of death sentence or dismemberment." In 1439, Duarte's and Henry's brother Pedro, regent for Afonso V, who succeeded his father Duarte as king in 1438, granted Henry the seven Azores islands then known (all except Flores and Corvo). A precedent was set. All that was needed now was one or more agents of the donatary out in the islands, a Minister of the Republic *avant la lettre*.

When Henry died in 1460, his nephew and heir Fernando (1433-1470), Duke of Viseu, Afonso V's brother, succeeded him as the second donatary. Fernando even inherited the Western Azores, discovered in the meantime. And within a month of Henry's death, Afonso V granted Fernando the known Cape Verde Islands.

The third and fourth donataries were, theoretically, Fernando's two sons, John and Diogo, respectively Dukes of Beja and Viseu. John died very young, in a year not known to historians. His successor Diogo was killed in 1484 by the very hand of his brother-in-law and first cousin King John II. Actually, their mother, Dona Beatrice (died 1506), Fernando's widow, acted for her two sons from 1470 until Diogo became of age in 1483.

After the murder of Diogo, John II granted the title of donatary of the Atlantic islands to Diogo's younger brother Manuel (1469-1521), who also became the new Duke of Beja. John II and Manuel were also first cousins and brothers-in-law. When the former died without an heir in 1495, the latter succeeded him on the throne. He incorporated the title of donatary within that of king. He also took unto himself as king the administration of the Military Order of Christ (discussed in Chapter 6).

These absentee landlords naturally needed agents out in the ocean. They hit upon the idea of dividing the archipelagoes, and on occasion a single island, into captaincies, granting each to a *capitão-do-donatário* (captain-of-the-donatary). They thus branded the islands with a hierarchical social stamp which Insular Portugal is only now outliving. The captains-of-the-donatary, needless to add, were gentlemen and soldiers, although possibly penniless.

The two names associated with the early peopling of Madeira—the Portuguese make a convenient distinction between *povoamento* or peopling of an uninhabited land and *colonização* or colonizing by white Europeans of a land already occupied by another people—are João Gonçalves Zarco and Tristão Vaz Teixeira. They shared the island, Zarco based on Funchal and Teixeira on Machico, and they are well commemorated by local statuary. Bartolomeu Perestrelo received Porto Santo. It was his daughter whom Christopher Columbus married in Lisbon in 1479. With her the Genoese moved to Porto Santo, and there Diego Colón was born. The Columbus's then moved to Funchal.

Early settlement of the Azores is associated with the name of Gonçalo Velho Cabral, who held Santa Maria and São Miguel in trust for the absent Prince Henry. Among others, Flemish captains were active in the Central Azores, as will shortly be seen.

But of donataries and their captains, marquesses, counts, viscounts, barons, and their lady opposite numbers this book is little concerned except in very negative fashion. It prefers to focus its attention on the lower class.

Portugal, leading Europe, expanded overseas to south, west, and east at the end of the Middle Ages. A medievally structured nation, it used medieval technology. A combination of several motivations impelled the Portuguese abroad: intellectual curiosity, a desire for trade, obtaining intelligence about the Moslem enemy for the central royal agency, union or reunion with Eastern-rite Christians who lived beyond the encircling Islamic crescent, a desire to save souls by conversion to Christianity, and, yes, and most importantly, the astrological influence derived from the "inclination of the celestial wheels" (to cite Henry's chief chronicler and panegyrist). These were the reasons why the Portuguese explored the African coast, rounded the Cape of Good Hope, proceeded to the Malabar Coast of India, continued on to Malacca, the Moluccas, Macao, and Japan.

Of this glorious epic activity concerning which orators boasted, poets sang, and tapestry weavers wove, the twentieth-century end-product was the Portuguese Republic's possession of a series of colonies. One was the Cape Verde Islands, unknown to Europe and uninhabited when come upon by Portugal-sponsored mariners, and subsequently peopled chiefly by men from Portugal and by African men and women brought in from the nearby Guinea coast. The others were real colonies, lands with native populations, and occasionally with mixed Portuguese and native populations, ruled by white Europeans: Portuguese Guinea, São Tomé-e-Príncipe (two small islands in the Gulf of Guinea), Angola and the associated Cabinda, Mozambique, Goa and the associated Diu and Damão in India, Macao on the China coast near Hong Kong, and Timor (the eastern half of the island of that name the other half of which belonged to Indonesia).

Nehru absorbed the three Indian enclaves into the Indian Union at the end of 1961. Once in power, the revolutionary government of 1974 immediately set about divesting European Portugal of the rest of its colonies. Portuguese Guinea became independent as Guinea-Bissau on September 10, 1974, and was admitted to the U.N. one week later. On June 25, 1975, Mozambique became independent, on July 5 the Cape Verde Islands, and on July 12 São Tomé-e-Príncipe, the Atlantic archipelago becoming known as the Republic of Cape Verde. All three were admitted to the U.N. on September 16, 1975. Angola became independent on

November 11, 1975, but was not admitted to the international body until December 1, 1976. Mainland China seems not yet to desire an independent or absorbed Macao, but Indonesia completed its takeover of Portuguese Timor on July 17, 1976.

Azores and Madeiras should not be viewed in a colonial context. They merit a different perspective. They have never been colonies in the accepted legal sense, however much Lisbon may have repressed their populations and ruled and taxed and otherwise exploited them from afar. Rather, these new territories to the southwest and west constituted a challenge for the impoverished genteel and a promised land for Continental Portugal's downtrodden.

Along with the captains-of-the-donatary and other island governors went common peoplers, late-medieval Portuguese in search of a better life, disposed to cease being a piece of the continent, a part of the main, in order to become islanders, entire of themselves. Because these clods, as it were, were washed away by the sea, Europe became the less. And the United States ultimately gained.

Portuguese families were enticed to Madeira, which soon prospered because of sugar cane imported from Sicily. As sugar for export declined in importance, wine rose. The first vines were brought in from Cyprus and Crete, and Shakespeare reminded Falstaff that he had sold his soul on Good Friday last for a cup of madeira and a cold capon's leg. The island of Madeira continued prosperous. Population increased, exploiters from abroad arrived—"explorers have always been followed by exploiters," says Jacques Cousteau—and grave social and economic problems arose. Nevertheless, the archipelago continued basically Portuguese. A foreign strain has been remarked, particularly in the Camacha and Santo da Serra area northeast of Funchal, in connection with the presence of British troops during the Napoleonic era. Whatever blond influence anthropologists may or may not discern, I have myself photographed blond children on the northeast side of the island.

Portuguese families did not at first view the more distant, more isolated, more humid Azores in quite so receptive a manner. This fact is surprising, for these islands are at the latitude of Continental Portugal, are physically similar in a general way, and enjoy roughly similar climate. But, I repeat, they are isolated. Portuguese did people Santa Maria and São Miguel, the easternmost islands, those first found. As for the islands of the central group, come upon next, the Crown faced difficulties and had recourse in part to foreigners, particularly foreign men, to fill the vacancies.

King John I ruled Portugal from 1385 to 1433. In 1386, he signed the Treaty of Windsor, in the name of which Great Britain's ambassador in Lisbon on June 16, 1943, appealed to Salazar for facilities of which the Allies stood in need in the Azores. In 1387, John married Philippa of Lancaster, an English lady, daughter of John of Gaunt. The couple had a series of children: Duarte (who succeeded as king), Pedro (the traveler and, from 1438 to 1448, regent of the realm), Henry (the so-called Navigator), Isabel (the only daughter to survive infancy), and two others. In 1430, Isabel married Philip the Good, Duke of Burgundy, of which Flanders was a part. She co-ruled as duchess for thirty-seven years and survived her husband by four.

The years of Duchess Isabel's considerable European influence were critical ones for peopling the Azores. In close touch by letters and ambassadors with her brothers, she was aware of the problem and encouraged the dispatch of Flemings from her Flanders to the islands, specifically to Terceira, São Jorge, and Fayal. There is no documentary evidence, however, that Duarte or any other king ever named her donatary of the Azores.

Among upperclass personages who went out into the Atlantic were Jácome de Bruges (Josué van den Berge), influential in the peopling of Terceira; Jorge d'Utra or Dutra (Josse van Hurtere), important on Fayal; and Guilherme da Silveira (Willem van der Haghe), active on São Jorge as well as the other two islands. It is possible that the city of Horta's name is derived from this Hurtere, although some writers believe it was due to a famous garden. In any event, the place-names Ribeira dos Flamengos (Brook of the Flemings) on Terceira and Fayal and Flamengos (Flemings) on Fayal, as well as certain family names, represent vestiges of the Flemish presence. Some of the family names follow. The numbers in parentheses are the occurrences in the 1978 Azores telephone directory: Brum from Bruyn (39), Bulcão from Bulscan or Bulscamp (3), Dutra from van Hurtere (20), Goulart from Govaert (46), Rosa from Roos, Roose, Roosen, Roosens, or Rooze (76, of whom 36 on Fayal), (da) Silveira from Van Der Haegen or Van der Haeghe or Van Der Haeghen (127), and Terra from van Aard or Aertrijcke (14). The distribution of the 325 occurrences by island is: Fayal (112), Terceira (79), Pico (53), São Miguel (47), São

Jorge (26), Santa Maria (4), Flores (3), and Graciosa (1). In the 1974-1975 telephone directory for the Zone of Bruges, by the way, there were 94 occurrences of Roose, etc., and 25 of Vanderhaeghen, etc.

In the latter part of the fifteenth century and for many decades thereafter, the Azores were known as the Flemish Islands. Fayal was early called New Flanders or Isle of the Flemings. Nevertheless, the over-all Flemish influence appears to have been slight. The Flemings were completely absorbed by the majority Portuguese element of the population. By 1507, even the Flemish language was completely dead on Fayal. In 1939, during four full-day research trips to Flamengos from Horta I was unable to detect a trace of Flemish influence on the language of the inhabitants. I could not even find support for the notion that blonds with blue eyes prevailed there. It is possible, as some believe, that the attractive row of windmills overlooking Horta from a ridge to the north represents a Flemish legacy. In any event, in October 1977 in Meetkerke just northwest of Bruges (Brugge) in West Flanders, I photographed a magnificent windmill which did give me *saudades* (nostalgia) for Fayal. And lace and the Beguine movement may have gone out to the Azores from Flanders.

It is indubitable that some Flemings in fact settled on Terceira, Fayal, and other Azorean islands. The same cannot be said of French, or Celts, or Armoricans on São Miguel. Superficial writers continue to say just that, however, and thereby hangs an amusing tale.

Two facts are in evidence. One concerns the pronunciation of the Portuguese language as spoken on St. Michael's, where several peculiarities remind the listener of French. The two most striking of these characteristics are the pronunciation of the sound depicted by the letter *u* (*escudo*, *Furnas*) as *ü*, the *u* of French *tu*, and the sound depicted by the written diphthongs *ou* and *oi* (*ouro*, *noite*) as *ö*, the *eu* of French *peu*, roughly the *ur* of New England English *Burt*. The other fact concerns a place-name, Bretanha (Brittany), designation of a locality in the northwest corner of the island.

The publicists quickly add two and two and obtain five. The "French" sounds in the Michaelese language must be due to a French influence. Bretanha must have been settled originally by Bretons from Brittany in France, possibly by shipwrecked sailors.

They go much farther. At the western end of São Miguel is a

place called Ginêtes, probably so called from a famous breed of jennets for which the island was noted. The name reminds some imaginative local citizens of the French word *genêt* "heather," as in the English royal house of Plantagenet (ruled 1154-1399). Royalty enters the Azorean picture. In early 1934, the well-known French magazine *L'Illustration* went so far as to suggest that Louis XVII of France, the Lost Dauphin, had lived on São Miguel. The article's author had heard of a family named Capeto who lived near Bretanha and naturally recalled the family name of the forty kings who in the course of a thousand years ruled France, whose progenitor may have received the figs from Corvo.

As for the pronunciation, the so-called French *u* also exists on Corvo and in parts of Madeira. The French *u* and *eu* are heard in Continental Portugal, specifically in the region known as the Upper Alentejo over on the Spanish border to the east of Lisbon. As for the place-name Bretanha, the sixteenth-century chronicler of Portugal's Atlantic islanders suggested that it was originally a common noun meaning a high piece of land, although he admitted the possibility that "a Breton," a solitary man from Brittany, may have lived there. Moreover, and most importantly, from the point of view of linguistic science the French *u* and *eu* are the result of the spontaneous phonetic evolution of the language. No appeal to an outside influence need be made. Indeed, if it were absolutely proved, on documentary grounds, that there had been a large colony of Frenchmen in Bretanha, it still would not follow that these foreigners were the cause of the changes of *u* to *ü* and of *ou* and *oi* to *ö*. Such changes are inherent in the language.

Moreover, if there had been washed-up Breton fishermen or pirates on São Miguel at the end of the fifteenth century or in later decades, they would have been Celtic-speaking and not French-speaking. Amateur Azorean philologists and their disciples must therefore examine the Celtic phonological system and not the French if they wish to confirm a theory of Breton influence.

During the late 1940's, I tried to lay this French or Celtic theory to rest, in a paper read at the Modern Language Association of America and in an article published in a U.S. learned journal. My efforts were to no avail. The guidebooks and popular travel books repeat it ad nauseam, even the usually authoritative *Guide Bleu*. Prime Minister Caetano introduced it, cautiously, during the speech he delivered in honor of Presidents Nixon of the United

States and Pompidou of France on Terceira on December 13, 1971. It turned up once again in 1973 in a volume reporting the papers read at an international congress held at Rennes in France's Brittany two years before. The theme of this congress was Brittany, Portugal, and Brazil. One paper was entitled "Bretons in the Azores." Its revelations were picked up by Continental Portugal's press and, in turn, cited uncritically by the Portuguese-language press in the United States.

An extraordinary coincidence involves the geographical location of Rennes, 48° 06′ N, 1° 40′ W. If a crow, or say, a missile, flew from there to Pointe-à-Pitre (16° 14′ N, 61° 32′ W) on France's Caribbean island of Guadeloupe by great-circle course, the bird would overhead Santa Cruz (39° 27′ N, 31° 08′ W) on the island of Flores. That fact explains much.

France desires an independent role in the modern world. France's culture fertilized that of all Europe over past centuries, including Portugal's from the Middle Ages on and Brazil's ever since that South American nation of Portuguese language acquired its independence from Portugal in 1822. France today does not admit inferiority to either U.S.A. or U.S.S.R. France understandably withdrew from NATO in 1966. France pursues her own policy in the Azores. She works independently on Flores and, with her supporting ships such as the missile-range-ship *Henri Poincaré*, elsewhere in Azorean waters. She cooperates, but outside the framework of NATO, in FAMOUS and also in the AFAR (Azores Fixed Acoustic Range) to be described in Chapter 11. Therefore, the theory that Frenchmen may have settled in the Azores very early naturally would have been welcomed in both Portugal and France. But there is no concrete evidence that Frenchmen did so settle, much less influence the pronunciation of Michaelese.

The matter of pronunciation impinges on that of provenience. Linguistic evidence strongly suggests that the early Madeirans and Azoreans—or at least their language—came from southern Portugal, chiefly from the Algarve but also, as just noted, from the Upper Alentejo. The theory of southern Portuguese origin is borne out by the large number of Algarve-type chimneys, particularly apparent to the visitor to Terceira as he rides across the island from the airport at Lajes to the city of Angra, and by the system of irrigation in use on the island of Madeira, notably the sluices known as *levadas*.

A *levada* above and behind Funchal

Other evidence, including that of physical anthropology, suggests that some Adjacent Islanders came from northern Portugal, following the original settlers but after the southern language habits had become so deeply entrenched as to cause later arrivals to conform. Still later emigrants from Continental Portugal to both Madeiras and Azores went forth from northwest Portugal, the region known as Minho, the great fount of the emigrants to Brazil.

White Portuguese families for the most part, then, peopled the Adjacent Islands. True, presumably a very small fraction of these Whites in their physical appearance did betray the centuries of juxtaposition to Moors or to black slaves within the Iberian Peninsula. Undoubtedly, on occasion, a white Portuguese male did go out to the Adjacent Islands accompanied by a child, or children, the product of some previous high living involving attractive women in Africa, India, China, Japan, or Insulindia. Traces of just such miscegenation turn up among the white Portuguese in the United States. The progenitors of the Portuguese community in America deserve praise and not blame for their acknowledgment of the fruits of their loves. They were never ones to sweep them under the rug. And they did love the ladies globally.

One suspects that some upper-class and educated Azoreans stress intermarriage with northern Europeans—Flemish and Bretons—in order to present as European-white an image as possible to a racist world once dominated largely by European Whites. These Adjacent Islanders rarely mention the presence of Moors in the past or of the handful of Gypsies seen today on São Miguel and even on Madeira. Nor do they readily acknowledge the possibility of a black presence in Insular Portugal. Their attitude is similar to that of sensitive Brazilians who stress their Portuguese and/or Italian descent in the belief that, so doing, they divert suspicion of black and/or American Indian origin. Sensitive Puerto Ricans or Peruvians stress their Castilian ancestry, and, also, sensitive Portuguese of a bygone generation in New England gave the impression that they were Spanish . . . or Brazilian. Little wonder that Blacks react by stressing that Black is Beautiful.

No human society is simon-pure. In its original efforts to people the Adjacent Islands the Portuguese Crown undeniably had recourse not only to foreigners but also to some very unsavory elements among white Portuguese men, to jailbirds to whom it gave the opportunity of exile in the islands, where they reformed and became solid citizens.

Several other groups were also represented in the fifteenth and sixteenth centuries: Blacks, Moors (both Moriscos and captives), baptized Jews (New Christians), Spanish priests, prelates, and others, and mercantile Italians, French, English, and Germans. Slaves were definitely present, Blacks and, to a lesser extent, captive Moors; and hanky-panky involving white men and female slaves resulted in the presence of some homegrown *mestiços*. The paucity of references in chronicles and documents to Jewish immigrants may well be due to the efforts of descendants anxious to destroy what to them were compromising statements. Revealing proper-names, however, prove the presence of "minority groups": Rua da Mouraria (Street of the Moorish Quarter) and Rua das Pretas (Street of the Black Women) which meet in downtown Funchal; Porto Judeu (Jewish Port) at the southeast corner of Terceira; and the Igreja dos Mouros (Church of the

Hauling agar, Porto Judeu, Terceira, July 1977

Moors), the parish church of Cedros on the north coast of Fayal which recently burned down.

The hard evidence for the presence of Blacks in the peopling of the Azores, a matter of great interest to some Americans of Azorean descent, is very hard to come by. This very paucity suggests that the outer limit of such presence was represented by a handful of black slaves scattered from Santa Maria to Corvo.

However many practicing Jews and New Christians there may have been over the centuries since the original peopling of the islands, the definitive abolition of the Inquisition in Portugal in 1821 resulted in the presence in the Azores of the prestigious Bensaúde family. The power of the Inquisition, originally introduced into Portugal in 1536, was already considerably reduced in the latter half of the eighteenth century. The first Bensaúde came to Portuguese territory from the Barbary Coast, that is, Morocco, in 1819. Family members prospered, some on Fayal, others on São Miguel. In 1873 the two sets of Azorean business interests merged to form the Casa Bensaúde (House of Bensaúde), particularly notable, as will be seen, in connection with support of shipping. Its headquarters is in Ponta Delgada.

In spite of strong reactions in recent years against the Bensaúdes in the Azores, their activity in Portugal in general has often been most enlightened. Thus, Alfredo Bensaúde founded the Instituto Superior Técnico (the M.I.T. of Portugal), later to become part of the Technical University of Lisbon. This latter, under the leadership of Mosés Bensabat Amzalak, was the only Portuguese university to join the International Association of Universities, founded in 1950. During the arrogant authoritarian years of falsely presumed self-sufficiency, the venerable University of Coimbra and the others did not deign to take advantage of a golden opportunity for self-improvement. This failure is all the more surprising as I was a member of the Association's first administrative board and from 1950 to 1955 never ceased to try to convince the Portuguese rectors to sign up.

To return to Azorean attitudes: Azoreans may have welcomed an opportunity to stress a North European connection for racist reasons. As Portuguese they are great admirers of French culture and, of course, understandably seize upon a possible French connection. Another reason, this one political in nature, has emerged for them to claim French and Flemish origins, or, to put it another way, to claim uniqueness.

The Lives of Azoreans and Madeirans   51

For many decades the inhabitants of the Azores have been dissatisfied with their relationship to Lisbon. The 1974 Revolution suddenly gave them an opportunity to manifest their sentiments, which range from a desire for true autonomy while yet remaining an integral part of Portugal to a desire for complete independence. Azoreans today are asking themselves all-important questions: who are we? are we Portuguese or are we Azoreans? To be Azoreans they must be different from Mainland Portuguese and from Madeirans. The affirmation that they are in fact a mixture of Portuguese, Flemish, and French would go a long way toward convincing the world—or at least themselves—that they are unique. New scholarly studies of North European presence in the archipelago accordingly must be examined carefully for a possible late-twentieth-century political twist, a slant diametrically opposed to that of studies of a dozen years ago which emphasized the Portuguesism of Azoreans. Moreover, the late Professor/Admiral Samuel Eliot Morison's remarks about his 1939 conversation with Dona Maria Isabel do Canto de Barcelos Coelho Borges in Angra must not be misconstrued to prove a political point. This descendant of Azorean explorers of old claimed to be Azorean and not Portuguese, yet she had portraits of the last few kings of Portugal in her salon!

The objective outsider concludes that white Portuguese origin predominates in the Azores and Madeiras. He should be forewarned, however, that we really know very little about the peopling of Insular Portugal, especially of the Azores, beyond the original settlements. Neurologists and geneticists are now concerned with the so-called "Azorean disease of the nervous system" (also known as "Machado disease" and "Joseph's disease"). Autosomal dominant, this inherited genetic disorder tragically affects members of one or more extended Azorean families in the islands and in the United States and is discussed further in Chapter 20. In order to gain deeper insight into the disease, medical doctors wish to know much more about the ultimate provenience of the population and about possible migrations from island to island. As each successive island was discovered and peopled, did settlers from Azorean islands discovered earlier move to the new one? Or did Continentals come directly out to the new one? Or both? How extensive was the Flemish presence in fact? Was there really ever a French or Breton presence of any magnitude? Was there any other human presence which has been overlooked? Was there significant movement among the islands after their original peopling? To such questions Ph.D. theses of the future will most certainly provide answers, but a generalization can be hazarded now. Once the original peoplers settled in their towns and villages, they stayed in them, except for emigrants who went abroad. And their descendants are in them yet. Knowledgeable local priests acquainted with parish vital statistics confirm this conclusion.

The question of provenience of the Insular Portuguese population should not obscure an important fact. Neither of the archipelagoes, not even a single one of their respective islands, has ever been invaded and occupied over an extended period of time by any foreigners. True, a Spanish military force was stationed on Terceira and other islands during the so-called Babylonian Captivity (1580-1640) and gave rise to a motto proposed for the new Azores (Preferably to die as free men than to live in peace subjugated) so reminiscent of the controversial statement on New Hampshire automobile number plates (Live free or die). In spite of the Spaniards, the Azores, like the rest of Portugal, although technically ruled during those years by three Philips kings of Spain and Portugal, were not invaded and occupied in the sense that Sicily and the Aeolian Islands have been on so many occasions over the years.

Although no full-blown Spanish occupation occurred, a definite Spanish influence is apparent on Terceira. Tourists invariably inspect the Spanish forts dating from that period. Especially around Midsummer Day (St. John's Day, June 24), they witness the running of the bulls, the type of macho-oriented bullfighting so reminiscent of Spain's Pamplona.

Azorean and general Portuguese denials to the contrary, differences between Portuguese and Spanish culture, and between Portugal and Spain as a whole, have often been exaggerated by some Portuguese. A rapprochement between the two Iberian nations now seems inevitable, for both face parallel political problems, even as regards Atlantic islands. As they both seek membership in the European Communities, their friends abroad sense an era of peace and unity in the making rather than a continuation of separation and isolation. Particularly does one feel this in Bruges, West Flanders, Belgium. Here Continental Portuguese were once active, to be followed by Spaniards. Here the Lusophile thrills to the many Portuguese coats of arms which decorate the tombs of Duke Charles the Bold (Duchess Isabel's son) and his daughter

Marie of Burgundy in the Church of Our Lady, the latter the great-granddaughter of a king of Portugal and the grandmother of a king of Castile. Here also the globetrotter recalls the Flemish presence in the distant Azores. The visitor acquainted with both Flanders and Azores even remembers the significant fact that, when the Spanish were ruling Portugal including the Atlantic archipelago, they were simultaneously heavily engaged in the Low Countries. Accordingly, he perceives another transmission belt for possible Flemish influence in the Atlantic, including even conceivably that of a lone defective gene.

Rulers from abroad aside, pirates and notably French corsairs have on occasion raided one or more islands, especially Madeira, relatively near the Moroccan coast. On Madeira the grandiose Curral das Freiras (Corral of the Nuns) attests to the attempt of local religious to flee from males by holing up in a huge crater. Back in 1597, Raleigh had sacked Horta and environs on Fayal. And during the Napoleonic era, British troops, as already outlined, served as a protective force on Madeira over a period of several years with Portuguese acquiescence.

The only true foreign-flag occupancy of Insular Portuguese space occurred in 1811. A tiny island suddenly emerged from the ocean depths between São Miguel and Terceira. British promptly claimed it and, in an apt Miltonian reminiscence suggested by the name of their ship, named it Sabrina. When they returned a few weeks later, it had dropped beneath the waves.

☆ ☆ ☆

The Insular Portuguese constitute a special people within world society. From several points of view a very homogeneous group, Azoreans and Madeirans live a life of Atlantic isolation beautifully sketched in the following Azorean poem:

> These grayish and very oppressive days
> Of an inexpressible void
> Which fall upon the island
> And leave us all close-lipped and seeming restless
> With a continuing yearning for the World
> Which even our ancestors never beheld renew itself

> This sea without end
> Which sails do not prefer
> And which is the highway always taken
> By those daydreams of ours of evasion
>
> These overlongish nights
> Of such gentle silences
> Which seem to set free our very hearts
> With the prospect of a returning world
>
> And this awakening always equal
> With one's head reposing upon the rock
> And one's eyes retaining the eternal bitterness
> Everything is and remains
> Little limited and uninteresting.

Atlantic, these islanders are also Portuguese. As such they reflect the culture primarily of southern Portugal and notably the Algarve. That culture was urban in character, with little human settlement between towns. Such is precisely the nature of life in the islands, where, with an exception on Madeira, people tend to congregate in villages and towns and to eschew living in isolated farmhouses.

The Algarve, like adjacent Spanish Andalusia, underwent Moorish occupation for centuries, from soon after the initial invasion of 711 until the middle of the thirteenth century, with Spain's Kingdom of Granada resisting Christian reconquest until January 2, 1492. But even here there is a difference. Both the short west coast and the extensive south coast of the Algarve are Atlantic. The coast of Andalusia is all south, but only that portion from the River Guadiana on the Portuguese border to Gibraltar is Atlantic; the rest is Mediterranean.

On the basis of Roman Empire, Latin language, Christianity, wine, olive oil, garlic, fig tree, carob tree (the fruit of which is the carob, called *la carrubba* in Italian), decorative tiles in which blues often predominate (*azulejos*), certain irrigation and water-raising techniques, and male dominance with attendant seclusion of women, it would be easy to conclude that the culture of not only the Algarve but of Portugal as a whole is Mediterranean. One distinguished Portuguese student of human geography writes: "In winter, wine warms and provides the comfort so often lacking in the houses; in summer, it refreshes, aids digestion, whets an appetite which decreases in the hot season. . . . Where cider or beer is drunk is another land and another people."

In the broadest sense, the culture of Portugal of course represents a fusion of the Mediterranean and the Northwest European (or Atlantic). When this same Portuguese geographer, however, writes that Portuguese culture is transitional and that beyond the Strait of Gibraltar the Algarve is the last Mediterranean land and the Minho is the first Atlantic land, and when he quotes approvingly an affirmation that "Portugal is Mediterranean by nature, Atlantic by position," we pause for reflection.

We think of the gay dances of Greeks and Italians and, today, Israelis and the happy songs of Naples and Sicily and quickly realize that triste fado-singing Portuguese dressed in black and bemoaning their fate are decidedly different. We find quite acceptable what an intelligent and experienced English lady has written:

> The Portuguese are predominantly an Atlantic not a Mediterranean people. Although they like to describe themselves as Latins, their temperament has very little in common with that of, say, the Italians. They are on the whole introverted, quiet, reserved, where the true Latin is an extrovert. The Italian phrase *far bella figura* has no equivalent in Portuguese, and indeed the Portuguese has a horror of making a spectacle of himself, a quality that belongs to the north of Europe rather than the south.

Reading this, we pause again. We think of the many Americans of Irish descent and birth in the very areas of the Northeastern United States where the Portuguese immigrants have settled. We can affirm with some authority that, while the Irish are undoubtedly Atlantic and are certainly Northwest European, the Portuguese bear little resemblance to them, not even in their Catholicism. On the other hand, we can also report that, deep inside, the Portuguese are by nature funloving, that at a Portuguese wedding in the United States the old folks respond to the playing of a polka exactly as do other Mediterranean folk, with bounce.

The logical conclusion is that the Portuguese departure from an original Latinity is not so much the result of Atlantic influence as an intra-Portuguese development occasioned by the social system which has prevailed in Portugal across absolute and constitutional monarchies, Republic of 1910, and right-wing dictatorship of Salazar/Caetano. Hopefully, this system is drawing rapidly to an end in spite of a number of indications that the 1974 Revolution is proving more political than social.

The Portuguese, to sum up, are unique. Indeed, Portugal is one of the oldest countries in Europe. It became independent of Castile and León in 1140. Its continental territory was completed by 1249 with the final reconquest of the Algarve from the Moors. The first major step in the creation of the France which we know today dates from 1515 and the incorporation of Brittany into the royal domain. Italy as such dates only from 1870 and Germany from 1871.

Ever since the twelfth century, the Portuguese masses have been dominated by a crushing social system, one imposed by fellow Portuguese, fellow Catholics, not by an outside ruler. The Portuguese people have never known anything but Portugal, not even, really, during the Spanish rule of 1580-1640. Unlike the Sicilians and Aeolians, they never knew Norman and French and Aragonese and North Italian rulers, real foreigners. The Portuguese never learned to thumb their noses at a ruling class and, protected by a mafia of their own creation, to go about their own business relatively unconcerned, poor, yes, and deprived, yes, but not broken in spirit.

Many humble Portuguese were clearly broken in spirit by the middle of the fifteenth century. That is why they were quick to take advantage of their geographical situation and the overseas proclivities of their upper class and embark on a first quest for betterment. But they were followed out into the Atlantic by Lisbon, or by the medieval equivalent of Lisbon. They could never shake off Lisbon. A number remained, or rebecame, subservient, docile, bent down, accepting, prone to bow and scrape, in fine ideal servants. Only as a result of a second quest for betterment, which brought them to the United States beginning in the early nineteenth century and now brings them to Canada as well as the United States, did some—not all—of them break loose and assert themselves as independent members of the human race. To those who remained behind on their islands the 25th of April, 1974, quite suddenly pointed out a new direction in which to seek the desired better life.

3

SUPERVISION FROM DISTANT LISBON

Prior to divesting itself of its colonies, Lisbon always considered Azores and Madeiras officially to be parts of what was known as Metropolitan Portugal, the mother country in Europe. The two archipelagoes formed Insular Portugal. They stood in opposition to Continental Portugal, the mainland territory. Although hardly adjacent, they were also known conveniently and descriptively as the Adjacent Islands.

In those days, Metropolitan Portugal was divided into twenty-two administrative districts, each named after its capital city. Continental Portugal accounted for eighteen—for example, the District of Faro, which consisted of and coincided with the Algarve. Insular Portugal comprised the remaining four. The Madeiras, including the Selvagens, formed the District of Funchal. The Azores were divided into three districts. The several islands were distributed as indicated in the following table, which gives the area in square miles and the population as reported by the most recent decennial census, that of 1970.

For purposes of comparison, the State of Maine has an area of 33,215 sq. mi. and population (estimated 1975) of 1,059,000, Rhode Island 1,214 sq. mi. and 927,000 inhabitants, Delaware 2,057 sq. mi. and 575,000, and Barnstable County, Massachusetts, (roughly Cape Cod) 399 sq. mi. and (in 1970) 96,656 inhabitants.

A glance at the map of the Azores in the endpapers demonstrates that the assignment of Azorean islands to districts did not correspond to the physical reality. While the Eastern Azores did coincide with the District of Ponta Delgada, the Central Azores included not only the three islands of the District of Angra but also Pico and Fayal of the District of Horta. The Western Azores belonged to the latter district.

Lisbon never labeled the Azores and Madeiras—officially—as colonies, although a case can be made that they were non-self-governing territories. And the Russians did make that case. The Soviet Union, to a greater extent than the United States, has perceived the true relationship of Insular Portugal to Lisbon. In connection with Article 73 of the Charter of the United Nations (on non-self-governing territories) and the U.N. committee on information from such territories, the U.N. General Assembly on December 15, 1960, adopted a resolution listing Portugal's territories, namely, the full panoply of eight overseas provinces including Goa. The Soviet delegations wished to add Azores and Madeiras to the list but failed to win majority support.

	Area	Population
CONTINENTAL PORTUGAL		
(18 districts)	34,170	8,124,019
INSULAR PORTUGAL		
(Adjacent Islands)	1,209	544,248
Azores	902	291,028
District of Ponta Delgada	329	159,360
Santa Maria	37	9,487
São Miguel	288	149,873
(City of Ponta Delgada)		(21,347)
District of Angra	272	90,409
Terceira	153	70,368
(City of Angra do Heroísmo)		(16,476)
Graciosa	23	7,188
São Jorge	92	12,853
District of Horta	301	41,259
Pico	167	18,014
Fayal	66	17,474
(City of Horta)		(7,600)
Flores	55	5,302
Corvo	7	469
Madeiras	307	253,220
District of Funchal	307	253,220
Porto Santo	16	3,927
Madeira	286	249,293
(City of Funchal)		(43,768)

In official Portuguese eyes the Cape de Verdes were associated with Portuguese Guinea, Angola, Mozambique, and all the other colonies. In the early Salazar days, this ensemble was known collectively and honestly as the Portuguese Colonial Empire, witness postage stamps of the late 1930's. Once the word colony became dirty in international circles, Salazar revived a very old term, province, and began to speak of Portugal's overseas provinces. The provinces taken together were known by the singular noun *Ultramar* (Overseas). This word derived from the Crusades of old. In French it was *Outremer*. It continued in use in the U.S. Marine Corps at least into World War II in official phrases like "temporary shore duty beyond the seas," a euphemism for a secret mission such as an invasion. Socialist Prime Minister Mário Soares early saw through this Salazaristic deception, however. In his volume of reminiscences he wrote: "The constitutional change approved in 1951 hurriedly transforming the 'colonies' into 'overseas provinces' and the 'empire' into a 'unitary multiracial and pluricontinental state' was a belated patching-up job which did not alter the underlying fundamental realities nor deceive anyone."

To sum up: at the time Dictator Caetano hurriedly left for Brazil in the spring of 1974, Portugal officially was divided into Metropolitan Portugal and Overseas Portugal, the latter (occasionally called Portugal Beyond Europe) into a series of overseas provinces. Unofficially, however, Azores and Madeiras were very often considered to be apart from Metropolitan Portugal. An example is contained on the program for the Miss Portugal 1972 beauty contest: "lindas raparigas da Metrópole, das Ilhas e do Ultramar" (beautiful girls from the Metropolis, from the Islands, and from the Overseas). Moreover, until November 1, 1969, Azores were officially distinguished from Madeiras in a most extraordinary way.

For my 1964 cruise abroad the Portuguese ship *Carvalho Araujo* from Lisbon to Madeiras and Azores and return via Madeiras to Lisbon, I was informed that Americans, Belgians, Canadians, and Luxembourgers needed a visa for the Azores but not for the Madeiras. My passport issued in 1962 shows that in Lisbon on April 4, 1964, PIDE—the international police later to fall into infamy—issued me a visa authorizing embarkation for the Azores. A five-year campaign on the part of Americans of Portuguese descent and birth was instrumental in bringing the anomaly to an end. They objected strenuously to paying the government of Portugal in Lisbon $4.77 for the privilege of visiting relatives in the Azores.

Stress on Lisbon's obvious putting down of Insular Portugal should not be interpreted to imply that the islanders were backwards in comparison with Continentals. To the contrary, in many respects islands such as Fayal for many decades were culturally and economically well advanced over outlying areas of Continental Portugal like the northeastern portion known as Trás-os-Montes or like part of the Alentejo, as will be seen in Chapter 19's statistics on illiteracy and Chapter 20's figures on births.

Continental patronizing, belittling, and neglect of Adjacent Islanders, especially Azoreans, was due in large part to ignorance. Salazar never visited the Azores, much less any overseas province. During my months of research there in 1939 the only Continentals I met were traveling salesmen and a handful of government officials. Even during the pre-Salazar Republic, the Azores were virtually unknown. In 1924, a Continental writer visited them and later published a book with precisely that title, *The Unknown Islands*, meaning unknown to him and fellow Continentals. Continentals were much better acquainted with Funchal, Madeira, and surrounding holiday zone because access was easy via the ships of many nations which passed through both Lisbon and the Madeiran capital en route to southern Africa and South America.

Lisbon considered everyone in all its lands as Portuguese and the entire territorial ensemble as Portugal. It insisted that all its school children everywhere be taught this terminology. Take the Angola-born white children of the white Angolan family which befriended me in Moçâmedes in the extreme south of Angola. In that year 1967, they reprimanded their Angola-born white parents for referring to a forthcoming holiday trip as a voyage to Portugal. "To the Metropolis," corrected the effectively indoctrinated children.

Lisbon attempted to sustain this fiction of a single nation by occasionally juggling around highly-placed officials of diverse proveniences, especially prelates of the Catholic Church. Thus, Portuguese bishops—perfectly sincere and possibly unaware of being used for a political purpose—would turn up in strange places. At one given moment there was an Azorean Archbishop of Goa (from Pico), an Azorean Bishop of Dili, Timor (also from Pico), an Azorean Bishop of Macao (from São Miguel), an Azorean Bishop of Nampula, Mozambique (also from São Miguel), a Madeiran Bishop of Coimbra on the Continent, a Goan Bishop of Santiago de Cabo Verde, and a Goan Bishop of Sá da Bandeira, Angola. There was no Cape Verdean-born bishop, however, a lacuna which confirms the conclusion that, on the racial prestige scale, blackness rated below Asiaticness in Europe as well as in America.

The fiction of intercontinental unity has been promulgated, naturally, by other European nations. I spent most of the year 1943 in Algeria, where it was constantly dinned into us that the three *départements* of that country formed an integral part of France whereas Tunisia and French Morocco enjoyed a different status. Moreover, a demand for island autonomy is not unknown to Paris even in the 1970's, witness Corsica.

The fundamental distinction between Metropolitan and Overseas Portugal was reflected within the Government in Lisbon. Continental and Insular Portugal came under the Minister of the Interior, the Overseas under the Minister of Overseas.

The Ministry of Overseas itself had grown to become a huge empire. As my invaluable series of Lisbon telephone directories reveals, it contained secretariats which together in effect formed a centralized government. Belying the doctrine that all territories formed a single integrated Portugal, the Ministry supervised banking and the issuance of bank notes and coins for the different overseas provinces, and postage stamps, and customs and visa regulations. It also had its hand in the naming of bishops.

In retrospect, the Catholic Church in her multisecular wisdom has proved cleverer than Portugal regarding the Atlantic archipelagoes. The Church treated Azores, Madeiras, and Cape Verde Islands coequally, as Americans have traditionally viewed them. Each group of islands formed, and still form, a single diocese, with sees in Angra, Funchal, and Praia (on Santiago) respectively, all three then and now suffragan to the Metropolitan Archdiocese of Lisbon.

The notion of associating Cape Verdeans ecclesiastically with Madeirans is nothing new, and a visit to the attractive cathedral in downtown Funchal proves dramatic. In 1514, Rome established the Diocese of Funchal. The new diocese embraced all Atlantic, African, and Asian lands into which the Portuguese had expanded except Morocco. In 1533, the reigning pope raised the status of Funchal to that of metropolitan archdiocese. At the same time, he created a series of suffragan dioceses: Angra (for the Azores), Santiago de Cabo Verde, São Tomé-e-Príncipe, and Goa. The latter diocese in its turn encompassed the whole of the Indian Ocean area from the Cape of Good Hope to the China Sea. In

1558, Goa became an archdiocese in its own right, independent of Funchal and with its own suffragan dioceses. Much later, Funchal reverted to diocesan status. Bereft of an imperial halo, it was subordinated to Lisbon.

In a November 1966 formal lecture in Portuguese in Lisbon, which was printed there shortly afterward, I raised the question of the administrative distinction which Lisbon was then making between the Cape Verde Islands on the one hand and the Azores and the Madeiras on the other. Before a former Foreign Minister and a number of other high dignitaries, I hinted that New Englanders and perhaps Americans in general were most interested in Continental Portugal, the three groups of Atlantic islands, their collective strategic importance, and their political future. In that pre-divestiture age, I implied that Americans were rather less interested in the mainland African provinces and tended to think of them as African and not Portuguese. What I was striving to put across was the idea that New Englanders might be interested in Portugal's continued dominion over the three archipelagoes, and that it behooved Lisbon, if it gave any weight to U.S. opinion, to detach the Cape Verde Islands from the Overseas and to do so pronto.

At an ensuing luncheon meeting, to which I was invited immediately following my impertinent presentation, kind and informed hosts hastened to refute my arguments. After a little groping, they settled on the single point of self-interest: the Cape Verdeans' own self-interest dictated that they remain in the overseas category, for they would benefit from the greater governmental largesse of the official development programs then being devoted to the overseas provinces.

What those highly-placed but short-sighted Portuguese did not realize at that 1966 luncheon was that they were admitting to me official neglect of Azores and Madeiras.

☆ ☆ ☆

Distant Lisbon neglected the Adjacent Islands. It kept them weak by maintaining the two archipelagoes administratively separate from each other and by dividing the nine far-flung Azores islands into three administrative districts. It pretended that the four insular districts were "autonomous" in contrast to those of Continental Portugal. It even stressed this autonomous nature in the title of the legal document which provided the basis for Lisbon's supervision: Statute for the Autonomous Districts of the Adjacent Islands. This document was originally issued in 1940. It reappeared as late as 1972 in an annotated edition published in Ponta Delgada. The following diagram, based on the Statute, attempts to illustrate exactly how Lisbon exercised its supervision and achieved its domination.

The direction of the arrows in the diagram reflects the numerous appointments from above and the few elections from below. The diagram must not be construed, however, as indicating that this particular feature of Portuguese national life was peculiar to the National Dictatorship of Salazar and the successor dictatorship of Caetano. The concept of centralization and authority from above dated back to the Roman Empire, of which in certain respects Portugal was the last surviving heir. The concept received its modern configuration from Napoleon Bonaparte, whose troops invaded and occupied portions of Continental Portugal (but not the islands) and left a lasting legacy of destruction. Many features of Portugal today should be credited to Napoleon and not to Salazar: the centralized system of public instruction which graduated into national education, for example, and the rigid administrative subdivision into *distritos* (districts), *concelhos* (municipalities), and *freguesias* (precincts).

The word *freguesia* is of particular interest. A *freguês* is a store's customer. The ensemble of customers, the clientele, constitutes the store's *freguesia*. In the days of old, a local Catholic church had its *fregueses* or parishioners. The ensemble of parishioners made up a *freguesia* or parish. At that time, the smallest administrative unit of the country was the *freguesia*, for the simple reason that birth, marriage, and death records were the Church's concern and therefore in the Church's hands.

With the laicization of Portugal in modern times, the *freguesias* became civil administrative units. The Church, divorced from civil administration to as great a degree as in the United States if not more so, came to call its basic unit a *paróquia* or parish. A similar evolution took place in the State of Louisiana where what other states call a county is named a parish. Inevitably, in Portuguese territory, coincidence exists on many occasions between the area of the civil *freguesia* and the zone of the Church's *paróquia*. In the islands the coincidence is practically total, yet it behooves the outsider to appreciate the difference.

Civil Administration in the Adjacent Islands (1928-1974)

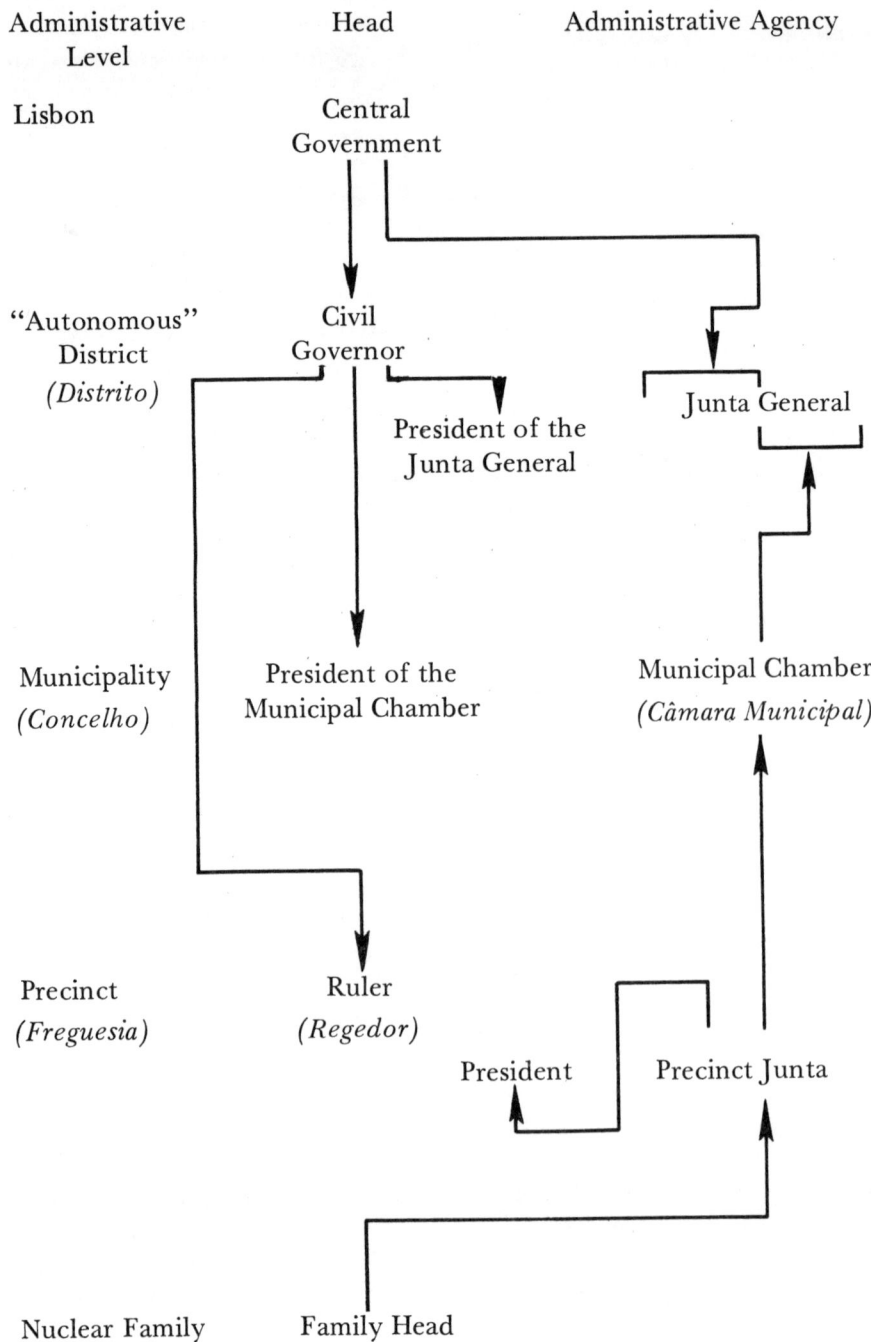

Prior to the 1976 Constitution, however, there were no precincts on the two adjacent islands of least population, Corvo and Porto Santo. In these unique cases, the island constituted a single undivided municipality. Today the municipality of Porto Santo consists of the single precinct of Porto Santo.

There did exist a measure of local self-government on those Azores islands which had precincts. The precinct was administered by its junta. Being a decidedly local administrative agency, this *junta de freguesia* always consisted of members who were local, elected by the heads of the nuclear families. Occasionally, in the Azores, the group had its own little building, as in the Angústias precinct at the southern end of Horta around Porto Pim, where the whales are brought in. In other places, they met in a church or school. Prior to the complete separation of Church and State following the advent of the Republic in 1910, the president or chairman of the precinct junta was often the parish priest. Still today, as a further example of the blending of *paróquia* and *freguesia*, the precinct junta is responsible for the establishment, enlargement, and administration of the cemeteries which exist within the confines of the precinct.

On the island of Madeira, although the ten municipalities were subdivided into a total of fifty-two precincts, there were no precinct juntas and there had not been since 1888. The reasons which used to be given by officials in Funchal concerned the nature of living on the island, namely, the spread-out distribution of dwellings due to the difficult nature of the terrain. Homes were not clustered into villages; therefore there was little awareness of village society, hence little need for juntas in the precinct. As there obviously were local Church parishes other than in the municipality seats, this explanation stood in need of amplification. Today the precinct juntas are being restored.

The Statute for the Autonomous Districts of the Adjacent Islands presented the fact that there were no precinct juntas on Madeira in charmingly indirect fashion typical of the administrative double-talk of that era. Article 120 stated that in each precinct of the archipelago of the Azores there would be a junta and a *regedor* (ruler). Article 123 stated that in each precinct of the Madeiran archipelago there would be a ruler. The Azorean-written annotation to the latter article pointed out that by "confronting this article with Article 120 of the present Statute one

South coast of Madeira from seaward

Interior of Madeira—Curral das Freiras

notes that in the Madeiran archipelago there are no precinct juntas."

The Statute for the Adjacent Islands was a supplement to the voluminous *Código Administrativo*. This Administrative Code applied to Continental Portugal, and also to Insular Portugal except where the special Statute applied. These documents and other relevant laws or decrees governed voting. Basically, the election of precinct juntas was the only one in which Continental and Azorean—but not Madeiran—citizens participated. And then only heads of families, including widows or other woman heads, voted. Everyone voted for the Deputies of the old National Assembly; but, as the candidates were handpicked and choices were limited or nonexistent, that particular universal suffrage was farcical. Through the Presidential election of 1958, when General Humberto Delgado was the opposition candidate, all voters had a voice. Salazar was frightened by the results of 1958, and President Admiral Tomás in 1965 and again in 1972 was reelected not by the people but by a body of electors.

The municipality was administered by a local *câmara municipal* (municipal chamber), elected by the members of the precinct juntas of the *concelho*. On the islands with no precinct juntas, there was in each municipality a municipal council named by the civil governor. This appointed council elected the *vereadores* or members of the municipal chamber, who were often but inappropriately called aldermen in English translation, just as the president of the municipal chamber was often and equally inappropriately called the mayor of his municipality.

The presiding officer or president of the chamber was most often, but not necessarily, a local man. Because he did not have to be local, the major islands of Insular Portugal, those with port cities which were in turn district capitals, could come to dominate the other islands, which almost by definition were the minor ones. Take the District of Ponta Delgada, consisting of huge São Miguel and relatively small Santa Maria. The civil governor and the junta general had their offices in Ponta Delgada, on São Miguel. St. Michael's, the Green Island, was divided into six municipalities: Ponta Delgada, Lagoa, Nordeste, Povoação, Ribeira Grande, and Vila Franca do Campo. The island of Santa Maria constituted but a single municipality, that of Vila do Porto. The entire island, in spite of its sprawling international airport, was coequal with one sixth of its neighbor forty-six nautical miles away. Here is the point: in pre-1974 days, the president of the municipal chamber of Vila do Porto, Santa Maria, was from São Miguel. An engineer, he was also the Azorean representative of Pan American World Airways. This, of course, is not necessarily to say that he was not an able man and excellent choice.

The municipality was a very old level of government, going back to the Middle Ages. The administrative building, the home of the municipal chamber, was often known as the *Paços do Concelho* (Palaces of the Municipality). Some of these palaces in Continental Portugal are magnificent structures, for instance in Tavira in the Algarve.

The municipality was old, and it was basic in the lives of the people. A scholar-priest who is pastor of Horta's Angústias parish goes as far as to affirm that the *município*, as the *concelho* used to be called, was in the past the moving force behind the entire social organization of the Azores, the agency which was most central and which, with its tentacles, dominated the entire life of earlier generations. It was even more basic than the Church, and it continues basic. The people look to the Câmara, as it is succinctly and affectionately known, for help in emergencies.

The primacy of the municipality within Portugal was made evident in the very first paragraph of the Administrative Code: "The continental territory is divided into municipalities, which consist of precincts and form districts." The same phraseology appeared in the first paragraph of the Statute for the Adjacent Islands.

Because of the prominence of the municipality and its administrative building, it was natural for the Portuguese who immigrated into the United States to perceive the importance of City Hall in that country. They promptly baptized it *Ceriol* in their native language and this word, in turn, worked its way back to Insular Portugal.

At the top of the administrative structure was the "autonomous" district, administered by a local *junta geral* (junta general). The juntas general consisted of seven members. Four were elected directly by the respective municipal chambers and certain corporate agencies, and the civil governor had to name one of them as the junta's president. In exceptional cases, however, the governor could select a president from outside the group. The other three members of the junta general were there ex officio: the rector of the district's *liceu* (State secondary school; see Chapter 19), the district's delegate from the National Institute of Labor and Welfare, and a public works engineer. As these three were named by Lisbon for their principal duties, only four-sevenths of the junta general resulted from an electoral process.

The members of the several governing bodies, or administrative agencies, then, were local, and the ruler of each precinct had to be a resident of the precinct. In spite of the local provenience of these officials, Lisbon in fact dominated the Insular Portuguese.

The Minister of the Interior in Lisbon named a civil governor for each "autonomous" district and, also, an alternate for him. The civil governor represented the central government, Lisbon, and was the de facto ruler. Often referred to in the adulatory press as the district chief, he could be either a local man or an outsider. In April 1972, the governor in Horta was a native of Flores (same district) and the governor in Angra a native of Terceira (same island), whereas the governors in Ponta Delgada and in Funchal came from the Continent. A year later, the same governors continued in service in Ponta Delgada and Funchal, but new governors had been appointed to Horta and Angra, both of them from the Continent.

The "civil" governor could be an officer of the armed forces, as in Ponta Delgada, where the Continental governor and the Continental alternate governor were both army colonels, or in Funchal, where the Continental governor was a colonel and a count and was subsequently exiled to Brazil. If the commanding officers of the three armed forces and the captains of the ports and the bishop in any one archipelago were also sent over from the Continent—and they were—the outside observer concluded that a given "autonomous" district possessed no autonomy whatsoever and that the civil governor was in fact an exarch, that the island districts were exarchies. Indeed, whenever I asked in the islands just what the word "autonomous" meant, I invariably received an all-knowing smile but no verbal answer.

Although they granted the Insular Portuguese precious little participation in their own government, Salazar/Caetano did not rule Insular Portugal militarily. Their Portugal was not a military state in the common meaning of the term. True, a large number of Portuguese men were under arms for the African wars, and some observers estimated that, keeping all factors in proportion, the nation's military involvement was equivalent to a U.S. presence in Vietnam of 1.4 million men. Portugal's military personnel were not training or serving en masse in the islands, however. The traditional Insular reluctance to strike out and innovate must be attributed more to innate character shaped by years or centuries of endurance of the system than to fear of immediate repression. The means of such repression were not at hand.

The head of the army, the so-called Military Governor of the Azores, formerly maintained his headquarters in Angra, the central district capital. In 1936, the headquarters was moved to Ponta Delgada, and during my 1974 visit the commanding general was a Continental. The Azores Naval Command was based on Ponta Delgada, where the ranking officer was a Continental commodore married to a São Miguel lady. The Azores Air Zone was naturally administered from Lajes on Terceira. The commanding general was of course a Continental. As a further example of Continental penetration of the islands, the commanding officer of Fayal's "Independent" Coast Defense Battery was from the Continent, the soldiers using as their barracks the monastery beside the old Church of Our Lady of Mount Carmel.

In all fairness I should add that, from what I observed, some at least of these outside officials sent from the Continent to govern or administer the islands were hard-working persons. They often came to be genuinely interested in the welfare of their Insular wards. Their posts were not political in the U.S. meaning of the word. They could hardly be called patronage posts, for, far from representing sinecures, they must have seemed to many holders a kind of exile.

Lisbon argued that it had to administer island affairs with the firm hands of its own officials because the islanders were unprepared to take care of them. To an extent, this was true. It was true because the islanders were not acquiring the necessary experience combined with responsibility and, above all, a disposition to act independently. The system stifled local administrative initiative, with the result that the precinct ruler depended on the president of the municipal chamber, who depended on the civil governor, who depended on the Minister of the Interior, who depended on the President of the Council of Ministers (Salazar or Caetano). In effect, a vicious circle was operative.

In general, elections and electioneering as Americans understand them were almost nonexistent. And here is an astonishing fact: elections were more nonexistent in the Adjacent Islands than in Continental Portugal. This condition becomes apparent from a detailed comparison of the method of selecting the effective heads and the junta presidents at the various administrative levels on the mainland with that in effect in the islands.

Again, in fairness, it should be said that in the normal course of Insular events the president of the municipal chamber nominated the precinct rulers for formal appointment by the civil governor, who presumably also listened to the opinion of the junta general's president concerning appropriate candidates for the several presidencies at the municipality level. On the other hand, it is true that from 1834 to 1928 (the year Salazar began to rule in earnest), the president of the municipal chamber was a local man elected locally, although each municipality also had its *administrador* (administrator), occasionally an outsider, appointed from above. In 1928, the post of administrator was abolished.

The unit underlying the entire Portuguese administrative structure in the pre-April 25 era was the nuclear family, which was represented, in the eyes of the government as well as in the eyes of the Church and of society in general, by its head. In other words, father was the apparent boss in Portuguese society, a fact which explains much of what goes on within Portuguese communities in the United States. Within the islands, that fact was translated into frequent abuse of the concept of authority at all levels from the home to Lisbon. Portuguese immigrant children in U.S. schools who have previously studied in Portuguese schools reflect the abuse when they tell of the respect in which they held their teachers in the old country, of the stress in the island schools on discipline, and of the widespread although forbidden use of corporal punishment. All the evidence points to an extensive use of the yardstick on the palm of the hand in Portuguese schools, in a country which used to pride itself on rarely resorting to capital punishment for crimes.

The net result of this cult of authority was often an inability, in the United States, to make personal decisions, whether in the realm of learning in school (where critical thinking must come into play) or of coping with a new social environment (with new rules about dating, voting, and like matters). And yet, when some of these very Portuguese immigrated into the United States and breathed the freer air, they became perfectly capable of expressing their personal views (often vociferously as if out of release), acting as community leaders, and participating in the American democratic process. The stagnation in the islands was not due to the Insular Portuguese people but to the pan-Portuguese system. A British writer strayed way off the beam when he wrote in his book on Salazar and "modern" Portugal: "It will be said, and rightly said, that the British or American democratic models will never transplant to societies inherently unattuned to them, . . ." with a reference to Salazar's writings.

Shortly after the 1974 Revolution, the civil governors of the Adjacent Islands were packed off and the secretary of each civil government took over as acting governor. On June 18, 1974, the presidents of the municipal chambers all resigned, and the senior *vereador* in each took over as acting president. The presidents and vice presidents of the juntas general, on the other hand, retained office for a longer period. Much confusion followed, with an attempt made to establish neighborhood and workers' committees as parallel powers to, and possible eventual replacements for, governors, *vereadores,* and others not considered representative.

4
THE BONES OF PETER AND MICHAEL

From 1928 to 1974, the Insular Portuguese were supplied a sufficiency of reasons for desiring administrative if not political reform. To this impulse was added the slight dosage of liberalism imparted to all Portuguese, but above all to Azoreans, by the changes which were instituted in the 1820's.

Over the centuries, the Insular Portuguese problem has stemmed in part from Lisbon's policy of separating Madeiras from Azores, yet the two archipelagoes are physically as near to each other as either is to Lisbon. Indeed, the distance between Santa Maria and the island of Madeira (454.3 n mi.) is only a little more than that from one end of the Azores to the other (332.6 n mi.). Unification of Portuguese Atlantic islands, however, now seems an impossible dream.

Over the centuries, the Azorean problem has stemmed in part from the attempted imperialism of Insular cities. The primacy of Angra in the early years led to the tripartite division and the three capital cities of the nineteenth and twentieth centuries. This division into districts, in turn, led to the present post-1974 concept of pan-Azoreanness with a single government distributed equally over the three cities. The new policy, however, is being challenged, this time by the attempted primacy of Ponta Delgada.

The island of Terceira once dominated the Azores. Portuguese fleets returning from India would round the Cape of Good Hope, pass St. Helena and Ascension, sail west of the Cape de Verdes, and make for Angra, thence to run down the latitude of Lisbon (almost exactly that of Angra). Vasco da Gama called at Angra in 1499 on the return from his first voyage, and his brother Paulo died and was buried there. Famous travelers to Asia of the sixteenth century, including an Italian early and a Dutchman late, stayed at Angra for varying lengths of time and included descriptions—or at least mention—of the city in their narratives.

When the single Diocese of the Azores was created in the early 1530's, Angra became the see city.

In Portugal the mid-eighteenth century was a period of great change, including administrative reform, especially after the disastrous earthquake which rocked Lisbon and other parts of Portugal on All Saints' Day, November 1, 1755. Thus, in 1766, the Azores were organized into a single captaincy general. The residence of the captain general was in Angra, in the sprawling building still known as the Palace of the Captains General (Palácio dos Capitães Generais).

☆ ☆ ☆

Several years ago, when we were both passengers aboard the *Carvalho Araujo* rolling heavily in the swells of the St. George Channel off Cais do Pico waiting to unload cargo, an Azorean called my attention to the Palaces of the Municipality. (Cais do Pico is the seat of one of Pico's three municipalities, the Concelho de S. Roque do Pico.) He informed me that the building had once been a Franciscan monastery, reminded me that the government had confiscated the property of religious orders back in 1834, and commented that the State would have gone broke erecting administrative buildings if it had not stolen them from the Church. I have since verified his observation in detail. Still today in the Adjacent Islands, many governmental administrative offices and other institutions are located on or in former Church property, specifically in ex-Jesuit schools or ex-Franciscan monasteries.

Horta exemplifies the situation to perfection. As one strolls through the city, one comes to the seventeenth-century Church of St. Francis, now the possession of the Santa Casa da Misericórdia (an establishment discussed in the chapter on doctors and midwives). Next to the church, in the former monastery, is a poorhouse, called in Portuguese an asylum of mendicity and dated 1906. Continuing on to the north, the visitor suddenly arrives at a huge structure of the 1600's which was once the proud possession of the Society of Jesus. In the center of the edifice is the principal parish church of the city, the Mother Church (Igreja Matriz). Its design is typical of the great Jesuit churches—Bom Jesus in Old Goa, the Gesù in Rome, São Roque in Lisbon—with a single nave and no pillars to hide either altar or preacher from full view of all the congregation. To the left or south of this church, in the supplementary Jesuit structures, were the offices of the civil governor and of the junta general, with separate entrances. To the right were those of the municipal chamber.

In Angra a similar fate befell the Franciscan and Jesuit buildings. For years, the Franciscan monastery contained the State secondary school. In October 1969, however, an elaborate new building went into service for the Liceu Nacional, whereupon the Museum of Angra took over the Franciscan church and monastery. The Church of the *Colégio*, that is, the church of the former Jesuit secondary school, famed for its beautiful Dutch *azulejos*, is now, due to the expulsion of the Jesuits from Portuguese territory in 1759, all but devoid of ecclesiastical functions, being a dependency of the cathedral. In 1974, the school itself housed various government agencies, including the civil governor's offices, the police (who were shortly to move to new quarters), and army offices. Beginning in 1766 and for as long as there was such an official, it had served as the Palace of the Captains General.

In Ponta Delgada the former Jesuit church, of magnificent façade, has been abandoned since the Jesuits were expelled. The former Franciscan church functions as one of the city's three parish churches (Church of St. Joseph), and the district hospital occupies the monastery. Quarters for the civil governor and the junta general were provided by the former monastery of Our Lady of the Immaculate Conception, of the middle of the seventeenth century. Later transformed into a "palace," it is today called the Palácio da Conceição.

In Funchal civil use of the Church's buildings was effected on a far less extensive scale. The Governo Civil (Civil Government), as the offices of the civil governor and his entourage were called, was in an elegant old waterfront fort, the Fortress of St. Lawrence, whither President Américo Tomás and Prime Minister Marcello Caetano were first consigned when evicted from Continental territory following the 1974 Revolution. Nearby, the Junta General of the Autonomous District occupied its own elaborate building. The Jesuit Church of the *Colégio* still stands, facing the square on which the building of the municipal chamber is located. To its left, the old Jesuit school functioned as an army barracks.

The municipal chambers of Angra, Ponta Delgada, and Funchal occupy beautiful buildings built specifically for them. The structures confirm the thesis that the municipality level of government is closest to the people. The Church did not have to be robbed in order for the State to provide office space for the respective sets of offices.

My friend off Cais do Pico implied that nothing less than robbery had taken place back in 1834. Talking in this fashion, an Azorean reveals not so much genuine affection for the Church and disapproval of the governmental action taken in the 1830's as a certain resentment toward distant Lisbon, a certain chafing at the bit as regards being driven from afar, in fine a certain liberalism. This liberal strain goes back at least as far as the period immediately following the French Revolution and Napoleonic era. A look at the origin of this strain proves instructive, for it elucidates one of the causes of the beginning of mass Azorean emigration to the United States following the war of 1812.

When Napoleon's troops invaded Portugal toward the end of 1807, the royal family and many of the court entourage fled to the capital of Portugal's greatest colony, Brazil. They left behind a Portugal which almost immediately began to oust the French and soon acquired an English commander-in-chief. In the New World, in 1808, the Portuguese visitors made of Rio de Janeiro the capital of the entire Portuguese-speaking world.

The royal family at the time consisted of a widowed and mad queen, Maria I, totally incapacitated, and her son João (John), the Prince-Regent, who in effect had ruled Portugal since 1792. With João went his Spanish wife and their two sons, Pedro and Miguel. Lest the reader deem this ménage a cozy little family, let him be disabused at once. Prince João and Princess Carlota maintained separate establishments. Worse, the two brothers were antagonistic one to the other. Older Pedro sided with the father, younger Miguel with the mother.

In 1816 in Rio, Queen Maria died. The Prince-Regent succeeded her as João VI. He continued to reign from Brazil, the former mother country having become the colony and vice versa. In 1817, his son Pedro married Maria Leopoldina, daughter of the last Holy Roman Emperor, Francis II, who had been deposed by Napoleon (his son-in-law, husband of Maria Leopoldina's sister Marie Louise) and was ruling as Emperor Francis I of Austria. The marriage was consummated in Rio, whither the bride traveled.

In 1820, well after the Napoleonic era and as an indirect aftermath of the French Revolution, the inevitable Portuguese revolution broke out, setting absolutists against liberals. The following year, King João and Queen Carlota journeyed to Continental Portugal accompanied by Prince Miguel. The king left Pedro as regent in Brazil. On September 7, 1822, the unavoidable happened once again: Brazil declared its independence from Portugal under this same Pedro, who accepted the change at a brook called Ipiranga. Pedro became known to history as an emperor, Emperor Dom Pedro I, in true Roman and Napoleonic style and in direct imitation of what had just momentarily happened in Mexico.

The father, King João VI, died in Portugal in 1826. Emperor Pedro was of course his heir, and he forthwith ruled Portugal in absentia as King Pedro IV. He was immediately challenged by his on-the-spot brother, Dom Miguel. In the meantime, the two rival political factions had become polarized around the two brothers—the liberals around Dom Pedro and the absolutists or conservatives or traditionalists around Dom Miguel and his mother. Due to the vicissitudes of Fortune, Miguel spent from May 1824 to February 1828 in exile, most of the time at the imperial court in Vienna, the court of his rival brother's father-in-law. The modern Lusophile desirous of appreciating the true historical dimension of Portugal in Mainland Europe visits not only Bruges in West Flanders but also Schönbrunn Palace in Vienna. Here he senses the presence of Maria Leopoldina and Miguel, and Emperor Charles I (buried on Madeira) and his son Archduke Otto as well. The latter are discussed in Chapter 13.

With King Pedro IV of Portugal still in Brazil, Miguel's forces soon gained some measure of effective control in the European territory. In 1828, Miguel had himself acclaimed King Miguel I, and the Holy See recognized his regime. Shortly thereafter, the captain general of the Azores resident on the island of Terceira openly sided with Pedro and provided a rallying ground for the liberals. The Azores, which never recognized Miguel as king, thus entered the conflict. The archipelago had been prepared for this role by the deportation of liberal writers from the Continent to the islands back in 1810. At the town of Praia on the eastern shore of Terceira on August 11, 1829, the liberals won their first military victory over the absolutists.

As a result of the island's role in this successful struggle, the names of the *cidade* (city) of Angra and of the *vila* (town) of Praia were expanded to Angra do Heroísmo (Bay of Heroism) and

Praia da Vitória (Beach of the Victory), two symbols of Insular Portuguese reluctance to accept right-wing domination from Continental Portugal or anywhere else. Praia da Vitória became prominent once again beginning in 1943 in another round of resistance to oppression from the main. It became the port of the new airport at Lajes, for advantage was never taken of the golden opportunity during and after World War II to build up the ancient port of Angra as a modest rival to Ponta Delgada. Today Lajes is supplied through Praia da Vitória, which now boasts a breakwater in addition to elaborate facilities for the unloading of petroleum products. Being given the central location of Terceira within the archipelago, the island's important role across the centuries, the availability of port facilities at Praia, and the presence next to Praia of the Azores's only international airport constructed on a major island, surely Praia da Vitória would be a principal candidate for capital of any united Azores of the future whether autonomous or independent.

Early in 1831, Dom Pedro abdicated his imperial throne in favor of his only son Pedro de Alcântara, too young to govern Brazil and therefore aided by a council of regency. Pedro the father proceeded via England and France to the Azores. For several months he remained in the archipelago, where a provisional government based on Terceira was functioning. It was this government which abolished the captaincy general and paved the way for the division into administrative districts. King Pedro IV was thus the first Portuguese monarch freely to set foot in the Azores, although his was hardly the paternal royal visit from Lisbon which the Azoreans had every right occasionally to expect and which finally materialized with King Carlos in 1901. In the seventeenth century, King Afonso VI, mentally and sexually incomplete, had been caught by a political squeeze and imprisoned for five years, 1669-1674, in the Fortress of St. John the Baptist just outside Angra on Mount Brazil (shades of a legend on medieval maps).

Pedro IV's expedition to Continental Portugal was fitted out in the Azores, and the task had its elitist social aspect. A niece of Charles William Dabney born on Terceira in 1848 wrote in the 1880's of the events of those exciting days:

> ... In the spring of 1832 the expedition was fitted out in the Azores to go to Lisbon, and place Donna Maria on the throne, in place of the usurper Don Miguel. Dom Pedro, her

father, who had resigned the throne in her favor, commanded the expedition in person, and with him were many noted men of Portugal, besides representatives of other nations, one of his aides being a grandson of La Fayette; and the naval part of the expedition was in command of Admiral Sartorius, of the British navy. The fleet fitted out in Fayal, where there was the best port. The army collected in the larger islands, St. Michael's and Terceira. The ex-Emperor went and came in his little steamer, the first which had been seen in those islands. He was greatly feted by the prominent citizens of the place, both native and foreign. . . .

Later in 1832, King Pedro IV left Terceira for Continental Portugal. By 1834 he had defeated Miguel and the absolutists and succeeded in having his fifteen-year-old daughter recognized as Queen Maria II. Miguel was forced into exile a second time. He lived for many years in Germany, married Adelaide of Löwenstein-Wertheim-Rosenberg, and died in 1866. He never returned, alive, to Portugal.

Pedro IV never returned, alive, to Brazil. Rather, in that same year 1834 he passed away in Portugal. As he had renounced both his thrones, he was simply the Duke of Braganza. He was buried in the Braganza family pantheon in Lisbon. A statue of him in the Rossio, the city's central square, lists the salient facts of his life: born October 12, 1798; granted a constitution to Portugal on April 29, 1826; died September 24, 1834; and received the tribute of the monument from the Portuguese people in 1870.

By 1840, Pedro IV's Brazilian son was of age and ruling in Portuguese America as Emperor Dom Pedro II. This Pedro visited Cambridge, Massachusetts, in 1876, had dinner with Longfellow in Craigie House on Brattle Street on June 10, and subsequently translated Longfellow writings into Portuguese. He was in the United States on the occasion of the nation's centennial celebration, the first royal visitor to come to U.S. shores, and spoke in Philadelphia on one end of the first long-distance telephone conversation, hence the Pedro the Voder (Voice Demonstrator) exhibited by Bell Telephone at the 1939 World's Fair in New York.

When the Church plays politics, the Church ultimately falls victim—a warning which is as important for Portuguese priests and prelates in Continental and Insular Portugal and the United States in the mid-1970's as it should have been a century and a half ago. The Church, or prominent members of it, had sided with Dom Miguel and the absolutists during the period of political struggle. In the year of liberal victory, the victorious liberals quite naturally decreed the confiscation of the property of religious orders, Pedro IV having already in May 1832 decreed the suppression of various religious establishments in the Azores.

These victors for a moment seemed bent on effecting the profound changes in the social system which were so badly needed. Curiously, they did effect one surprising change. As a result of Pedro IV's doing away with convents, fine ladies worked, reports the *Annals of the Dabney Family in Fayal*. An ex-convented nun "was the first lady in Fayal, who ever came out boldly before the public, to work for pay. She used to sew straw bonnets."

They did not effect the needed changes, however, and in retrospect we see that they had no serious intention of so doing. Their changes merely substituted one gang in power for another. As Almeida Garrett, the early-nineteenth-century Portuguese romantic writer who had spent his youth on Terceira and sided with the liberals during the Pedro-Miguel contentions, phrased it, the barons succeeded the friars. This author, himself a viscount, called these barons, who were still very much in evidence in island society as late as April 24, 1974, especially on São Miguel, the Sancho Panzas of the new social system. All that was accomplished, in the words of a more recent writer, was to create "a new class of capitalist rural proprietors with a vested interest in the régime, and to confer the social status of landownership on the aspiring bourgeoisie." The American TV commentators who accompanied Humberto Cardinal Medeiros, Archbishop of Boston, to his native Azores in the summer of 1973 repeatedly called the descendants of this group the "landed gentry."

Another attempt was made ostensibly to change the social system in 1910 with the Republic and its expulsion of religious orders. The new regime followed this action with an assault on the secular Church and separated Church and State. Again, a new gang came to power. And so on through 1926 and 1968 and 1974 and. . . .

A principal lesson from all these early-nineteenth-century facts concerns the later Azorean political stance. Azoreans in general became pro-Catholic liberals. They were liberals in the normal political acceptance of the term and therefore in principle against absolutist rule from Lisbon and against having their sons "serve the king"—that is, bear arms—on the distant Continent for illiberal regimes. They were pro-Catholic in the sense of resenting the confiscation of Church property to support a civil administration based on Lisbon. At least, such appeared to be the view of my acquaintance off Cais do Pico in 1964.

There is, however, an opposing point of view. Because of the general poverty of the masses of the people in the islands over the centuries, it is legitimate to conclude that the religious orders had done a little robbing of their own. There had always been an excessive number of religious in the Azores. For example, in 1720 about eight percent of the population of Ponta Delgada were members of religious orders, whereas in 1644 the percentage for Rome was 6.6. These religious had extracted large sums in little quantities from the people in order to build ornate churches and spatious monasteries and convents. In 1834, the people retaliated by taking back what was in reality theirs and proceeded to devote it to their own benefit. So doing, the people avoided being taxed to erect new administrative buildings.

The aftermath of the so-called liberal struggles continued on in an extraordinary way.

In 1966, the body of Dom Miguel was returned from Germany to Lisbon, amid great monarchical enthusiasm (which seemed suddenly to collapse when Salazar was stricken in 1968) and amid great clerical rhetoric. This cadaverous migration took place in the very year in which a Cultural Treaty Between Portugal and Brazil went into effect. From 1966 on, therefore, the bones of the rival brothers coexisted in Lisbon. Then, in April 1972, the sesquicentennial year of Brazil's independence from Portugal and of the acclamation of King João VI's son Pedro as emperor, the mortal remains of this Pedro were transported by ship to Rio de Janeiro amid considerable pomp and circumstance. It was the paternal gesture of the mother country toward its ex-colonial daughter during an anniversary year, aimed, of course, at strengthening that sense of community in relation to the former fatherland which, with respect to the Insular Portuguese in the United States, constitutes a recurring theme in this book's companion piece.

Ironically, this latter osseous shipment, under the direct supervision of none other than the President of Portugal, Admiral Tomás (subsequently exiled in Brazil with Caetano and the civil governor of Funchal, and, later, General Spínola), denied Insular

Portugal the badly needed services of one of its few major passenger vessels, the *Funchal,* built in 1961 for the Lisbon-Funchal-Ponta Delgada-Angra-Horta run and normally so employed. Within Brazil the bones went on tour, and on September 5, 1972, during Fatherland Week, they were laid to rest in the Ipiranga Independence Monument in São Paulo.

As was inevitable, in 1972 Portugal issued a series of postage stamps commemorating the 150 years of Brazilian independence; one contained the portrait of Dom Pedro, whom it designated "Dom Pedro IV." Moreover, coincident with the arrival of the bones and Admiral Tomás in Brazil, a new document went into effect, a Convention on the Equality of Rights and Duties Between Portuguese and Brazilians.

☆ ☆ ☆

A specific Azorean political stance was visible at the very commencement of the Peter-Michael struggles: the people, or at least the leaders, on Fayal were objecting to being ruled by Terceira. Apparently West-Central and West Azoreans deemed the captaincy general not so much a pan-Azorean institution as a symbol of Terceiran supremacy. The ensuing division into three administrative districts in effect serves notice on post-Revolutionary Azorean governments that there must be One or Nine, not Three, not perhaps even Two. Indeed, back in 1821, as the districts were shaping up, Pico let it be known that she would not be subject to Fayal!

The Dabney *Annals,* about one of the families of Boston Brahmins in the Azores, are replete with references to Azorean discontent with Lisbon, to the exhorbitantly high taxes the Azoreans were forced to pay, to the absurd quarantine regulations imposed on local ports from without. One entry tells of a revolution on Pico in 1862: "the women are the prime movers in it; the poor things are desperate and think this new system of taxation will be the end of them." (No wonder my maternal grandmother emigrated not long after.) Another entry tells of a similar revolution over taxation on Fayal on July 28 and 29 of the same year, this one in Castelo Branco, the people killing three soldiers.

The desire was rife not for independence but for outright attachment to the United States, or at least for "the protection of" the United States, so near (Boston is 1,930.2 n mi. from Horta), so friendly. Terceirans in particular, who had had a Spanish experience during the reigns of the Philips, were not enchanted by the ideas anent an Iberian Union with Spain current in the late 1860's. They expressed their preference for being American.

The fear of just such an annexation became a theme for super-patriotic Portuguese Republicans of the 1920's and monarchists of the 1960's. They evoked the wave of American imperialism of the Spanish American War era which resulted in annexation of the Philippines and might have resulted, they suggested that Portugal feared, in annexation of the Azores. All of this concern was à propos of the visit to the Adjacent Islands of the king and queen in the later spring of 1901.

Yachtsman King Carlos and his French Queen Maria Amélia arrived at Horta on June 28, 1901, with the royal yacht *Rainha Dona Amélia,* after having first called at Funchal between June 22 and June 25. They departed Ponta Delgada on July 11. The Museum of Angra possesses several mementoes of the memorable visit between which and the desire of some Azoreans for annexation by the United States an amazing link exists.

Milk distribution, north side of Pico, Spring 1964

In the late 1920's, a well-known Portuguese historian who began writing under the Republic prior to Salazar's advent informed his readers of the extraordinary cupidity of the United States of 1898 and years immediately following. So doing, he gave the lie to the view that the Azores are an integral part of Portugal and revealed that he considered them a colony, those very Azores which had produced the first or provisional President of the Republic (Teófilo Braga of São Miguel) and the first elected President (Manuel de Arriaga of Fayal):

> The United States were also intent on taking possession of the Azores, just as they had taken possession of the Philippines and were considering taking possession of Fernando Póo [Spanish, former Portuguese, island in Gulf of Guinea]. Due to the convergence of fortunate circumstances and principally the personal action of King Carlos, the plot against the Portuguese colonies was successfully frustrated.

In 1964, during a period of renewed monarchical fervor in Portugal when the pretender's photograph in red jacket graced many a Portuguese living room, an apologist published a volume of essays about King Carlos as an object of great calumny. (Carlos and his heir apparent were assassinated in 1908 by Republicans whose movement attained success two years later.) One of the essays is entitled "A page of history in which is evoked the visit to the Azores of King Carlos by which it was possible to save the archipelago from American covetousness."

The author mentions the earlier historian's passage. He adds many embellishments of his own, however, reflecting the considerable anti-Americanism or at least anti-Kennedyism of many upper-class Portuguese of his day. Thus, he tells how King Edward VII and his imperialistic England opposed this aggrandizement of the United States, their "former colony which had crowbarred its way to independence," and how Edward backed Carlos's decision to effect the first "sovereignty voyage" of a Portuguese monarch to the Azores by sending two English battleships, *Australia* and *Severn,* to Azorean waters. The Government of Brazil, the author continues, also got in on the act by dispatching the warship *Floriano* to match the British battleships. The United States received the message and backed down. Carlos was the hero of the day and his voyage a great national triumph, a veritable apotheosis, for they had saved the beautiful and most Portuguese ("portuguesíssimo") archipelago of the Azores from a planned rape.

What the author does not point out is that Azoreans at that moment, and for decades before and after, were emigrating to the land of the rapists, that the Azores had just been linked by submarine telegraph cable for the first time to the United States with the full approval of the Portuguese government (see Chapter 9), and that Azoreans were asking to be raped. Indeed, the *Boston Post* of 1902 reported that the newspaper *O Telégrafo* (The Telegraph) of Horta was publishing a series of articles on the idea of separation from Europe.

The lesson for the United States of the late-1970's seems clear. The American nation, its citizens, and its permanent residents should avoid involvement with any independence movement in the Azores or Madeiras, above all with any Insular Portuguese demand for annexation. If they become involved, they will be accused by the government in Lisbon, the world Communist press, the U.N. General Assembly, and possibly even France of planning the rape of the Adjacent Islands. If Azoreans and Madeirans wish independence, a natural and understandable aspiration in view of that of the Cape Verde Islands, they must achieve it for themselves. And in 1931 they did make an attempt.

In that year a military revolt against the Salazar regime broke out in the Azores, Madeiras, and Portuguese Guinea. The Madeira uprising lasted for almost a month. In the Azores, military aircraft played a minor role but, nevertheless, an important one for the history of aviation in the Azores. This affair of the early Salazar years is actually more of a warning to present-day Insular Portuguese super-autonomists and separatists than a precedent for their legitimate aspirations. The revolt was apparently engineered not by islanders in opposition to Continentals but by mainland Republicans who had fled to the islands in opposition to Salazarists.

Island opposition to mainland as exemplified by the Peter-and-Michael episode seemed to wane with the advent of the Republic. It was the masses of strongly Catholic citizenry in the center and north of Continental Portugal who resented the new and anticlerical regime. They manifested their resentment by emigrating, many to the United States, where they formed new nuclei to be distinguished from the great centers of the earlier Insular Portuguese immigration.

Curiously, these conservative Continentals of the lower class were followed in the interwar period and especially in 1940 by another group of conservative European Portuguese who perceived the desirability of fleeing Nazidom. The newcomers were members of the exiled royal family of Braganza, descendants of that Michael who had died in Germany in 1866. Some got out of Europe on Pan American clippers via Lisbon and Horta (see Chapter 10). The widow of Michael's grandson, Miguel, Duke of Viseu (1878-1923), herself an American lady, settled on a beautiful estate in Newport, Rhode Island, where she still lives on as the Duchess of Viseu. One of her sons had become a Pan American pilot.

After the short-lived Republic came forty-eight years of intensive authoritarian propaganda, rightist in the extreme. The Insular Portuguese, by and large, accepted the New State of Salazar and the Social State of Caetano, as they were known. The legacy of authoritarianism in the event proved stronger than that of the nineteenth-century liberal stance. With the 25th of April, as Continental Portugal moved markedly to the left, Insular Portugal moved only slightly in that direction. So doing, Azores and Madeiras placed themselves in opposition to Continent and bade fair to cut themselves off from the new developments.

The new political position of the Insular Portuguese is all the more surprising as the bones episode pointed up the dehumanizing absurdity of authoritarianism Continental-Portuguese style. I continue to be shocked at the 1972 newspaper photograph of an old acquaintance decked out in striped trousers, cutaway coat, and plug hat, acting as a pallbearer for the bones of Peter. The power of authoritarianism was great indeed to have cajoled him into accepting such a role. Portugal was ripe for Revolution on many fronts, social and economic as well as political.

5

THE NEW POLITICS

During the last days of the authoritarian regime, General António de Spínola's mildly revolutionary book was allowed to appear. Entitled *Portugal e o Futuro* (Portugal and the Future), it soon became of the highest importance, for Spínola was named by the Revolutionaries as President of the Republic immediately after the 25th of April. He remained in office until overthrown on September 30, 1974.

In his book Spínola dismissed Insular Portugal in exactly thirteen words: "Adjacent Islands would continue linked to present metropolitan territory without alteration in Statute." He dreamed of a Federal Portuguese Republic to consist of eight "states": Lusitania (the Metropolis, that is, Continental and Insular Portugal), Angola, Mozambique, Portuguese Guinea, Cape Verde Islands, São Tomé-e-Príncipe, Macao, and Timor. The Cape de Verdes would thus have had equal status with Continental and Insular Portugal combined. Within Spínola's "Lusitania"—a name stemming from the Roman province of old and once applied to an institution which was torpedoed and sank—the Azores and Madeiras would have been swallowed up, obviously by design.

Portugal and the Future missed the mark rather completely. Its author revealed the limited nature of his predictive powers on another occasion. Speaking at the Boston Committee on Foreign Relations on November 21, 1975, he affirmed, according to my handwritten notes, that the Communists, based on Algeria, had a four-point program: (1) first take Vila Real de Santo António, at the mouth of the Guadiana River in the southeasternmost corner of Portugal; (2) then on February 24, 1976, take over power in Portugal (presumably while Catholic Lisbonese were busy feting St. Matthew); (3) foment a separatist movement in Catalonia, followed by such movements in the Basque country, Galicia, and

Aragon; and (4) combine the six Peninsular lands, including Castile, into a Union of Iberian Socialist Republics.

The 1940 Statute for the Autonomous Districts of the Adjacent Islands, to which Spínola alluded and which he would not alter, in fact stood in need of complete alteration. Many enlightened Azoreans and Madeirans within the islands were well aware of this need. Once the Revolution came, their thinking centered on four solutions to Insular problems: little or no change, much greater autonomy within Portugal, complete independence, and annexation by the United States. A rationale for the latter view lay in the obvious fact that the remotest corner of the Azores (Ponta do Castelo, Santa Maria) is only 2,125.7 n mi. from Boston as compared with the 2,186.7 between San Francisco and the remotest point in Hawaii (Niihau Island).

Few adhered to no change and equally few, apparently, to annexation. Autonomy vs. independence became a particularly acute question during the middle months of 1975, as the Communists increased their power in Continental Portugal and increasingly alienated Insular Portugal, although on June 20, 1975, I visited a bookstore in Funchal which assembled more Communist literature than I had ever seen together in one place in Portuguese-speaking territory. When the power of the Communists seemed broken by a political coup on November 25, 1975, cogent reasons argued for autonomy within a renovated Portugal.

In the meantime, on the first anniversary of the Revolution, the people of Portugal elected representatives to a Constituent Assembly, which promptly met in Lisbon, worked hard, and produced a new Constitution of the Portuguese Republic. The document went into effect on the second anniversary.

A total of 250 deputies were elected on April 25, 1975, to the Constituent Assembly: 235 from Continental Portugal, twelve from Insular Portugal, two from Overseas Portugal, and one from emigrants abroad.

In this as in subsequent elections, four principal parties were active. From left to right along the political spectrum they lined up as follows: Portuguese Communist Party (Partido Comunista Português or PCP), Socialist Party (Partido Socialista or PS), Popular Democratic Party (Partido Popular Democrático or PPD), whose name was changed in October 1976 to Social Democratic Party (Partido Social Democrático or PSD), and Social Democratic

Center (Centro Democrático Social or CDS). In the 1975 voting PS elected 116 deputies with 37.8% of the vote, PSD 81 with 26.4%, PCP 30 with 12.5%, and CDS 16 with 7.6%.

Azores and Madeiras showed their new colors in this election, and they were surprising. The party affiliation of the deputies elected, and the party vote, were as follows, with totals for Insular and Continental Portugal supplied for comparison:

	PCP	PS	PSD	CDS
District of Angra	0 - 2.3%	0 - 22.9%	2 - 62.8%	0 - 6.1%
District of Horta	0 - 2.3%	0 - 22.9%	1 - 67.6%	0 - 0
District of P. D.	0 - 1.5%	1 - 30.3%	2 - 54.8%	0 - 3.1%
District of Funchal	0 - 1.6%	1 - 19.4%	5 - 62.0%	0 - 10.0%
Insular Portugal	0 - 1.8%	2 - 23.4%	10 - 60.6%	0 - 6.6%
Cont. Portugal	30 - 13.1%	113 - 38.6%	70 - 24.7%	16 - 7.7%

In addition to the 241 deputies accounted for in this table, there were six from two other parties (one UDP and five MDP) and the three representing Overseas Portugal and the emigrants.

The 1976 Constitution of the Portuguese Republic which these deputies drew up and adopted provides for a President of the Republic, elected by universal suffrage for a five-year term. It also provides for an Assembly of the Republic consisting of Deputies elected by voters in electoral "circles" in proportion to the number of registered voters. The Deputies are elected for a four-year term; they, in turn, elect their own presiding officer, the President of the Assembly of the Republic.

A Council of the Revolution, primarily military but including the President of the Republic and also, if an armed-forces officer, the Prime Minister—which Mário Soares was not—functions on a permanent basis to guarantee the success of the Revolution. In addition to President and Prime Minister, the Council includes the Chief of the General Staff of the Armed Forces, the Chief of Staff of each of the three services, eight additional Army officers, three additional Air Force officers, and three additional Navy officers.

The "Government" consists of the Prime Minister, Ministers, and Secretaries and Undersecretaries of State. The Prime Minister and the Ministers themselves constitute the Council of Ministers or Cabinet. Because the word Government has this specific meaning in Portugal as in Great Britain and other countries but not in the United States, in this book the word when capitalized refers to the Prime Minister and his group and when with a lower-case *g* refers to "Lisbon" or the ensemble of rulers (Government, Assembly, judiciary, Council of the Revolution, et cetera), in other words, to what Americans mean when they say "Washington" or the federal government.

The Prime Minister is named by the President of the Republic after he has listened to the Council of the Revolution and the parties represented in the Assembly of the Republic and has taken into account the party complexion of the results of the elections to the Assembly of the Republic. The remaining members of the Government are named by the President of the Republic after being nominated by the Prime Minister. A Deputy who is named to the Government cannot at the same time function as a Deputy.

The Constitution provides for an administrative subdivision of the country into *regiões* (regions), *municípios* (municipalities, the former *concelhos*), and *freguesias* (precincts). In Continental Portugal the regions are called administrative regions. In Insular Portugal they are called autonomous regions, there being two (the Azores and the Madeiras).

Each region will have its Regional Assembly elected by universal suffrage, the members in each Assembly electing their own presiding officer or Assembly president. The Constitution specifies that each Regional Assembly of Insular Portugal will draw up a new Politico-Administrative Statute for the approval of the Assembly of the Republic in Lisbon. The pair of new Statutes will take the place of the old Statute for the Autonomous Districts of the Adjacent Islands.

So far so good. Great progress, from a Western democratic point of view, was made. The two autonomous regions are like, say, Hawaii. They send their representatives to the national capital. At the same time they have their own elected legislature with its speaker. There is a difference, however. Hawaiians elect their own governor, who appoints his fellow executive officers by and with the advice and consent of one house of the bicameral legislature (namely, the senate). In the new Continental Portugal, however, each region is assigned a representative of the Lisbon Government named by the Council of Ministers, in other words, an official not unlike the civil governors of old, the *intendentes* of Getúlio Vargas, the *intendants* of Louis XIV. In the new Insular Portugal, each region is assigned a "Minister of the Republic," named by the President of the Republic after being nominated by the Prime Minister, the Council of the Revolution having been heard. This Minister, presumably a Continental and quite possibly an armed-forces officer sent out from Lisbon, is in fact a true Cabinet Minister. As a true member of the Government he has a voice in the Council of Ministers for matters which affect his "autonomous" region. Presumably, also, he would fall if the Government of which he is a member falls.

Hawaiians, then, elect their governor, who appoints his cabinet. The citizens of each region of Insular Portugal have their Minister of the Republic appointed by Lisbon and possibly—probably—sent out from Lisbon. This appointed outsider in turn names the President of the Regional Government after having taken into account the party complexion of the results of the elections to the Regional Assembly. The remaining members of the Regional Government are named by the Minister of the Republic after being nominated by the President of the Regional Government.

In each autonomous region there is one Minister and two presidents (with a lower-case *p* in the Constitution). The one president presides over the Regional Assembly and is a member of it. The other president heads the Regional Government; if he is already a member of the Regional Assembly, he must forego his legislative function when named to the executive post. Of potentially great interest is the fact that, in the event the Minister of the Republic is absent or prevented from exercising his functions, it is the president of the Regional Assembly and not the president of the Regional Government who takes his place.

With reference to the two new autonomous regions, the 1976 Constitution warns that "regional politico-administrative autonomy does not affect the integrity of the State's sovereignty and is carried out within the framework of the Constitution." Another warning is contained in the article which prohibits the formation of those political parties "which, by their name or by the objectives contained in their programs, are of a regional nature or area of concern."

The Constitution thus renders explicitly illegal such groupings as the Movement for Autodetermination of the People of the Azores (MAPA), which emerged in 1974 immediately after the Revolution, the Front for the Liberation of the Azores (FLA), which seems to have supplanted MAPA, and the Front for the Liberation of the Archipelago of the Madeiras (FLAMA). The visitor to Portugal in the summer of 1977 noted that FLAMA was

Superposition of graffiti on a Funchal wall, June 1975

indeed recognized as clandestine and illegal on Madeira but that FLA functioned openly in the Azores, especially on its native habitat of São Miguel, indeed, in Ponta Delgada's Café Royal across the street from the police station. He also observed that the numerous graffiti on the islands trended to the right, those in Lisbon to the left.

On the day the new Constitution went into effect, the people of Portugal went to the polls for a second time. They elected their definitive Deputies to the Assembly of the Republic.

A total of 263 Deputies were elected: 247 from Continental Portugal, twelve from Insular Portugal, two from emigrants in Europe, and two from emigrants elsewhere, the latter distinction correctly analyzing the difference between the Portuguese migrant workers in Northwest Europe without protection of permanent-residence visa and the Portuguese immigrants with full legal protection into such countries as Brazil, Venezuela, the United States, and Canada.

The same four parties were active. In the new voting PS elected 107 Deputies with 34.9% of the vote, PSD 73 with 24.4%, CDS 42 with 16.0%, and PCP 40 with 14.3%.

Azores and Madeirans continued to show their new colors, that is, their trending to the right of the mainland:

	PCP	PS	PSD	CDS
District of Angra	0 - 1.4%	1 - 30.4%	1 - 51.8%	0 - 12.1%
District of Horta	0 - 1.6%	0 - 34.2%	1 - 57.0%	0 - 4.3%
District of P. D.	0 - 1.5%	1 - 35.4%	2 - 45.7%	0 - 11.8%
District of Funchal	0 - 1.5%	1 - 24.9%	4 - 53.0%	1 - 13.3%
Insular Portugal	0 - 1.5%	3 - 29.5%	8 - 51.2%	1 - 11.9%
Cont. Portugal	40 - 15.1%	103 - 35.2%	63 - 22.8%	40 - 16.2%

In addition to the 258 Deputies accounted for in this table, there were one Deputy from another party (UDP) and the four representing the emigrants. Subsequently, five PS and one CDS Deputies withdrew from their parties and became Independents. Accordingly, the composition of the Assembly became:

UDP	1
PCP	40
PS	102
PSD	73
CDS	41
Independents	6
TOTAL	263

On June 27, 1976, 61.5% of the voters of Portugal elected a politically neutral and highly respected figure as President of the Republic—General António Ramalho Eanes.

On that same June day, the voters of Insular Portugal elected the Deputies of their Regional Assemblies. A surprise occurred in the Madeiras, where seats were won by two members of the left-of-Communist party known as the Popular Democratic Union (União Democrática Popular or UDP), which had one seat in the Constituent Assembly and had one in the Assembly of the Republic. The following table lists the number of Deputies, by party, of the two Regional Assemblies of Insular Portugal. It reveals that the Socialists are a greater threat to the Social Democratic majority in the Azores than in the Madeiras.

	UDP	PS	PSD	CDS	Totals
São Miguel		5	7	1	13
Santa Maria		1	2		3
Terceira		3	5		8
Graciosa		1	2		3
São Jorge			2	1	3
Fayal		1	3		4
Pico		1	3		4
Flores		1	2		3
Corvo		1	1		2
TOTAL AZORES		14	27	2	43
Madeira	2	8	28	2	40
Porto Santo			1		1
TOTAL MADEIRAS	2	8	29	2	41

Events now moved ahead rapidly. General Eanes was installed as President of the Republic on July 14, 1976. Two days later he named the head of the Socialist Party, lawyer Mário Soares, as Prime Minister. Soares, in turn, promptly nominated the members of his Government (Socialist, Independent, Military), a minority Government and not a coalition Government. The new Government was installed on July 23.

Finally, on December 12, 1976, the elections of local officials, at the precinct and municipality level, in both Continental and Insular Portugal took place. The over-all party percentages conformed pretty much to the 1976 pattern which determined the composition of the Assembly of the Republic, namely, PCP and allies 18%, PS 33%, PSD 24%, CDS 17%. The islanders, however, voted more conservatively than Continentals, preferring PSD candidates. And Madeirans reacquired precinct juntas.

Soares presumably could have nominated Socialists as Ministers of the Republic. He wisely chose, however, to nominate politically neutral individuals. They both turned out to be Continental armed-forces officers: for the Azores, General Galvão de Figueiredo, an infantry officer of the Army with extensive service in São Tomé, Macao, Mozambique, and Portuguese Guinea in the authoritarian days; for the Madeiras, Colonel Lino Miguel, an Air

Force officer with service in Portuguese Guinea and Mozambique.

Events also moved with dispatch in the Adjacent Islands. Each Regional Assembly elected its president, Álvaro Monjardino in the Azores and Emanuel do Nascimento dos Santos Rodrigues in the Madeiras. Each drafted a provisional Politico-Administrative Statute, neither of which, however, was immediately approved by the Assembly of the Republic in Lisbon in its definitive form. For the Azores I use the Provisional Statute issued in mimeographed form in Angra in July 1976 and still being distributed a year later. For the Madeiras I use the Proposed Statute (*Projecto de Estatuto*) issued by the Regional Assembly on May 17, 1977, and given me in July of that year. For the Madeiras I also have the Provisional Statute published in the *Diário da República* (Daily of the Republic, which took the place of the old *Diário do Governo* or Government Daily of earlier regimes) of April 30, 1976.

The Azorean text sets up each island as an electoral circle. It provides that each will elect two Deputies to the Regional Assembly, plus one additional Deputy for each 7,500 voters or fraction above 1,000. The provision guarantees Corvo its representation regardless of tiny population. The Madeiran text establishes each of the eleven municipalities as an electoral circle. It provides that each elect one Deputy to the Regional Assembly for each 3,500 voters or fraction above 1,750, circles with less than 3,500 voters being guaranteed one Deputy. The latter provision guarantees Porto Santo its single Deputy.

In both regions the Deputies are elected to four-year terms. The Azorean draft makes no mention of Deputies for emigrants. The Madeiran draft, however, proposes two electoral circles for emigrants, one for Madeirans resident in Portuguese territory outside the Madeiras, the other for Madeirans resident abroad, each circle to elect one Deputy. This proposal, however, was not applied in the 1976 elections.

The Madeiran text further provides that the Regional Government, based wholly in Funchal, may, if it deems such action necessary, name a Regional Undersecretary for Porto Santo. This ensures the participation of both islands of the archipelago in the Government as well as the Assembly. Similarly, the Azorean text provides for the possibility of a representation of the Regional Government on each island.

Another most enlightened concept introduced into the 1976 Constitution and the two Regional Statutes affirms that the

Deputies represent the entire country or region and not just the electoral circles which elected them. Surprisingly, this idea is not expressed in the Constitution of the United States of America. Today, more than ever, it is needed to inhibit U.S. Senators and Representatives from representing specific vested-interest groups such as the increasingly vocal ethnic groups of their constituencies.

Simultaneously with the getting into harness of each Regional Assembly came the action of the Ministers of the Republic in naming presidents for the Regional Governments: João Bosco Mota Amaral in the Azores and Jaime de Ornelas Camacho in the Madeiras. These two heads of Regional Governments, both PSD, then nominated the members, called Secretaries, of their respective Governments, all of them PSD. In the Madeiras, Alberto João Jardim, also PSD, later took the place of Camacho.

In the Azores the Regional Government consists of nine Secretaries with offices as follows:

Ponta Delgada
   President of the Regional Government of the Azores,
   Regional Secretary of Commerce and Industry,
   Regional Secretary of Social Necessities,
   Regional Secretary of Finances,
   Regional Secretary of Labor;
Angra do Heroismo
   Regional Secretary of Public Administration,
   Regional Secretary of Education and Culture,
   Regional Secretary of Social Subjects;
Horta
   Regional Secretary of Transportation and Tourism,
   Regional Secretary of Agriculture and Fishing.

In the Madeiras the problem of headquarters was simple, as obviously all Secretaries would have their offices in Funchal. The president of the Regional Government and four Secretaries are installed in the excellent building which used to house the Junta General and is today called the Palace of the Regional Government. The other Secretaries have offices in appropriate places elsewhere in the city. The list of Secretaries follows:

President of the Regional Government of the Madeiras,
Regional Secretary of Labor,
Regional Secretary of Social Necessities, Transportation, and Communications,
Regional Secretary of Social Subjects and Health,
Regional Secretary of Education and Culture,
Regional Secretary of Planning, Finances, and Commerce,
Regional Secretary of Agriculture, Industry, and Fishing.

The Assembly of the Autonomous Region of the Madeiras meets in the same ex-Junta General building which houses most of the Regional Government of the Madeiras. In the Azores, however, the wise practice being followed is necessarily different. As recognition that the president of the Regional Government has his office in Ponta Delgada—even though the Government meets four times in Ponta Delgada for each three times in Angra and each two times in Horta—the Regional Assembly is now meeting in Horta (in the beautiful Club Amor da Pátria or Love of Fatherland Club).

As for the Ministers of the Republic, he of the Madeiras resides and presides in the waterfront Fortress of St. Lawrence. It was there that the civil governor of old held forth. The Fortress is therefore a symbol of Lisbonese power and control. He of the Azores has vacillated in his selection of a headquarters. At first setting himself up in Ponta Delgada, he soon realized that he was in a hotbed of separatism. He then moved to Angra, residence of the captains general of old, another symbol of Lisbon's sovereignty.

☆ ☆ ☆

At the time of the first Soares Government's fall, Azoreans and Madeirans seemed to be on their way to an orderly constitutional autonomy based on sound democratic principles. Seeds of conflict with Lisbon, however, were planted early. In the election of April 25, 1975, to the Constituent Assembly, that of April 25, 1976, to the Assembly of the Republic, and the local elections at the end of 1976, Insular Portugal voted far more conservatively than Continental Portugal. The Atlantic archipelagoes set themselves apart from what was obviously a progressive mainstream of Portuguese political life. They did so despite the nineteenth-century liberal tradition in the Azores, despite the experience of decades of conservative absentee rule emanating from Lisbon, and despite an administrative arrangement under conservative Salazar and Caetano sitting in Lisbon which conferred even less freedom of voter expression on the islanders than on the Continentals.

The President of the Republic and the Government in Lisbon are sworn to uphold a Constitution which looks askance at any suggestion of separatism. The Insular Portuguese had a voice in the formulation and adoption of that Constitution, as they have had a voice in the Assembly of the Republic created by it. It is, therefore, not surprising that President Eanes on June 28, 1976, the day after he was elected President, pronounced himself rather precisely: "These separatist groups will be easily neutralized with decisive action."

An Insular Portuguese movement for independence is understandable, but only after the new Lisbon has been given an opportunity to exercise its sovereignty over the islands and prove itself deficient. There has not yet been time for that Lisbon to be judged. Nevertheless, the independence movement in the Azores, centered on São Miguel, was rampant in the summer of 1977.

This observer goes as far as to affirm that the movement, at that juncture in history, was positively harmful to Azorean progress. Everyone should have been pulling together in the direction of a renovated Azores within a renovated Portugal. Instead, fear and the concomitant reticence to reveal one's true feelings were widespread. Individuals were reluctant to side openly either with the constitutional government in Lisbon or with the independence movement. On São Miguel I found more such reluctance than I had ever found during my many visits in the authoritarian era. In this sense São Miguel was a less open society than I had ever known it to be, and therefore more frightening to an American. True, Azoreans, like other Portuguese, have learned the consequences of open adherence to a form of government. After the 25th of April they observed the firing of many public officials, including even teachers, whom the new regime deemed fascist, and some of them jokingly referred to the new situation as democracy Portuguese style. In 1977, therefore, they did not show their hands. As a result the January-February 1977 issue of *Freedom at Issue* published by Freedom House in New York was absolutely correct, perhaps unwittingly. It rated Continental Portugal's Status of Freedom as F (free). On the other hand, it listed the Azores and Madeiras, along with Macao, under Portugal in a table of territories and dependencies; it gave the two Atlantic archipelagoes PF (partly free). This latter rating actually referred to the partial lack of political rights, but it did reflect that other aspect of freedom. The January-February 1978 issue upped the rating of the Status of Freedom in both archipelagoes to F, reflecting an increase in political rights.

Reluctance to speak out naturally carried with it a reluctance to act. I noted some of the old dependence on higher authority. A specific example concerned the domestic flights of TAP between São Miguel and Lisbon and between São Miguel and Madeira. There was no assigned seating. Standing in line within the nonairconditioned terminal building in sweltering heat, I asked why? Because they are domestic flights. What difference does that make? Shrug of shoulders and the suggestion that there was no authorization for such seating.

What surprised me in particular was the lack of desire to stay within and improve the new post-Revolutionary system. If I were an Insular Portuguese, I would naturally resent the presence of a Minister of the Republic imposed from without. But, instead of grumbling, I would fight for a locally elected Minister of the Region—or Governor—as the supreme local executive authority, ideally with a voice in the Council of Ministers in Lisbon for matters which affected his region. I did not encounter open discussion of issues such as this one.

I did find within the Regional Government of the Azores a keen desire to advance the Azores as a single entity. The balanced use of the three cities for Governmental purposes was noteworthy. I was very impressed by the gratitude toward Lisbon for allowing aircraft—especially helicopters—of the Portuguese Air Force and small vessels of the Portuguese Navy to assist the Regional Government in matters involving civilians: in the movement of the sick or injured, for example, from a smaller island to a city with major medical facilities. I was reminded of a statement made in 1859 by the civil governor of the District of Horta. At a time of great famine he was distributing corn sent and paid for by generous persons in Boston, and he sent some of it to São Jorge. He wrote: "... although this Island lies outside of my District, I understand, that in the Community of Misfortune—Charity does not permit of terrestrial divisions." A great vision has always existed within the Azores.

Whence comes the intense conservatism of today's Azoreans, specifically of the São Miguelians? Only a secret agent can answer the question accurately. My own guess is that the rightist spirit has been carefully nurtured by the remnants of the local landed gentry of old, in alliance with those of their number who have sought refuge in Brazil or elsewhere and also in alliance with extreme conservatives and their Portuguese-language press within the so-called Portuguese "colonies" of the United States. I hasten to point out, however, that Boston's Cardinal Medeiros, a son of São Miguel, does not figure in this group. On his native island I learned that in certain quarters he was considered to have fallen into the hands of the Socialists!

The conservatism of emigrants established and doing well abroad is widely recognized. Just before his assassination, King Carlos is said to have toyed with the notion of visiting Brazil to solicit political support and possibly money from the conservative Portuguese emigrants resident there. Mário Soares himself has referred to the traditionally reactionary nature of the Portuguese "colony" in Brazil, that is, those of Portuguese birth who have settled there. The recent South American conservatism is perhaps understandable because from 1930 to 1945 and again beginning in the spring of 1964 Brazilians have lived under an authoritarian regime. Not so North American conservatism, which has blossomed in an atmosphere of relative freedom. Apparently, recently immigrated Azoreans are influenced by the incessant propaganda and dream of saving money, owning property in the home land, and returning there to live well in retirement. This dream represents a powerful force pushing to the right.

Independence may, in the event, prove a necessary and a wise solution for the Azores and the Madeiras. To be viable, however, certain fundamental transformations will be necessary. Or, to put the matter differently, six major arguments militate against independence at this time. I limit this discussion in general to the Azores, for the independence movement in the two-island Madeiras appears much less active and, indeed, less required.

(1) There exists at present little Azorean identity, little Azorean unity, little sense of Azoreanness. Memories of domination by a

captain general in Angra and by three civil governors in Angra, Horta, and Ponta Delgada promote division, islandness, the cult of one's island, "islism." Terceirans still poke fun at São Miguelians. Rivalry still exists between Terceira and Fayal. The net result is that there is no agreement on so fundamental an issue as the site of the capital of a united Azores. São Miguelians naturally expect it to be Ponta Delgada, and they have the predominance of political and economic power. Citizens of the other islands have other ideas, however. They may not agree on Praia da Vitória, yet they should ponder the experiences of Americans, Australians, and Brazilians. These peoples moved their capitals from great centers to new sites—Washington, Canberra, and Brasília—and strengthened their national lives. The analogy is valid, for the Azores, like the United States, Australia, and Brazil, is a federation. It is a commonwealth of nine entities.

(2) Although there is little Azorean unity, there does exist the unity conferred by being Portuguese. In spite of a minor Flemish and probably nonexistent Breton/French influence in the Azores, Insular Portugal in ancestry, language, religion, and general culture is Portuguese. This unity militates against separation. Rather, it strengthens the desire for autonomous regions within Portugal, regions already provided for by the 1976 Constitution. The case of the Cape Verdeans is not parallel, for Cape Verdeans are of mixed European and African ancestry and culture. Their independence is natural, for they are sui generis. I repeat, sui generis. They do not constitute "an emerging African state," as a Church World Service news release would have it in an announcement of a formal agreement between this relief arm of the National Council of Churches and the Government of the Republic of Cape Verde.

Even the case of the Canarians is different, for there was once an indigenous, or at least pre-Spanish, population there. Movements for "national liberation" under such circumstances have been the order of the day since World War II. They are deemed "liberal," and they tend to come from the left. The Azores do not fit into this pattern. Fear of the left is the dominant theme there, fear of a leftist Lisbon. The theme forms the basis of FLA's propaganda and could be a legacy of the Cold War. More likely, it reflects a remembrance of things past, of the good old days of monarchy. Hence the liberation front's blue and white flag, followed in early 1978 by the completely different blue and white flag proposed for the Autonomous Region of the Azores (with the new Azorean shield in its center, containing an *açor* and nine stars).

(3) Rivalry among the so-called Great Powers constitutes a strong deterrent to independence. Once independent, the Azores would inevitably fall under the sway of the United States, by accident if not design. France, itself esconced on Flores and making a notable contribution to the progress of that island, would hardly welcome such a development. Nor would the Soviet Union, which realizes full well that the air base on Terceira, AFAR on Santa Maria, and NATO's use of Azorean ports and the field on Porto Santo are aimed at her. France and the U.S.S.R. would thus prod Lisbon into resisting separatism. Moreover, a larger Portugal is able to keep subordinate the several foreign armed-forces installations in the Azores. These installations, and the governments behind them, like tempted international conglomerates, might swallow up an independent mini-nation.

(4) A fourth argument against independence at this time is provided by the new Lisbon itself. Portugal has lost its overseas empire. It is groping toward complete reintegration within the European society of nations, its society. It cannot afford to lose any more territory, especially an archipelago which for over half a millennium it has proclaimed to be an integral part of the homeland. Lisbon controls the available military, naval, and air power, not to mention civil air service and telecommunications between Insular Portugal and the outside world including Continental Portugal. The Adjacent Islands have no such power and, due to the Great Power rivalry, probably will not be able to acquire modern arms and armor in the immediate future. They are forced to bow to Lisbon. Unless, of course, Lisbon wishes to rid itself of Atlantic headaches!

(5) A fifth argument is provided by the need for political education of the masses of Insular Portuguese. Just freed from a half-century of totalitarianism, many cannot seem to resist new rightist propaganda. They do not discuss politics rationally. They are impressed by repetition, effected via graffiti and, in the Azores, the photograph of FLA's head (José de Almeida) displayed all over Ponta Delgada and elsewhere. Azoreans, and also, I suspect, Madeirans, need considerable education in political action before they are ready to make a real move. It is to be hoped that the new institutions of higher education in the two archi-

pelagoes will recognize such education as of the highest importance and not limit themselves to purely vocational training.

(6) A sixth and last argument concerns the class structure of island society and the islanders' economic life. Neither can sustain true independence at this time. The experience of the past several centuries demonstrates that the two-class system does not promote the common weal. Rather, it leads to emigration and ever greater weakness at home. This class structure and sexism in the islands are discussed in the following chapter. Similarly, the experience of many decades makes clear that much is radically wrong with the islands' economic system. It also has led to emigration and the resulting debilitation of the home archipelagoes. The nature of island economic life—the strengths, weaknesses, and potentiality which would ultimately provide the bases of independence—is treated, following the discussion of sex and class, in a series of chapters on the use of the archipelagoes for international shipping, communications, and aviation, on the facts concerning imports and exports, and on the potential for international tourism.

Vila do Porto, Santa Maria—Teófilo Braga Street

6
SEX AND CLASS

The preamble to the 1976 Constitution of the Portuguese Republic constitutes a clear socialist manifesto. It talks of the overthrow of the "fascist" regime and continues: "Freeing Portugal from dictatorship, oppression, and colonialism represented a revolutionary transformation and the beginning of a historic change of direction for Portuguese society." The new direction is explicitly democracy, to be followed by socialism.

The text of the Constitution first speaks of transforming the sovereign Republic of Portugal into "a society without classes," then shifts to "the power of the working classes." The theme of the "working classes" recurs, as does mention of socialism.

The Portuguese Constitution thus stresses a classless society of the working classes in its opening articles, but in the part on fundamental rights and duties is an article entitled "Principle of equality" which reads:

1. All citizens have the same social dignity and are equal before the law.
2. No one can be privileged, benefited, injured, deprived of any right, or exempted from any duty by reason of ancestry, sex, race, language, territory of origin, religion, political or ideological convictions, education, economic situation, or social condition.

In this article the Constitution clearly recognizes the most obvious basis of discrimination within Portuguese society—class—a subtle mixture of ancestry, political or ideological convictions, education including accent in spoken language, economic situation, and social condition. Consequently, the present chapter is devoted mostly to class. But throughout the Portuguese territory there has also been discrimination based on sex. Sex accordingly is here discussed as well.

Portugal traditionally—at least since 1820—has not known diversity due to religion (except for the few Jews) nor to national or ethnic origin, although returnees from former colonies such as Whites born in Angola of Portuguese parents may in the future lead to a new type of discrimination, one anticipated and prohibited by the 1976 document. And under Salazar and Caetano there were no party politics, and nobody—or everybody—was discriminated against on this score. Nevertheless, the new Constitution wisely rules out discrimination because of all these factors. It fails, however, to take cognizance of age as a factor in discrimination, although it does devote an entire article to what it calls "Third Age," about the elderly, the senior citizens.

Moreover, the Constitution does not specifically mention "gays" and their rights. Homosexuals of both sexes have certainly been present in both Continental and Insular Portugal since time immemorial. They are now more visible. In the second half of the 1960's, they began to assert themselves openly in the upper portions of Lisbon's aptly named Avenue of Liberty. Moreover, in a 1977 list of words commonly used on St. Michael's, the presence of *zabela* tends to suggest the existence of gays on that island. The word is defined as "maricas, efeminado," and another word in common use is *invertido*.

☆ ☆ ☆

A remarkable fact concerning women over the centuries in Portugal involves the word "senior." In Latin, *senior*, or, in one of its forms, *seniorem*, connoted advanced age. As Latin developed into the Romance languages, *seniorem* became *Senhor* in medieval Portugal and meant Mr., Mrs., Master, or Miss. It was a sexually and maritally neutral word, distinguished as masculine or feminine only by an accompanying adjective, as in these verses:

> E que queria eu melhor
> De ser seu vassalo
> E ela minha senhor?

> And what better could I wish
> Than to be her vassal
> And she my liege?

Eventually, a new word *Senhora* was coined as feminine on the model of *amigo* "male friend" and *amiga* "female friend." *Senhor* became limited to males. But, and here is a second remarkable fact, *Senhora* meant either a married or an unmarried woman. Portugal has kept its *Senhor* and *Senhora* but, unlike Spanish, Italian, French, or German, never developed a *Señorita*, *Signorina*, *Mademoiselle*, or *Fräulein*. In other words, *Senhora* is today the equivalent of modern America's Ms., as *Senhor* means Mr. With their Ms., the Portuguese have long been way ahead of the Americans, although it is true that in some social circles they do have a special title (*Menina*) for an unmarried girl or woman.

In male-female relations, Portugal is advanced in other ways as well. For years, it has been possible for distinguished upper-class women to rise to positions of eminence, to a professorship at the ancient University of Coimbra, for instance, or to a professorship and deanship at the more recent Classical University of Lisbon. As will be noted in due course, the role of women is considerable and influential within the Portuguese family, especially in the family's money-transference function. In the eyes of the law, the woman household head—e.g., a widow with minor children—has enjoyed full equality with her male opposite number, as in voting. Lastly, upon marriage a woman could retain her own family name, or at least combine it equitably with her husband's in such a way as to project an image of sexual equality. Thus, the famous German philologist Carolina Michaëlis could marry the equally famous Portuguese art historian Joaquim de Vasconcellos and be thereafter ever known as Carolina Michaëlis de Vasconcellos. Or she could quite properly combine the title Dona with her first name and be known, even to strangers, as Dona Carolina in a way which among males was limited to noblemen and bishops.

Women could become airline flight attendants (if young and pretty). But here is an amusing point: upper-class women tended to enter this glamorous occupation, and then, accustomed to being served rather than to serve, they would on occasion slough off and require the vigilance and intervention of the TAP captain himself to keep them in line and the passengers satisfied.

Yes, some upper-class women and females of the upper-middle class could rise. They could vote and be elected to the National Assembly and to municipal chambers, and in 1970 a woman was appointed Undersecretary of State for Health, that is, a member of the Government. In general, however, women, in particular lower-class women, were much discriminated against in pre-1974 Portugal. For example, prior to the adoption of the New Civil Code at the end of 1966, the first revision since the code of 1867, a wife could not travel abroad without her husband's permission, nor could she carry on an occupation or profession and freely dispose of the income thus earned, nor could she, without her husband's authorization, contract debts, buy or sell property, administer her own possessions, or dispose of her own income.

Portugal used to be a man's world. At mixed social gatherings and official functions the wives sat demurely on the sidelines while the husbands held forth on their feet, prominently, pompously, and vociferously. A widow was branded, often for life, whereas a widower, after suitable acknowledgment of his loss, became a free agent once again.

A woman was dominated by males—father, brothers, husband, and sons—literally from puberty to menopause, and often on the outer sides of those events. Above all was her sexual life supervised, yet the male was free to roam. The three initial shocks I suffered upon visiting Portugal for the first time were caused by the omnipresence of prostitutes, the frequent references to mistresses, and the young men's curious custom during movie and theater intermissions of moving to the front of the orchestra and brazenly staring at the legs of the Senhoras in the balcony. Of course, New England males brought up in the Irish-Catholic tradition stared at legs, too, but more discreetly.

A form of male domination is refusal to allow one's woman to work, for a working woman can be the object of attention of other men. Therefore, it is not surprising that, in a (reliable?) report at the end of 1975, out of twenty-one countries Portugal had the smallest percentage of working women, 25% as against Italy's 29%, United States's 49%, Sweden's 59%, and so on up to the Eastern European countries and finally the Soviet Union with 82%. When a woman did work such as cleaning out the Lisbon airport's public rooms, she wore very moral slacks rather than the possibly immoral skirt. The Portuguese working woman was thus well in advance of the American woman as regards this item of fashion.

Courageous individuals spoke out long ago in defense of women. One was the Brazilian lawyer Frederico Dabney de Avelar Brotero, grandson of John Bass Dabney (1767-1826), U.S. consul in the Azores from 1806 to 1826, and son of John Bass's daughter

"Portugal used to be a man's world"—country scene on Fayal

Nancy (1803-1872). In a noteworthy speech delivered in Minas Gerais in 1868 on the education and emancipation of women, he blamed the Metropolis, Portugal, for the ideas current "in our country, where the majority seem to think that the only mission of woman is to people the world, and be a perfect automaton of domestic accomplishments."

The whole matter of women's rights was ventilated within the Metropolis in the debates which preceded promulgation of the New Civil Code. A thick volume entitled *Proposed Civil Code* circulated. It affirmed, as does the final version, that the husband is the family head, it being his role to represent the family and make the decisions concerning "all the acts of the common conjugal life," and that the wife, during the life in common, is responsible for domestic affairs in accordance with the customs and condition of the spouses. This clear differentiation in the sex roles was hotly debated, the proponents having recourse among others to St. Paul and his statement about wives being subject to their husbands as to the Lord.

The opponents of the traditional female role in Portuguese society, in large part enlightened women, were aware that in those years Portugal was waging its three African wars and was in effect in the international doghouse. And I, observing all of this at rather close range, used to predict to friends and my relations that, when the Revolution came, it would be brought about by women and that the first victims would be bishops and priests.

Technically, the Revolution was not brought about by a revolt of the masses nor yet by a revolt of women. Rather, it was precipitated by dissatisfied armed-forces officers of the company and field grades who perceived a hopeless morass in Africa. Women, however, played a most notable role in laying the broader groundwork, and especially the famous Three Marias, whose book, *New Portuguese Letters*, was published in 1972. Promptly banned by the authorities, this book, among many other things, revealed to the world the sexual suffering—both physical and emotional—of women left at home by husbands fighting wars abroad or working on a distant continent. In accordance with the lopsided mores of some Latin Christians, the men could indulge themselves sexually while away from their wives' beds, but the women at home were expected to remain as pure as the driven snow, not even to be pitied, and at the same time to sustain sexist abuse even in letters from the distant spouses.

Consider the feelings of the wife, Mariana, residing in Lisbon, when she receives this missive from her accountant husband in Africa:

> How happy you made me and how proud I felt when I received your news! We finally have a baby! It's too bad that it's not a boy, because as you know, having a boy was what I wanted most, but it was God's will that it was a girl instead, and we must bring her up too amid the loving atmosphere of our house and the glowing warmth of our hopes.
> . . .
> May she be able to follow your example, Mariana, one day offering to her life's companion not only a virgin body but also all the virtue of her spirit, all the tranquility and innocence of a woman who has nothing to hide from her husband. And above all, may she learn to be forgiving! A woman who can forgive her husband for his faults, who is understanding, tender, and generous is a model to set before her own daughters later.

Or ponder the feelings of this illiterate Maria Ana in central Portugal as she has a letter written to her emigrant husband in Western Canada:

> ... My beloved and never forgotten António I am taking advantage of our cousin Luisa's visit to me today to send you this letter that she's kindly offered to write for me to tell you how much I miss hearing from you. Listen António you havent been back to see us for two years now and this only makes things worse even though youre very good about sending money—our Jorge cashes your money orders in Aveiro every month and may Our Lord repay you for working so hard and your children and I are very grateful to you because others there where you are do nicely but only send home as little as they can. ... Everybody around here keeps asking about you and so did the new parish priest who came to give me his blessing and I dont complain because the helping hand you give me makes me hold my tongue and I'm only telling you this because its Luisa who's writing this letter for me but even though youve spared me the many hardships and miseries that so many people around here are suffering and even send me enough to help them out and this makes me more respected, still and all its as though I were wearing widow's weeds because I'll be thirty-eight this year and I bore you three children before you went away and raised them and now theyre all grown up and in all these years that youve been away I've never done anything to tarnish your reputation and when I shed so many tears last time you left again you gave me your word youd send for me to join you there in that faraway place because I'm not the sort of woman who's afraid of the cold or hard work but then you wrote me a letter telling me to wait till you'd set aside enough to make your children rich and could come back here with more money than anybody else around. But listen António what good does it do me for you to come back here and lord it over everybody and for us to be able to spend money like water and be filthy rich. ...

The movement personified by the Three Marias acquired many adherents. The Miss Portugal 72 bathing beauty contest in the Estoril Casino was a particular object of their attention. A Miss Madeira participated, as well as beauties representing the Cape

Verde Islands, Portuguese Guinea, Angola, Mozambique, and Macao, but no Miss Azores. Other young women, some of them reported to be more beautiful than the contestants, protested in the rain in front of the building. A sign read "NO to the thingification [*coisificação*] of women." And in Angra that April I copied down a sign in front of the Liceu Nacional which proclaimed that "Woman is not an object of decoration."

The Revolution came. Portuguese women are on their way to being liberated, although they are still lagging behind men in public service. Thus, in the Regional Governments the president and all nine Secretaries in the Azores are men. In the Madeiras, the president and five of the six Secretaries of the original Regional Government were men, the Regional Secretary of Education and Culture a woman. But in the latter part of 1977 she resigned and was replaced by a man. In the Madeiras, five of the forty-one Deputies in the Regional Assembly are women (four PSD, one PS). In the Azores, five of the forty-three Deputies are also women, but the party affiliation is significantly different (three PS, two PSD).

Natália Correia, São Miguel-born and a leading woman writer of the new Portugal who served as Cultural Adviser to the first Soares Government, informed me in the summer of 1977 that a Statute for Women was being drafted to be included in a revision of the Civil Code. Among other things, she told me, it confers on a wife the right to give her name to her husband, on a mother the same right to recognize a child as is possessed by the father, and on a common-law wife of two or more years standing the right on separation to a subsistence allowance from the man. The revisions were published in the *Daily of the Republic* on November 25, 1977, to become law in the course of 1978.

The post-Revolutionary liberation of women in Portugal includes the right and the possibility to place their plight on public view. In February 1976 a well-known Azorean lady of distinguished family took full advantage of the new opportunities. She witnessed publication of her innermost thoughts and feelings in a courageous and honest book which makes the *New Portuguese Letters* pale by comparison.

Margarida Victória, Marchioness of Jácome Correia, had a female dog—a *cadela*, that is, in the king's English, a bitch—named Pura ("Pure"), and so she entitled this first volume *Loves of the Bitch Named "Pure"* with a laconic subtitle *Confessions*. The book focuses on what one Portuguese critic calls "an erroneous sexological pedagogy," which is a nice way for a Portuguese male to summarize generations of repression of young women, held in ignorance until the great disillusionment of physical marriage opens their eyes and, in this case, their soul. "Nothing was explained; everything was implied. I was already accustomed to this type of proceeding on the part of my mother: hiding the truth, she established confusion; that was ever her great mistake."

This is not to imply that I have not known very normal, happy, and well-adjusted couples on the Continent and in both archipelagoes. It is no longer necessary to risk generalizations in either direction, however, for the new Portugal of the Revolution is changing rapidly on the sexual front. Young women are even chasing the bulls on Terceira. When that happens, men and boys no longer have any reason to strut, to lord it over the other sex.

☆ ☆ ☆

Insular Portuguese, above all Azoreans, frequently thought of themselves as second-class citizens of Portugal. This self-characterization stemmed from the isolation and abandonment which they sensed. The feeling, however, applied only to those who remained in the islands. If the islander went to the mainland and became assimilated, if he melted into Greater Portuguese society, he was accepted. His island origin was not held against him. An Azorean from São Miguel even served as Foreign Minister in the first Soares Government until he resigned not long before that Government fell.

The concept of class, however, normally embraces not a horizontal or geographical ranking but a vertical or social one.

In 1945, at the end of a war which profoundly shook practically every human institution, an untouched Lisbon firm named the Maritime-Colonial Publishing House brought out a biography which has been admired even within U.S. Portuguese circles. It is entitled *Servidor de Reis e de Presidentes* (Server of Kings and Presidents). It is about a well-known figure, Vital Ferreira Fontes, who was then in his eighties and had served exalted masters for over half a century beginning with King Luís (reigned 1861-1889). The book's paper cover bears a striking photograph of the *servidor*, a word which my all-Portuguese dictionary defines as *obsequiador*. This picture depicts Fontes in full regalia standing at what seems to be attention, but with head obsequiously bowed. No better exemplification of Portugal's two-class system can be found.

The mentality of a Vital Fontes and of a publisher who could issue a book with such an illustration was Portugal's root problem. A Lisbon example of as late as 1970 is provided by the elegant and wealthy ladies who used to drive in their limousines with liveried chauffeurs to the Chiado, the chique shopping area. Each Senhora would enter a boutique leaving the car awaiting her at the curb. The resplendent chauffeur would proudly stand beside his vehicle, which would be a Volkswagen Beetle. Yes, uniformed chauffeurs came cheaper than appropriate automobiles in those days, those far-off days.

A linguistic vestige of the two-class mentality prompted the Portuguese, be they Continental, Insular, or Ultramarine, to address a social superior as Your Excellency, or Mister Engineer, or Mister Architect, or Mister Ambassador, or even (with reference to all who have graduated from or attended a university and including, it is said, the bootblacks of the city of Coimbra) Mister Doctor, and to address a presumed inferior as Thou or by means of a nickname. Significantly, the New-World Brazilians have long since given up these forms of address, although both Germans and Italians retain vestiges of the system on their calling cards and letterheads.

This matter of "treatment," as the Portuguese call the several varieties of direct address, looms large in the eyes of the immigrant in the United States. An anecdote serves to illustrate. An ex-primary school teacher from the Azores came to a New England city and found employment in one of the factories. She was amazed to discover a former pupil of hers working in the same plant, and she was doubly amazed when the ex-student came up to the ex-teacher and exclaimed: "We're in America now, and I'll address you by Thou and not by 'Senhora'."

It is this stratified mentality, well known to those in touch with the U.S. Portuguese, which led an Azorean lady visiting an American home to ask concerning the attractive widow who lives next door: "É formada?" (Is she formed, that is, is she a college graduate?)

It is the hierarchical mentality which caused Insular Portuguese as well as Continentals to admire *fidalgos* and *morgados* (male aristocrats or minor noblemen often imagined by adulating females to be particularly handsome) and to talk about their *criadas* (domestic help). The references to *morgados* are all the more amusing as the institution of the *morgadio* was abolished in the 1830's, at the time the property of religious orders was confiscated. Initiated in the early fifteenth century, the system provided that only the eldest son, or *morgado*, could inherit certain lands granted by the Crown, and he inherited everything. In other words, the lands were not to be divided and subdivided ad infinitum but rather were entailed. In the absence of a legitimate male heir, the property was to revert to the Crown. The *morgado* inherited property but he could not dispose of it. And he inherited the moral obligation of supporting his entire family.

It is the mentality under discussion, alas, which led one who rises not to wish to bring his former peers up with him, but to keep them in their place and lord it over them, like the husband in distant Canada. This manifestation of the mentality might be denominated the king-of-the-hill complex. It accounts for the widely recognized fact that within clubs and associations of the Portuguese in the United States there are too many *morgados* and not enough *criadas*. In reverse, it accounts for a related trait highly visible among the Portuguese in America, one which definitely holds up progress within the group: proneness to criticize, or make fun of, or even campaign against, a peer who rises. The explanation lies in the tendency of the one who rises to cease paying any attention to his brethren left behind and below. Or else he who rises looks down on others. In my opinion, the Portuguese look down even on other Portuguese, their blood brethren, because they have no one else—no ethnic minorities like the Lapps in Norway—on whom to look down. Thus, the Portuguese in Portugal look down on "Portuguese-Americans" who visit them, the traffic police on occasion being particularly rough with them once they recognize them, whereas the police are very polite with "regular Americans." And Americans descended from the earlier wave of immigrants from Portugal look down on the recent arrivals, the "greenhorns."

It is undoubtedly due to this mentality that some Portuguese, including many Islanders, impress foreigners as being devoid of a sense of humor. In marked contrast to the Italians, often as poor and downtrodden, the Portuguese do not appear happy but, rather, sad, like Vital Fontes in his photograph. In accordance with the characteristic they label *saudade*—the German *Sehnsucht*—they unsmilingly look backward in time or space to what they deem a better world and are never more content than when listening to a fado (song of fate) expressing their mood. Or else, or in combination, their Sebastianism comes to the fore, that acceptance of wishful thinking for reality. This characteristic goes back to the days following the battle of Alcazarquivir on August 4, 1578, and the refusal of large segments of the Portuguese populace to accept the news that their King Sebastian had been killed in the Moroccan encounter. The occasional Insular Portuguese lady clothed in black, with black shawl over her head, a hand ever ready to bring a portion of the shawl up over her mouth in typical Moorish fashion when she descries a male, represents the epitome of this sadness.

What they lack in a tarantella-type gaiety, Portuguese men of the lower class make up for with their traditional politeness, which they manifest toward foreigners, toward their own upper class, and, as will shortly be exemplified by a bus episode on Madeira, toward their peers. Trolley-car starters and conductors in Continental Portugal, and waiters and lottery-ticket salesmen everywhere, to name only a few, go out of their way to be helpful in a manner which is all but lost throughout much of the rest of Europe and almost totally lost in America.

Cult of social-class differences manifests itself in several ways in Portugal. On São Miguel and to a certain extent on Madeira, but very little on the other islands, a veritable cult of nobility exists. Thus, on the Azorean Green Island there are, or recently have been, marquesses and marchionesses, earls and countesses, viscounts, and barons. On July 5, 1974, the last titled person was buried in Horta, the daughter-in-law of the first Baron of Ribeirinha, a title granted by King Carlos during his 1901 visit. Other titles exist, occasionally as components of street names. One is *Conselheiro*, strictly speaking a counselor, a name applied to judges of the Supreme Court in Lisbon. Another, *Comendador*, necessitates an extended explanation which is most relevant to the chapter on culture heroes in the companion volume.

In Europe at the time of the Crusades (1095-1291), quasi-military religious orders were formed, the Knights Templars, for example, the Knights of St. John of Jerusalem (the Hospitalers), and the Knights of the Holy Sepulcher. In those days, the knights performed specific duties, such as succoring Crusaders and pilgrims. The Knights of St. John evolved into today's Knights of Malta, and new Church orders have been established such as the

Knights of St. Gregory. Membership in these orders is now largely honorific.

Medieval orders like the Knights Templars became very wealthy. Tourists in London invariably visit the Temple and see its so-called Round Church (circular chapel), dedicated in 1185, where the knights sat. In Portugal, the Templars had their headquarters in Tomar in central Portugal, where one still admires their chapel of similar shape named the Charola dos Templários. Greedy monarchs aspired to control the wealth of these orders, and at the beginning of the fourteenth century they convinced the pope that he should abolish the Order of Knights Templars. Aware of allegations of sodomy made against the knights, he did so, whereupon the heads of state promptly sequestered the Order's properties. King Dinis (reigned 1279-1325) made of their possessions within Portugal a national Portuguese order, the Military Order of Christ. Its headquarters continued in Tomar, in the buildings henceforth known as the Monastery of Christ. The cross of the Knights Templars was transformed into the angular red Cross of Christ, which came to symbolize militant religion devoted to national purpose. The Cross of Christ is thus not the cross of Christ crucified, but the cross of the national military order which bears His name. The Cross of Christ is a symbol of the State, of *étatisme*, of a Church subordinate to the State.

Prince Henry the Navigator became the administrator of the Military Order of Christ. He never became its Grand Master, as is often asserted, because he was not a professed knight, that is, a priest or monk. He devoted the order's income to his maritime endeavors, wherefore the Cross of Christ became an ornament on the billowing sails of Portuguese vessels and on stone constructions throughout the Portuguese world. The modern Portuguese Navy school ship *Sagres II* displays the Cross of Christ, as did the preceding *Sagres* in which in 1960 I made my only voyage under square sail.

During the centuries following that of Henry's death, the kings of Portugal held jurisdiction over the Military Order of Christ. Today, the State, meaning in effect the Government, controls it.

Traditionally, in the orders with medieval roots, such as the Knights of Malta, there is, on the one hand, an inner circle corresponding to the professed knights of old and, on the other hand, the masses of members. In modern times, the Governments of the various countries with national orders confer the latter type of membership on many persons at home and abroad who have rendered conspicuous service to those countries—scilicet those Governments—in either a military or civilian capacity. Thus, Napoleon founded the French Legion of Honor in order to reward meritorious individuals.

The Légion d'Honneur, which is typical, consists of five ranks: Grand-Croix, Grand Officier, Commandeur, Officier, and Chevalier. The Portuguese equivalent of Commandeur is Comendador (the Italian Commendatore), hence the street names on São Miguel.

In addition to the Military Order of Christ, Portugal has other decorations at hand to confer: Military Order of Santiago of the Sword, Order of Prince Henry the Navigator, Order of Meritoriousness, and Order of Public Instruction. The hierarchy within the orders is the international one—Grand Cross, Grand Officer, Commander, Officer, and Knight—and recipients proudly wear the respective insignia on a lapel of their civilian suit coats.

The whole idea behind these decorations differs markedly from traditional American conceptions. The Founding Fathers' views were expressed succinctly in the U.S. Constitution, where, in Article I, Section 9, among the powers denied to the Federal Government, they provided: "No title of nobility shall be granted by the United States; and no person holding any office of profit or trust under them shall, without the consent of the Congress, accept of any present, emolument, office, or title, of any kind whatever, from any king, prince, or foreign state."

Titles and decorations are not the only manifestations of class-consciousness and hierarchy among the Island Portuguese. Another is the charming and picturesque custom that used to require the waiters in Ponta Delgada's superb Hotel de São Pedro to wear white gloves when serving dinner. In the olden days, the dining-room stewards aboard the *Carvalho Araujo* also wore white gloves in first class. The ship was then São Miguel-owned.

Whether the waiters liked to display enforced subservience by wearing white gloves is another matter. There is considerable evidence to suggest to the discerning visitor that Insular Portugal for long has been in partial social revolt. Some youngsters have refused to marry cousins, and some brides design their wedding costumes in such a way as to eliminate the traditional lace veil. Modern young Azoreans object to the publicity given the antiquated whaling techniques. So-called regional costumes are hardly ever seen in everyday use. The old-fashioned men's straw hats on sale in the Santa Maria airport's Turismo are strictly for the tourists, although on Madeira, where it can get cold up in the highlands, the men's headgear replete with ear flaps continues to be worn. Interest in folk music, folk dances, and probably even folk literature is waning on the part of the island young, who want to live in the modern international jet age to which in fact their island airports have contributed so much.

Pending fuller revolution, the lower class has its methods of defending itself. The normal international way of course is to steal from the rich. Portuguese people, however, are honest. They extract their due in other more subtle ways. The two best examples which I dare relate without betraying confidences happen to be respectively Peninsular- and Island-Spanish and not Portuguese, but they are illustrative and typical.

At Christmas time in 1934, I traveled by train from San Sebastián slowly and inexpensively via Burgos, Valladolid, Ávila, and El Escorial to Madrid. The locomotives had a pet cock on the outside. As we pulled into successive stations, local women would be lined up on the platform each with her large jug. With the engineer's permission and connivance, they would proceed to fill their utensils with piping-hot water badly needed for domestic use, and with disastrous results for the railroad's timetable.

For a month at the end of 1955, including Christmas and the Feast of the Three Kings, I stayed in Puerto de la Cruz on Tenerife. On many occasions I took the local bus to the University of La Laguna and on to the capital city of Santa Cruz. The bus company did publish a schedule, and occasionally I seriously counted on its being followed. At an open field along the road, however, the bus would stop and a waiting peasant lady would give a package or a load of laundry to the driver for free delivery a few kilometers away. The bus naturally stopped a second unscheduled time for the delivery to the second peasant. Again, the schedule was ruined. I let myself be aggravated until I perceived exactly what was going on, namely, retaliation against the social system.

The lower class respects its own members. Exactly seventeen years before the Canaries sojourn, I took many bus trips around Madeira. In those days, some of the roads would permit only one bus to pass. As two approached head on, one would pull over to the side. All the peasant gentlemen in the favored bus, at the moment they passed the mass of humanity parked by the side of the road, would, as if by signal, simultaneously tip their hats as an expression of gratitude.

All these admirable qualities, foibles, and defects have been perfectly well known to intelligent, forward-looking, and genuinely patriotic young business men, priests, teachers, and doctors, even under the 1928-1974 dictatorship. For example, the members of the Azores Regional Planning Committee, based in Angra, were very active preparing long-range studies in anticipation of the Fourth Development Plan (which was to cover the years 1974-1979). They were speaking of both economic and social development of the Region and announced the objectives of the Fourth Plan as a whole to be (a) a raising of the standard of living and (b) greater opportunities to participate in all levels of education and in the benefits of medical and social assistance. They had very specific and excellent suggestions concerning the school system.

The Azores Regional Planning Committee correctly diagnosed a major problem of Portugal as a whole and an acute problem within the archipelagoes: social-class distinctions. Lack of economic development in the Portuguese Atlantic Islands has been due not exclusively to royal or dictatorial or paternal government, not to lack of talent or industriousness, but to the stratified nature of society. This social characteristic accounts fully as much as the mere hope of personal economic betterment for the desire to emigrate.

It is essential for Americans to ponder this point, for one segment of Portuguese society has suggested that the islands are paradisiacal although lacking in opportunities for earning large sums of money, that the United States is virtually uncivilized but a good place to earn money, and therefore that Insular Portuguese emigrate to America merely to earn money and then return to Portugal. Another segment has been more honest and in reality far more patriotic. Made up of such persons as the members of the Planning Committee and the anonymous authors of the *Survey of the Portuguese Economy* published by the Portuguese Government in 1971, this group recognized the existence of a social problem and even of a specific retrograde mentality, and the *Survey* mentioned creation of "a different mentality which believes in the validity of modern techniques of working at the entrepreneurial level."

Because of the deeply-ingrained social system within Portugal, upper-class Portuguese, including recently ascended kings-of-the-hill, do not mix well with Portuguese immigrants in the United States. Psychologically, it is too much to expect that, say, a university-trained professional person from Portugal would be sympathetic to the problems encountered by Insular Portuguese children in an American bilingual program. Experience has already shown that conflicts can arise when Portuguese university students, for example members of choral groups or orchestras, are housed with Portuguese families in America. The university students are, almost by definition, upper-class or on their way up. The Portuguese in America, on the other hand, are, within the Portuguese cultural context, lower-class and probably speak what their guests would deem to be broken Portuguese.

University students either are upper-class or are lower-class on their way up. The latter group is already constituting a middle class, which will be enlarged as opportunities for higher education are expanded, as they began to be expanded in both Azores and Madeiras in 1976.

For several decades, all the Islands have given evidence of a middle class, small, to be sure, but real: professional people including teachers (even husband-and-wife combinations), shopkeepers and other entrepreneurs, and taxicab owners. On many an occasion the rise from lower to middle class has been assisted by money from America.

Recently in Ponta Delgada, a taxi driver proved most belligerent with regard to the United States. He had spent several years in New Bedford and could not stomach the place. He returned and bought his taxi. Further conversation developed the points that he had completed the fifth year of the technical high school in his native city before emigrating and that the money with which he paid for the taxi had been earned in Massachusetts.

A more spectacular example is provided by the biography of José de Almeida, the "representative of the Provisional Clandestine Government of the Azores," who was once very active in promotional activities among the Portuguese in the United States. He was born in Bretanha on São Miguel, the youngest of eighteen children. Until he entered the fourth class of primary school he had gone barefoot and worked in the fields like any other rural laborer. Due to the help of brothers who had emigrated to America, however, he succeeded in "forming himself," that is, in

Three social classes on a Funchal street in 1964

earning a university degree (in history and philosophy at the Classical University of Lisbon). He followed a career in teaching, first in Continental Portugal (where he also served for six months as an elected Deputy in the National Assembly), later on São Miguel.

But then, Salazar himself was of humble origin.

That three classes have, in fact, long existed in the Azores is clear from the account written by Rose Dabney Forbes. This reflects knowledge of the social situation prior to the beginning of 1892, when the last Dabney left Fayal:

> The inhabitants of the Azores may be said to be divided into three classes, viz., first (and not necessarily best) the aristocrats, who are usually educated in Lisbon or Paris, proud of being "real blue-bloods," and usually averse to much work; second, the poorer townspeople, who have a certain amount of schooling but early turn to shopkeeping and other trades; and last but not least, the peasants, who are

to be found in all the villages, and who, with their modest ways, their devotion to friends, and hospitality to strangers, are especially attractive.

☆ ☆ ☆

In 1967, I photographed a statue of two Africans at the entrance to the beautiful and modern railroad station in Beira, Mozambique, the Indian Ocean terminal of the famed trans-African railroad whose Atlantic terminal is in Lobito just north of Benguela, Angola. The posture of the two figures, amazingly, was exactly that of Vital Fontes on the cover of his book. The two widely separated works of art reflect but a single phenomenon, not racism but classism. Over the centuries, the white masters of Portugal beat down their own lower-class Whites as well as the Blacks of their African territories. Just as Cape Verdeans chose not to continue under Portuguese rule, so lower-class Continental and Insular Portuguese will surely not be content to continue subject to an upper class. The days of class, the days of the two distinct orders of *dominatori* and *dominati*, are over.

Lawn of Hotel de São Pedro, Ponta Delgada, São Miguel

7
SAILING SHIPS AND STEAMERS

The modest, devoted, hospitable, and attractive Portuguese Islanders of the lower class are agriculturists who live in the middle of the sea, who see the sea without end, who dream of evasion via the sea. But they are not seamen. Some become temporary seamen upon evading. Others like my paternal grandfather become seamen and remain professional seamen for decades on end. The seamanship, however, is an acquisition learned aboard U.S. vessels. It was not a prior skill. These Islanders by and large are not even local fishermen, whatever their emigrant brethren may have become in Provincetown and Gloucester. They are farmers. But they are aware of the sea and its effects.

Sailing ships, piston-engined airplanes, and dirigibles share a feature which distinguishes them from powered vessels, cables, radio, and jet planes. For the former, the least-time track between two points is not necessarily nor even normally a straight line (that is, the shortest distance). The reason lies in the influence of winds. The intermediate places at which these carriers touch are determined by location in relation to the prevailing winds, and in the case of sailing vessels also by location in relation to the ocean currents. Steamers, motorships, cables, radio waves, and jets, on the other hand, tend to move in straight lines, although jets are also subject to the influence of strong winds. The intermediate ports of call are accordingly determined by their relation to the straight-line track, which in the case of east-west or west-east travel may be rhumb lines (loxodromes) or great circles (orthodromes) depending chiefly upon the latitude.

All these bonds between peoples are absolutely dependent upon intermediate stops if their range is limited. Sailing ships, dirigibles, radio, modern jet planes, and the most modern coaxial submarine telephone cables enjoy very long range. The earlier powered vessels, submarine telegraph cables, and propellor planes had very limited range; and they had to be refueled, or, in the case of cablegrams, relayed.

On both counts, the Portuguese Atlantic islands score high. They lie athwart prevailing winds and ocean currents, and they sit astride the straight-line tracks between continents. One or more of them has therefore been important for sailing and powered vessels, for telegraph and telephone cables, and for piston and jet airplanes and even the navigation of transoceanic dirigibles.

The basic pattern of wind and current in the Atlantic Ocean has been likened to a figure 8 drawn as follows:

The top and bottom of the figure lie at roughly 40° N and 40° S latitude respectively. When the figure is fitted onto a map or chart, the recommended sailing (and slow-plane flying) routes become obvious, subject to some seasonal variation. (Columbus and Vasco da Gama were aware of them.) The reasons for the nature of the flow of wind and current are complicated and lie outside the scope of this book. They involve the earth's rotation and the location of high or low pressure areas in the atmosphere, for example the famous Azores High or anticyclone so well known to North Atlantic navigators.

The Azores lie astride or near the eastbound track from the United States to Europe (which takes advantage of the prevailing westerlies of the northern hemisphere) and northbound track from southern Africa to Europe (which first takes advantage of the southeast trade winds and finally the prevailing westerlies of the northern hemisphere). The ghost ship *Mary Celeste*, a brigantine eastbound from New York, was very near the Azores when found sailing without a crew aboard on December 4, 1872. The Madeiras and the Cape Verde Islands lie astride or near the southbound track from Europe to Brazil and other South American countries (which takes advantage of the northeast trade winds). On his third voyage, Columbus stopped off at both these latter archipelagoes and, between them, at the island of Gomera in the Canaries before heading southwest.

The latter-day whaling ships out of New Bedford, of the early twentieth century, confined their hunting to the Atlantic and perfectly exemplified this pattern of circular sailing. A typical voyage would take the vessel with its largely Portuguese crew (including Cape Verdeans) to the Hatteras Grounds, thence to the Western Grounds between the Gulf Stream and the Azores, into Horta to offload oil already taken (whence it would be shipped to the United States), to the Cape Verde Islands, to the South Atlantic, to either Barbados or Dominica in the Caribbean's Windward Islands to offload again, to the Western Grounds; and around again, and possibly again.

The tradition of crossing the Atlantic by sail is far from dead. Every year, hundreds of well-constructed, small yachts, beautifully equipped and expertly handled, sail from the U.S. east coast or Caribbean northeast and east via the Azores to Europe. Others sail from Europe south and southwest via the Canaries to Barbados or other Caribbean port, thence to a U.S. destination. Readers of course recall the three-leg transatlantic race of the "tall ships" in mid-1976 en route to the Bicentennial: Plymouth to Tenerife to Bermuda to Newport.

Aware of the influence of winds and currents, one can appreciate the consternation with which Azoreans in March and April 1972 greeted the news that drums containing highly toxic chemicals had been washed overboard from a ship off Nova Scotia, or how the entire North Atlantic community received the intelligence that on December 7, 1972, about 330 miles east of Cape Henry, Virginia, thirty-six 55-gallon drums of poison were lost overboard from a U.S. merchant vessel. One can also understand why a note and dollar bill dropped overboard from a cruise ship between Bermuda and New York on April 13, 1976, elicited a reply dated July 24, 1977, from a fisherman in Vitória, Graciosa. What one does not understand is why, after the breakup of the tanker *Argo Merchant* off Nantucket in December 1976, the U.S. National Oceanic and Atmospheric Administration chose to drop plastic float cards into nearby waters with instructions printed only in English, French, and Spanish.

In the earliest days, Angra was of the utmost importance as an Azorean port because of its location on the return route from India via the South Atlantic. After Spain came to rule Portugal in 1580 and Elizabethan England challenged Spanish naval might, English men-of-war lay off the Azores awaiting the rendezvousing of the fleets from the Spanish Main with Portuguese ships returning from India or Portugal's Brazil. It was in this area that one of England's greatest mariners met the death immortalized not only by Tennyson's "At Flores in the Azores Sir Richard Grenville lay" but also by a sixteenth-century Portuguese poet who witnessed the 1591 battle and described it in Spanish.

The calls at Angra by the ships returning from the Indies contributed relatively little to the economy of the Azores because, in accordance with Crown regulations then in force, the cargoes had to continue on to Lisbon for unloading. Lisbon's exploitation of the Atlantic islands thus began very early.

The Azores felt a much more substantial impact from world trade via Horta, Fayal. As European commerce with the English colonies of North America grew, and eventually commerce with the United States, Horta became an increasingly significant port of call on the eastbound passage across the Atlantic. As a matter of fact, in that pre-breakwater era, Horta possessed the only safe anchorage in the Azores. Angra had never been a safe year-round anchorage, and it continues uneven to this day.

Horta—transatlantic yachts and view of Pico

Horta today is the Mecca of the eastbound transatlantic yachts. The local newspapers report each day's arrivals, assigning a serial number and giving name, flag, captain, port of departure, length of crossing, and destination. About 80 called during the 1971 season, 100 in 1972, and 120 in 1973. Some 150 were expected in 1974, and by July 10 numbers 96 and 97 had arrived. By July 6, 1977, the season's total had reached 164, including one which, sixty miles from Fayal with crew asleep, collided with a sleeping whale, with the results that can be conjectured. Passengers (if any) and crew, once ashore, make for the waterfront Café Sport to pick up accumulated mail and then for a hotel to get unsoaked or soaked depending upon condition and mood at arrival.

Many famous ships of the past stopped at Horta, and their owners or passengers have described the city and island of Fayal and facing view of Pico.

In the Peabody Museum of Salem, Massachusetts, the visitor enters a scale replica of the interior of the yacht *Cleopatra's Barge*, a hermaphrodite brig of about 185 tons built for Captain George Crowninshield, Jr. (1766-1817). Long since lost, the original went on "a voyage of pleasure" to the Western Islands, Madeira, and the Mediterranean in 1817. The yacht's complement first sighted Flores, then Corvo. Members went ashore on Flores and for a much longer while on Fayal. Salemites of that era, with their special racial and religious orientation, were hardly able to appreciate a Portuguese Catholic island, however. Nor was Miss Harriet Low of Salem able to appreciate the Portuguese and Chinese features of the Macao in which she dwelled for over four years in the early 1830's.

Crowninshield's journal, privately printed in Boston in 1913, states:

> Fayal itself is a small town, the streets narrow, the houses in general mean, and the populace ragged. The streets are not so dirty as those of Lisbon, nor the beggars so numerous.

The journal also reports that on August 24, 1817, having departed the Strait of Bonifacio (between Corsica and Sardinia), *Cleopatra's Barge* overtook the two "Portuguese 74's having a Princess of Austria on board who is to be married to the Prince Regent of Portugal [who had become king in 1816] on her arrival at Brazil, whither she is going in the above Ships."

It was about Horta that Mark Twain wrote years later in *The Innocents Abroad*, after he had stopped off there in June 1867 on the paddle-wheeled liner *Quaker City*:

> The community is eminently Portuguese—that is to say, it is slow, poor, shiftless, sleepy, and lazy. . . . The people lie, and cheat the stranger, and are desperately ignorant, and have hardly any reverence for their dead.

Still later, Mark Twain, in reality Samuel Langhorne Clemens (1835-1910), built a splendid Victorian home in Hartford, Connecticut. There he lived with his family from 1874 to 1891 little realizing that the Connecticut capital would later emerge as a center of those very Portuguese whom he so eloquently disparaged.

Americans of Portuguese descent, especially those whose forebears came from Fayal, react rather vigorously when they come upon passages like the afore-cited and others equally malicious or worse, for they sense the presence of bigotry and smart-aleckness rather than objective reporting. The existence of such passages has not contributed to the easy assimilation of Portuguese Catholics into Yankee Protestant communities.

Horta became a first port of call for the long-range Nantucket, New Bedford, and other whalers outward bound, as it was for Joshua Slocum in the *Spray* in 1895. It and nearby Pico are delightfully depicted on the Purrington-Russell panorama of a whaling voyage round the world 1841-1845. Called by Samuel Eliot Morison "a pictorial counterpart to Herman Melville's classic *Moby Dick*," the panorama measures eight and a half feet high and 1,295 feet long and is the proud possession of New Bedford's Whaling Museum. Another view of Horta, one of the most artistic of them all, is contained within a treasure of the Nantucket Historical Association's archives, the journal kept by boatsteerer Joseph Edward Ray aboard the Nantucket whaleship *Edward Cary* during a voyage to the Pacific 1854-1858.

With the coming of oceangoing steamships toward the middle of the nineteenth century, Horta, like Funchal, became an important coaling station. It was not long, however, before the city's importance for commercial shipping began to diminish and Ponta Delgada's to increase.

An early factor in the shift in economic interest from Fayal's port to São Miguel's was the deleterious aftereffect of the plant disease which attacked the former's grape vines and orange trees in mid-century. Actually, two blights were involved. Oidium is a fungus. Phylloxera is a root louse native to the United States which one authority on wines calls "the all-destroying Transatlantic louse." One or both damaged São Miguel's orange groves as early as 1844, fatally damaged them in 1895. They both destroyed Fayal's orange trees and Pico's vines in 1852. Oidium cut down Madeira's vines in 1852; in 1873 phylloxera wiped them out once again and within five years was attacking the vineyards of Continental Portugal and of France. The solution to the twin problems proved to be sulfuring in the case of oidium and, for phylloxera, grafting the native vine on stock imported from the United States and already inured to the louse's attack. Ironically, the California vine, often maligned by amateur connoisseurs, thus turned out to be the salvation of Europe's most famous vines in a grand example of cooperation between the Insular Portuguese and the United States.

Except for the coaling station, Horta's commercial life thereafter declined. In 1891, by which date Ponta Delgada had established itself as the Azores's number one port, the U.S. consulate moved from Horta to the São Miguel city, there to remain to this day. The number of Eastern Azorean emigrants to the United States naturally increased, for expanded commerce does not necessarily mean improved living for the masses.

Although it failed to provide ships a sheltered anchorage, Ponta Delgada already in the seventeenth, eighteenth, and early nineteenth centuries was an important port because of the worth of its island's products—pastel dye, wheat and flax, and oranges. Wheat as an early item of export is particularly noteworthy in view of present-day Azorean and Madeiran dependence on imported wheat. Great Britain used to be the most significant market for the oranges. Ponta Delgada in those days was thus commercially linked with Britain, whereas Horta was tied to the United States. For instance, a report out of Boston of 1873, undoubtedly reflecting a slightly earlier state of affairs, affirmed that sweet Fayalese oranges "every winter are hawked about the streets of our city, or met with at almost every fruit-stand."

Ponta Delgada became a U.S. naval base during World War I, and Admiral Dunn Square on which the Hotel de São Pedro is located commemorates the name of the American commanding officer. Much improved, the port serves NATO today. (Portugal is a founding member of the North Atlantic Treaty Organization, established in 1949.)

In his capacity as Assistant Secretary of the Navy, Franklin Delano Roosevelt went to Europe beginning in July 1918 to inspect U.S. naval establishments. He first called briefly at Fayal on July 15 and wrote: "It is one of the westerly Islands of the Azores and is the place where the Dabneys of Boston were so long as Consul General, also the scene of the famous fight of the privateer *General Armstrong* in the War of 1812 against two British Men-of-War. . . . Tell Anna and James to look up these Azores places on the map."

Roosevelt spent July 16 and 17 in Ponta Delgada. "We visited a wonderful park of a family named Canot [*sic* for Canto]—a collection of trees, plants from all over the world and especially of curiously marked and colored leaves. Almost anything will grow in the Azores—for the temperature is about the same at all times—and one sees bamboo next English oak and even White Pine." At a formal noon banquet in the Palace of General Machado, to whom he refers in the grand British tradition as the Portuguese High Commissioner (obviously the civil governor), he "managed to struggle through ten courses and many different kinds of cakes and sweetmeats and relishes and to make a speech toasting the Republic of Portugal." Insular Portuguese hospitality has ever been as generous and as fattening.

Roosevelt did more than write enthusiastically home about the Azores. He commissioned a painting of his destroyer, U.S.S. *Dyer,* anchored off Ponta Delgada in 1918. Today it hangs in his study in the Franklin D. Roosevelt Library, Hyde Park, New York. (See frontispiece.)

F. D. R. was not alone in recognizing the superb geographical location of the Azores. Presidents Pompidou of France and Nixon of the United States did likewise when they agreed to hold their summit meeting there in December 1971. But they chose not São Miguel but Terceira with its great airport, to which Pompidou flew in record time in a Concorde.

The selection of the mid-Atlantic island led one American newspaperwoman to refer to the Azores as "the birthplace of the devalued dollar." It also confirmed the reasonableness of a view which I held and orally proclaimed at the end of World War II: the new United Nations should set up its main headquarters in the Azores and not New York City. Although I did not know it at the time, President Roosevelt in part shared my views. As early as January 5, 1940, he had suggested the Azores as the capital of a proposed Atlantic Union, the famous "Union Now" between the United States and the British Empire. He had stressed that they were "impregnable," had an excellent climate, and were centrally located. In a press conference on February 19, 1945, he discussed likely U.N. sites. Remembering his visit there of July 1918, he stated: "Although I don't think I will get it, I want to get a building like Al Smith's Empire State Building, just for the records and the records staff, and then have the conferences meet half the time in one of the Azores Islands. I was there once. In front of my house were royal palms and Norwegian spruce, growing side by side. It's a wonderful climate." Asked if it would not turn into a resort after a while, he replied: "I wouldn't let anyone on it, not even the press."

In 1966 I was even more temerarious. Referring to that future day when Catholics throughout the world would no longer wish their spiritual leader to be identified with the Roman Empire, *Latinitas,* and Western Europe, I suggested that the Church Universal should maintain its Holy See in a location universal, the Azores.

An important later factor in the definitive shift in maritime significance from Horta to Ponta Delgada was the Fayalese coaling interests' failure to meet the era of oil, the new fuel which was discovered in quantity in Pennsylvania in 1859 and soon thereafter began to threaten New Bedford's thriving whale fishery. Although the Royal Navy began converting to oil in about 1910, steamships in general switched from coal to bunker fuel oil in the years following World War I. It was at this time also that motorships, consuming marine diesel oil, began plowing the high seas in numbers, the first oceangoing motor vessel, the M/S *Selandia*, having been built in Copenhagen in 1912. This change from coal to oil reached its height with the Depression and the concomitant reduced shipping activity. Ponta Delgada thus was very courageous in furnishing the bunkering facilities, preparing for the new age, whereas Horta failed to meet the challenge. Indeed, Ponta Delgada's breakwater, begun in 1861, was built in large measure before Horta's, another element in the shift. Although Horta's, begun in 1888, was eventually completed first, it came to serve a relatively restricted harbor. A recent extension of Ponta Delgada's has made of that city a major commercial port.

Ponta Delgada's huge breakwater, on the inside of which several large ships can tie up one astern of the other, used to be called Salazar Pier. Its name served as one of the few reminders in the Azores of a dictator who, during forty years in power, never deigned to visit them. Royalty had been almost as neglectful. Prince Luís did visit the Azores in 1858 shortly before he succeeded his brother, Pedro V, as king, and once one royal couple visited them, as has been noted.

King Carlos and Queen Maria Amélia called at Madeira en route to the Azores. This island lies near the outward sailing-vessel track from Europe south and west, and over the years therefore Funchal has been the port of call for many ships, both sailing and powered. Many famous persons have stopped off there, including Benjamin Franklin in 1762 en route from Europe to America. In recent years, however, the port of Las Palmas on Gran Canaria in the Canaries has managed to take away from Funchal its ship-servicing function. Here again, the reason was the Spanish port's ability to adjust rapidly to the use of oil. But there was another reason. When the New Bedford whalers at the end of the whaling era were increasingly offloading en route, their owners discovered that the authorities on Fayal were charging the ships ever greater dues each season. They therefore dispatched the "mother ship" to Las Palmas to effect the rendezvous.

The emergence of the French port of Casablanca in Morocco after World War I dealt a further blow to Funchal. It should also be pointed out that Funchal's breakwater was completed only after World War II. When I first arrived there, aboard the *Carvalho Araujo*, in December 1938, the ship anchored off the city and we went ashore in launches. True, the open roadstead was sheltered from the northeast trades, but surprises could blow up from a different direction. When we arrived there in June 1975 aboard the *Leonardo da Vinci*, the liner of course tied up. Nevertheless, we went from the breakwater across the harbor to the old landing in launches, less expensive than taxis and more fun.

Funchal's location accounts for a most extraordinary accretion to the Protestant population of the United States.

In 1838, a ship outward bound from the British Isles carried as passengers a missionary of the Free Church of Scotland and his wife, both headed for the China fields. The vessel touched at Funchal. Mrs. Robert Reid Kalley's illness was the reason for the husband's decision to remain on Madeira. Soon he was subtly converting Madeirans to Scotch Calvinism and, as was inevitable, promptly collided head on with the local authorities.

In 1845, Kalley's place was taken by another Scot, William Hepburn Hewitson, who formally organized a church, said to be the first Protestant church of Portuguese ever established. Persecution followed, and in 1846 a large number of the converted Madeirans emigrated as exiles to Trinidad. Here they suffered all manner of privations. Their plight came to the attention of the American Protestant Society in New York. One of its missionaries, a Madeiran who was doing the work of his Lord among the Portuguese along the New England coast, "to the number of five or six thousand," so goes the story, was dispatched to Port of Spain to look into the matter.

The upshot of the affair involves the American Hemp Company of Illinois. The Trinidad Madeiran Protestants journeyed to the Springfield-Jacksonville area of West Central Illinois to work for the company, but the arrangements fell through. The twice-exiled migrants found other work, prospered, and left descendants who are there yet. One of their number was once a maid in Abraham Lincoln's household, Frances Affonsa, described in Irving Stone's novel *Love Is Eternal* almost inevitably as "a dark-haired, dark-skinned young girl," Stone thus continuing an American literary stereotype.

It is most likely that the early migration of Madeirans to Bermuda was a spin-off from the Protestant proselytism on the home island. A press statement of August 28, 1849, tells of a Bermudian sending his vessel to Madeira for immigrants as a result of the favorable reports emanating from the Governor of Trinidad about the immigrants arriving on that island.

Not only missionary influences from abroad but also foreign commercial interests have entered the ports of Insular Portugal. Ship-coaling services in both archipelagoes, for example, were quickly developed by and remained in the hands of outsiders, some of them actual foreigners.

In the harbors of both Horta and Ponta Delgada, the Bensaúde family has been well known. My 1968 *Brown's Nautical Almanac* carries a full-page ad of Bensaúde & Co. Ltd. of St. Michael's and Fayal announcing the availability in Ponta Delgada of bunker fuel and lubricating oils and in both Ponta Delgada and Horta of the best spring water, well-equipped repair shops, and wireless telegraph stations. It is presumably due to the influence of this firm that *Brown's* carries a double-page spread expounding the virtues of the port of Ponta Delgada, "The only bunkering station and port of refuge in the CENTRAL NORTH ATLANTIC OCEAN area, between NORTH AMERICA, BERMUDAS or the CARIBBEAN ports and EUROPE directly on the routes of the great air and shipping lines." This ad sounds like a salvo in the barrage in favor of a great international airport on São Miguel to eclipse Santa Maria's and Terceira's. And the pair constituted the only ad for an Island Portuguese port.

The Bensaúdes and their coaling and other interests displaced members of the American Dabney family, to whom F. D. R. alluded and who personified U.S. shipping in Horta and provided three generations of U.S. consuls there. The Dabneys represented the Boston Brahmin tradition at its best and, along with Prescotts, Hicklings, Websters, Cunninghams, Olivers, Lothrops, and Forbeses, are discussed in the following chapter.

The family and firm to reckon with in Funchal is Blandy, at whose country estate King Carlos and his queen were royally entertained during their 1901 visit. The first Blandy arrived during the Napoleonic wars. This English family became famous not only as shipping agents but for madeira wine. Charles Blandy, and also Thomas Slapp Leacock (1817-1883) of another English family famous for madeira, were instrumental in effecting the island industry's recovery from the nineteenth-century blights. Indeed, the Leacocks were there before the Blandy family. John Leacock (1726-1799) arrived on Madeira in 1741. In 1759, he founded the commercial firm which still bears his name: Leacock & Co., Ltd.

Another family achieving notoriety at the present time is formed of descendants of William Fisher, born in Norfolk County, England, around 1640. This Fisher arrived in Angra an indigent young man and in 1658 married a local girl. The liberal Regional Secretary of Education and Culture, José Guilherme Reis Leite, a direct descendant, has recently published an enlightening monograph on the Fishers, a veritable manual on how to get ahead in the Azores: (1) make money in commerce, chiefly by selling abroad—in those days to Brazil—at higher prices than could be commanded locally and thus depriving locals of necessities; (2) marry well; (3) withdraw from commerce and become a landholder; and (4) through marriage, purchase of land, and service in public positions, somehow achieve standing within the nobility. This is what Secretary Reis Leite calls "the perfect alliance between the ownership and exploitation of land in the manner of the *grands seigneurs* and the exploitation of local commerce and business in the modern capitalistic manner."

It is not clear to me that the contribution to the Azores of Thomas Amory (1683-1728) in any way equalled that of Hicklings or Dabneys. English, Amory was born in Ireland and brought up on Barbados and in England. In 1706, he went to Terceira as a merchant. There he was associated with Fishers, and he remained there until 1719. The following year, he settled in Boston, where he continued to make money and died. A "Fisher/Amory Trail" should definitely be worked out for Angra.

☆ ☆ ☆

Due to their location, the Portuguese Atlantic archipelagoes, in particular the Azores, serve ships and airplanes not only directly as ports of call but also indirectly as suppliers of basic data on which marine and air navigation depend. Portuguese awareness of the need for such information goes back to the very beginning of the overseas expansion. An early true scientist was Dom João de Castro (1500-1548) who made many observations at sea of the phenomenon we know as compass variation. Little wonder that in the nineteenth century individual Portuguese savants accompanied international developments and appreciated the value of islands as in effect immovable ships anchored in midocean.

In 1853, a meteorological and geomagnetic observatory was created in Lisbon and named for the Infante Dom Luis, the sixteenth-century princely patron and friend of Dom João de Castro. In 1864, its director asked that meteorological stations be set up in the four Insular Portuguese cities.

Much had happened between 1853 and 1864. At the beginning of that period, meteorology was in fact climatology, the accumulation of local records. With the Crimean War (1854-1856) and the availability of land telegraph, it was realized that accumulated knowledge plus fresh observations sent to a central agency could be utilized for forecasting and the issuance of warnings to ships. The new service became centered on Paris, and the Lisbon observatory collaborated from 1857 on. It was in 1857 that Lisbon was linked by land telegraph to the rest of Europe, and five stations in Continental Portugal were tied into the meteorological network.

The 1864 request to the Islands reflected the double realization that observations made out in the Atlantic would greatly improve European weather forecasting and that the newly-developed submarine telegraph cables would be the only means of communicating this invaluable information to forecasting centers. Advantage was taken of the Carcavelos-Madeira-São Vicente-Recife cable (see Chapter 9) almost as soon as laid. Meteorological cablegrams were sent from Funchal to Continental Europe beginning on June 20, 1874, and from São Vicente beginning on August 1, 1884.

The obstructionist, alas, proved to be the Azores, or more accurately the nature of the relations between Lisbon and that archipelago. There was an international call for a cable to the Azores beginning at least as early as 1866, and the farther west the line stretched the better for meteorological purposes, even to Flores or Corvo. The years passed, however, and no cable materialized. A convergence of personalities and an international friendship finally contributed proper conditions.

Carlos succeeded his father as king in 1889. He was greatly interested in sailing on the high seas. Even as prince he was naturally interested in winds and currents and in the prediction of winds. Because of his close friendship with Albert of Monaco (1848-1922), who ruled as Prince Albert I of Monaco from 1889 to his death, Carlos also became interested in physical oceanography. Furthermore, he prided himself on his knowledge of marine botany and zoology and was an excellent marksman, as his French acquaintance Baron Henri de Rothschild has pointed out. Moreover, he was an artist of no mean ability and a gourmet.

Albert of Monaco in his turn visited Azorean waters on several of his scientific expeditions—in 1885, 1886, 1887, 1888, 1895, 1896, 1897, and later years. In Horta's Porto Pim (a kind of back bay) in the summer of 1888 he was greatly impressed by the manner in which a whale was harpooned by men in the service of Samuel Wyllys Dabney (1826-1893), U.S. consul in the Azores from 1872 through 1891. The mammal was towed ashore and then cut into pieces, a procedure followed to this day. During the 1896 voyage aboard his yacht *Princesse Alice*, Albert's men discovered a bank southwest of Fayal which he promptly named for his vessel. Princess Alice Bank is located at 37° 58′ N, 29° 18′ W, and has a least depth of sixteen fathoms. A supertanker drawing ninety feet obviously has to be on guard.

Albert, of course, was among the many who realized the importance of the Atlantic islands for meteorology. In 1892 before the Academy of Sciences of Paris he outlined his idea of establishing observatories on various islands, particularly the Azores, which he apparently realized were about to be connected with the European mainland by cable.

The cable, from Carcavelos to Ponta Delgada thence to Horta, was laid in the summer of 1893, the connection being completed on August 22. At 3 P.M. on August 27, King Carlos sent the first cablegram from Carcavelos to Ponta Delgada, whence it was retransmitted to Horta. Here is its text:

> I feel truly happy connecting the Mother Fatherland [mãi pátria] by means of so intimate a link as the thought which ties us to the valerous Azorean people. The telegraph cable between Lisbon and the Azores is open to traffic.

Clearly, to Carlos as to his later monarchist biographer and to many other Continentals, the *Mãi-Pátria* or Metropolis did not embrace the Adjacent Islands.

Ponta Delgada sent its first meteorological bulletin the next day, August 28. The development of a proper forecasting system in Western Europe could begin. The key is the Azores High, which hovers over and around the archipelago and consists of a very stable air mass. The exact location of this extensive zone of high pressure together with the polar front to the north is most important for defining the nature of the weather in West and Southwest Europe. Thus, if the high moves northward, its clockwise and outward-blowing winds flow from the northwest to the northeast over western France, Spain, and Portugal. Dry and warm, they confer fine weather on that area, and even on the Madeiras and Azores. If, on the other hand, the high moves southward accompanied by the polar front with its lows whose winds blow counterclockwise and inward, moisture-laden winds from the west and southwest strike Western Europe, and the weather is poor.

In accordance with the original Lisbon request, meteorological stations in Ponta Delgada, Angra, and Funchal began to function on a regular basis beginning in that very year—1864. Horta did not step onto the world meteorological stage until much later, but when she did, she did so in the grand manner.

The 1893 cable was laid from Carcavelos to Ponta Delgada. An extension continued to Horta, the end of the line. Ponta Delgada was the key point. As will be seen, pressure had been mounting not only for a cable from the European mainland to the Azores but also from the Azores to North America. In the summer of 1900 not one but two cables were laid between the archipelago and that continent. The U.S. cable to Canso, Nova Scotia, was completed on July 27, the German cable direct to Manhattan Beach (next to Coney Island) in New York on August 28. The German transatlantic cable had been preceded by a cable link from Borkum island, near Emden in Germany, to the Azores completed on May 27, 1900. The U.S. transatlantic cable was followed by a link from the Azores to Waterville, Ireland, completed on November 23, 1901.

The Azorean end of all these cables was Horta. Transatlantic communication could now be effected between the financial and political capitals of both continents via Fayal with no reference to the 1893 cable via Ponta Delgada to Lisbon. Horta was about to become a world-famous cable relay station on its own. Ponta Delgada became a cable backwater. Meteorological bulletins began to be sent from Horta on October 1, 1901, to both Europe and America.

At first a small meteorological station functioned in Horta's Civil Government building, part of the Jesuit complex of old. Something better was obviously needed. During their stay in Horta, King Carlos and Queen Maria Amélia witnessed the laying of the first stone of the definitive new Horta Meteorological Observatory atop Monte das Moças (Mount of the Girls) just behind Horta. Delays ensued, however, and it was not until July 1915 that the new building became serviceable. And today it merits the tourist's visit. It is fully equipped with the usual meteorological instruments. It sends its observations several times a day to the Santa Maria airport, where they and other observations from all over the Azores are coordinated and the results disseminated as needed. It also records geomagnetic observations daily and is equipped with a heliograph (to indicate the number of hours of sunshine daily), three seismographs (two electromagnetic and one mechanical, to record earthquakes), and, at the end of the breakwater, a nilometer (tide gage, to record the extent of the rise and fall of tides). As a bonus, a platform atop the observatory provides a most magnificent panoramic view. In 1923, after Prince Albert's death, the institution's name was changed to honor him.

Although radio took the place of the cables and Santa Maria has become the Azorean meteorological center, the Horta radio station (CTH) plays a key role in the worldwide network of marine weather broadcasts. Its weather reports cover the area of eastern North Atlantic waters between 30° N and 44° N and between 20° W and 40° W. Since 1946, these Azorean services have been a regional activity of the Serviço Meteorológico Nacional (National Meteorological Service) based on Lisbon.

Geomagnetic observations are akin to those concerning weather, for they also require fixed locations in isolated areas. Accurate observations in the North Atlantic have been needed in particular because of the great range in magnetic variation from Europe to North America. Thus, flying a great circle from Lisbon to New York one finds that the variation is 8°.5 W in Lisbon and 12° W in New York. However, during the flight it increases to over 24° W at about 45° N, 51° W, then decreases.

Geomagnetic observations therefore have to be made in various localities at any one time in order to determine the amount of the variation. But this phenomenon also varies with time in any one place, and it varies at a different rate in different places. Thus, at Lisbon it is decreasing by a few minutes annually. The rate of change decreases down to no change at about longitude 71° W (where the variation is just under 16° W). At New York it increases slightly every year. The geomagnetic stations on Atlantic islands thus make an invaluable contribution to navigation, for they measure the rate of change.

The accumulation of data underlying the magnetic variation given on today's nautical charts represents international collaboration going back over many years. In 1899, a distinguished son of São Miguel, Afonso Chaves, made observations of both magnetic variation (horizontal or lateral deflection, important for conventional compasses) and magnetic inclination (vertical deflection). The Prince of Monaco paid for the instruments he used in this reconnaissance. Chaves continued his observations almost until his death in 1926. The construction of a suitable Observatório Magnético de São Miguel was begun in 1903; the magnetic observatory was inaugurated in 1911.

Afonso Chaves was also a key figure in setting up the meteorological services of the Azores. He was involved in yet another activity, but this one, alas, came too late to make a great international contribution.

Ptolemy had utilized a prime meridian running north and

south through the Fortunate Islands (Canaries). Centuries later, the English-speaking and much of the rest of the world was using the one running through the Greenwich Observatory in London. By the time the Greenwich meridian was adopted, navigators were well acquainted with virtually the entire globe and they counted longitude as east and west of Greenwich up to 180° in each direction. Where the E and W longitude meet at 180° is the International Date Line, in the Pacific.

In a world which was still far from internationally-minded but rather was composed of a host of distinct nationalities, some proud nations and notably France did not relish the idea of a prime meridian running through the English capital. Accordingly, a whole series of different national prime meridians came into use. I can recall my own horror when, during the planning stage of the Moroccan invasion of November 8, 1942, I discovered that the U.S. Army was designating its shore targets using maps (based on French maps) with 0° longitude through Paris and that the U.S. Navy was plotting these targets for its naval gunfire on charts using 0° longitude through London! The Paris meridian, by the way, lies 2° 19′ 51″ east of that of Greenwich. At the latitude of Casablanca this difference of longitude amounts to 116.8 n mi. of what navigators call "departure."

The 1884 conference in Washington debated the ideal prime meridian. Curiously, Portugal had no delegate in attendance, perhaps because of preoccupation with the coming scramble for Africa. Nevertheless, the internationally more or less neutral location of the Azores was noticed and discussed, all the more as to the north there was only the bleak eastern coast of Greenland and to the south, barring a few tiny islands, only Antarctica. It was felt, however, that the prime meridian had to run through an observatory connected by land telegraph lines and submarine cables with the outside world in order for the necessary time signals to be transmitted. The Azores in 1884 had no such connecting links, and no Azores meridian came into international use.

A century earlier, a distinguished mariner had made navigational observations in the archipelago. At the end of his second voyage round the world, Captain James Cook of the Royal Navy had doubled the Cape of Good Hope and stopped at St. Helena and Ascension and on June 9, 1775, had passed close to Fernando de Noronha. On July 13, he made Fayal, moored in Horta harbor next day, and stayed until the 19th.

Cook's sole purpose in stopping, he affirmed, was to enable his astronomer to check the chronometer's rate, in order to determine more accurately the longitude of the several Azores islands. Accordingly, observations were made on shore as well as at sea.

Cook was struck by the lack of glass windows, the large number of religious edifices, and the satisfactory nature of the harbor as an anchorage. He also told how the local wine came from Pico, and from Horta was shipped abroad, chiefly to America, where it acquired the name of fayal wine.

Hickling home near Rosto de Cão, São Miguel

8

BOSTON BRAHMINS IN THE AZORES

The family name of Dabney was long identified with the trade between Fayal and New England. The Dabneys were not the only Americans in the Azores, however. The Hicklings of St. Michael's, who ultimately became inextricably linked with the Dabneys by marriage, reached the archipelago first.

In 1764, Thomas Hickling of Boston (1745-1834) had married Sarah Green, fifteen years his senior. By her he had two children. One, Catherine Green Hickling (1767-1852), in turn married William Prescott (1762-1844), son of Colonel William Prescott of Bunker Hill fame. William and Catherine had a number of children, the most famous of whom was historian William Hickling Prescott (1796-1859), author of four monumental books on Spain, Mexico, and Peru.

Even before his wife's death, Thomas Hickling perceived the commercial opportunities open to an enterprising merchant on St. Michael's. Accordingly, in 1769, without his family, he moved to Ponta Delgada. Immediately upon hearing of his wife's death in 1774, he married again. The second Mrs. Hickling, Sarah Falder (1760-1849), fifteen years his junior, was from Philadelphia and was passing through the Azorean port with her father when love struck. In 1776, Hickling was appointed U.S. vice consul on St. Michael's. He prospered, built three magnificent homes on the island, had sixteen children by the second Sarah (including two sets of twins), and lived until the age of eighty-nine. St. Michael's was good to him.

Hickling's city home was located in the parish/precinct of São Pedro (St. Peter) toward the eastern end of Ponta Delgada at the water's edge. A veritable palace, with master bedroom on the third floor overlooking a broad balcony, beautiful lawn, and harbor entrance, the building was remodeled and enlarged in great good taste by the late Vasco Bensaúde. It now stands as the elegant

Hotel de São Pedro, the island's finest. The master bedroom is available as the most luxurious suite, with Hickling coat of arms above the master bed.

On the same south coast about two miles east of the city home, a curious rock formation amuses passersby. It is dubbed Dog's Face (Rosto de Cão) because it looks like one. Just east of it and slightly inland close to Livramento, Thomas Hickling acquired a second home. It still stands, resplendent with its curved northern side and graceful set of curved outer stairs leading to what must have been another well-kept lawn. The grounds today are inhabited chiefly by hens and cows. Nevertheless, this Hickling home, however dilapidated, still merits a visit.

In the great Furnas crater within the village of Furnas northeast of the lagoon, Hickling built a summer home, Yankee Hall. Situated on high ground, it faces a large pool to its north, The Tank. It is this warm-water pool which local youth and guests in the Terra Nostra Hotel used for swimming. A later owner added his embellishments to the property. Unfortunately, in the 1970's, Yankee Hall itself is used as a storage bin for potatoes. A bust of Thomas Hickling stands beside it.

According to Fayal Dabneys who frequently visited them, Thomas and Sarah Hickling spent half the year near Dog's Face (probably spring and fall), four months in the city, and the balance of the year in Furnas. All Americans who visit St. Michael's must of course view the crater of the Seven Cities. They should also tread the "Hickling Trail": eat their luncheon in the Hotel de São Pedro, examine the home near Dog's Face, stroll through the grounds surrounding The Tank and Yankee Hall in Furnas, and dine in the Terra Nostra.

Several of the vice consul's children died young. Others married English spouses. Two daughters married Americans. Yet other Hicklings married local Azoreans—for example, Frances Hickling (1789-1865) in 1813 married medical doctor Joaquim António de Paula Medeiros—and descendants have achieved great distinction. In two cases, two daughters married the same Azorean man, that is, the widowers of older daughters married younger daughters—for instance, William Ivens first married Elisabeth Flora Hickling (1783-1832), then Mary Ann Hickling (born 1800). Harriet Frederica (1793-1853) and Amelia Clementina (1796-1872) met their American husbands on St. Michael's, for the Hicklings were accustomed to receive many visitors from America.

Yankee Hall, Furnas, São Miguel

An early visitor was Boston-born William Jarvis, who served as U.S. consul and acting chargé d'affaires in Lisbon over the critical years 1802-1811 during which the royal family fled to Brazil. He visited Ponta Delgada for a week or two before the turn of the century and engaged in a sharp business deal involving a cargo of corn. He became very friendly with Harriet Frederica, then four or five. He claimed to have taught her the alphabet.

As a young man, the future historian William Hickling Prescott spent six months with his grandfather, his uncle, and his several aunts, Harriet Frederica being three years older than he, Amelia Clementina the same age. Cited by a biographer as "the only moment that he studied an Iberian culture face to face," this sojourn took place in 1815-1816. In part it represented an attempt to improve Prescott's eyesight and relieve his chronic headaches. A well-known letter of his dated March 15, 1816, to his parents in Boston reveals a good deal:

> ... Much of this time has been beguiled of its tediousness by the attention of Amelia and Harriet, particularly the lat-

ter, who is a charming creature and whom I regard as a second sister.

I have had an abundance of good prescriptions. Grandfather has strongly urged old Madeira as a universal nostrum; and my good Uncle the doctor no less strenuously recommended beef-steaks....

A somewhat stuffy postscript of April 4 adds a tidbit about "my dear Harriet":

> ... since the match of Barnes has been dissolved, it has been thought inexpedient for her to visit England. Barnes is a dashing young fellow of very good family, and with person and manners so engaging that he was permitted to pay his address to Harriet until his pretensions should be examined. Upon investigation, however, it was found that early extravagancies had so deeply involved him that he has been very wisely discarded.

Extravagance and male indebtedness were to beset Harriet for most of the rest of her life, although she probably had no way of foreseeing this when, on March 16, 1818, on the lawn of her father's Ponta Delgada home, she married John White Webster, A.B., Harvard, 1811, M.D., 1815. He was exactly her age. Years later, after his execution by hanging on August 30, 1850, it was rumored—I believe maliciously—that he had been quite a bounder in his youth. A private communication dated October 4, 1850, from Massachusetts to St. Michael's affirmed:

> ... Dr. Reynolds was with Dr. W[ebster] in England and France. He committed a rape on a girl and was obliged to fly the country—he then engaged himself to a young lady and would probably have married her but he was engaged by Mr. Thorndike to go to St. Michaels where he soon engaged himself to Harriet and left the lady in the lurch so you see he has been a very bad man from the beginning....

Actually, Webster was possessed of the highest credentials. He was spending the year 1818 in the Azores doing geological research principally on St. Michael's. In 1821 in Boston, after he and his bride returned to the United States, the fruits of this Azorean research were published in book form in *A Description of the Island of St. Michael, comprising an Account of its Geological Structure; With Remarks on the Other Azores or Western Islands.* Probably the first published U.S. book on the Azores, it still makes superb reading, although geologically it is reported to be passé if not in error. It does mention the volcanic obsidian and pumice for which Lipari in the Aeolian Islands is famous. Pumice was being exported from the Mediterranean to Germany at a great rate in the summer of 1972 and could conceivably figure in the Azorean economy of the future.

For many years the Websters lived at 22 Garden Street, Cambridge, in a large house built in 1837 which still stands. Early in his career John White practiced medicine. Beginning in 1824, he taught chemistry in the Harvard Medical School, which was located at that time in the West End near Massachusetts General Hospital. The couple became the parents of five children. The only son died young. The four daughters lived to ripe old ages: Sarah Hickling (1821-1909), Marianne (1825-1925), Catherine Prescott (1827-1909), and Harriet Wainwright (1830-1924).

In Cambridge the Websters lived well, that is, well beyond the means of a Harvard Professor. Connected as she was to Boston's high society, Mrs. Webster persisted in entertaining graciously and lavishly. Professor Webster fell badly into debt.

Whereas Harriet Frederica's marriage ended in tragedy, her sister Amelia Clementina's began with one. In October 1822, Amelia married Hugh Chambers of Philadelphia, a widower. Almost immediately after the wedding, while en route to St. Petersburg, he was accidentally killed at sea. In 1823, Amelia gave birth to his daughter, Emma Chambers. Then in 1827, Amelia married Thomas Nye, Jr., of New Bedford, Massachusetts. There the Nyes settled, with Emma, and, in 1830, had their daughter Eliza Williams Nye.

Emma Chambers married Edward C. Jones of New Bedford, who purchased a fine house for her at 396 County Street, to this day a landmark in that city. The Jones's had a number of daughters, one of whom, Sarah (1838-1891), in 1873 married John Malcolm Forbes of Milton, Massachusetts, just south of Boston.

John Malcolm Forbes (1847-1904) was a descendant of a great family active in shipping, especially the China trade. His father, John Murray Forbes (1813-1898), was widely knowledgeable within Atlantic shipping circles; he even visited Buenos Aires when only nine years old. In 1843 with "Governor" W. W. Swain he purchased Naushon Island, one of the Elizabeth group southwest of Cape Cod and north of Martha's Vineyard in Massachusetts. He later became sole owner; and, on Naushon, many Forbeses and also Dabneys enjoyed their vacations. John Murray Forbes's older brother was Captain Robert Bennet Forbes; it is his old Milton home which is today the Museum of the American China Trade.

In the meantime Emma Chambers Jones's half-sister Eliza Williams Nye grew up in New Bedford. At the age of seventeen, she accompanied her father in one of his ships on a journey to the Azores, to Horta and Ponta Delgada. She wrote a journal of that trip, still in typescript.

Over the years, Amelia Clementina Hickling Chambers Nye also retained a link with the Azores, especially by means of letters to her sister Mary Ann Hickling, living in Ponta Delgada as the second Mrs. Ivens. Some of the letters have been deposited in the Massachusetts Historical Society. They are revealing, but they are also possibly family-serving. And she did not maintain contact only by mail. In 1862, during the Civil War, Mrs. Nye crossed on a Dabney ship to Horta, thence to St. Michael's, to visit her beloved sister. Amelia Clementina was sixty-six, Mary Ann was sixty-two.

☆ ☆ ☆

Modeling himself, perhaps, after successful merchant Thomas Hickling, John Bass Dabney of Boston decided to try his fortune on Fayal. Of a French Huguenot family originally named d'Aubigné, he first visited Fayal in 1795 and perceived the opportunities the island offered. He settled there in 1804 and sent for his wife, Roxa Lewis (1772-1845), and their five living children. Five more children were born on Fayal.

In 1806, President Jefferson appointed Dabney U.S. consul in the Azores, a rank higher than that of Thomas Hickling and his successor Thomas Hickling, Jr. (1781-1875). This first Fayal Dabney retained the consulship until his death in 1826. His oldest son, Charles William Dabney, succeeded him in the position and retained it, with one brief hiatus, until 1869. In 1872, Charles William's third son, Samuel Wyllys Dabney, became the third Dabney to serve as consul.

The Lives of Azoreans and Madeirans

In January 1892, the last consul, his wife, three of their children, and his very literate maiden sister "Roxie" (Roxana Lewis Dabney, 1827-1913) left Fayal forever, the last of the Dabneys to have lived there. They departed because there were no other branches of the family remaining on the island and they realized their day had come. A contributing factor may have been a new rule of the U.S. Department of State which prevented a full-time consul from engaging simultaneously in private business. They moved to a place they had purchased in California at the foot of the mountains inland from San Diego. Nostalgically they named it Fayal Ranch.

The male Dabneys who lived in the Azores served both the Azores and the United States in many ways. They imported and exported, especially significant items of export being oranges and wine. U.S. congressional legislation which preceded the War of 1812, and the War itself, had provided an exceptional opportunity for John Bass Dabney to develop a flourishing commercial house at the beginning of the Dabney era. To quote a granddaughter of his: "an immense business was done in those islands, simply in transferring United States products from American to British ships, and *vice versa* the products of the old world to the American vessels."

The Dabneys acted as ships' agents, taking particular care of the Yankee whaling fleet. The same granddaughter has written glowingly of the heyday of whaling, the 30's, 40's, and 50's:

> At this time the whaling business was in its palmiest days. Nearly 700 vessels sailed on this business from New Bedford, Nantucket, Falmouth, Holmes' Hole, Sag Harbor, Providence, Newport, New London, New Haven and other ports between New York and Cape Cod. These, or those of them who made the Atlantic their cruising ground, made Fayal a regular stopping place every spring and summer, landing oil to be shipped to the United States, and supplying themselves with water and fresh provisions. This business was in the hands of the Dabneys, and gave ample occupation for all the brothers, and many clerks and employees, some Portuguese natives of the islands, others American and English. . . .

The Dabneys ran their own passenger-freight sailing vessels between Boston and Horta, the names *Harbinger, Io, Azor* (renamed

Fredonia during the American Civil War), and *Azorean* being especially well known. They brought in coal when steamers came into service, and they shipped offloaded whale oil to Massachusetts in the returning empty colliers. They introduced silkworm culture; they pressed very early—at least as early as 1838—for construction of a breakwater in Horta; and they accompanied the expansion of the Atlantic network of submarine telegraph cables from 1858 on. Indeed, Charles William Dabney received a letter from W. W. Swain dated Naushon, September 29, 1855, and in it read the following:

> . . . How long before you will be connected with this country and Europe by telegraph? We deemed ourselves insulated almost as much as you are, but lo! they are coming next week to put up poles and stretch a wire that will connect Tarpaulin Cove with Boston and all creation, running a submarine cable across Woods Hole; it is already in operation from the latter place to Boston. . . .

The Dabneys encouraged Azoreans to fit out their own whaleships, and they encouraged Azoreans including their own employees to develop the offshore or "open boat" whaling which has lately received so much publicity. Lastly, the Dabneys were generous to a fault. They provided at cost food for the local population during famine years, for instance the corn which the civil governor in 1859 sent to St. George, outside his district.

The Dabney women did not lag behind their men. They cared for the sick. They translated from English into Portuguese, and from Portuguese into English. They wrote creatively. They taught or promoted crafts: the knitting of the finest of white stockings; the making of shawls and head dresses of aloe, the fiber of the century plant, which was beaten into gossamer threads and made into exquisite lace; and the making of crivo, the famous Fayal drawn-thread work. Above all, they provided a model of what women are capable of contributing if only they are allowed to do more than "people the world, and be a perfect automaton of domestic accomplishments."

What is most remarkable, the Dabneys knew everything that was going on in the entire Atlantic world, North and South, and in the Mediterranean, Baltic, and South China Seas and Indian Ocean as well. The whole world literally came to the doors of their

Horta homes for almost nine decades and made of that city one of the world's best informed and most cosmopolitan centers, a description I found still appropriate in 1939.

One of the last ocean battles of the War of 1812, the affair of the *General Armstrong,* was fought in front of Horta on September 26 and 27, 1814. In 1824, Nancy, Bordeaux-born daughter of John Bass and Roxa, married a Portuguese—the only Fayal Dabney to marry outside the Brahmin circle—José Maria de Avelar Brotero. The couple settled in Brazil, raised a distinguished family, wrote letters back home to Fayal, and received relatives from Fayal, thus keeping the home base au courant with Brazilian affairs. One bit of gossip thus sent back concerned Emperor Pedro I's second German-language marriage, which in fact took place in 1829, when he married Amalie, the daughter of Duke Eugen von Leuchtenberg, by whom he had a daughter, Amalie (1831-1853).

The political struggles over the years 1821-1834 took place in part at the Dabneys' doorsteps. The Dabneys were aware of steamboats from 1821 on. In 1822, a ship called at Fayal en route from Baltimore to "the new Colony on the coast of Africa," that is, Liberia, and of the fifty-two Blacks on board, "the greater number of them came up here to walk in the garden." The Dabneys became familiar with the early signaling system known as "Telegraph," flags from shore to ship and vice versa, and they visited Fayal's "signal hill" on May 8, 1832. They knew of the famous burning "by a savage and fanatical mob" of the Ursuline Convent of Charlestown, Massachusetts, and, later, were informed of the move of the Madeira Protestants to Illinois. They were in intimate touch with Harvard College, which many Dabney young men attended; and they knew of life in Cambridge from Samuel Longfellow (brother of Henry Wadsworth), who had been a tutor on Fayal in the early 1840's. They knew of whaling other than by New Englanders, for Bremen and Prussian whalers called at Fayal. They were informed of Spanish and Mexican politics, for General Prim stopped off in 1862; and they had news of Garibaldi in the same year. They fought the Civil War in part by controlling the supply of coal in midocean, and their ship *Azor* once had a close call with the Confederacy's *Alabama.* They were knowledgeable concerning St. Michael's because of their Hickling connection, concerning Terceira because John Bass's youngest son William Henry (1817-1888) served as U.S. vice consul there over the years 1844-1848, and concerning the Canary Islands because this same William Henry after a sojourn in the United States served as U.S. consul on Tenerife for many years beginning in 1862. Lastly, they maintained correspondence over many decades with the Forbes family, the warm friendship between John Murray Forbes and Charles William Dabney being particularly productive, in Fayal oranges sent to Forbes, in wideranging information sent to Dabney.

Over the years 1811-1814, in other words during the War of 1812, when Continental and Insular Portugal were ruled from Rio, John Bass Dabney had a magnificent home built in the northern section of Horta. He named it "Bagatelle," and it still stands almost as in yesteryear. Here his Fayal-born children saw the light of day and grew up—Frederick (1809-1857), Emmeline (1811-1885), Olivia (born 1815), the afore-mentioned William Henry, and one other son.

The journal of *Cleopatra's Barge*'s voyage of pleasure tells of George Crowninshield, Jr.'s visit to Bagatelle in 1817. It includes the following description, partially valid after 160 years:

> The garden of our Consul is an enclosure of about three acres, subdivided into smaller apartments, conforming to the character of the ground. There are three principal gradations, on one of which the house stands with a small postern ornamented with myrtles, roses, jessamine, grape-vines, Pride of India, pomegranates,—with their beautiful red flowers,—passion flowers, and geraniums. In the lower garden there was a field of wheat, a cluster of sugar-cane, olive trees in blossom, several plants which produce the gum Trajacanth, tree of Paradise, mimosa, two small magnolias (imported from St. Michael's), pears, apples, citron trees, the camphor tree, soft shelled almonds, and lemon trees.
>
> In the back garden were weeping willows, poplars, supporting grape-vines, Faia trees (a shrub which gives name to the island), sycamore, fig, bananas with fruit, coffee trees, English walnut, and orange trees, one of which produced last year 12000 oranges.
>
> Our Consul built his house during the late war. The stone work was done by the Masons of the country, but he sent to America for his carpenters. It is of two stories. The Faia produces the same effect on the soil of Fayal, that the prickly pear does on the soil of Sicily. . . .

It was in the Bagatelle garden that the ex-slaves walked. It was in the ballroom of Bagatelle, today its main living room, that ex-Emperor Pedro I of Brazil was feted on April 8, 1832, as is narrated in this continuation of the lengthy Dabney quotation contained in the chapter on the royal bones:

> . . . Among the many balls which took place, one was given at "Bagatelle," where the Emperor, who was very fond of dancing, opened the ball with Miss Emmeline Dabney, then a great beauty. The eldest brother and his wife were then in the United States, so that the office of host devolved on Frederick Dabney, a young unmarried man. He was assisted in entertaining by his sisters Emmeline and Olivia, and his cousin Roxana Stackpole, whom he afterwards married. Mrs. Dabney, the widowed mother, was still living, but had become somewhat of an invalid. This was an exceedingly gay and exciting time in the history of the little island, and the events of it made a very deep impression on the Dabneys of that generation, most of whom have now passed away.

It was at Bagatelle that another great social event took place. From September 22 to 28, 1834, a very special midshipman of the French Navy visited Horta aboard the frigate *Sirène*. The Prince de Joinville, third son of King Louis-Philippe, was only sixteen at the time. He was so royally entertained by the Dabneys that two years later the grateful Queen sent the American family a handsome gift, a tea set of Sèvres porcelain in vivid green and gold. Consul Charles William wrote Congress about accepting it, and in 1843 he received the necessary permission. Several parts of the set are now dispersed across the United States in the proud possession of Dabney descendants.

In London in 1835, Charles William's brother Frederick (Harvard class of 1828) married Roxana Stackpole of Boston, she who had already stayed at Bagatelle and met the Emperor. Because Frederick and Roxana planned to reside in Bagatelle and because that dwelling was off center, away from the Dabney commercial interests, Charles William purchased a stately mansion much nearer town. Thither he moved his seven Fayal-born children and their mother, Frances Alsop Pomeroy of Brighton, Massachusetts (1797-1862). The new home became known as "Fredonia," and how the Marx Brothers knew of it mystifies me.

Fredonia functioned as U.S. consular residence from 1835 until the last family members departed. It also received royalty. On November 7, 1858, twenty-year-old Prince Luıs of Portugal arrived unexpectedly in Horta aboard the *Bartolomeu Dias*. He was the second son of Queen Maria II. An appropriate ball was given. The excitement of the occasion was increased by the realization that the Prince was expected to visit St. Michael's first, that (in the words of the Dabney *Annals*) the "St. Michaels people were terribly mortified at his giving them the 'go-by,' as they had made extensive preparations for his entertainment."

The Dabneys' acquaintance with the Azores was obviously most intimate with respect to Fayal. There they came to have three city homes, a summer house on the hill known as Monte da Guia overlooking Porto Pim (the back bay), and, later, a small retreat known as Woodcock Lodge in Capelo in the western part of the island. The Dabneys also knew St. Michael's through frequent calls on the Hicklings, although, apparently, the reverse was not as true. They also called off at Terceira, especially during the years when William Henry was vice consul. And they could not have failed to become acquainted with Pico.

From the day Bagatelle was finished, the Dabneys enjoyed a superlative view of Pico—"The glorious prospect from the windows of Bagatelle cannot very easily be matched on earth," a New Bedfordite wrote in 1858 upon learning of Frederick's passing. Inevitably the Dabneys acquired a summer home on that island's western shore from which they could enjoy a view of their beloved Fayal. In 1834, Charles William took advantage of the dissolution of monasteries and convents to purchase the vineyard and house which had belonged to the Carmelite friars in Areia Larga, just south of the little port of Madalena. It was known as The Priory and was the delight of young Dabneys for many a year. The Horta households shared it. Thus, Frederick and his family from Bagatelle used to spend the early part of the summer there, Charles William and family from Fredonia the time of the vintage in August and September.

☆ ☆ ☆

It was not long before the Fayal Dabneys established a solid Boston connection. In Bagatelle in 1822, Roxalina (1799-1872), oldest daughter of John Bass, married Charles Cunningham of Boston.

Having set up their residence in Boston, the bride and groom became very friendly with the Websters of Cambridge, or at least with Mrs. Webster and her four daughters.

Transatlantic visiting ensued, and in Boston in 1829 Roxalina's widowed mother Roxa wrote to her son Charles Williams: "I find Mrs. Webster as amiable as ever; they have a beautiful garden and are very pleasantly situated; she has retained her youthful looks surprisingly; they have four [!] daughters who promise to be fine women, but I doubt whether they will be as beautiful as their Mother." Reciprocally, the Cunningham and Webster families visited Bagatelle in 1835. A ball was given which Sarah Webster, the oldest daughter then in her early teens, attended. Inevitably, Sarah met her hosts' oldest son, John Pomeroy Dabney (1821-1874).

In 1841, Marianne ("Mollie"), the second oldest Webster daughter, the only one who never married, spent two or three months in Horta, then went on to spend the winter with the Hicklings. The following summer Charles William Dabney, Jr. (1823-1870), a student at Harvard, returned to his native Fayal on the *Harbinger* accompanied by Sarah Webster. Sarah disappointingly stayed in Fredonia only a few days, then proceeded to St. Michael's to join her sister and be with her grandmother and cousins. By 1843 John Pomeroy Dabney was actively courting Sarah Webster.

In the spring of 1844, Roxana Lewis Dabney, one of John Pomeroy's three sisters, was in the Boston area. She saw much of her brother at Harvard (who graduated that June) and his classmates and also her cousin Frederic Cunningham (1826-1864) son of her Aunt Roxalina, who graduated from Harvard in 1845; and she visited the Websters regularly. Inevitably she saw the Prescotts, and it is significant that in that very year Edward Goldsborough Prescott (1804-1844), the historian's younger brother, sailed for Fayal on the *Harbinger*. He died of heart trouble during the voyage and was buried at sea.

All the evidence confirms the conclusion that the Prescotts in Boston and the Websters in Cambridge were close friends. Indeed, during the agonizing months from November 1849 through August 1850, historian William Hickling Prescott and his brother-in-law Franklin Dexter, as well as Charles Cunningham, were constantly at Dr. Webster's side and available to him for assistance. Dexter (1793-1857) had married Catherine Elizabeth Prescott in 1819.

In 1845, John Pomeroy Dabney sailed to Massachusetts to seek his bride. The Fayal Dabneys, the St. Michael's Hicklings, and the Cambridge Websters now became formally related, for John and Sarah Hickling Webster were married in Cambridge. An old friend of Dr. Webster performed the ceremony, the Reverend Francis Parkman (1788-1852), father of another distinguished American historian also named Francis Parkman (1823-1893) and famed for his book *The Oregon Trail*. Reverend Parkman had baptized all four of the Webster daughters and buried the Webster son.

John and Sarah proceeded to Fayal in October 1845 and at first lived in Fredonia. The summer of 1846, Mrs. Webster and her third daughter Catherine ("Kate") visited Sarah and the other Dabneys on the island. In the *Annals of the Dabney Family in Fayal* covering the years 1806-1869 which Roxana Lewis Dabney compiled and on which I rely most heavily—but always with circumspection—it is stated that Mrs. Webster was much beloved by Charles William Dabney and his wife. The *Annals* go on:

> ... How often I have heard my mother speak of her exquisite taste in dress, such refinement and finish in every thing about her. She had the beautiful Hickling eyes, teeth, and smile, and was very fascinating to old and young. She made a little visit in St. Michaels, returning here, and was here when the first grandchild was born, Sept. 20. What a glad day was that! never I am sure was child more warmly welcomed. He was named Charles, but always called Karl.

Mrs. Webster returned to Cambridge in the autumn, leaving Kate behind to spend the winter in the Azores. Kate was interested in all conceivable topics and, *mirabile dictu*, wrote her younger sister Harriet at length about Catholic liturgy.

In 1848, Consul Dabney, his wife, and their youngest daughter Frances Alsop Dabney (1833-1926) visited the United States. On June 18, Mrs. Dabney wrote back to Fayal that Mrs. Webster and Marianne had called on them, Marianne had stayed for dinner, and her daughter Frances ("Fan") had returned with Marianne to pass the night in Cambridge. When the Consul and his family returned to Fayal later in 1848, they were accompanied, prophetically, by Harriet Webster and also by Susan Heard Oliver and George Stewart Johonnot Oliver, children of Francis Johonnot

Oliver of Boston. One wonders if many of these transatlantic missions in Dabney ships did not have as their primary objective the localization of appropriate spouses for sons or daughters, sisters or brothers. The danger of allowing love to blossom between a Dabney and a local Azorean-Portuguese Catholic youngster was to be avoided at all cost.

In the spring of 1849 the *Monte Christo* sailed to the United States with quite a crowd aboard: Harriet Webster (already wooed and won by Samuel Wyllys Dabney, John Pomeroy's brother and future consul); Charles William Dabney, Jr., and Susan Oliver (the two of them engaged); Susan's brother George; John Pomeroy Dabney, his wife, and their son Carl (1846-1861), and William Henry Dabney, his wife, and their baby daughter born on Terceira. Charles William, Jr., and Susan were married soon after arrival. They settled in Roxbury. His sister Frances and her brother George were married in King's Chapel, Boston, a decade later.

John Pomeroy Dabney and family represented the Fayal Dabneys at the 1849 wedding and stayed on. Reverend Francis Parkman baptized three-year old Carl in September in the Webster home in Cambridge, where expenditures for entertainment must have increased by leaps and bounds. The family was joined by John's sister Roxana Lewis, who spent the winter of 1849-1850 in Greater Boston. John, Sarah, and Carl, however, returned to Fayal in October 1849.

☆

By combining a reading of the printed—but in part not widely available—sources and Mrs. Nye's manuscript letters with an understanding of sex and class on St. Michael's, one is led inexorably to the conclusion that the attitudes of Nyes and Ivens's and Father Hickling himself were in part responsible for the tragedy which ensued.

Harriet Frederica Hickling Webster was brought up on St. Michael's in the lap of luxury, in the city home across the street from the Church of São Pedro, in the villa near Dog's Face, and in Yankee Hall. She was fawned over by the great of her day who passed through Ponta Delgada, including William Jarvis. She was waited on by maids and footmen, gardeners and cooks, all of them perchance wearing white gloves. Her family, possibly sensing

Harvard prestige, as obviously permitted her marriage to Dr. Webster as they had clearly objected to the Barnes affair. Yet what did she, or they, really know of Dr. Webster? Certainly not that he was a rapist, if he really was.

The Websters lived in the grand manner in Cambridge, as already noted. When an indigent Harvard professor marries a lady of high social rank, it is normally expected that she will fund the ménage. But old Hickling back on St. Michael's had many other children to support, plus three costly homes; and he died in 1834. Moreover, why should Azorean money finance a young lady who had presumably married into Boston society, whose Prescott half-sister was well connected and could lend a helping hand?

To make ends meet, Dr. Webster borrowed from literally everyone, from—it is reported—Charles Cunningham, Mr. Nye (obviously Amelia Clementina's husband), Mr. Prescott (presumably the historian), and Mrs. Prescott (presumably his mother), and from Dr. George Parkman.

Charles Cunningham was of course Charles William Dabney's brother-in-law. He had the care of the Dabney concerns in Boston and, also, in a way, of Webster's. His son Frederic later joined with Charles William Dabney, Jr., in establishing a firm to run the Boston end of the Dabney business; it was known as Messrs. Dabney & Cunningham, Boston.

Wise Mrs. Nye knew the score all too well, and she wished to absolve Hickling extravagance by downgrading Webster. On March 2, 1847, this sister of Mrs. Webster wrote the sister on St. Michael's in most hostile fashion about John White Webster and his debts, and she revealed the hatred which, she said, the Prescotts and the Hicklings felt toward him. "I think it was a most fortunate thing for Harriet to have one daughter so well settled, but the Dr. will have nothing to do with her or John [Dabney]. I hope Sarah will keep Kate with her for some time." On October 3, 1847, Mrs. Nye continued in the same vein: "I expect it will be painful to Harriet not to be able to invite the Dabneys to her house to dinner, but they will not think anything of it as they are probably aware of the circumstances of the family as Mr. Cunningham has the care of their concerns."

On November 23, 1849, Dr. George Parkman of Boston disappeared. A few days later his bones were found in the Harvard Medical College in the basement below Dr. Webster's laboratory.

Dr. Parkman (1790-1849) was the brother of Reverend

Parkman. He was a wealthy medical doctor who had received his A.B. degree from Harvard in 1809 and M.D. from the University of Aberdeen, Scotland, in 1813. He had become a staunch financial supporter of the Harvard Medical School. He was well known for his moneylending activity, as Dr. Webster was well known for being chronically in need of money.

Dr. Webster was indicted for the murder on January 26, 1850. Arraigned on February 9, he pleaded not guilty. His trial began on March 19. He was convicted eleven days later and sentenced on April 1. He was hanged on August 30.

Of the entire affair Judge Robert Sullivan has written: "Excluding the three presidential assassinations, the tragic Lindbergh kidnap-murder, and probably, but not certainly, the Sacco-Vanzetti case, few, if any, American crime stories so completely engrossed the public press, so totally grasped the attention of the American people as did the trial and execution of Harvard Professor John White Webster at the halfway mark of the nineteenth century."

In her *Annals*, Roxana Lewis Dabney states that, upon arrival in Boston to spend the winter of 1849-1850 there, "I went, much to my joy, directly out to Cambridge, where were J.P.D. and family. It was always delightful at the Websters', and I had the best of times." She then reports that in the spring of 1850 her brother John Pomeroy (J.P.D.) and her unmarried aunt Olivia (John Bass's fourth and youngest daughter) came to Boston. John stayed but a short time, for his wife was about to give birth (on July 10) to their third child, Catherine Prescott, who died fourteen months later. Aunt Olivia, however, remained for the summer, and she and Roxana visited Alsops in various parts of the country. But of the murder, arrest, trial, conviction, and execution, not a word in Dabney print.

Mrs. Nye managed to keep St. Michael's abreast of this "gravest scandal in the history of the University"—Harvard historian Morison's words—as is revealed in her letter to Mrs. Ivens of June 14, 1850: "Poor sister Prescott [in reality their half-sister] finds it quite a task to go to Cambridge as she with all of us thinks the Dr. guilty and Harriet and the girls do nothing but talk of the shame of keeping an innocent man in jail and Kate says '*that Papa is very good and cheerful*'—which is very annoying to one who knows his bad qualities." Daughters Marianne, Catherine, and Harriet, by the way, had all three given testimony at the trial.

In her letter of October 4, 1850, the one which brings up the youthful raping, Mrs. Nye provides Mary Ann with details of Dr. Webster's end. In one of February 9, 1851, she callously goes farther:

> His death has been a great relief to them. Harriet has not been as happy as now for years—the manner of his death alone clouds her brow occasionally although I am sure she will never acknowledge it. It will be a very long time before they can learn economy. . . .

On February 15, 1854, Amelia Clementina makes a final revelation: "It was not till very long after his death that even his friends knew where he was laid, in an empty tomb under Trinity Church Boston." That would have been the old Trinity Church at Summer and Hawley Streets, destroyed in the Boston Fire of November 1872. Earlier that year, in anticipation of plans to build the present structure in Copley Square, the Massachusetts legislature required "all bodies and remains interred in tombs under said church" to be removed. Many remains were moved to Mt. Auburn Cemetery, Webster's probably being among them, arrangements possibly having been made by a Cunningham.

I find Mrs. Nye to be overreacting. She was after all a Hickling. Realizing that the Webster women needed lessons in economy, she sensed that they—a Hickling and a Hickling's daughters—could be partially blamed for the Harvard professor's crime. Cleveland Amory in *The Proper Bostonians* succinctly outlined Mrs. Webster's share of responsibility by referring to her as "a socially aspirant woman, particularly for her two daughters of debutante age." I should go as far as to add that only the guest in the Hotel de São Pedro who has occupied the luxury suite can really understand the chain which ended in the Boston bludgeoning.

☆ ☆ ☆

Those were trying months for the engaged couple—Harriet Webster, in Cambridge, and Samuel Wyllys Dabney, on Fayal. Later in 1850, Samuel went in the *Io* to fetch Harriet. In the spring of 1851, after their marriage, he took her to Fayal, along with her mother and her sister Kate. Marianne ("Mollie") was already on Fayal, having gone there slightly earlier.

And they must have been trying years for Francis Oliver Dabney (1830-1858), youngest son of consul Charles William, for he was attending Harvard College, where he graduated in 1851.

The day had obviously come for John Pomeroy Dabney and family to move out of Fredonia, the abode of Consul Charles William which now housed Samuel Wyllys and bride. John Pomeroy rented a house temporarily, and it was there that Mrs. Webster and two unmarried daughters joined him and Sarah. But their stay was not for long, as they soon returned to Cambridge. He then planned and built a new home for himself, his Webster wife, and their growing family. He occupied it toward the end of 1856. Up the Rua Beleago—in 1863 renamed the Rua Consul Dabney—above and beyond Fredonia and the specimens of Norfolk Island pine (araucaria) which Charles William had planted, it was called "The Cedars." It still enjoys the most beautiful view of all three homes, overlooking Fredonia, the pines, the harbor, Pico Channel, and Pico itself, about which island the following has been so accurately penned:

> The view of the mountain at sunset from Horta is beautiful beyond description. Often it is bathed from crown to base in a rosy glow that deepens into purple and is gone. Sometimes a bright red spot, like a dome of burnished copper, suddenly appears in the midst of the clouds that all day have shrouded the mountain. Instantly the cloud-curtains are drawn aside, as if by an unseen hand, and the peak, all aflame, is revealed. As we watch, it seems actually to flash redder and mount higher, the glow of it creeping down to the shoulders of the mountain, whose base is murky black. Alternately meeting and parting, as if to display the gorgeous spectacle, the clouds roll on, and the peak, now lifted up into infinite height, now thrown back into infinite depths of space, is transfigured with an unearthly glory.

A three-cornered Dabney social whirl ensued. In Fredonia lived Consul Charles William, wife, unmarried children in Horta, and married Samuel Wyllys and family. The Cedars served John Pomeroy and immediate family, who had received additional guests in the autumn of 1853 before occupying the new residence, for Molly and Kate Webster moved to Horta after the sudden death of their mother. Historian Prescott narrates the move in a warm note dated Pepperell, Massachusetts, October 21, 1853, to his cousin Thomas Hickling, Jr., on St. Michael's:

> You will doubtless before this have heard, through Mary Ann and Catherine Webster of the sad news which they bear with them to Fayal. To me it came about as sudden as it will have done to you. I heard of dear Harriet's illness only a day before I learned her death, and her burial—which was hastened to enable the girls to embark for Fayal. . . .
>
> The girls have gone to join their sisters in Fayal, which I understand was Harriet's last wish. . . .

Bagatelle continued as the home of Consul Charles William's brother Frederick, Frederick's wife Roxana, and their children. Young Thomas Jackson Lothrop (Harvard '54) went there immediately following graduation to serve as tutor to the boys who had survived infancy. He returned to Boston in May 1857, having fallen in love with Kate Webster, several years his senior. The two were married in 1858 and made their home in Taunton, Massachusetts.

Frederick Dabney passed away in 1857. Four years later, his widow and her three youngest living sons moved to America. She was determined to see that they received the same Harvard education her two oldest sons were receiving. What is most remarkable is that all five boys did graduate from the university in Cambridge: Lewis Stackpole Dabney in 1861 as number ten in his class, George Stackpole Dabney in 1863, Walter Dabney in 1865, Frederick Dabney, Jr., in 1866, and Alfred Stackpole Dabney in 1871. Not only did Frederick's five sons attend Harvard but also Dabneys of two additional generations: Lewis Stackpole Dabney's sons Frederick Lewis Dabney (1868-1920, class of 1891) and George Bigelow Dabney (1880-1939, class of 1902), Frederick Lewis Dabney, Jr. (1901-1978, class of 1926), and Alfred Stackpole Dabney, Jr. (1885-1944, class of 1909). Moreover, Frederick's numerous descendants have retained an interest over the years in Horta and, above all, Bagatelle. Thus, Lewis Stackpole Dabney, a distinguished Boston lawyer, in his later years kept a print of his childhood home on the desk in his study, and shortly before his death visited that home after an absence of nearly fifty years. The late Frederick Lewis Dabney, who resided in

Dartmouth, Massachusetts, between Fall River and New Bedford, paid his only visit to Fayal as recently as 1975.

The Harvard-Horta connection was reinforced during the first few months of 1858 by a significant visit paid Fayal. The Dabney guest was the well-known New England artist William Morris Hunt (1824-1879), whose brother Leavitt married the granddaughter of William Jarvis.

Hunt had entered Harvard College in 1840 and remained there for three years. He was thus a classmate of Charles William Dabney, Jr., with whom he maintained a close friendship over the ensuing years. Charles's sister Roxana Lewis Dabney witnessed the development of this friendship, and she and their brother Francis Oliver ("Frank") were particularly close to Louisa Perkins, whom Hunt married in 1855.

The author of the *Annals* spent much of 1857 in the United States. She and Marianne Webster sailed from the Azores to New Bedford in October 1856, and she stayed with Charles, Jr., and his family in their new home "Stanhurst," on grounds which were later to be part of Boston's Franklin Park. And then, on May 16, 1857, the *Azor* arrived in Boston from Horta not only with Thomas Lothrop but also with Consul Dabney, his wife, and their daughter Fan.

The usual traveling took place. During the summer when en route from Middletown, Roxana called on "cousin Lizzie Hoppin" in Providence. This lady was presumably the wife of Thomas Frederick Hoppin whose portrait Hunt's friend George Peter Alexander Healy painted the following year and who, one would like to believe, was a forebear of Martha Jay Hoppin, author of an invaluable Harvard Ph.D. thesis of 1974 on Hunt. Roxana then went on to see the Hunts in Newport, their place of residence from 1856 to 1862. "They had just lost their beautiful little boy, Morris, and were feeling very sad," writes Roxana, "but I had a charming visit, and the result of it was that the Hunts went with us to pass the winter in Fayal."

Consul Dabney, his wife, his sister-in-law Roxana (wife of Frederick Dabney) and her son Frederick, Jr. ("Fritz"), the consul's children Roxana, Frank, and Fan, Marianne Webster, Mr. and Mrs. Hunt, and a number of others all sailed from Boston aboard the *Azor* on November 24, disembarking in Horta on December 8. Hunt described his role in the return of the consul as his first experience of "being in the train of a Prince, or Monarch." The end-of-year festivities were suddenly marred by Frederick's death on December 29.

The amiable Hunts departed Horta aboard the *Azor* on May 25, 1858, with the idea in mind of sending Roxana Lewis and Fan Dabney and Marianne Webster some small plaster of Paris figures to serve as drawing models. From the professional point of view, the artist's sojourn on Fayal had proved most productive. He had done portraits of the consul and his wife—which family members found not altogether satisfactory—and had sketched shipwrecks and other scenes. Possibly after his return, he painted his famous portrait, now in the Toledo (Ohio) Museum of Art, of Mrs. Francisca Paula Terra Brum, obviously from a photograph, for she had died on June 4, 1857. Later, he finished two oils dated 1864 of Fayal doorways, quite likely of Fredonia; they remained the possessions of Mrs. Charles William Dabney, Jr., after her husband's premature death. Slightly thereafter and perhaps because of a continuing affection for Fayal Dabneys, Hunt did the portrait of *Mrs. Beevor as a Child*, in Harvard's Fogg Museum. This young girl was Susan Heard Oliver Dabney, born in Roxbury June 11, 1857. Unfortunately, what was deemed "a speaking likeness," the first charcoal sketch made for the portrait of Consul Dabney, was burned in the 1872 Boston fire which consumed Hunt's studio.

Bagatelle was closed down. It remained closed until 1868, when the Olivers, George Stewart Johonnot Oliver and his wife Frances Alsop Dabney, moved there.

Charles William Dabney died in 1871. His son Samuel Wyllys became consul the following year. Then, most tragically, in 1874, John Pomeroy Dabney was killed at sea aboard the *Fredonia*. He was buried in the special Dabney corner of the Foreigners' Section in the Horta Cemetery up behind the Church of Our Lady of Mount Carmel. He was the last of fourteen Dabneys to be laid to rest there, as the pilgrim learns who studies the headstones:

John Bass Dabney, 1767-1826, the first consul;
Roxa Lewis Dabney, 1772-1845, his wife;
Son of John Pomeroy and Sarah Dabney, born and died January 28, 1849;
Catherine Prescott Dabney, 1850-1851, daughter of John Pomeroy and Sarah Dabney;

John Lewis Dabney, 1801-1853, unmarried son of John Bass and Roxa Dabney who, after living a number of years in Rio de Janeiro, returned to Fayal;

Wyllys Pomeroy Dabney, 1854-1855, son of John Pomeroy and Sarah Dabney;

Frederick Dabney, 1809-1857, son of John Bass and Roxa Dabney;

Carl, 1846-1861, son of John Pomeroy and Sarah Dabney;

Richard Alsop Dabney, 1856-1862 (November 5), son of Samuel Wyllys and Harriet Dabney;

Frances Alsop Pomeroy Dabney, 1797-1862 (November 10), wife of Consul Charles William Dabney;

Harriet Frederica Dabney, 1857-1862 (November 12), daughter of Samuel Wyllys and Harriet Dabney;

Clara, 1861-1864, daughter of Samuel Wyllys and Harriet Dabney;

Charles William Dabney, 1794-1871, the second consul, son of John Bass and Roxa Dabney;

John Pomeroy Dabney, 1821-1874, son of Charles William and Frances Dabney.

Another fact makes John Pomeroy Dabney unique. He was the only member of the Dabney family to have lived in all three of the family's Horta mansions.

Not long after John Pomeroy's death, his widow, two sons, and four daughters left for America. They lived at first in Cambridge, where daughter Edith (1852-1876) died almost immediately. Shortly after the departure of the family from The Cedars, the Olivers left Bagatelle. By 1880 only the family in Fredonia remained. Horta's days appeared to be numbered, what with the disastrous aftereffects of phylloxera and oidium, the establishment of the House of Bensaúde, and the emergence of Ponta Delgada as a major protected port. New technology, however, was about to give the Fayal city a new lease on life.

Memory of an earlier Fayal has never vanished from Dabney minds, and several members of the family, loyal to their motto Fidèle et Reconnaissant, have given concrete expression to it.

After returning to the United States from the consulship on Tenerife, William Henry Dabney collected family materials, chiefly about the Virginia branch of the family. The fruits of his labor were published in Chicago in 1888 with the title *Sketch of the*

Dabneys of Virginia, with some of their Family Records. The book, which contains considerable information about Fayal, includes an outline of William Henry's life by his daughter Olivia Frederica Dabney (she who was born on Terceira in 1848), an introduction by the compiler (who died February 16, 1888), and a note by Frances Susan Dabney (1856-1918, daughter of John Pomeroy Dabney) dated Englewood, Illinois, August 9, 1888. It was obviously the latter who saw the book through to publication.

Earlier, in the summer of 1880, a great gathering of the Dabney clan had taken place in Horta. Those already in residence there were Consul Samuel Wyllys, his wife, his older unmarried sister Clara (1820-1904), his younger sister Roxana Lewis, his oldest child Alice (1852-1923), and second oldest Herbert (1853-1920). On June 11, aboard the *Azorean* from Boston, Captain Jacob Samuel Davis—quite likely the bark's maiden voyage—came the following Dabney and Dabney-related passengers, all women except for one male youngster: Mrs. John Pomeroy Dabney and her three daughters Frances Susan, Sarah Hickling "Jr." (1861-1930), and Ellen (1863-1940); Miss Rose Dabney (1864-1947, younger daughter of Samuel Wyllys who in 1892 became the second wife of John Malcolm Forbes); Rose's younger brother Charles William (1867-1936); Miss Harriet Eleanor Lothrop, oldest child of Kate Webster, born 1859, to become an M.D. by the University of Zurich; and Emma B. Hathaway of New Bedford, daughter of Eliza Williams Nye by her first husband and therefore a granddaughter of Amelia Clementina Hickling. On June 28, the more distantly related Misses Lothrop and Hathaway continued on to St. Michael's, for they were of Hickling descent and not Dabneys. The rest stayed in Horta. In October the entire group except Miss Lothrop sailed in *Azorean* from Horta for the return to Boston.

I have in my possession the photograph/autograph album of that round trip. The gift to me of a Dabney descendant, it will eventually go to Harvard. In addition to invaluable photographs of local Azorean costumes, it contains drawings (one of a sailing vessel signed F.S.D.), a chart of the *Azorean*'s eastbound track with daily positions, a manuscript and highly personal poem by Frances Susan Dabney entitled "The Priory," and a page of autographs. The latter page was signed by all but Emma Hathaway. In addition it includes the signature of Anna Lowell Dunbar, another round-trip passenger.

The literarily talented Roxana Lewis Dabney realized that in that summer of '80 she had around her all her living nieces but two, Mary Oliver Alsop Dabney ("May") and Susan Heard Oliver Dabney ("Zay"), the two daughters of her deceased brother Charles William Dabney, Jr. They collectively emphasized this fact by urging her to write out a sketch of the life of their grandfather Charles William Dabney, certainly the greatest Dabney of them all. The two absent nieces as well as the two present and three absent nephews warmly seconded the suggestion, one of the absent nephews being Samuel Wyllys Dabney's son Ralph Pomeroy Dabney (1859-1899) of the Harvard class of 1882. Roxana Lewis rose to the occasion. She had already seen in print her Portuguese translation of English writer Mary Botham Howitt's *Strive and Thrive: A Tale*. It was published in Lisbon in 1867 with the closely parallel title *Quem Trabalha Tem Alfaia*. The Portuguese book contained no name of translator, only the indication "por uma senhora" (by a lady). Roxana was to witness publication in Boston in 1891 of her English translation of Júlio Diniz's well-known novel *The Fidalgos of Casa Mourisca*. The result of the 1880 gathering was her monumental *Annals*, privately printed in three volumes paged continuously (Boston, ca. 1899).

Years later, widowed Rose Dabney Forbes composed a digest of the *Annals* with additions bringing the narrative down to January 1892 and her departure from Fayal. She called it simply *Fayal Dabneys*. She had her book, also intended for private circulation, beautifully engrossed and illustrated by Vida Lindo Guiterman of Arlington, Vermont, and New York, who thus revived the ancient art of the scribe over the months June 1931-February 1932.

In the meantime, poet Frances Susan Dabney had written a little volume of *poèmes en prose* in English about the Azores. Appropriately entitled *Saudades*, it was likewise privately printed, by Boston's Merrymount Press in 1903. One of the eighteen sections is headed "The Vintage: Arêa Larga," another "The Priory Gate: Arêa Larga." The first, "Saudades: The Azores," cast a spell over a Horta audience when I read it there on July 8, 1977:

> Long, long ago, when the first garden was deserted, an Angel saw the flowers weeping there, and her heart was filled with pity and love.
> Spreading her wings like summer clouds, she left her starry home to gather the lovely things in her arms, and bear them back to Heaven whence they had come.

Over the gleaming water she flew, and the sea reflected the bright vision as it passed, for one brief moment, and then it palpitated with a strange joy, for on its breast lay nine rare and wondrous blossoms that had fallen from her close embrace.

And the sea clasped them and held them in its faithful arms for evermore, and brought all things beautiful to lay beside them. And when the Angel saw this she smiled and said, " 'Tis well," and her smile blessed her beloved flowers.

Another memento of the Dabney presence on Fayal is of quite a different genre. The three youngest daughters of John Pomeroy and Sarah Dabney lived on well into the twentieth century. Never having married, they lived together in later life on Boston's Beacon Hill. Each had a special talent. Frances Susan was the poet and Sarah Hickling the financial manager. The youngest of all, Ellen, became a sculptor. A Dabney descendant owns a superlative bronze bust done by her which was exhibited by the Boston Society of Sculptors in 1920. It is of the young Portuguese daughter named Lauri Anna of a maid of one of the Dabneys. This same descendant also owns the Gilbert Stuart marriage portrait of Frances Alsop Pomeroy, done in 1819 on the occasion of her marriage to Charles William Dabney. It had once hung in Fredonia. Years later it was owned by the sisters on Beacon Hill.

The four printed books of family information described above are invaluable to the scholar. They must be used with caution, however, for as stressed above, they share a remarkable characteristic: not one of them breathes a word of Dr. Parkman's murder or of Dr. Webster's arrest, conviction, and execution. It is difficult, as Roxana Lewis must have found out, completely to cover up a widely celebrated murder case, one which, because based on circumstantial evidence, became a classic in the curriculum of U.S. law schools. Roxana Lewis in fact made one great slip in her *Annals*. She quoted a long letter dated March 24, 1851, from Samuel Longfellow to his former tutee Samuel Wyllys Dabney about the latter's marriage to Harriet Webster:

> ... I have been glad to feel what sunshine your coming must bring to the home at Cambridge; a Dark and sorrowful baptism, but I know they have found it a most sanctifying one and have learned deep and holy and beautiful lessons of

Trust and Peace from this dark angel. It will be a satisfaction to you to feel that your affection and fidelity and ever thoughtful kindness and cheerful spirit may weave brightness and joy into their lives. You receive now a heart hallowed and purified by that experience of suffering, which alone, as it seems, can open the deepest springs of the soul. It is a richer treasure now....

Even more remarkable than the failure of the Dabney books to mention the murder—none of them is possessed by Harvard, by the way, except *Saudades*, which is in the Amy Lowell Collection—is the fact that news of the Dabney-Hickling tragedy never reached Fayal. Because of what was perhaps one of the greatest Portuguese journalistic omissions of all time, and one of the Azores's greatest scholarly oversights, Horta learned of the event only in the summer of 1973. A Dabney descendant—I believe a Virginia Dabney—journeyed there and spilled the beans.

Years before, when I was studying Portuguese in Harvard's graduate school, a descendant of the Fayal Dabneys requested me never to tell the tale in Horta. I respected the point of view. Never, in the winter of 1939, nor in that summer, nor in 1964 or 1972, did I ever breathe a word of Dr. Webster and Dr. Parkman. Nor did I write of it in letters to the archipelago. When I returned in 1974, however, I was immediately queried on all sides: "Is it true?"

I broke my silence. After my return, I sent over copies of Helen Thomson's 1971 book *Murder at Harvard*, conveniently remaindered at one dollar. I regret that I have never sent Judge Sullivan's more technical book of the same year, *The Disappearance of Dr. Parkman*, for it takes the position that Dr. Webster's guilt was never established.

Three quarters of a century before I first visited the Azores as a Sheldon Traveling Fellow, another traveler may have been asked to keep the secret. Manuel Borges de Freitas Henriques was born on Flores in the Azores about 1810. He or a relative was certainly the Mr. Borges mentioned in the *Annals* as the American vice consul on Flores in 1830. After a full life aboard American whaleships during which he became a harpooneer, he settled in Boston. There he became a merchant, importing Azorean products and attempting to establish regular ship service between the Azores and New England. He served as the vice consul of Portugal and Brazil in New England and may have been the aspiring "King of the colony" who got in the hair of the Azorean priest brought to Boston at the time of the establishment of the city's first Portuguese "national" Catholic parish in 1873. We know that his writings appeared in two 1873 issues of the *North-End Mission Magazine*, hardly Catholic. Freitas Henriques committed suicide in Boston on September 20 of that very year 1873, and the news of it reached Flores on November 7 via the bark *Fredonia*.

In the summer of 1866, not having seen his homeland in eighteen years, Freitas Henriques embarked on a visit to the Azores. The following year his charmingly written little book *A Trip to the Azores or Western Islands* was published in Boston. I have been given Eliza Williams Nye's copy, signed "Eliza N. Dana 1867," for her second husband's name was Dana.

Freitas Henriques had apparently been in Boston at least since 1848. He obviously knew everything that was going on. He could not have missed the eleven-day trial of Dr. Webster, attended by sixty thousand spectators each allotted ten minutes. Yet of Websters, Hicklings, and Dabneys in his book there is not a syllable. For failure to mention "that untitled prince," "a pacific Rajah Brooke," Charles William Dabney, Freitas Henriques was upbraided by Thomas Wentworth Higginson in *The Nation* of that same year 1867, a reprimand repeated in the Dabney *Annals*'s report of the Higginson review. Higginson was a proper Bostonian himself. He had contributed "Fayal and the Portuguese" to the *Atlantic Monthly* of 1860 and repeated it in his *Atlantic Essays* of 1871. In the article he praised the Dabneys to the skies, pointing out that almost every good institution or enterprise on Fayal was the creation of Charles William Dabney.

Why did not Freitas Henriques so praise? Because of commercial rivalry, or a national Azorean stance against foreigners? Or because he had been asked to refrain from tying the Hicklings and the Dabneys to the murder? Yet he must have mentioned the homicide in conversations on Fayal and St. Michael's. His confidants obviously never betrayed his trust, and this in spite of three magnificent homes on each island continuing to stand as silent reminders.

In Horta the three residences went on to distinguished futures. In 1899, the widow and other heirs of Samuel Wyllys Dabney sold Fredonia to the Europe & Azores Telegraph Co. It thenceforth served as the residence of the Horta superintendent of the first submarine telegraph cable company to link the Azores with the outer world.

In 1900, widow Sarah Hickling Dabney sold The Cedars to the Commercial Cable Co. It became the residence of that company's Horta superintendent.

Bagatelle was eventually acquired by the distinguished Goulart de Medeiros family. It did yeoman service during the Pan American clipper days of World War II by entertaining many of the greats who passed through Horta. Its autograph album of that period lists among others Clement Atlee, the Queen of Sarawak, Inez Robb, William A. Winston, Leland Stowe, Francis M. Rogers, Edward G. Robinson, Carole Landis, Mitzi Mayfair, John C. Winant, Louis Mountbatten, and Amelia Forbes Emerson, the latter the daughter of John Malcolm Forbes by his first wife Sarah Jones and therefore a great-great-granddaughter of Thomas Hickling. And how coincidental that the Queen of Sarawak should have called at Horta after Higginson's likening of second consul Dabney to Rajah Brooke!

The Cedars, Horta home of John Pomeroy Dabney

9
DOTS, DASHES, AND SUBMERGED WIRES

The idea of a submarine cable appears to have been suggested first in 1795 by an Iberian, a native of Catalonia named Salvat. To serve as a conduit for cablegrams, however, an undersea wire required a suitable insulator. Eventually, the substance known as gutta-percha was tried, and it proved ideal. A Portuguese engineer named José de Almeida is said to have brought the first specimens of this substance to Europe from Malaysia, where it is found. He presented them to the Royal Asiatic Society in London in 1843.

Man seems fated to have the paths of his progress dictated by the needs of the military. Portugal entered the exciting new world of cables because of the Sepoy Rebellion of 1857, the English Crown's take-over of the reins of government in India from John Company in 1858, and the subsequent British desire for a fast, secure, and all-British line of communication between London and Bombay. By June 1870, this latter objective was attained through a chain of cables beginning in Porthcurno in Cornwall near Land's End and ending at Bombay itself. The successive links took advantage of places over which the English then exercised political control: Gibraltar, Malta, Alexandria, Suez, and Aden.

The Portuguese government knew of the English cable plans and remembered the close relations which had existed between England and Portugal since the second half of the fourteenth century. It insisted that the Porthcurno-Gibraltar cable planned for its coastal waters be brought into the Greater Lisbon area. The cable was therefore led into Carcavelos, today a resort community at the mouth of the Tejo and within the shadow of Fort St. Julian. King Luís of Portugal participated in the initial exchange of congratulatory messages.

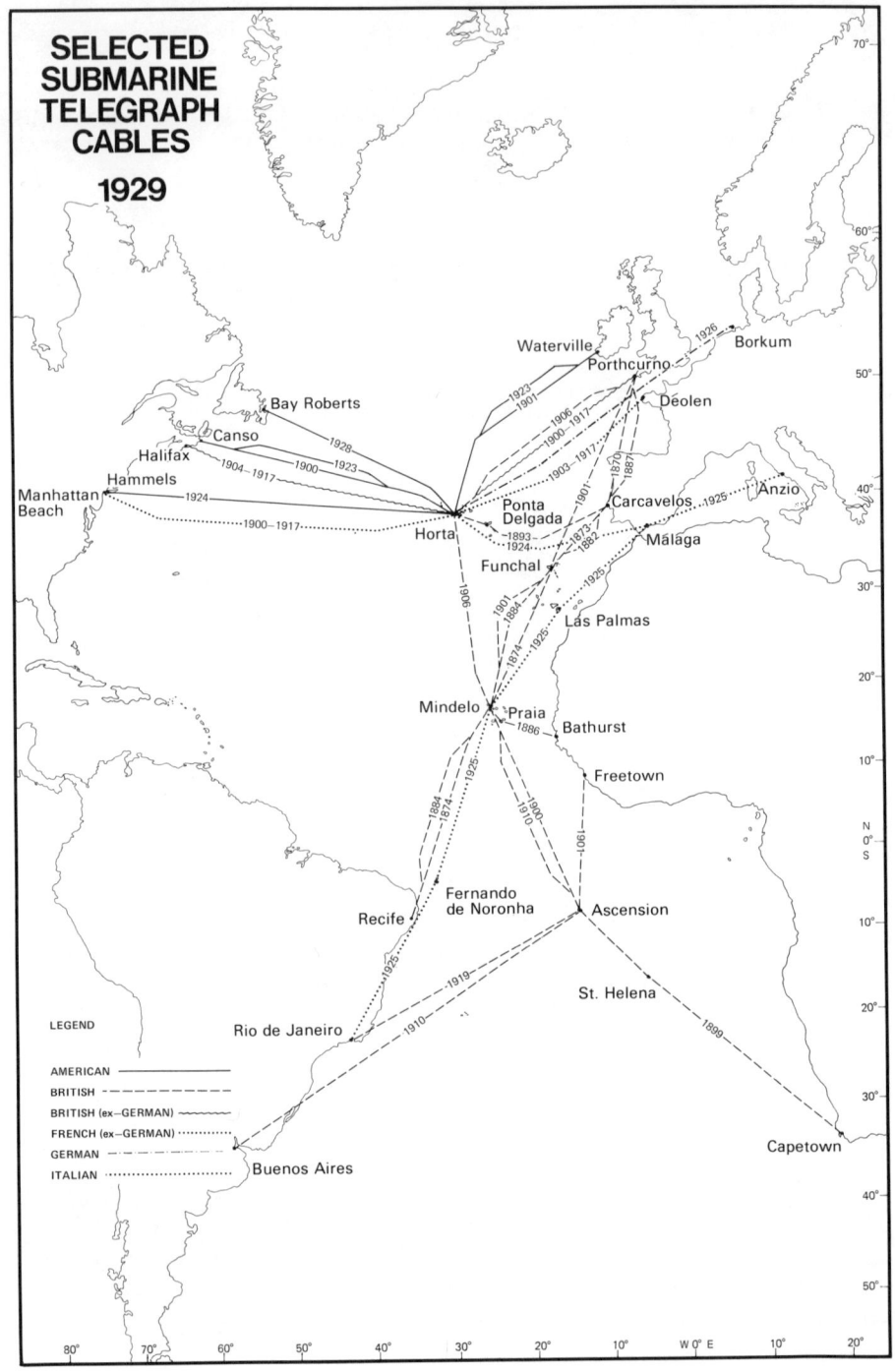

This cable is the first in date of those shown on the accompanying map, which includes all Atlantic cables passing through Portuguese islands which were in operation in 1929 (the year after the last of them, Horta-Bay Roberts, Newfoundland, was laid).

Portugal's English connection is important for an understanding of Portugal's role in later telecommunications. The submarine telegraph cables were almost exclusively an English development. English firms manufactured the cables, and these firms employed their own cableships to lay them, even for companies of other major countries including the United States's Western Union Telegraph Co. and Commercial Cable Co. Because of the Treaty of Windsor, it was natural for the English to consider Portuguese territory through which their cables passed as friendly. Madeira, the island of St. Vincent in the Cape de Verdes, and Fayal in those days were to England as Ascension, St. Helena, Gibraltar, and Malta.

The English cable employees who went out to Portugal soon constituted a thriving English colony in Carcavelos. Their impact on the local community was considerable and included the establishment of a good English school, St. Julian's School, which continues to be a reason why many English-speaking people decide to settle in Carcavelos. The impact of the 1870 cable must have been enormous, coming as it did amid several other technical advances: the postage stamp 1853, land telegraph 1856 (to Spain 1857), railroad 1856 (Sud Express to Paris 1887), and telephone 1882 (in Lisbon). Little wonder that great literature was written at precisely that period and that literary historians speak of a Portuguese Generation of 1870, one which included a famous poet who was born and committed suicide on São Miguel, Antero de Quental.

In 1872, the various English cable companies which contributed to establish this first viable cable connection with India merged to form the Eastern Telegraph Company, eventually the world's largest. The Eastern Telegraph Co. sponsored the formation of many other cable companies, and together they became known as the Eastern and Associated Telegraph Companies. In 1929 these "Eastern" companies became part of Imperial and International Communications Ltd., which in 1934 became known as Cable & Wireless Ltd. or simply C & W. Fortunately for thousands of refugees from Nazism whom Portugal welcomed and assisted, the C & W station at Carcavelos was in existence during the early

1940's. In communication with Brazil via Madeira and São Vicente, and with the United States and Canada via Fayal as well as via Porthcurno and the more northerly cables, Carcavelos served the stateless, newspaper correspondents, spies, and countless others.

The next and predictable step was taken in January 1873. The Brazilian Submarine Telegraph Co. was formed by the same Englishmen who already had entrée into Carcavelos. As Brazil was an ex-colony on amicable terms with Portugal, and the mecca for huge numbers of Portuguese emigrants, this extension to Brazil was effected within the family, so to speak.

The company laid a first cable between Carcavelos and Funchal in 1873, but a fault developed and the cable did not become operational until April 1874. Immediately thereafter, the Funchal-Mindelo (the city on St. Vincent) and Mindelo-Recife sections were laid. This task was completed on June 21, 1874, and the cable was operational the next day. The formal opening of service between Funchal and Carcavelos took place on September 26, 1874, with an exchange between King Luís and the civil governor of the District of Funchal. Suddenly, distant Madeira and remote St. Vincent were capable of communicating in a matter of minutes with their capital city of Lisbon and were linked with Paris and London and even, via transatlantic cables stretching from Ireland to Newfoundland, with New York and the great whaling port of New Bedford.

Funchal and Mindelo, like Carcavelos, welcomed substantial colonies of British cable employees and their families, who reinforced the preexisting coaling and—in the case of Madeira—wine colonies, conferred an international aura of sophistication on these mid-Atlantic cities, and incidentally created new employment opportunities for local citizens. In Funchal, for instance, at one time there were more than one hundred British cable employees and fifty Portuguese.

The staff of the Brazilian Submarine Telegraph Co. on Madeira at the end of 1883 went so far as to found a little monthly magazine entitled *The Monthly Correspondent* which appeared forty-nine times (December 1883-December 1887). It was "issued mainly for the purpose of inaugurating a new departure in the social intercourse existing among the staffs of our three cable-stations of Madeira, St. Vincent, and Pernambuco." (Today the Venice-like city of Recife is the capital of the State of Pernambuco, but then the city was also named Pernambuco.) Perusing its pages, one appreciates the insularity and aloofness of an English colony implanted among "natives," its cult of cricket and lawn tennis, its intense interest in local excursions, its looking forward to the calls of passing English men-of-war and passenger ships. Whereas service on Madeira was agreeable enough, St. Vincent, the "Cinder-heap," was considered a place of banishment, and Pernambuco was highly prized by bachelors.

The Monthly Correspondent contains invaluable tidbits relevant to central themes of this book. The December 1885 number outlines the misdeeds of the Funchal customhouse, pointing out that an order had recently come from Lisbon lowering considerably the salaries and emoluments of its officials, "the money thus deducted to be devoted to the Azores." The January 1886 issue tells of the vicissitudes of emigration from Madeira to the Sandwich Islands: the *City of Paris*, "chartered by a London Jew Bill-Broker of German extraction," had seven hundred cases of measles, including two hundred deaths, during the voyage. The June 1886 number contains a report from St. Vincent concerning an insurrection that had broken out on the neighboring Cape Verdean island of Santo Antão and the rumor that the military were being summoned from Praia (the archipelago's capital) and Lisbon. Of greatest interest is the continuing discussion of Home Rule for Ireland, defined as the rule "of a state belonging to a confederation, which manages its own local affairs, leaving the interests it has in common with the other states of the confederacy, to be dealt with by a confederate parliament." The participants probably did not realize that they were outlining one viable form of government for their host country's Atlantic archipelagoes.

In 1882, the Brazilian Submarine Telegraph Co. duplicated its cable between Carcavelos and Funchal and in 1884 the cable between Funchal and Recife via Mindelo. In 1899, it merged with the company which owned the Brazilian coastal cables and changed its name to Western Telegraph Co. One of the Eastern and Associated Telegraph Companies, it ultimately formed part of C & W. In Carcavelos, Eastern and Western included within their compound a beautiful building, typically Portuguese, with imposing entrance stairway, today the principal building of St. Julian's School. A distinguished staff telegrapher assigned there for many years was the Cape Verdean novelist Manuel Lopes.

A logical next step for the English was to tie in this Atlantic

Ocean cable system with a projected African coastal system which eventually extended south via Luanda and Moçâmedes in Angola to Cape Town. Therefore, in 1885, the African Direct Telegraph Co. was formed by the "Eastern group," and the following year a cable was laid from Bathurst in Gambia to Praia on Santiago, thence to Mindelo. It, too, ultimately became part of C & W. The company, significantly, was created just as the scramble for Africa was getting into high gear.

The international importance of the location of the Azores for submarine telegraphy was appreciated very early, and by commercial as well as weather interests. In 1855, there had been talk within and outside of Portugal, possibly stimulated by Charles William Dabney, concerning the promotion of a cable through the Azores to the United States. For almost forty years thereafter, a series of proposals, counterproposals, contracts, prorogations, and revocations ensued, all coming to naught. Even the Bensaúde interests entered the cable scene: on November 28, 1885, they signed a contract for a Lisbon-Azores cable and the following year transferred the rights to an English company which wished to continue the wire to Bermuda. In 1892-1893, French interests were discussing very seriously the possibility of laying a cable Brest-Lisbon-Azores-Haiti, but the French government did not go along.

Finally, in the summer of 1893, the government of Portugal had the Telegraph Construction and Maintenance Co. of London lay the Carcavelos-Ponta Delgada-Horta cable. Among the several elements involved in the decision to put down this line, one would have been pressure from the Bensaúdes, anxious to promote the port of Ponta Delgada as well as to continue exploitation of Horta's.

At the end of August 1893, the isolation of centuries was suddenly broken. Not only could meteorological information flow to Continental Europe but news from abroad could flow to the Azores. In that very year 1893, the newspaper *O Telégrafo* was founded, appropriately named.

Immediately, whaleship owners in New England began to communicate with their agents in the Azores, and through them with their ships, and vice versa. There is still record of a cablegram of early March 1895 to New England from "Silveira, Edwards & Company, agents, Fayal."

Whales, by the way, resented the entry of cables into their

watery domain. In at least fourteen recorded instances they managed to become entangled with the intruding wires, on occasion at tremendous depths.

In 1893, the Europe & Azores Telegraph Co. was founded in England under the aegis of the "Eastern group" to exploit the Lisbon-Azores cable. Only in 1895, however, did the Portuguese government turn over the Azores concession to the new company. Thereafter, Eastern Telegraph operated the cable of Europe & Azores Telegraph, a company which, like African Direct Telegraph, ultimately formed part of C & W. Moreover, Europe & Azores Telegraph, that is, the "Eastern group" and later Imperial and International and finally C & W, was the sole cable concessionaire to operate into and out of the Azores for many years. The American and German companies about to be mentioned, and later the other companies, were all considered to be subconcessionaires of Europe & Azores Telegraph. Among other things, this meant that all the companies had to operate out of the same building, which building was the property of Europe & Azores Telegraph.

As provided for in its contract with the Portuguese government, Europe & Azores Telegraph laid cables Fayal-Pico, Pico-São Jorge, Pico-Terceira, and São Jorge-Graciosa, and service was inaugurated on November 1, 1893. No cables were ever laid to Flores and Corvo in the far northwest nor to Santa Maria in the southeast. In 1906, however, radio communication was established by the Portuguese between Flores and Fayal, such a link obviously being essential for a better flow of weather reports, which began to be transmitted on September 23, 1913. The interisland cables were given up in 1931, when the government's radio system took over completely. Thereafter, radio in various forms was the only means of communication among the islands.

In November 1899, the Europe & Azores Telegraph Co. acquired Fredonia and adjacent land in Horta. As Fredonia was located near the site of the cable station, the cable company desired it as the residence for part of its English staff. The English were looking ahead, for they knew that employees of the Americans and also Germans would soon be looking for villas in which their officials might be properly housed, in anticipation as it were of the famous Battle of the Villas in Algiers in 1943 involving Allied generals, admirals, and air marshals. The very next year, both the Commercial Cable Co. and the Deutsch-Atlantische Tele-

Entrance to Horta's *liceu*, with Fredonia in background, 1974

graphengesellschaft (German Atlantic Telegraph Co.) inaugurated services which made use of Horta. Quite logically, the Commercial Cable Co. in April 1900 purchased the newer and more ideally located Cedars.

The two new transatlantic services connecting the Old World with the New supplemented the thirteen other cables then in use via more northern routes. These new services embodied some interesting features, not least of which was the transit tax of one cent a word owed to the Portuguese government, which in its turn granted no subsidy and obligated the companies to send its own messages at half rates. Another feature provided that local traffic between the Azores and North America belonged, not to Commercial, but to Deutsch-Atlantische. On the other hand, Commercial handled the New York end of the German cable, and also later of the second German cable (of 1903-1904). In other words, the German cables and Commercial's cables from Canso (Nova Scotia) all came into the same cable station at 184 Oxford Street, Manhattan Beach, adjacent to French Cable's terminus at 180 Oxford Street. This business tie-in between Commercial Cable and the

Germans is significant, especially in view of later alleged ITT dealings with the Nazis. In 1928, Commercial Cable came under ITT.

In February 1913, all Commercial's cables, including the two German cables, were transferred from Manhattan Beach to a new station at 1414 Caffrey Avenue, Far Rockaway, just inland from the Atlantic Beach end of Long Beach. This change was made because the War Department stated that it wished to dredge at the mouth of Jamaica Bay and the cables were in the way. The landing point at Manhattan Beach of the U.S. extension of the French cable from Déolen (next to Brest) direct to Orleans on Cape Cod was not changed, however, nor was that of the cables associated with the Commercial Cable Co. which continued to come into the latter's partially abandoned Manhattan Beach station from Haiti and Cuba.

As if convinced that the new cables would permit him to remain in close contact with his capital and also, if need arose, with other capitals on both sides of the Atlantic, King Carlos chose precisely this year 1901 to visit the Azores. As a new American commercial firm was entering the archipelago under conditions which guaranteed His Majesty's government badly needed revenue, and as the whole cable and meteorological atmosphere at that moment exuded an aroma of friendly international cooperation, it seems unlikely that Carlos feared the U.S. political takeover discussed in Chapter 4.

On October 30, 1903, Deutsch-Atlantische's (or DAT's) second cable from Borkum to Horta was completed, and on May 26, 1904, the continuation to Manhattan Beach. Commercial Cable curiously did not duplicate its service through Horta until 1923, yet in 1905 it laid its fourth direct cable between Waterville and Canso. The question arises: why? On the one hand, cables from Europe via the Azores direct to New York were desirable because they avoided the extensively used fishing grounds between Newfoundland and Nantucket where they stood in danger of being hooked and broken by fishermen. On the other hand, the Portuguese government's tax for use of the Azores was undoubtedly considered high, so high that it seemed more advantageous for the U.S. company to expand its service direct from Ireland to Nova Scotia, thence to New York.

In any event, the advent of English-speaking and German personnel at the turn of the century to join the English employees and families already there, combined with the Bensaúdes and their shipping interests, with the heritage from the earlier Dabney dynasty, and with whatever meteorologists and oceanographers were either stationed or visiting there, made of Horta a true cultural nucleus. Indeed, a well-known Azorean literary figure has written that at the end of the nineteenth and beginning of the twentieth centuries the Fayalese city was the principal center of Azorean intellectual activity, that Walt Whitman, Balzac, and Henry Wadsworth Longfellow were being translated by local intellectuals, often earlier than in Lisbon.

In those early cable years there was only one foreign cable colony in Carcavelos, Funchal, and Mindelo, the English. In Horta there were English, Germans, and employees of the Commercial Cable Co. And they had to work together, for in its original concessions, as already noted, the Portuguese government wisely stipulated that the three companies (Europe & Azores, Commercial, and DAT) were to work together in a single building. Therefore in 1902 a new and larger cable station was built and suitably equipped to replace the original Europe & Azores building located nearby. The new edifice, still standing, was most aptly named Trinity House.

In the meantime the Boer War in South Africa (1899-1902) was breaking the Pax Britannica. The English were dissatisfied with their complicated and roundabout submarine and land telegraph lines to the war zone and initiated feverish activity on the part of the Eastern Telegraph Co., which in 1899, 1900, and 1901 linked Cape Town with Porthcurno via St. Helena, Ascension, Mindelo, and Funchal as indicated on the map, and subsequently laid other South Atlantic cables.

Of the entire Atlantic network of submarine telegraph cables laid in the nineteenth and early-twentieth centuries and touching at Portuguese Atlantic islands, only the German cables Borkum-Horta-Far Rockaway became war prizes at the outbreak of the 1914-1918 war. All the other cables belonged to the Allies. The English and the French appropriated the German cables for themselves in a complicated crisscross fashion, and the Treaty of Versailles in 1919 confirmed their actions.

In July 1917, three months after the United States entered the war, the English diverted the European end of the 1900 Borkum-Horta cable into Penzance (in Cornwall, very near Porthcurno) and the American end of the 1904 Horta-Far Rockaway cable into Halifax (Nova Scotia). The English General Post Office then operated this Penzance-Horta-Halifax cable until 1929, when it was run into the great Porthcurno cable station and became part of Imperial and International Communications (C & W in 1934).

In October-November 1917, the French diverted the European end of the 1903 Borkum-Horta cable into Déolen and moved the American landing point of the 1900 Horta-Far Rockaway cable from Far Rockaway back to Manhattan Beach, but this time to French Cable's station at 180 Oxford Street and not to Commercial Cable's station next door at 184 Oxford Street. A period of silence ensued. After the end of the war, French Cable took over operation of this Déolen-Horta-Manhattan Beach cable. The French ran the two portions as a unit but with manual relay in Horta. This French action provoked considerable reaction from the Commercial Cable Co., as can be imagined and as is evidenced by a statement made before the Senate Committee on Interstate Commerce in 1921 by Clarence H. Mackay, who in 1902 had assumed the presidency of the company upon the death of his co-founder father John W. Mackay. After all, the French had no staff in Horta and Commercial had handled the New York ends for DAT from the beginning. Mr. Mackay got nowhere, and the Eastern staff in Horta handled the French business there until 1930, when Commercial Cable took it over.

But Commercial never got back the New York end of that particular business. It is clear that Commercial wanted what promised to be a lucrative postwar business via Horta with the German Republic. From the point of view of those American-German interests which saw no point in the United States's entry into World War I, it was a shame that a cable connection via Horta had been lost. Ironically, in 1926 those interests were to get such a connection back, as will be seen, but not via Commercial Cable Co.

In his 1921 statement Mackay also complained about the fact that from the beginning the Portuguese government granted all landing rights in the Azores only to the Europe & Azores Telegraph Co. and another company had to obtain its rights by assignment from the English company. "As the Azores is the natural gateway to southern Europe," he continued, "we trust that the United States Government will succeed in inducing the Portuguese Government to grant landing rights direct to American companies, so that the latter will have an independent status at the

Azores." What Mackay did not appreciate was the truism that, whereas Lisbon divided the Azores administratively in order to govern them, it did find union on occasion—and the concept of the Trinity—a convenient device by which to dominate completely.

Mackay further revealed that Commercial Cable had arranged to lay a cable from New York via the Azores to England or France before World War I but hostilities had forestalled the plan.

In 1923, Commercial established via Horta its last cable link between Waterville and Canso. This transatlantic cable was of high speed and was noted for the thickness of its copper conductor, as thick as a pencil and the heaviest per mile of any transatlantic cable laid.

The very next year, a new company entered the Azorean cable picture. For many years the Western Union Telegraph Co. had been carrying on its transatlantic business via a series of cables over the northern route. From Canada the messages continued to the United States, to the Western Union station at 260 Beach 84th St., Hammels, Rockaway Beach, New York. But these northern cables were old-fashioned, slow, and relatively uneconomical. Moreover, by the early 1920's an automatic relay called a "regenerator" had become available to speed up transmission through intermediate points such as Horta, Funchal, and Mindelo. Installed at the relay station, this device not only amplified but reconstituted the received signal and sped it on its way automatically and virtually instantaneously. Once introduced, the regenerator naturally led to a reduction in the number of cable operators. During the summer of 1938 I lived for three months in a *pensão* in Portugal's Monte Estoril, not far from Carcavelos. Among the other guests were a number of members of the so-called B.O.P. (British Observers in Portugal). They supposedly took turns watching the Portuguese-Spanish border to see that neutrality regulations—the Spanish Civil War was raging—were being complied with. I recall that they were unemployed cable operators who had once served Eastern Telegraph in Portuguese territory. A hard-drinking crowd, they regaled me with tales of crates of machine guns crossing the border labeled as typewriters.

Moving into this technically more advanced age, then, Western Union laid a cable in 1924 between Hammels and Horta. The connection was completed on September 20. The cable itself was a new type of "simplex" cable which permitted the simultaneous operation of five 300-letters-per-minute channels in one direction and was the fastest long-distance cable in the world at the time. In point of fact, however, it was apparently never used continually at its full capacity.

The next step in the development of the Atlantic network involved Italy for the first time. In 1921 the Compagnia Italiana dei Cavi Telegrafici Sottomarini was formed in Rome. In 1924, it laid a cable from Málaga in southern Spain inside the Strait to Horta, completed on October 30. The next year, it connected Rome with Rio de Janeiro by laying a cable in five sections: Anzio (just south of Rome)-Málaga-Las Palmas-Mindelo-Fernando de Noronha-Rio de Janeiro. No Italian cable employees ever resided in Horta, where Western Union staff members, just entering the Azores, worked the cable. In Mindelo, however, a substantial number settled in, supplemented by local Cape Verdeans.

When first put into operation, messages involving the Hammels-Horta cable of Western Union were manually relayed to or from the other cables converging on the cable station on Fayal. Such manual relay was also used between "1 HO," as the Western Union cable was called, and the new Italian cable, for this latter was in fact not of a modern design. It should be pointed out, however, that "manual" means "nonelectrical." A manual relay in the later decades of the telegraph cables could, and in the case of 1 HO/Italcable did mean, automatic perforating of a tape by the incoming message, automatic movement of the tape (say, through a hole in the wall between one company's room and the other's) to the transmitter, and automatic transmission. The process was manual in the sense that a human being was standing by. Indeed, I stood with cable employees in Horta in the midwinter and the summer of 1939 and watched them absorb the passing and saddening news, later to spread it around town and make of the modest city the best because first informed in the world.

Only in October 1926, when DAT laid its new cable between Borkum and Horta and when German personnel reappeared on Fayal did 1 HO have an appropriate mate. The German cable was in its construction identical to 1 HO, and messages were relayed automatically via electrical connection from one cable to the other. Indeed, Western Union reserved one or two of its five channels for messages to and from Germany over the German cable, another example of that inter-war U.S.-German business collaboration already noted in connection with the Commercial Cable

Co. And of course Nazi Germany cherished its outpost in the Atlantic. In any event, it sent its Ship-of-the-Line *Schlesien* there in February 1939, and the ship's band regaled us with a concert.

On September 2, 1928, Western Union completed the laying of a final Azorean cable. Of the highest traffic capacity of all, 2 HO ran from Horta to Bay Roberts, its length 1,341 n mi. as compared with 1 HO's 2,022 n mi. Unlike the 1924 cable, the design of 2 HO permitted "duplex" operation (simultaneous transmission in the two directions) over five 300-letters-per-minute channels.

Apparently the 1928 cable was never fully utilized either. For most of its life (until Western Union's transatlantic telegraph cable system closed down completely in late 1966) it handled only two New York-Horta channels, and at Horta its traffic was passed on manually to one of the other companies.

There is some evidence to support the conclusion that Commercial Cable, which also handled the French (ex-German) cable to Manhattan Beach beginning in 1930, and Western Union, which handled Italcable's line to Málaga and Rome, tended to avoid routing via the Azores the many messages which flowed between the United States and Europe. The subject needs a complete investigation, one which would get to the bottom of the belief that the Portuguese government charged an excessive transit tax.

The golden cable year in Horta was thus 1928, when there were about 150 foreign cable families in the city, Englishmen, Germans, and the staffs of the two American companies. Ironically, in the Azores the latter employed, not Americans, who demanded high wages out of line with the going scale, but Canadians, Newfoundlanders, Irishmen, and Scots. In that year, also, Stone & Webster completed three construction projects for Western Union, the first of which the American company immediately turned over to the English company, the sole concessionaire:

> Joint Cable Station and Power House, April 1, 1926-April 19, 1928. The station connected with Trinity House at the latter's southeast corner. It was of reinforced concrete, including foundations which rested on rock. The power house was built to the east of the cable station to replace the old Eastern and Commercial power installations. Total cost $295,419.63.

Housing Development, December 20, 1925-May 2, 1928. Traffic Director's house, Superintendent's house, Chief Electrician's house, five two-family houses, a garage, and two tennis courts. Total cost $304,913.20.

Additional buildings, yard work, and yard structures, December 1, 1926-April 10, 1928. Infirmary, recreation building, staff house (that is, bachelors' "mess"), and other work. Total cost $155,180.72.

As the ensemble of the Western Union staff buildings recently became the magnificent Hotel Fayal, discussion of these structures will be found in Chapter 13, where an outline of Horta's "Cable Trail" is also included.

Then came World War II. The British cut the 1926 German cable early in September 1939. In later 1944, the European landing point was moved to Cherbourg, and the through channels from New York served the U.S. armed forces. The cable was restored to commercial service after World War II and remained in service for a brief period. Meanwhile, in 1943 the Allies received permission to set up land air facilities in the Azores, notably at Lajes on Terceira. The German personnel who stayed on in Horta after the outbreak of the war were promptly whisked away by the Portuguese. In accordance with the agreement signed in Lisbon on August 17, 1943, two special cables were laid between Horta and Terceira. They were removed after the war.

Within twenty-four hours after the Italians entered World War II in 1940 the British cut all the Italian cables passing out of the Mediterranean. They moved the European landing point of the Málaga-Horta cable to Gibraltar, where it continued to function until 1947. Moreover, they laid a special Gibraltar-Funchal cable, claiming that it was needed because of the more than two thousand Gibraltarians on Madeira during the war.

Italy did get its cables back eventually. Improved, the South American chain remained in service until the early 1970's, providing C & W with stiff competition. In 1952 the Italians took their cable into Recife between Mindelo and Rio de Janeiro and gave up their relay station on the Brazilian island of Fernando de Noronha.

The telegraph cables were phased out of service over the 1960's and early 1970's. By December 31, 1969, with the closing down of

C & W, Fayal was no longer in the cable business. C & W closed down the same day in Funchal, on December 31, 1970, in Carcavelos, on April 25, 1973, in Recife, and on April 30, 1973, in Mindelo.

A significant era had ended, consisting of exactly one century of a close and physical connection between Portuguese Atlantic archipelagoes and the United States, a link provided by strands of wire lying across the bottom of the sea, a link far more tangible than radio waves and airplane routes. One may still locate the old Western Union station at Hammels, trace the route of 1 HO down the street via a series of manhole covers lettered W U T CO to the water's edge, and then look south and east toward Horta. One may experience a similar nostalgic thrill at the old Manhattan Beach station, where the only other Azorean umbilical cord was tied to the U. S. shore.

10
FLYING BOATS AND WHEELED PLANES

Well before World War II, the submarine telegraph cables suffered from the effects of the Depression of 1929 and following years and from the competition of transoceanic radio and transoceanic air mail. After World War II, they received their death knell from the new coaxial submarine telephone cables of enormous capacity and, finally, from the communications satellites and associated earth stations of even greater capacity which included the capability not possessed by the telephone cables of transmitting live TV programs.

On July 17 and 18, 1922, Guglielmo Marconi (1874-1937) visited Horta, Fayal, for the second time. He was traveling aboard his white yacht named *Elettra* en route to England from Newfoundland, the site of his memorable 1901 experiment. On September 14, 1922, the Companhia Portuguesa Rádio Marconi (Portuguese Marconi Radio Company) was established. CPRM's first radio circuits between Continental Portugal and Adjacent Islands were inaugurated on December 19, 1926. And in 1927, the first commercial transatlantic radio telephone conversation took place, between New York and London.

Portugal had granted a concession to CPRM to handle telecommunications (but not mail) between Continental Portugal and Azores and between Continental Portugal and Madeiras. No longer could a businessman in Horta take a cablegram destined for New York or anywhere else including even Lisbon directly to the office of a readily available foreign-owned cable company. Eventually, CPRM's radio in the Adjacent Islands took over completely—radio telegraph (dot-dash messages via radio) and radio telephony (voice transmission by radio)—but via Continental Portugal rather than direct to foreign lands. All U.S. visitors to the Azores who suddenly needed to telephone home were well acquainted with the unsatisfactory nature of the radio telephony.

In other words, from end of 1926 on, the Adjacent Islands were, from the point of view of telecommunications, treated as colonies.

Be that as it may, certainly the airplane and its mail, in the years following the concession to CPRM, was the more important of the telegraph cables' two competitors, especially in strengthening family ties between Portuguese Atlantic archipelagoes and the United States, for ordinary folk did not send cablegrams or use long-distance telephone.

☆ ☆ ☆

The four-engined flying boat *NC-4* borrowed the routes of the early cables for its pioneering crossing of May 1919 from the United States to England. The flight began at Rockaway (near Hammels) and ended at Plymouth (near Porthcurno). The accompanying map of transatlantic flights indicates the intermediate stops.

In 1921 and 1922, the Portuguese naval officers Sacadura Cabral and Gago Coutinho effected their spectacular flights involving Atlantic islands.

In part, these early fliers were attempting to work out feasible airmail routes. Success was achieved first in the South Atlantic, and for two reasons. The minimum interport distance between Africa and South America is less than across the northern North Atlantic: Freetown (Sierra Leone)-Natal (near Recife, Brazil) 1,569 n mi.; Monrovia (Liberia)-Natal 1,594; Bathurst-Natal 1,601; Gander (Newfoundland)-Foynes (Ireland) 1,690. The interport route is equatorial and its weather therefore more favorable for flying.

The French were the great pioneers in the European airmail service to South America, as is well known to avid readers of Antoine de Saint-Exupéry's *Courrier Sud (Southern Mail)*, *Vol de Nuit (Night Flight)*, and *Terre des Hommes (Wind, Sand, and Stars)*. At first they flew from France south along the West African coast to St. Louis (Senegal), and from Natal south along the South American coast as far as Buenos Aires (Argentina). The oceanic gap was served by a fast mail ship. Finally, on May 12-13, 1930, Jean Mermoz closed this gap by flying nonstop from St. Louis the 1,716 n mi. to Natal in a float plane. The cables to South America were definitely threatened.

The Germans also wished to carry the mails to South America. In 1927, an affiliate on the latter continent was flying southward from Natal and possessed the rights to a base on Fernando de Noronha. On the other side of the Atlantic, Lufthansa was groping southward and by 1929 was flying from Berlin to Gran Canaria via Seville and the island of Tenerife. In July 1930, the German company established a regular Berlin-Rio de Janeiro service: planes from Berlin to Las Palmas and from Fernando de Noronha to Rio, transatlantic steamer between the islands.

To eliminate their ship link, the Germans resorted to the use of a mother ship midway between Bathurst and Natal. This vessel trailed a flexible ramp onto which a small hydroplane could taxi to be picked up for refueling and then catapulted aloft and sped on its way. The first such ship was the *Westfalen*, and the first scheduled flight began on February 3, 1934. The mail was flown by land plane from Germany via Seville to Bathurst and from Natal on south. A Dornier Wal flying boat flew from Gambia to Brazil via the midocean rendezvous, thus eliminating natural Atlantic islands. Later in the 1930's, the Germans used two motherships, one of them the *Schwabenland*, to speed up the service.

The Italians in 1939 became the first fliers to transport passengers all the way across the South Atlantic commercially using heavier-than-air land planes. This service provided by L.A.T.I. (Linee Aeree Transcontinentali Italiane) continued on a weekly basis, notwithstanding the British blockade attempts. In 1941, L.A.T.I.'s was the only South Atlantic service, its flights constituting the first regular passenger service since the *Graf Zeppelin*'s beginning in 1930. In September 1941 the route was extended to Buenos Aires. On December 27, 1941, the United States being at war with Italy, Brazil forced L.A.T.I. to suspend its South American run. Two hundred and eleven flights had been made, with only the 108th (January 15, 1941) ending in disaster. A total of 1,804,982 miles had been flown, with 1,784 passengers, 266,336 pounds of mail, and 316,174 pounds of cargo. And the Nazi political officer aboard the *Graf Spee* had returned to Europe as an incognito passenger.

As noted on the map of transatlantic flights, L.A.T.I. used the island of Sal in the Cape Verde Islands as a stopping-off place.

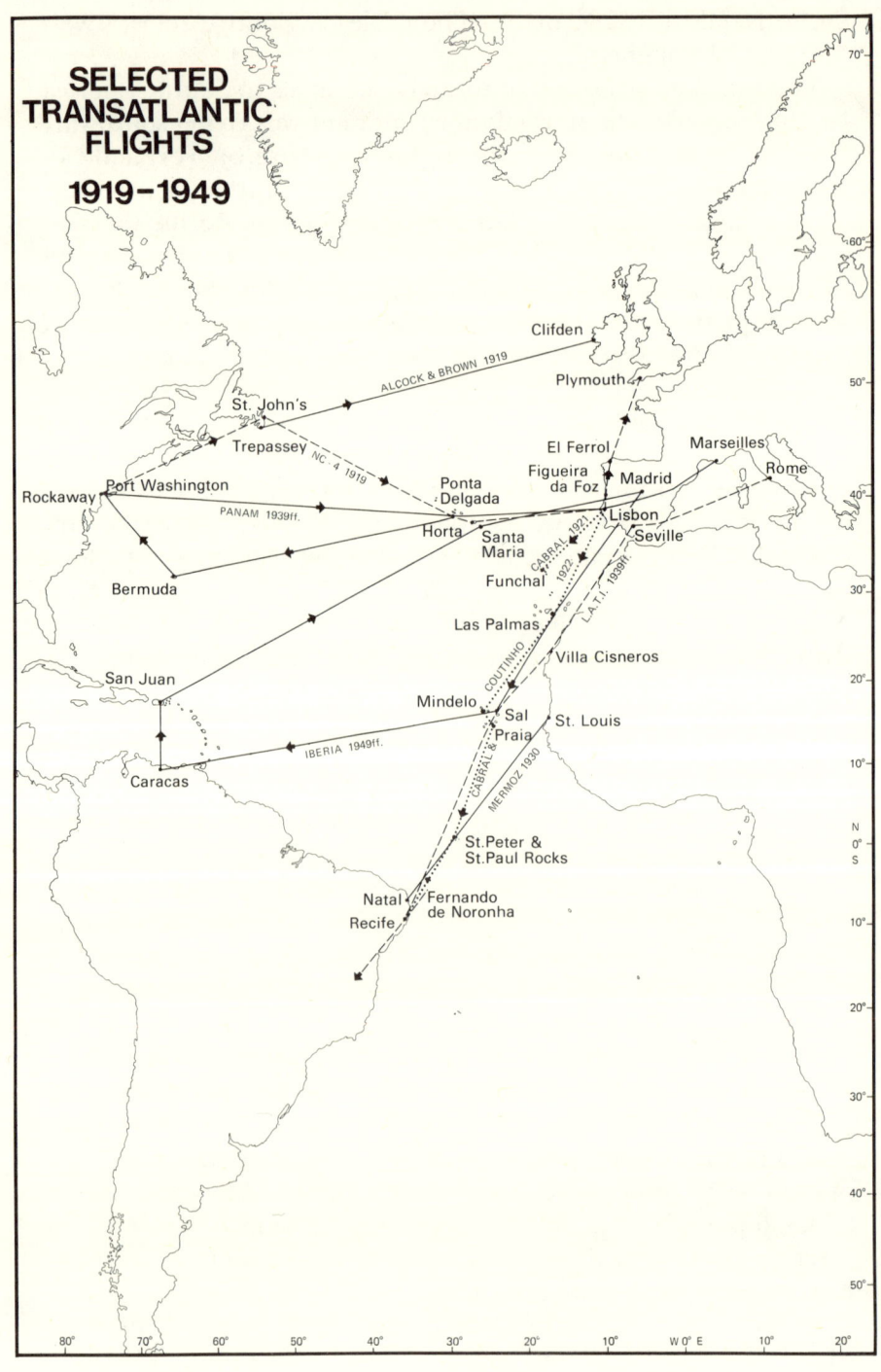

Actually, it was the Italian company which built the airport there in the first place, creating a "new aeronautical city" out of virtually nothing.

Although the very first transatlantic flights involved the North Atlantic, this treacherous body proved far more difficult to conquer than the South Atlantic, especially westbound against prevailing winds. Throughout the 1920's, several attempts via Horta were made to fly between Europe and North America in both directions, but they all came to naught. Either an eastbound plane was forced to come down short of the Azores—like Pinedo's Savoia-Marchetti flying boat in May 1927—or a westbound plane actually reached Horta but could not make it the rest of the way—like Fritz Loose's and Rolf Starke's Junkers flying boat with the Viennese actress Lilli Dillenz in October of that same year. The first plane after the *NC-4* to land in Horta in the course of a full transatlantic flight was the gigantic twelve-engined Dornier Wal flying boat known as the *DO-X*. Completed in 1929, the plane had had a long career of flying by May 21, 1932, when it crossed from Holyrood, Newfoundland, to the surface near Ribeirinha, Fayal. The next day it flew on to Vigo in Spain.

In 1933, Italo Balbo led a mass flight of twenty-four Savoia-Marchetti boats from Rome to Chicago for the World's Fair. Returning, they flew from Newfoundland to the Azores. On August 8, 1933, fifteen, with Balbo, landed at Ponta Delgada, and nine alighted at Horta. The next day they continued to Lisbon, one crashing on takeoff from Ponta Delgada. The age of experiment was over and that of air might upon the world. Then, on November 21, 1933, Colonel and Mrs. Lindbergh arrived at Horta from Lisbon on their commercially-oriented survey flight for Pan American. They left on November 23 for Ponta Delgada, thence to the Canaries (overflying Madeira), and on to West Africa and South America.

In the meantime, both French and Germans had resorted to a still different technique to expedite the transatlantic mails. Beginning in 1928, the French catapulted a mail plane from their liner *Île de France* some four hundred miles off New York or Cherbourg. On July 22, 1929, the Germans launched a seaplane from their speedy *Bremen* some 280 miles off New York, and on August 1, on the return, they catapulted the same plane from a position five miles west of Cherbourg for the flight to Bremerhaven. In 1930, the *Europa* was fitted with a catapult, and this service continued through 1935, again eliminating islands. Then the Germans changed method and took advantage of Fayal.

Over summer and autumn months of 1936, 1937, and 1938, Deutsche Lufthansa carried out catapulting and recovery in Horta and New York so as to have short takeoff runs unaffected by sea conditions and also to take advantage of the mother ship for rest and repair facilities. Horta was particularly convenient for the Germans because of the direct DAT cable to Borkum and the presence of a German cable staff in very comfortable quarters. In all, two ships (*Schwabenland* and *Friesenland*) and five planes were used, plus a sixth plane which shuttled between Horta and Lisbon, thus completing air mail service across the North Atlantic.

During the summers of 1938 and 1939, Air France, whose predecessor company had pioneered in carrying the mails between Europe and South America, experimented with transatlantic service via Horta using two six-engined Latécoère 521's, *Lieutenant de Vaisseau de Paris* (one round trip Lisbon-Horta-New York in 1938, the westbound portion of which was the first flight from Horta to the United States direct with the plane taking off under its own power, plus flights in 1939) and *Ville de Saint Pierre* (flights in 1939).

On May 20, 1939, Pan American began the first regularly scheduled flights across the North Atlantic. The very first, mail only, departed Port Washington, on the north side of Long Island, stopped at Horta and Lisbon, and continued to Marseilles. Leaving the French port on May 25, this *Yankee Clipper* called at Lisbon, Horta, and Bermuda before reaching Port Washington. The first passenger flight, *Dixie Clipper*, left Port Washington on June 28 and Marseilles on July 2, stopping at Horta and Lisbon in both directions and omitting Bermuda altogether. Thereafter, Bermuda was used as Nature's forces dictated. And Captain Bill Winston of the *Yankee Clipper* once told me that he would rather fly across rugged Iberian terrain between Lisbon and Marseilles in a strong-hulled flying boat than in a land plane, for the chances were better of a safe forced landing in the event of an emergency.

With the Pan American clippers, supplemented by the French planes which also dropped in, Horta in the summer of 1939 suddenly received its new lease on life. Pan American ground personnel had gone out there in the winter of 1938-1939 and enlarged the foreign colony hitherto consisting largely of the cable staffs. Inevitably, relations between the Pan American people and

The Lives of Azoreans and Madeirans

the Americans (or Canadians) with Western Union and Commercial Cable were close, and the Pan American crowd seemed to have the run of the Western Union compound.

Over the seven-year period 1939-1945, Pan Am planes landed in Fayalese waters a total of 656 times. They carried 9,729 passengers in transit plus 986 who disembarked and 1,931 who embarked. With development of the fields on Terceira and Santa Maria and the use of transoceanic land planes for passengers and mail at the end of World War II, Horta's importance to international aviation dwindled to zero. Today the only reminders of Pan Am's presence are the remains of its radio station behind the Horta Cemetery and its old waterfront offices opposite the Estalagem de Santa Cruz (Inn of the Holy Cross) in the harborside fort. On the other hand, since 1971, Fayal has had its own very fine little airport for the land planes of the interisland service.

Among the more notable episodes of the Pan American transatlantic flying-boat service was a delay of many days in Horta at the end of 1939 of two westbound flights due to an excessive and continuing swell which made takeoff impossible. The exasper-

Horta's hospitable Bagatelle

ated, bored, and highly talented group of thirty-six passengers, bent on being in the States for Christmas, were thus marooned on Fayal. Rallying, they pooled their abilities and produced an English-language newspaper. Named the *Horta Swell*, it is today a collector's item which the present owner of Bagatelle kindly allowed me to peruse along with her autograph album.

Six numbers were printed by the press of the local paper *O Telégrafo*: December 30 and 31, 1939, and January 1, 3, 4, and 7, 1940. The first number begins:

> ENTER THE SWELLS. Was there anybody here who wanted to get home for Christmas? If so, we seem not to have heard of it, but there was a general feeling in Pan American circles that this might be the case and determined but unsuccessful efforts were made toward transporting our brilliant gathering across the remaining miles of ocean-Swell!
>
> Having now spent a *swell* Christmas in Horta, regardless of unconfessed desires and herculean endeavors of our Twentieth Century Clipper Ships, we feel that everybody is settling down to the brilliant winter season of Fayal. So that nothing should lack in an otherwise perfect community we bring out this, we hope, daily paper, daily as the swells and bad weather reports of the Atlantic.
>
> In the age of censorship, we are free. In the age of propaganda we promise to be truthful (don't wince). We hope that in an island of apparently perpetual storms we are not too stormy. Cave dwellers, for once we come out to the light, to live for one short winter, till the summer months and the resumed Pan American service sends us, for lack of public, back to the dark recesses of the cavern from whence we sprung. May the Horta Swells to which we owe our birth, roll majestically inshore for many a long day.

Perusal of all six numbers reveals a most interesting passenger list. It includes Charles Munch ("Maestro Munch," later to conduct the Boston Symphony), Edgar Mowrer, Viscount Pedro Domecq, and Mrs. Denise Perrier. The latter, whose blue coat was reported to be envied by the Horta Schiaparellis, later married my beloved colleague and distinguished teacher of French language, literature, and civilization, André Morize (1884-1957).

The Lives of Azoreans and Madeirans 199

☆ ☆ ☆

France fell in the late spring of 1940, and the Atlantic world became a rumor mill concerning Germany's aggressive capabilities. One fear involved the Panama Canal, for German bombers were deemed capable—except by those who understood planes' ranges and the problems of navigation and refueling—of flying down the African coast to Dakar, across to Brazil, and along the north coast of South America. Hence U.S. Marine guard companies were sent from the United States to Recife, Natal, and Belém do Pará in Brazil on January 1, 1942. Another and very real fear involved the Azores, for the Germans were known to have Focke-Wulf Fw 200 (Condor) bombers based on Bordeaux with a range of 2,400 miles, enough with luck to bomb the archipelago and ships passing it.

During the critical summer of 1941, the United States had no intention of sitting by idly and witnessing an Axis takeover of either the vitally located Azores or the equally strategically situated Cape Verde Islands. The Amphibious Corps, U.S. Atlantic Fleet, consisting of the 1st Marine Division (Marine Corps) and the 1st Infantry Division (Regular Army) and capable because draftee-free of being sent abroad, was prepared so to move in spite of earlier Rooseveltian promises to the parents of American boys. Its staff had elaborate plans drawn up to counter any Axis threat to Iceland, Azores, Canaries, Cape Verde Islands, Dakar, Brazil's Northeast, or Vichy-ruled Martinique. Its Intelligence Section even had a highly trained group of interpreters knowledgeable in Portuguese, Spanish, French, and German to meet all linguistic contingencies. This little team reflected probably the first foreign-language program of U.S. participation in World War II.

Although I was not aware of his so doing at the time, F.D.R. publicly and very clearly outlined what I thought was the Top-Secret mission of our Amphibious Corps in an address reported in *The New York Times* on May 28, 1941. Delivered the preceding day, this policy statement spelled out America's strategy for defense:

> [The Nazis] have the armed power at any moment to occupy Spain and Portugal; and that threat . . . extends also . . .

to the island outposts of the New World—the Azores and Cape Verde Islands....

Control or occupation by Nazi forces of any of the islands of the Atlantic would jeopardize the immediate safety of portions of North and South America, and of the island possessions of the United States, and therefore of the ultimate safety of the continental United States itself....

Under German domination those islands would become bases for submarines, warships and airplanes raiding the waters that lie immediately off our own coasts and attacking the shipping in the South Atlantic....

Our national policy today therefore, is this:

First, we shall actively resist wherever necessary, and with all our resources, every attempt by Hitler to extend his Nazi domination to the Western Hemisphere, or to threaten it. We shall actively resist his every attempt to gain control of the seas. We insist upon the vital importance of keeping Hitlerism away from any point in the world which could be used or would be used as a base of attack against the Americas.

Secondly, ... we shall give every possible assistance to Britain and to all who ... are resisting Hitlerism.... Any and all further methods ... which can ... be utilized, are being devised by our ... technicians who, with me, will ... put into effect such new and additional safeguards as may be needed.

Fortunately, few of our plans were implemented, and then only those involving Iceland, Brazil, and Martinique. In the summer of 1942, the Corps was broken up. The Marines, with a single exception, went off to Guadalcanal. The Army staff and most of the Navy staff, including one lone Marine officer, planned and executed the Allied invasion of Northwest Africa of November 8, 1942, thereby diverting German attention to Europe's soft underbelly and ending the threat to the Island Portuguese.

The days of lumbering flying boats were numbered, except, as will be noted, on the tourist route between England and Madeira; and in mid-1943 the British and Americans obtained their rights to Azorean fields. And therein lies an amusing contrast in the critical spirit of recent writers.

Retired Lieutenant General Vernon A. Walters, U.S.A., has just written that "before the Portuguese gave permission to use the bases in the Azores, the Allies contemplated using Portuguese-speaking Brazilian troops to seize the islands for use against the German submarines." Fortunately, I do not have to point out the absurdity of that scheme, for an ex-Royal Air Force senior officer has already done so. Air Commodore R. E. Vintras in 1974 wrote: "Apparently, unknown to us, President Roosevelt had had the crazy notion of approaching the Government of Brazil to act as an intermediary with the Portuguese. A course of action more likely to infuriate our oldest ally could not be conceived and to imagine that the Spaniards would be happier because of Brazilian intervention staggers the imagination."

Lajes became a major British base used for antisubmarine patrol and other purposes, and there is today an impressive and beautifully maintained English War Cemetery outside the airport gates to remind one of the British presence and war contribution in mid-Atlantic. After the war, the field became Air Base No. 4 of the Portuguese Air Force, and the Portuguese allowed the Americans to use it in peacetime. Because of the U.S. presence and Terceira's location, Lajes came to serve humanity in a most dramatic way: as a base for air-sea rescue.

A typical example took place in early April 1972. The 45-year-old radio officer aboard the Dutch freighter *Ares* became seriously ill when the ship was at 32° 07' N, 39° 08' W, roughly 700 n mi. southwest of Terceira. An HC-130 of the U.S. 57th Air Rescue and Recovery Squadron at Lajes was soon airborne. Shortly thereafter, medics parachuted from the plane. The next day they reported that the man's condition had stabilized. Two days after the original radio message had been received, *Ares* reached Ponta Delgada. The patient was hospitalized, and the pararescuemen were returned to their station.

The Lajes airfield has served not only the international maritime community but also the Azoreans themselves, most specifically the Terceirans. The U.S. presence has contributed dollars, yes, but also a new way of life ranging from local television broadcasting to miniskirts. I well remember the two American teenagers in miniskirts in Angra's main square at noon on Easter Saturday 1972. They literally paralyzed the heavy flow of traffic. Moreover, Angra obtained its beautiful new *liceu* building because the secondary school's rector called Lisbon's attention to the excellent high school at the base and shamed the capital into matching it.

Even the quality of cattle on the island has been improved by the action of the U.S. doctors of veterinary medicine and officials

Angra do Heroísmo, Terceira—noon on Easter Saturday 1972

of the People-to-People program. Thus in 1974 Sally and Amber, two 500-pound six-month-old registered Holstein calves, flew from Madison, Wisconsin, direct to Lajes, the gift of people in Wisconsin to help upgrade milk production in the Azores. Incidentally, that flight of a cargo Constellation was the first overseas flight direct out of Madison's Truax Field.

Santa Maria became a major military transport field for the American armed forces. The original plan envisaged it as a staging area for the redeployment of troops from the European theater via the United States to the Pacific after the defeat of Germany. Once the war was over, it became a Portuguese civil field and was much used for years by airliners not quite capable of crossing the entire Atlantic without refueling. It was the French aviator Louis Castex who first realized that the Santa Maria site was suitable for land planes. He discovered it during his visit of December 21, 1935, and reported his find to local officials. They showed me the terrain in 1939. I passed the word to Washington in 1941. Whether Washington already knew of it is still a question in my mind.

After World War II, Sal assumed great importance for airliners not able to fly nonstop between Europe and South America. (The Canaries never developed an airport which was used extensively for the intercontinental flights except for Las Palmas, put to limited use.) The Italians refueled at Sal upon resuming their South American run, using that era's longer-range planes with four piston engines. In similar fashion, the Spanish national airline, Iberia, once took dramatic advantage of Sal and precisely exemplified the circular cruising described at the beginning of Chapter 7.

Iberia actually was the first airline to establish an air link between Europe and South America after the war. In October 1946, using a DC-4, it began service between Madrid and Buenos Aires via Villa Cisneros (Spanish Sahara), Natal, and Montevideo (Uruguay). When the Portuguese government opened the airport on Sal to international commercial traffic, Iberia used it instead of Villa Cisneros. In 1949, Iberia opened service to Venezuela and Puerto Rico, with route as indicated on the map. The stop in the Canaries was more for passengers than for fuel, for there was extensive emigration to Venezuela from that archipelago as well as from Madeira. The distance from Sal to Caracas was considerable, some 2,600 n mi. by great-circle track. If the DC-4 could not quite make Caracas, it had Port of Spain available for refueling. The distance from San Juan to Santa Maria amounted to about 2,400 n mi. Bermuda was available as a fuel stop if the winds so demanded.

Of all the Portuguese Atlantic islands, then, only two have proved important for international civil aviation, Santa Maria and Sal. In the mid-1970's, however, Lajes was opened up to limited scheduled transatlantic commercial service, initially only by TAP, in mid-1978 also by TWA. At first, the military terminal was used for civilian passengers, then a new civilian terminal was built. Its post-Revolutionary sign proclaimed the field as Lajes, Terceira, Azores. The terminal building built on Santa Maria in authoritarian days identified that field as Santa Maria, Azores, Portugal.

Occasionally, other islands are used for the intercontinental movement of aircraft. During World War II, Ascension played an important role in the airlifting of planes from the United States to the Middle East via Brazil and the Gulf of Guinea region of Africa. Since that war, Iceland has played a very significant role in transatlantic air service, especially for the economy-minded.

All three Island Portuguese international airports were much in the military news in the mid-1970's, and the ramifications of the incidents have not yet been fully perceived.

In the fall of 1973, during the fourth Arab-Israeli war, the United States staged a military airlift through Lajes in order to aid Israel. Valued at one billion dollars, this operation took place between October 14 and November 15. U.S. transport planes departing from widely separated Air Force bases in the United States refueled and rested crews on Terceira—with the full approval of Caetano's government—and continued to Tel Aviv. As an example of the advantage derived from use of the Azores, a C-5A jet could carry 148,000 pounds of supplies to Israel, as against 67,000 pounds on a nonstop unrefueled flight.

With the 1974 Revolution and a move to the left in Portugal, the Portuguese attitude toward this kind of use of the Azores changed. Whatever the final agreements between the United States and Portugal over Lajes turn out to include, an extraordinary repercussion of the 1973 airlift is visible in the 1976 Constitution of the Portuguese Republic. Article 229, 1, (*1*), lists the following among the powers of the two autonomous regions (Azores and Madeiras) to be spelled out in the respective Statutes now being elaborated: "Participation in negotiations about the treaties and international agreements which directly concern them as well as in the benefits which derive from them."

The other major military incident possibly, even probably, involved the airport on Santa Maria, the one on Sal, or both, but official information has so far been denied me. During the winter of 1975-1976, thousands of Cuban soldiers—revealed in 1978 to have been a division—went to Angola to aid what turned out to be the victorious faction in the post-independence struggle for control. Presumably, a large number went by ship. How did those who flew get there? Possibly on Russian IL-62 four-engined jets (with two engines on either side aft, as on the British VC-10). At which intermediate fields did these jets refuel? For suggested answers, see the accompanying map.

At least since early 1972, Cubana Airlines has flown a regular service between Havana, Cuba, and Prague, Czechoslovakia, with an intermediate stop at Madrid, flight CU 476 eastbound, flight CU 477 westbound. The planes have been IL-62's, the cabin crew Cuban, the cockpit crew Russian. Presumably these planes assisted in the exodus of some of the refugees from Castro's regime, ref-

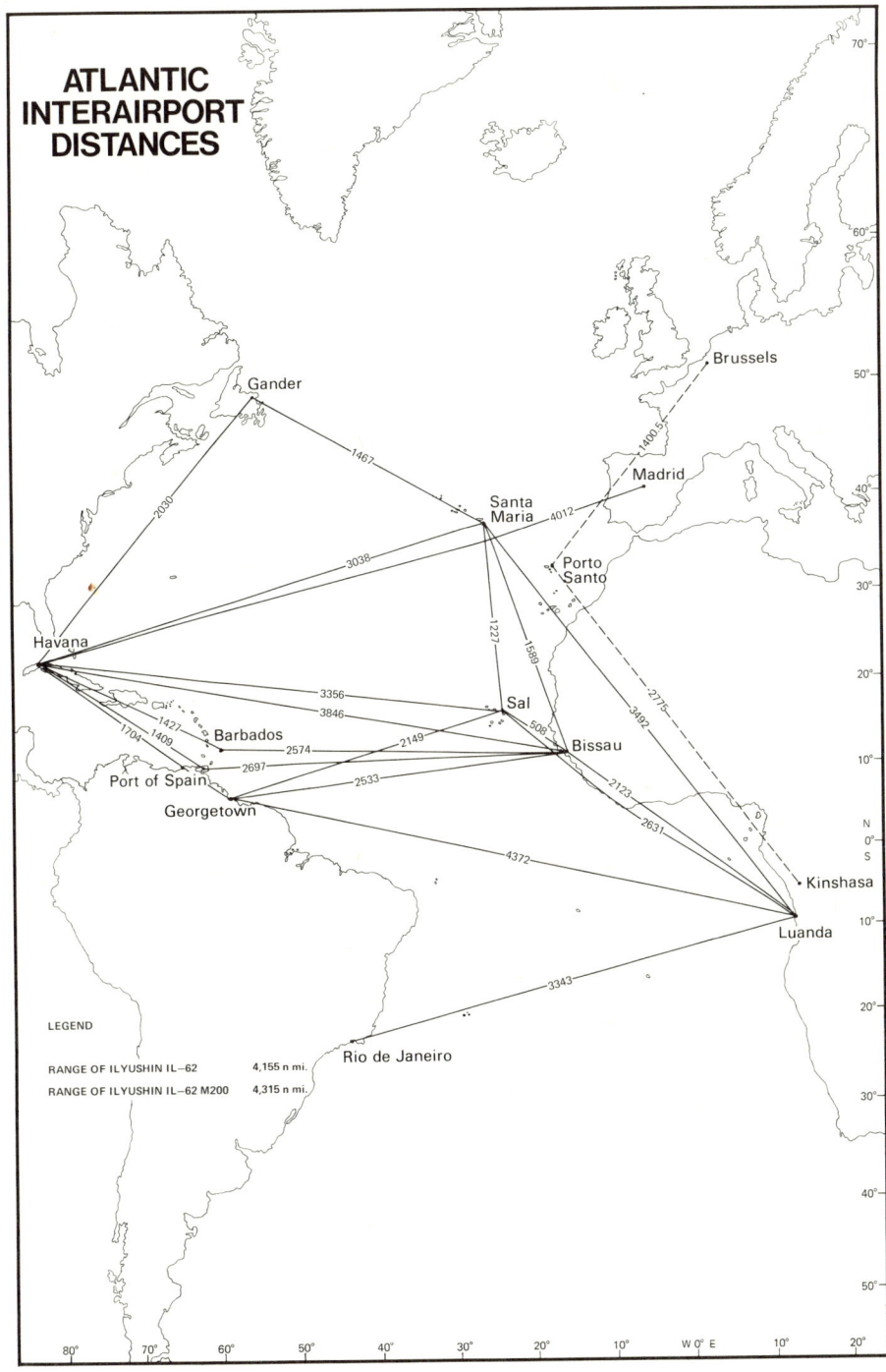

ugees who in turn immigrated into the United States listing Spain as country of last permanent residence. In such a capacity, they would have been in competition with the stretch-DC-8's which Iberia now flies between Havana and Madrid nonstop (IB 942 and 948 eastbound, IB 941 and 947 westbound).

The great-circle distance of 4,012 n mi. between Havana and Madrid represents close to the maximum range of the Russian planes, especially westbound against prevailing winds. Santa Maria has therefore served as an operational stop, for refueling only, with no passengers transferred. For the westbound flights Santa Maria is in fact a scheduled operational stop. Accordingly, Russian pilots have come to know one corner of the Azores, and some Azoreans have partly learned the Russian language from them.

For the airlift to Angola, then, Russian pilots and their aircraft already possessed Portuguese Atlantic Island know-how. On December 31, 1975, *The New York Times* quoted an Angra newspaper as saying that Soviet-built jets were transporting Cuban troops to Angola refueling on Santa Maria and in Guinea-Bissau. Possibly the reference was to flight CU 476.

Rumors about use or attempted use of Santa Maria and even of Gander in Newfoundland were rife at the time. More likely, the IL-62's took the southern route and refueled at friendly Georgetown in independent Guyana (ex-British Guiana). Unable to use any field in the Northeast of anti-Communist Brazil, the pilots still faced another refueling stop, probably Bissau or another friendly field on the West African mainland. If I had been the plane's captain and were under pressure to deliver troops rapidly, I would have opted for a single stop between Havana and Luanda, at the Cape Verdean Sal. This airport, following the 25th of April, was renamed the Amílcar Cabral International Airport in honor of the leader of the Cape Verdean independence movement.

It is of course possible that the airlift was not accomplished by modern Russian jets at all, but rather by antiquated Bristol Britannias, a British four-engined turbo-prop aircraft which seemed spectacular in the 1950's. Of interest is an entry in the International Airline Guide of September 1977: on Sundays, Cubana Airlines' flight CU 490 departs Havana for Barbados, Conakry (Republic of Guinea, ex-French Guinea), Freetown, and Luanda. On

Tuesdays, flight CU 491 leaves Luanda on the reverse route. The plane is a Britannia.

Domestic politics and international business rarely adhere to the same loyalties. Cubana Airlines' new scheduled service through Barbados (independent of Great Britain in 1966) is somewhat ironical. A greater example of politico-commercial realism has recently been furnished by South African Airways. Before the 25th of April, that line flew jets between Johannesburg and London with an operational stop on Sal (but with no passengers embarking or disembarking). It also used to run a jet service between Johannesburg and New York via Rio de Janeiro. Suddenly, it discontinued the Rio-New York portion of the latter service and, beginning in September 1977, placed a sensational ad in Portuguese-language newspapers in the United States. The ad, directed at Americans of Cape Verdean descent and birth, announced a new service, the only direct air service between the United States and South Africa. On Thursdays and Fridays, a Boeing 747 departs Johannesburg for JFK (SA 209 and SA 207), and, on Fridays and Saturdays, departs JFK for the return (SA 210 and SA 208). The planes stop at Sal, Republic of Cape Verde, for one hour in each direction, and do let off and take on passengers!

Today, Cape Verdeans have direct air connections with Lisbon and Bissau via TAP, with New York and Johannesburg via South African Airways, and, yes, with Budapest and Moscow once a week northeastbound via Aeroflot. This latter flight (SU 414, Ilyushin IL-62) originates in Conakry and calls at Dakar before Sal. Azoreans and Madeirans must conclude that independence of Lisbon certainly profited the Cape Verdeans.

The question of the strategic importance of Sal's airport to either West or Soviet bloc is thus still debatable. The Caetano regime had made a strong propaganda pitch to the effect that Sal was vital to the West, a veritable unsinkable aircraft carrier. In that regime's first year as successor to Salazar's, Sal became strategically important for a second reason. The submarine telephone cable known as SAT-1 (South Atlantic Telephone Cable No. 1) went into service linking Portugal with South Africa. Its intermediate terminuses were Tenerife, Sal, and Ascension. The cable, capable of transmitting both telephone conversations and dot-dash telegrams, was of a totally new type. It would be ironic, indeed, if the Republic of Cape Verde were to become a satellite not of left-oriented Guinea-Bissau but of the right-oriented Republic of South Africa.

The onward march of events has now placed yet another airport of Insular Portugal on the pan-Atlantic strategic stage. As will be noted, Porto Santo's field has been international because of its Caracas dimension, a fact of which I was aware when I visited the minor Madeiran island in June 1978 (my second visit, the first having taken place nearly forty years earlier). But I was not prepared for what I suddenly learned.

With a single runway 8,005 feet in length in low and flat territory, the field is in fact a NATO emergency base. I was told that NATO had subsidized construction of the runway, parking ramp, and extensive plane-refueling facilities, although the entire airport is Portuguese. I was further informed that Porto Santo was used in the sudden airlift from Northwest Europe to Zaire in May 1978, and transport planes of at least one NATO nation were continuing to use it. After all, if such a nation wished to accomplish a military mission to Africa-South-of-the-Sahara without overflying possibly hostile African territory or refueling at a supposedly unsympathetic airport, what better place to call in at than Porto Santo?

Airport's single runway, Porto Santo, June 1978

11

VOICES FROM DEEP DOWN AND HIGH UP

The visitor to the Transatlantic Cable Terminal operated by AT&T Long Lines under the symbol of the Bell System in Green Hill, Rhode Island (on Shannock Road in the Town of South Kingstown just north of Route 1 west of Perryville) is at once struck by a sense of double cooperation.

The Terminal, the only one of its kind in New England, houses the U.S. end of TAT-5 (Transatlantic Telephone Cable No. 5), a coaxial submarine cable in which AT&T Long Lines has a controlling interest. TAT-5 began operation in 1970. It consists of 845 voice-grade circuits, that is, is capable of transmitting 845 telephone conversations simultaneously. As each such circuit can handle some twenty-two telegraph or telex or other low-speed data-transmitting circuits which make a printed record at the receiving end, the total capacity is 22×845 or 18,590 circuits, in the hypothetical case of their full utilization for telegraph channels. This capacity contrasts with the ten circuits of old 2 HO (Horta-Bay Roberts).

TAT-5 extends for 3,650 n mi. south of the Azores to Conil on Spain's southwestern Atlantic coast between Cádiz (and the nearby U.S. Polaris submarine base in Rota) and the Strait of Gibraltar. It is designed to place the United States in direct voice and record communication primarily with Spain, Portugal, and Italy, earlier and more northerly telephone cables having linked America and Northern Europe beginning in 1956. Microwave radio circuits connect Conil with Sesimbra just south of Lisbon and with Estepona on Spain's southern coast between Gibraltar and Málaga. From Estepona, another cable, MAT-1, covers the thousand miles to Palo outside Rome. At the Green Hill end, TAT-5 is connected by both microwave radio and buried coaxial cable to major U.S. communications centers.

TAT-5 is not as vulnerable as the telegraph cables of old to the disrupting activities of New England fishermen. Off Rhode Island the shore end is buried for 94 n mi., up to a depth of three hundred fathoms. The Green Hill Terminal itself is deep underground and is protected from all natural and most man-made disasters. About a dozen staff personnel are on duty there. The facilities are spacious and also accommodate the 4,000-voice-grade-circuit TAT-6 laid in 1976 for a distance of 3,402 n mi. to St. Hilaire de Riez on the west coast of France between St. Nazaire and La Rochelle.

On the one hand, the four-way international cooperation represented by TAT-5 is immediately evident at Green Hill. The U.S., Spanish, Portuguese, and Italian flags are prominently displayed, as are maps and photographs. A brochure has the four flags in color on its cover, and its text is in the four languages.

On the other hand, the inter-company cooperation which makes of TAT-5 a viable business item is likewise evident in the prominent listing of the several owners:

> Compañía Telefónica Nacional de España,
> Companhia Portuguesa Rádio Marconi,
> Italcable Servizi Cablografici, Radiotelegrafici e Radioelettrici, S.p.A.,
> American Telephone and Telegraph Company,
> ITT World Communications, Inc.,
> RCA Global Communications, Inc.,
> Western Union International, Inc.

Portugal comes off particularly well in the publicity because of an endearing cultural trait which extends not only to architects but even to engineers. The Portuguese are understandably reluctant to give up their traditions in the wake of advancing technology. Whereas the Americans dot their landscape with small dish-type microwave antennas mounted on modern-type towers, the Portuguese incorporated their antennas wherever possible rather unobtrusively on old and modernized windmills. They did so in order to prevent destruction of the mills and also to avoid a change in the nature of the landscape. The microwave connection between Conil and Sesimbra consists of eight repeaters. Those in windmills are in Palmela and in Santana, the latter above

Sesimbra. And of course every early spring the Companhia Portuguesa Rádio Marconi celebrates, or used to celebrate, the feast of the archangel St. Gabriel, patron saint of telecommunications (March 24).

In fine, the Green Hill Terminal is an installation of which any Portuguese, or American of Portuguese descent, can truly be proud. It is in part his. Ironically, it lies only 2.5 n mi. as the crow navigates from Fort Ninigret (in Charlestown just south of Route 1). I discuss this allegedly Portuguese fort in my chapter on culture heroes in the companion volume. When in the Green Hill area, I prefer to worship at the coaxial shrine.

TAT-5 passes south of the Azores but does not call in there. As indicated on the telephone-cable map, SAT-1 (360 channels, laid in 1968) omits St. Helena and stops at Santa Cruz on the Spanish Tenerife rather than at Funchal on the Portuguese Madeira. It continues to the attractive and spacious CPRM station in Sesimbra, whence in 1969 a regional cable was laid to Goonhilly Downs (Cornwall, England). CPRM has an interest in both these cables as well as in TAT-5 and TAT-6.

The new BRACAN-1 (160 channels, laid in 1972 between Recife and Agüimes on Gran Canaria) omits the Cape Verde Islands and terminates at the other Canarian isle, which is linked to Conil as Tenerife is linked to San Fernando (between Cádiz and Conil). (The commencement of BRACAN-1's operations explains C & W's closing out of its telegraph cables to Brazil in the spring of 1973.)

The very new and felicitously named "Columbus" extends for a distance of 3,240 n mi. from Agüimes on Gran Canaria direct to Camuri in Venezuela, thence to serve the capital city of Caracas and other places. Consisting of 1,840 channels and opened to service in 1977, it was inaugurated on—naturally—October 12. My colleague Professor Juan Marichal, of Canarian birth who was on Gran Canaria at the time, tells me that the ceremonies there were attended by none other than the King of Spain himself, accompanied by the President of Mexico. The cable should prove a boon to the many Canarians in Venezuela. It may well be utilized also by the Madeirans there, via PENCAN-2 (and in the near future by a PENCAN-3 of 5,520 channels from the Canaries to San Fernando), microwave radio to Sesimbra, and CAM-1 to Porto Novo. Its name recalls Columbus's third voyage, from the

Canaries to Trinidad off the coast of Little Venice. Admiral Columbus, however, did stop off, en route, in the Cape Verde Islands. Cable Columbus does not.

Two questions are posed. Why do the international telephone cables fail to utilize strategically located Portuguese Atlantic islands, with the single exception of SAT-1, which calls in at Sal? Why, when they do go ashore, do they concentrate on the Spanish Canaries and go into southwestern Atlantic Spain?

The basic answer to the first question is technical. It involves the enormous range of the new cables, which incorporate amplifying "repeaters" at regular intervals. Thus, TAT-5 has 361 rigid transistorized repeaters spaced ten n mi. apart. The cables could extend almost indefinitely were it not for the power needed to supply the repeaters. The intermediate shore stations are thus not relay stations as were the telegraph stations of yesteryear but rather sources of power for the repeaters. As the supplying of this power is largely automatic, the number of employees needed is very small indeed in comparison with the large staffs of the pre-regenerator telegraph cables.

If business warrants so doing, one or more groups of voice-grade circuits or channels—sixteen to a group—may be dropped off at the island, as for instance happens on Sal from SAT-1.

Tourist-heavy Madeira with its spectacular terrain and curious straw huts employed to house the cows need not worry that no international telephone cable passes through it. That island is served by its own cable, CAM-1, 120 channels, laid for CPRM in 1972 at a cost of nearly 150,000 contos ($5,555,556 in that year). Madeira is the only Portuguese adjacent island so served. As a result of CAM-1, a person in the United States can direct-dial, toll free, the Sheraton Hotel reservation center (part of the "Worldwide Service of ITT") and immediately reserve space in a magnificent hotel on Madeira, the Madeira-Sheraton. He used to be able to do so in two other hotels, before the Madeira Hilton became the Madeira Palace and the Holiday Inn the Atlantis. He can also telephone directly to Continental Portugal, or, via CPRM's Sesimbra terminal, over CAM-1 to Madeira or over SAT-1 to Sal. For one's voice to continue from Continental Portugal to the Azores, however, the old radio telephone, until December 18, 1977, had to be utilized, from the mainland to CPRM's radio station outside Ponta Delgada, thence via the Post Office's microwave relays to other islands.

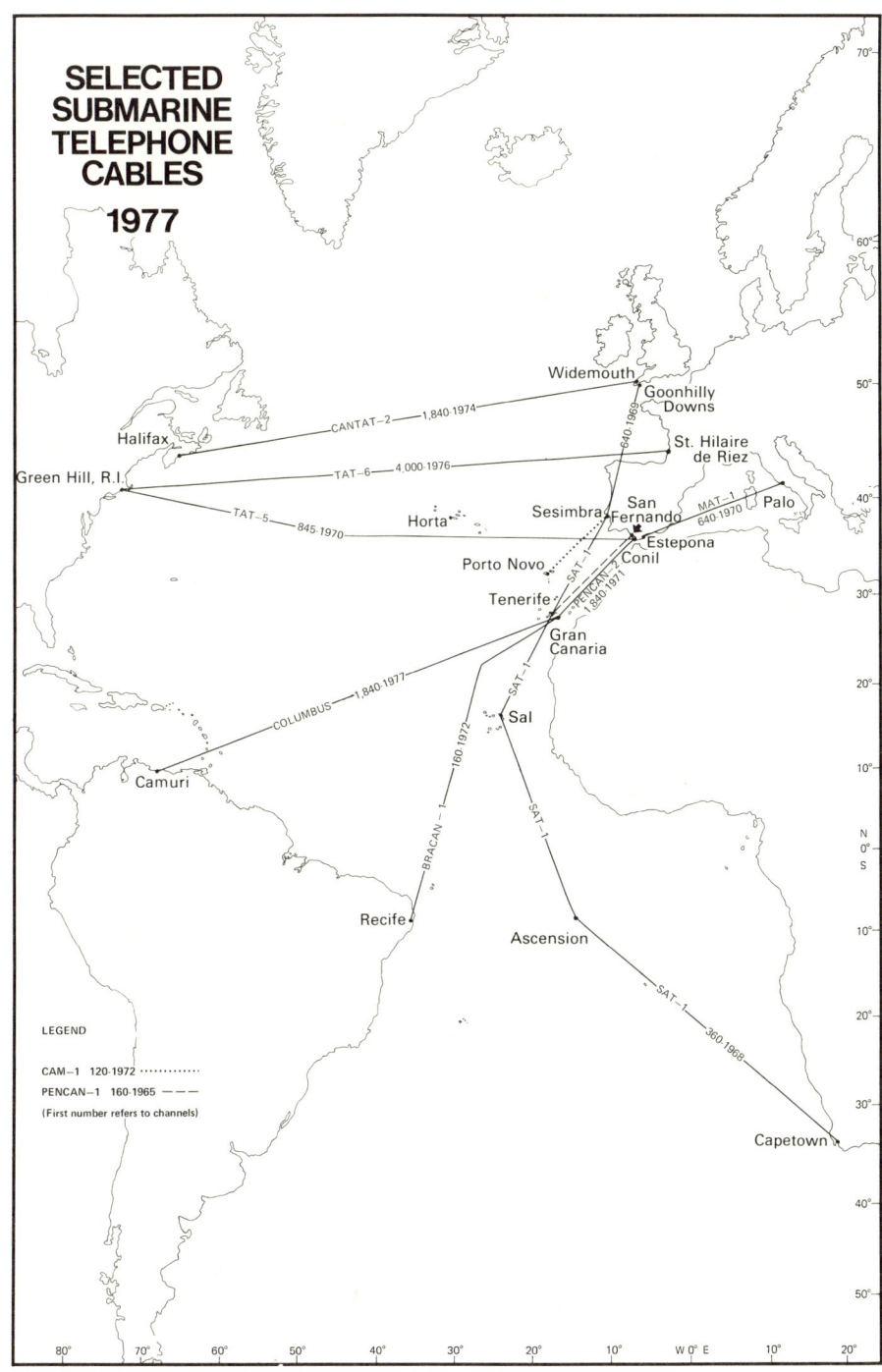

Tourist-heavy Madeira—spectacular terrain and products

The answer to the second question is more complicated, subtle, and risky for an outsider such as myself to formulate. It is deferred until the end of the following section. In a preliminary way it may be stated that back in 1929, long before Francisco Franco's regime or NASA, experiments with telephone cables had been carried out by an ITT affiliate in Canarian waters. Technical attention was already directed to the Islas Canarias.

☆ ☆ ☆

The Russians launched Sputnik in 1957. Among other things this event precipitated a widespread educational revolution in the United States which greatly increased the teaching of the Portuguese language. In 1958, the National Aeronautics and Space Administration (NASA) was activated, and soon satellite tracking stations were spotted around the globe, including one on Gran Canaria. None was placed on Portuguese territory.

From tracking a NASA satellite to communicating with or via a special communications satellite proved a logical next step. On July 10, 1962, Telstar I was launched, the world's first active communications satellite. On August 31 of that year, President Kennedy signed the Communications Satellite Act (Public Law 87-624). A space-age development was transformed into a huge business enterprise marked by a new type of government/business collaboration.

The current model of communications satellite moves in a so-called synchronous orbit some 22,300 statute miles above the earth's equator. Its speed is so adjusted that the satellite keeps pace with the earth's rotation and therefore appears fixed. The satellite receives microwave signals transmitted to it in the six-gigahertz range (six billion cycles per second) by a huge dish-type antenna at a station on earth on one side of the ocean. The satellite amplifies the signals and retransmits them in the four-gigahertz range to an earth station on the other side of the ocean—or even on the same side or on an island—in a position to receive them. A particular antenna points to only one of the several satellites in operation and actually tracks it in its minor wandering through space.

The earth station of the global system nearest to the Portuguese communities in the northeastern United States is the Andover station, located well northwest of Lisbon, closer to Peru, just northwest of Mexico, and somewhat north of Norway and Paris, all within the State of Maine. It is the oldest U.S. station, first used commercially in 1965 for service via the satellite known as Early Bird, which began live TV transmission across the Atlantic. It is a far more spectacular installation to visit than Green Hill. On the other hand, it is exclusively American, as a large sign at the entrance to the grounds makes clear. It is owned jointly by COMSAT, AT&T, RCA Globcom, ITT Worldcom, and WUI. It, like other earth stations and the terminal stations of the submarine telephone cables, is linked via land cable or microwave radio relay to major traffic centers. The other east-coast earth station of the continental United States is at Etam, West Virginia.

The communications satellite system has grown to constitute a formidable rival to the telephone cables. A total of 191 antennas on 154 earth stations in 86 countries were operational at the end of October 1977. They were owned and operated by designated telecommunications entities of the countries in which located, for example CPRM in Portuguese territory. The one on Gran Canaria is located at Agüimes, in the southeastern section of the island, where BRACAN-1's and Columbus's terminals are situated. It is to be distinguished from the NASA tracking station at Maspalomas, at the southern tip. Similarly, C & W's earth station on Ascension is to be differentiated from the NASA tracking station on that South Atlantic island. Indeed, the earth station was built in 1967 specifically to support the Apollo program. Once SAT-1 went into operation, NASA also used it for communication to Sesimbra, thence to its Madrid switching center.

Satellites are positioned above Atlantic, Pacific, and Indian Oceans. The advanced model satellite now in service above the Atlantic, at longitude 24°5 W, became operational on February 1, 1976. Known as the INTELSAT IV-A, this model has an average capacity of 6,250 two-way voice-grade circuits plus two TV channels. A more advanced model, INTELSAT V, is scheduled for launch in 1979.

A specific hookup is called a satellite pathway; see the satellite map. Such a pathway might be Etam-Atlantic satellite-Gran Canaria and could be likened to a supercable in space. As of October 1977, there were about 544 such pathways, 80% of their combined use being for telephone traffic, about 18% for record, data, and facsimile services, and slightly less than 3% for TV.

The communications satellites themselves are owned by an international consortium known as the International Telecommunications Satellite Organization (INTELSAT), formed in Washington, D.C., on August 20, 1964, as a result of Resolution 1721 (XVI) of the U.N. General Assembly. They are launched for INTELSAT by NASA at Cape Canaveral on a cost-reimbursable basis. The U.S. signatory within INTELSAT is the Communications Satellite Corporation (COMSAT), incorporated in 1963 as a result of the previous year's law. The Portuguese signatory is CPRM. INTELSAT shares many of the features of the United Nations, with a Director General and with headquarters in the United States, in Washington, D.C. The Board of Governors numbers 26 members. Portugal and Brazil are jointly represented on it by one Governor, who is appointed at the present time by Brazil, for the South American country holds a larger investment share in INTELSAT. One alternate Governor is appointed by Portugal. Thus, a citizen of the former colony represents the mother country, an arrangement which pre-Revolutionary Por-

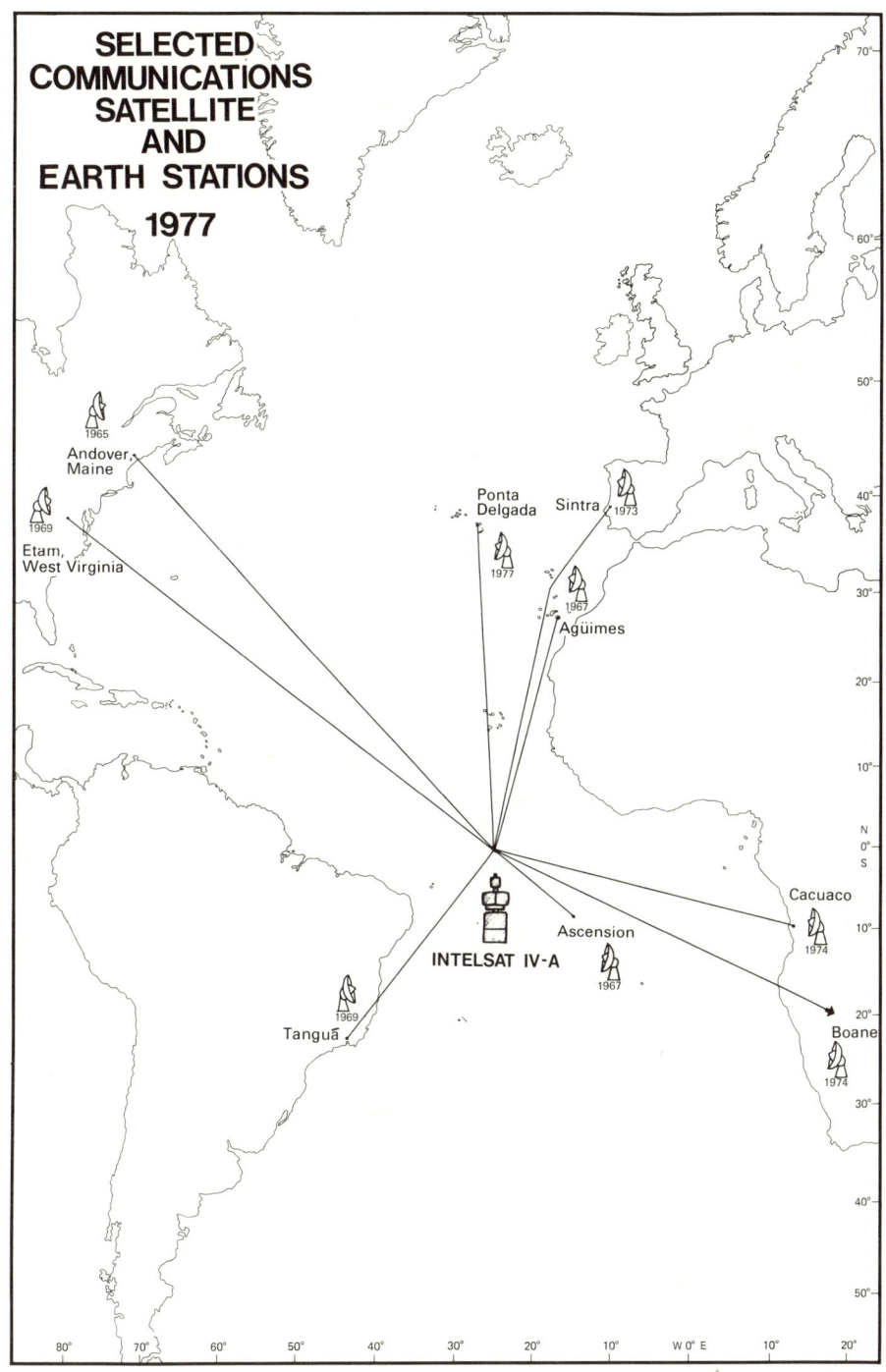

tugal found eminently satisfactory. Indeed, in anticipation of full-scale operation of its earth stations outside of Lisbon, Luanda, and Lourenço Marques respectively, that Portugal was fond of calling attention to the uniqueness of this joint representation of two countries with earth stations on three continents.

INTELSAT receives income by charging the various national agencies like COMSAT and CPRM for use of its circuits. In the case of the United States, COMSAT, being a "carriers' carrier," in turn charges its users for the circuits they employ. The principal U.S. users, or "carriers," are the single international voice carrier (AT&T Long Lines) and three international record carriers (ITT Worldcom, RCA Globcom, and WUI).

☆

In 1972, CPRM let a contract with ITT Space Communications, Inc., of New York for the construction of three earth stations.

The Sintra station, near Lisbon and originally known as "Continente," entered service in mid-1974. Once it became operational, telephone conversations and telegrams could be transmitted between the United States and Continental Portugal via either cable or satellite using exclusively Portuguese facilities at the European end. Even before its own earth stations were ready for service, however, CPRM had availed itself of the satellites by routing its traffic through Spanish and Italian stations.

The American customer has no choice as to type of service (cable or satellite), for the traffic is distributed automatically in such a way as to give each system what is presumably its fair share of the load. In the case of record traffic, the American customer does have a say. He may, if he chooses, specify that his message be sent via ITT Worldcom, RCA Globcom, or WUI. The Western Union Telegraph Co., which he telephones from his home or office to start a message on its way, incidentally, has no corporate relationship to Western Union International, which is today an independent company.

In mid-1974, also, CPRM put into service its other two earth stations, at Cacuaco near Luanda in Angola and at Boane near Lourenço Marques (today Maputo) in Mozambique. Boane continues to belong to and be operated by CPRM as a telecommunications entity officially appointed by the government of Mozambique. This country has not joined INTELSAT. Angola, on the other hand, has joined the international body. Angola's new government has nationalized the Cacuaco earth station, whose operation, however, continues to be carried out with the cooperation of CPRM technicians.

In similar fashion, Mozambique and Angola each now has its own international airline, respectively DETA (code TM) and TAAG (code DT). The former has a weekly DC-8 flight to Lisbon, the latter two 707 flights. Would that Salazar had seen the light in 1950! He would have avoided a quarter-century of international friction and aggravation plus three extended colonial wars. Portugal would have ended up no worse—perhaps much better—than it is today.

Cuba, by the way, has no earth station functioning within the INTELSAT system. At the end of 1977, though, the U.S. press reported that the Soviet Union had installed "eavesdropping antennas" in that country to intercept messages between the Andover and Etam earth stations and the respective satellite.

Had the 25th of April and the end of the wars in Africa not come about, Portugal would have had its own internal or "domestic" communications satellite network between the Metropolis and the two principal African provinces, one involving an international satellite. Pre-Revolutionary publicity stressed the domestic nature with phrases like "Lisboa-Luanda-Lourenço Marques" (the three L's) and "a Metrópole e o Ultramar." The entire development demonstrated how deep and ongoing was Caetano Portugal's commitment to its overseas provinces in Africa in spite of objections voiced nearly all over the globe and particularly in the United Nations.

When the Azores earth station, known as "Ponta Delgada," became operational on December 18, 1977, Portugal came to have a true domestic network, for legally and from INTELSAT's point of view the Azores, like the Madeiras, are within Portugal and therefore within the Country Code of Portugal. The Portuguese domestic satellite pathway is Sintra-Atlantic satellite-Ponta Delgada.

What a particular member nation of INTELSAT does with its earth stations and satellite pathways is strictly its private affair. After all, it does own its earth stations and does participate in the ownership of the satellites. All that is required is that it pay INTELSAT charges, use the frequencies assigned to it, and maintain certain technical standards with its earth stations. Thus, France maintains circuits to its Martinique, including daily TV broadcasts.

A perspicacious *citoyen du monde* can discern a rich potential for abuse in the direction of propagandizing nationals residing in foreign countries and possibly their descendants. Once technology succeeds in making of one's home TV set a miniature earth station capable of receiving broadcasts direct from a satellite—in the way that short-wave radio receivers in the home capture transmissions broadcast from a different country thousands of miles away—without the intervention of a genuine earth station nationally supervised by the host country, world living may change radically in nature.

Just such a possibility became reality on May 30, 1974, when NASA placed an Applications Technology Satellite in synchronous orbit above the Galápagos Islands in the eastern Pacific. For its first year of operation, it was to beam televised health and training programs to rural areas of the United States. It was then to be moved into stationary orbit over Kenya in eastern Africa, when the Government of India was to use it for a year to transmit educational, medical, and agricultural programs to its own population. For this purpose, India was to place in schools and town halls TV sets which are specially equipped to receive signals beamed directly to them from this very special satellite. Among the programs to be transmitted, family planning was included. *The New York Times* wisely sounded a cautionary editorial note:

> Opening the skies domestically and internationally for such idealistic and practical goals can lead to a better and healthier life, without artificial boundaries and communications roadblocks. At the same time, the technology of almost instantaneous communications raises cautionary flags. Since governments are fundamentally involved in satellites, there must be assurances here and elsewhere that regulatory agencies and international agreements build public purposes into programming and communications.
>
> Private as well as public access is needed to insure a multiplicity of voices beyond the parochial sounds of governments. The new educational satellite marks the main direction that must be followed if open skies are to mean ceiling unlimited for the human adventure.

Within the year, a broad coalition of Communist and third-world states in the United Nations were pressing for limitations on the use of direct TV broadcasting. A U.S. representative was arguing for more rather than less.

On July 12, 1977, Mrs. Rogers and I visited the site of the Ponta Delgada earth station, climbed all over the units under construction, and watched the highly skilled workers putting together what will certainly prove to be a great tourist attraction, as Andover has been for years in the summer months. We were taken there by two specialized CPRM engineers, one originally from Funchal (Engineer José Graciano Mendes de Góis, the Station Manager), the other a Lisbonese, and we were allowed to take photographs. The site is Charco da Madeira, just northeast of Ponta Delgada and above Fajã de Cima. The earth station including the antenna is Portuguese-made and Portuguese-built, except for the electronic equipment, delivery and assembly of which was done by the Japanese firm of Mitsubishi. Its total cost approached 200,000 contos ($5,200,000 in 1977's dollars). Once the earth station became operational, CPRM's short-wave radio installations on São Miguel passed to a standby status to keep the license alive and to serve in emergencies.

By the end of 1977, then, a telephone conversation originating in an American home of Azorean background in, say, Fall River passed to Green Hill, thence via cable TAT-5 to Conil, microwave relay to Sesimbra, and a combination of cable and microwave relay to Sintra. From Sintra the conversation traveled via the domestic satellite pathway to São Miguel. From the Azorean earth station it moved via microwave relay to CPRM's new satellite terminal building within the city of Ponta Delgada, at the corner of Rua Manoel da Ponte and Rua Machado dos Santos. From this center it entered the Post Office's network of domestic communications and continued by microwave relay to the Azores island of destination.

Conversations from Azoreans in Brazil and Canada and from the thirty-three Azoreans who emigrated to South Africa over the years 1965-1975 also converged on Sintra, coming in over other recently laid transatlantic telephone cables. These cables are Brazil-Canary Islands No. 1 (BRACAN-1), which ties into Peninsula-Canaries No. 2 (PENCAN-2, 1,840 voice-grade circuits) laid the year before to Conil; Canada Transatlantic Telephone No. 2 (CANTAT-2, 1,840 voice-grade circuits), put down in 1974 between Halifax, Nova Scotia, and a site in Cornwall near the terminus of the cable from Sesimbra; and SAT-1. Telephone calls and written telegrams destined for the Azores thus crossed the Atlantic Ocean by cable so as to avoid two round trips to the Atlantic satellite and the resulting diminution in the quality of transmission.

Technically, it would be possible, if Electronic Switching System (ESS) equipment were installed at all points, to direct-dial a station-to-station call from, say, Fall River to a private number in the Azores. Continental Portugal is served by International Direct Dialing from certain exchanges in the United States as well as from other countries. It has its Country Code (351) and, within its borders, its City Routing Codes, what Americans would call "area codes" (for example, Coimbra 39, Lisbon 19, Oporto 29). Thus, to direct dial the Casa dos Açores (House of the Azores) in Lisbon, one proceeds as follows: 011 (International Access Code) plus 351 (Country Code of Portugal) plus 19 (City Routing Code of Lisbon) plus 66 60 35 (Phone No.).

As of this writing (May 20, 1978) International Direct Dialing is not available from the United States either to the Azores or to the Madeiras. Funchal does have its City Routing Code (10), but the U.S. international operator has to do the dialing. To get the Azores the U.S. operator must ask the Lisbon operator for a circuit. The point is that the Azores and Madeiras continue to be integral parts of Portugal. To call them one must pass through the international communications centers located in the Lisbon area.

On the other hand, the International Direct Dialing capability is not yet widespread in the United States. Downtown Boston exchanges do have this capability, as do several in Cambridge, New Bedford, and Fall River.

The Ponta Delgada earth station, if the necessary arrangements were made, could function as the eastern terminal of a direct and, viewed superficially, a much more logical pathway Andover-Atlantic satellite-Ponta Delgada. Actually, and leaving political considerations aside, there may not be enough traffic between the United States and the Azores to justify the rental of the circuit or circuits required to constitute such a pathway. The merging at Sintra of traffic via cables from Canada, the United States, and Brazil with the more intense traffic originating within Continental Portugal and elsewhere in Europe does constitute sufficient volume to justify economically the new Portuguese earth station.

The Ponta Delgada earth station has the capability of receiving live TV programs, even in color (but only to the station itself, since Portugal as a whole does not yet have color TV). The determining factor is apparently cost. The cost to CPRM of renting the necessary TV channel from INTELSAT in order for the Azores to receive TV programs direct (as distinguished from the present airmailing of videotapes from Lisbon to Madeira and Azores for local TV stations) is reported to be high. Perhaps the best that can be hoped for at the present time is the occasional transmission of a very special **TV program such as Olympic Games or Benfica vs.** Sporting via a channel rented on a short-term basis.

The TV advantage possessed by the Azores is perhaps balanced by one possessed by the Madeiras. During our January 1973 visit to Funchal, we observed that Madeirans listened to TV programs from the Canary Islands; they gave the impression of doing so clandestinely, as if Portugal's authoritarian regime did not wish them to receive uncontrolled entertainment. And at that time, Funchal's newspaper *Diário de Notícias* listed only the TV programs of the local Portuguese station. In June 1975, however, we noted that the same Madeiran daily also listed the more extensive Canarian programs.

Be that as it may, at the end of 1977 the Azores were suddenly provided with telecommunications service not equal to that provided the Madeiras and the Cape Verde Islands but with more possibilities, involving greater circuit capacity and a TV capability. December 18, 1977, will long be remembered in the annals of the Azores.

☆

A partial answer to the second question raised at the end of the section on telephone cables may now be hazarded. These cables and the earth stations tie the Canary Islands and southwestern Spain (the strategically sensitive Cádiz area) into the vast U.S. military-industrial-space complex. They involve the many space programs. They involve U.S. use of naval and air bases in Spain outside the framework of NATO, to which that country has not yet been admitted. Apart from geographical considerations, they have developed in the face of a possible double reluctance on the part of Americans to use Portuguese islands, and this in spite of U.S. advantage taken of the Portuguese air base at Lajes on the

Azorean Terceira and guarded U.S. cooperation with Portugal via NATO.

Commercial carriers may have been reluctant to become involved any more than necessary with Lisbon in view of its reputation for taking advantage of its own Atlantic islands. The reputation goes back to the sixteenth century, as has been noted. In the Azores, the Bensaúde interests have enjoyed widespread fame for high prices. A book on the five so-called disgraceful features of the Azores (*As Cinco Desgraças do Arquipélago dos Açores*) used to circulate semi-clandestinely in Salazar-Caetano days within the archipelago. It singles out as disgraceful the Bensaúde shipping line (which ran the *Carvalho Araujo*), the port of Ponta Delgada, and the firm of Bensaúde & Co. Ltd. Written first in newspaper-article form in 1958 and brought out as a book at the end of 1961, it was authored by a São Miguel businessman in a position to know, and it stressed overcharging. Indeed, it went so far as to affirm that, after World War I ended, the U.S. Shipping Board sent radio messages to its ships prohibiting them from stopping at Azorean ports. We have already seen how the New Bedford whaleship owners shifted their rendezvous port from Horta to Las Palmas because of the increasingly higher port charges imposed by officials of the first years of the Portuguese Republic.

Reference has also been made to the transit fee of one cent a word assessed the Commercial Cable Co. by the Portuguese government when it began through service in 1900-1901. As the rate per word to the customer must have been around 25 cents at the time, that fee was considerable, all the more as the Portuguese contributed nothing to the cable but the island itself. (The Arab nations do supply the oil.) Another transit tax deemed extremely high was the landing fee charged foreign airplanes touching down on the commerical airport on Santa Maria. Said at one time to have been U.S. $270, it had to be paid by cash on the barrelhead, I was told, except in the cases of PAA and TWA, which had charge accounts. At a later date, namely in 1974, the Santa Maria landing fee for a Boeing 707 came to $290, plus a $1.93 per-passenger-charge paid by the airline, and it has never been clear to me what fraction of the fee went to local government. The Lisbon landing fee was $233.60, plus the same passenger charge. Bermuda's was a $172.50 fee, plus a $3.00 per-passenger-charge paid by the passenger. The landing fee in Keflavik (Iceland) was $319.50 total.

In addition to this reluctance resulting from the virtually colonial status of Azores and Madeiras over the centuries, a second braking force operating on U.S. companies and on the U.S. government stemmed from Portugal's reputation on the international political stage—deserved or undeserved—beginning in 1961.

Henrique Galvão, a Portuguese political showman who was active in the opposition to Salazar, seized the Portuguese luxury liner *Santa Maria* in the Caribbean in the wee hours of Sunday, January 22, 1961. His purpose was to call the world's attention to the nature of Salazar's rule, and in this he succeeded admirably. And the moment of his hit was aptly chosen: only one day following John Fitzgerald Kennedy's inaugural ball.

Portugal thus received adverse publicity from literally the very beginning of the Kennedy administration. Within two months it faced revolt—or "terrorist activity"—in Angola, and on December 18 of the same year lost Goa and the other territories of its State of India. In spite of the obvious correctness of U.S. official position, which centered on the doctrine of selfdetermination, the Portuguese felt that Kennedy was hostile to them. Certainly a large segment of U.S. liberal public opinion was just that, and it continued to be, expanded by the addition of U.S. black opinion.

The submarine telephone cables and the related communications satellite system were creations primarily of the Kennedy-Johnson years. In the United States those were anti-Portuguese years, and American corporations closely allied with the government and official Federal agencies would understandably have trod carefully.

At that time, the Azores seemed to have been left out of it all. They were not, however, forgotten.

TAT-1 and TAT-2 went into Newfoundland, from Scotland and France respectively. The first telephone cable to connect Europe directly with the United States was TAT-3, 178 channels, laid in October 1963 between Widemouth (Cornwall) and Tuckerton (New Jersey). In that same month, AT&T asked the Federal Communications Commission (FCC, created by the Communications Act of 1934) for permission to run a fourth transatlantic telephone cable, this one between France and the United States. The request was granted, and TAT-4, 138 channels, was laid in 1965 between St. Hilaire de Riez and Tuckerton.

In its Memorandum Opinion and Order dated March 17, 1964,

and released the next day, the FCC answered a number of applications and a petition, including AT&T's request for TAT-4. It granted the latter request on the basis that there would be a need by the summer of 1965 for additional service to northern and central European points, a need to which France and Germany also agreed. But before doing so, it had to consider a double proposal submitted by an ITT subsidiary: (1) that this company lay a direct cable from Massachusetts to France, or (2) that it lay a cable from New Jersey to France via the Azores, with an extension from the Azores to Portugal. The proponent stated that it had discussed the matter with the "Portuguese Administration" among others and conceded that its first proposal could not be realized before 1966 whereas its second could meet the target date of the summer of 1965.

The FCC thus had to face squarely the issue of the Azores at the very moment when the French were preparing to set up their installation on Flores, assuming the FCC knew about it. Neither the Department of Defense nor the Department of State entered any objection against either the AT&T or the ITT proposal, but DOD significantly did make clear that it had ample broadband transatlantic channels to meet its current requirement (obviously radio channels). FCC arrived at its decision on the grounds that AT&T's planning was at a more advanced stage than ITT's and that France and Germany had not at that time expressed a desire to participate in another cable through another country, namely Portugal's Azores, parallel to TAT-3's service via the United Kingdom.

Insular Portugal emerged into the modern age of telecommunications only after the advent of the Nixon administration and its apparent policy of sympathy toward ITT. A dramatic example at the highest level was the Nixon-Caetano meeting on Terceira on December 13, 1971, as part of the Nixon-Pompidou meeting. A few days earlier, on December 9, in Brussels, the U.S. Secretary of State and the Portuguese Minister of Foreign Affairs had exchanged notes which extended the arrangement permitting the rentfree peacetime stationing of U.S. forces at Lajes and which assured Portugal of U.S. economic assistance, particularly in the long-awaited strengthening of the educational system in Continental and Insular Portugal.

At precisely this moment, Sheraton hotels were being constructed in Lisbon and on Madeira, the one in the capital in a particularly prominent location. Hitherto, both places had prided themselves on their genuinely Portuguese hotels, so attractive to foreigners. The American tourist, however, was now being aggressively sought after, in part under the auspices of ITT, for The Sheraton Corporation was, and is, a wholly-owned subsidiary of that international conglomerate.

The added commercial possibilities on the Pearl of the Atlantic, as Madeira is known, attracted cable CAM-1, wholly owned by the Portuguese and significantly, and in accordance with the multisecular tradition, manufactured and laid by the British (Standard Telephones and Cables Limited, a "British Company of ITT"), as were SAT-1 and its extension to England, BRACAN-1, Columbus, and the intra-Spanish PENCANs. The telephone cable to Madeira comes in at Porto Novo, in the precinct of Gaula, municipality of Santa Cruz, just below the airport. The landing place is thus very near the imposing ex-Holiday Inn.

It is possible that the Portuguese did not desire the proposed entrée into their Azorean archipelago of ITT back in the summer of 1965. It is true, however, that in early 1973 some Azoreans seemed excited by a new ITT proposal to engage in the meatpacking business there. With frozen beef, they may well have reasoned, might come other trappings of late-twentieth-century living including coaxial cable, perchance an earth station with associated TV, maybe an Azores Sheraton Hotel, and just possibly an honest-to-goodness university.

Out of all this complicated interlocking of nations and corporations, one fact became very clear in October 1973 during the Seventeen Day War: it was Portugal and its air base on the Azorean Terceira which stood by the Nixon administration's policy concerning the proper way of achieving peace in the Eastern Mediterranean. At that critical moment, Spain, in spite of its military, industrial, and spatial links with the United States, chose not to go along.

☆ ☆ ☆

A number of modern electronic installations, in addition to cables and wireless, take advantage of island locations. Those in Portuguese archipelagoes, however, are limited almost exclusively to the Azores.

Loran (for LOng RAnge Navigation) is purely pacific and is

widely used by ships and planes within range. Old-fashioned Loran-A, now being phased out, is the particular system installed on Continental and Insular Portuguese territory. It involves receiving transmissions from the two stations of a pair (a master and a slave) in order for a marine or air navigator to establish a line of position. Reception from two pairs enables him to fix a position.

The three Portuguese pairs consist of four different installations: one each on Flores and Santa Maria in the Azores, one on Porto Santo in the Madeiras, and one in Sagres in Continental Portugal. The station on Santa Maria is a double master, for it is coupled with two slaves (Flores and Porto Santo), whereas Sagres is a single master, coupled only with Porto Santo. Porto Santo is thus a double slave and Flores a single slave. The pairs have the following designations, well known to navigators of many nations:

1S5 Sagres (master), Porto Santo (slave);
1S6 Santa Maria (master), Porto Santo (slave);
1S7 Santa Maria (master), Flores (slave).

The loran station on Flores is at the southeastern corner of the island. Still on the east coast toward the northern end, next to the town of Santa Cruz, is the new French compound.

In early 1964, Portugal conceded the rights for this installation. They were not totally clarified in the Portuguese press at the time and were of a mysterious nature even, it seemed, to some portions of Lisbon's U.S. Embassy. In fact, they involved a missile-tracking station.

France had constructed an experimental guided missile center in Les Landes in southwest France south of Bordeaux. In conjunction with it France needed a land-based tracking station. Spain, so the story goes (and I was told it by a seemingly knowledgeable priest in the Azores), refused to permit such French activity on its soil. Salazar let the French use Flores because, when the war broke out in Angola, Portugal had no troops trained in guerrilla warfare and asked De Gaulle for some and he sent them at once.

The French have built an airport near Santa Cruz and a road to their site. They have a hotel and restaurant and also a hospital with French doctor. They have also built a residential compound of recreation building, sports field, duplex houses, and, for bachelors, a trailer park. The airport has proven a boon for the

Azoreans, for in the summer of 1975 the interisland airline began regularly scheduled service to it. In the summer of 1977, flights were increased to two a week between Fayal and Flores.

The Azoreans seem quite reluctant to talk about the French on Flores—at least to an American—and also about the *Henri Poincaré*, which I observed anchored off Angra in June 1974. The reason is undoubtedly that they have been told next to nothing of these subjects and therefore consider them secret. *Jane's Fighting Ships 1974-75* spares no details, however. Rather, it makes clear that the vessel, built in 1960 in Monfalcone as the Italian tanker *Maina Marasso*, was converted by the French primarily into a missile-range-ship. She is fitted out with three tracking radars, whose domes are very obvious to an observer, and with a telemetry station.

The attentive traveler of 1970 was aware of additional intriguing activity in Azorean waters together with mysterious construction ashore on Santa Maria. The local population, who used the undefined word *polígono* (polygon) when queried, were in fact thoroughly mystified, not to say annoyed for not being brought in on the local secrets.

In a dispatch to *The New York Times* filed by Marvine Howe and published on March 5, 1972, the wraps were finally lifted, and on the following May 19, in the presence of high-ranking NATO officials and others, including Portugal's Minister of National Defense, the Azores Fixed Acoustic Range was inaugurated. AFAR is under the direction of an executive headquarters at Cascais, near Lisbon. As for its purpose, no less an authority than *Parade*, the widely read Sunday newspaper magazine, revealed it on March 2, 1975: "These sonars monitor submarine traffic through the Strait of Gibraltar and other waters and are linked by computer to Washington. They are designed to prevent an enemy nuclear attack upon the U.S." In no less blunt fashion did the invaluable *Parade* on August 6, 1978, confirm my theory of the Cuban airlift to Africa: "Cuban troops are flown in Cuban or Angolan transports from Havana to Sal.... They are then flown to Luanda. ... Ironically enough, the airport at Sal is also used by South African Airways as a refueling station."

A final example of the international importance of the Azores is related, one trusts, to peace. The U.S. Department of Commerce's National Ocean Survey established a global network of satellite-triangulation sites in connection with the production of more accurate land maps and nautical charts. This worldwide geodetic network consists of seventy-eight stations. Number 7 is, or was temporarily, at Lajes Field on Terceira, number 55 on Ascension. The typical Azorean know-nothing attitude even embraced the Terceiran installation. The U.S. public relations officer at Lajes was adamant in 1974 in denying that any such thing existed.

Therein lay a grave problem of the Azores and of the other Portuguese Atlantic islands: a legacy of remote control. The land of these islands, their waters, and their airspace belong to the islanders, yet the *ilhéus* used to be kept in darkness, ever made to fear relating whatever bits of truth they may have known. No wonder that, in an amusing act of retribution, Azorean authorities on São Jorge in August 1976 seized and held for a week a Continental Portuguese fishing boat from Peniche. The Azoreans charged foreign invasion of Azorean territorial waters. In that year, they had to give in. But in mid-1977, a new agreement between France and Portugal was signed. This time, and in accordance with the specific provision of the 1976 Constitution already quoted, the Azores are receiving their share of the financial benefits, to the tune, it is reported, of 144,000 contos ($3,613,097).

12
FARMING IN SIGHT OF THE SEA

Their location has conferred a great importance on the Azores and Madeiras in the past, some would say a strategic importance. From this importance certain economic benefits have flowed. Certainly the greatest of all in terms of foreign currency has come from the British and, later, the American presence at the Lajes airfield on Terceira.

Unfortunately, servicing ships, cables, airplanes, and satellite pathways cannot form the basis of an archipelago's economy. Such activity, like reliance on remittances from emigrants and migrant workers abroad, stands as a supplement. It can even be thought of as a crutch. Something more substantial and more basic is vitally necessary, for example the growing of all foodstuffs and the manufacturing of as many necessities as possible for local consumption, and the cultivating of products—such as tourism—for export in order to earn the credits abroad with which to purchase the indispensable imports.

The preceding is not to imply that the two archipelagoes are or should be independent economic units. As integral parts, albeit autonomous regions, of Portugal, they share in the economic vicissitudes of the country as a whole. They do expect to contribute whatever may be deemed their fair share to the national economy. Reciprocally, they expect that the nation as a whole will contribute to the solution of their peculiar economic problems. One such contribution might be compensation for their oceanic isolation and consequent increased shipping charges by subsidizing the shipment of items to or from the mainland.

Over the years, Continental Portugal has sold Continental goods within the mainland territory at certain prices but at increased prices to the Adjacent Islands. What has seemed lacking is the use of the government's power to tax everyone in order overtly to favor citizens of economically deprived islands. Why should a can of Continental orange juice be one price in Continental Portugal, a higher price on St. Michael's (whose port of Ponta Delgada receives cargo directly from the mainland), and a still higher price on Santa Maria (to which cargo very often has to be transshipped from Ponta Delgada)?

Martha's Vineyard and Nantucket once again provide a case in point. The ferries of the Woods Hole, Martha's Vineyard, and Nantucket Steamship Authority supply those islands in such a way as to endeavor to keep at reasonable levels what might otherwise prove an exorbitantly high cost of living for the islanders. This quasi-public organization is mandated by the state legislature to provide the residents of the two islands all year round with safe and economical transportation for people and the necessaries of life. In spite of competition from other carriers who tap off some of the lucrative summer business, the Authority should not incur an operating loss. If a deficit does occur, it is charged in the following proportions to the communities involved in the service: Martha's Vineyard Island 50%, Nantucket Island 40%, and the Town of Falmouth (the mainland base) 10%. This deficit is thus not passed directly on to the common people by higher prices. In 1978 in its eighteenth year of operation, the Authority ran at a loss only during its first three years. Its efficiency, and the ensuing benefit to the islands, is due in large measure to the island representation on the governing board, the public nature of all meetings, and the close scrutiny given every phase of the operation by literally every island citizen.

One would expect Continental Portugal to run a passenger/ freight service to Insular Portugal on a similar basis, possibly even at a loss, in order to spare Azoreans and Madeirans, already in general poor enough, excessive charges for vital commodities. One also looks to the central government to ensure interisland service, subsidized by the Nation, so that those on the smaller and more remote islands would not be charged even more than those on the larger and economically more productive islands for comparable items.

Insular Portugal can thus look to Insular Massachusetts for a model, all the more as Americans of Portuguese descent and birth have contributed considerable to the Martha's Vineyard and Nantucket steamer service. Within the Authority a pertinent story goes the rounds. A Labor Day weekend not long ago saw one steamer broken down and confusion reigning supreme. A very elegant lady in genuine Yankee accent demanded of the agent on the pier to know when her auto would arrive from Nantucket. The agent, a retired U.S. Coast Guard commander of Portuguese descent, tried to calm her, to no avail. "Why," she exclaimed, "I can remember the efficient steamboat service of the good old days when the goddamned Portygees ran the line. Now, with you finely clothed gentlemen replete with name tags, things are in a mess." "Lady," the agent replied, "I am a goddamned Portygee," whereupon she smiled and regained her customary composure.

☆ ☆ ☆

There was little political autonomy in the Islands because of the paucity of economic autonomy, and it is the latter which explains in part the many departures for Pasargadae. Except for some foodstuffs in Azores and Madeiras and the beginnings of manufacturing on the Azorean St. Michael's, the two archipelagoes were largely dependent on imports.

Unfortunately, both economic and vital statistics concerning Insular Portugal are very difficult to come by. Figures on the Azores and Madeiras, when taken into consideration at all, are—or have been—often merged with those on Continental Portugal. Or they are omitted completely.

Another problem stems from Salazar/Caetano organizational theory. Insular Portugal was considered distinct from Continental Portugal yet was supposed to be an integral part of Portugal. Therefore, if a family left one of the Adjacent Islands to take up residence on the mainland, the members did not emigrate. They merely made an internal move. Figures for such moves, and returns, were accordingly not included in migration statistics. Nor was the movement of goods between the Adjacent Islands and Continent and vice versa considered foreign trade. Thus, the highly important movement of beef from Azores to Madeiras and from Azores to Continent did not count as an Azorean export.

Because of an overzealous administrative theory, published comparisons between "Portugal" and other countries could involve Greater Portugal (which included the Overseas Provinces), Metropolitan Portugal, or Continental Portugal. Most probably, they concerned merely Continental Portugal, although occasionally Continental plus Insular Portugal. An example is furnished by the estimates of per capita gross national product (GNP) compiled by the Agency for International Development and published annually in *The World Almanac & Book of Facts*. Of ten roughly comparable European countries in recent years, "Portugal" has always ranked number ten after Sweden (number one), Denmark, Norway, Belgium, Netherlands, Italy, Ireland, Greece, and Spain (number nine). But what does "Portugal" mean?

A glance at the statistics on the foreign trade of Azores and Madeiras over the past decade serves to place the Insular Portuguese economy in perspective. The accompanying table of the dollar value of Insular Portuguese foreign trade over the years 1970-1976 gives the full story and needs little comment:

Dollar Value of Insular Portuguese Foreign Trade, 1970-1976

	Azores				Madeiras
	District of Ponta Delgada	District of Angra	District of Horta	TOTAL AZORES	District of Funchal
Imports 1970 $1=28$750	$5,463,617	$995,930	$318,852	$6,778,400	$11,123,026
Exports 1970	2,369,878	838,330	450,886	3,659,096	10,423,165
Imports 1971 $1=27$560	6,549,601	1,647,134	413,861	8,610,595	18,600,871
Exports 1971	2,074,202	463,824	491,800	3,029,826	11,667,707
Imports 1972 $1=27$000	8,731,000	1,400,852	502,111	10,633,963	19,135,185
Exports 1972	2,546,815	332,185	528,111	3,407,111	13,988,037
Imports 1973 $1=25$845	12,873,090	1,616,599	632,966	15,122,654	18,394,970
Exports 1973	2,860,128	687,599	1,259,083	4,806,810	18,139,369
Imports 1974 $1=24$596	17,110,465	2,858,229	1,230,607	21,199,301	25,748,455
Exports 1974	4,800,537	909,335	2,518,133	7,821,434	20,705,684
Imports 1975 $1=27$472	13,641,380	2,252,657	578,808	16,472,845	16,012,813
Exports 1975	5,933,678	562,791	531,086	7,027,555	17,207,957
Imports 1976 $1=31$549				20,577,895	22,059,970
Exports 1976				8,276,364	15,562,141

These figures do not include movement of goods among islands within an archipelago, or between archipelagos, or between Insular and Continental Portugal, what might be called the intra-Metropolitan trade. They do, however, include the small trade with Portugal's existing overseas provinces. The figures, as given, reflect a continuous increase in the volume of trade through 1974, at least for the Azores, and then a decrease. They also show that the foreign trade of the Madeiras was much more significant than that of the Azores, although less so with the passing of the years. Within the Azores, the District of Ponta Delgada was the most active economically, as might be expected from the size of its population and principal port.

The table's outstanding revelation concerns the consistently unfavorable trade balance throughout Insular Portugal with the notable exception of the District of Horta and with the exception in 1975 of the Madeiras. Ponta Delgada's balance was the least enviable and was steadily growing worse through the year of the Revolution. Horta, on the other hand, was consistently exporting more than it imported, in 1973 just twice as much but in 1975 slightly less. Its level of imports was extremely low, however, and therefore the comparison is relatively meaningless. One wonders, incidentally, how accurate these figures are in general and those for 1975, Portugal's most leftist year, in particular.

The islands were importing the obvious: foodstuffs (especially wheat but also corn, refined cane sugar, and dried codfish), petroleum products, building materials, and machinery including automobiles, among many other items. The Madeiras were also importing meat from abroad, for animals are raised only with great difficulty on the rugged terrain of the main island of Madeira. The islands were importing these items from the obvious countries: chiefly from the United States and the United Kingdom but also from France, West Germany, Italy, the Netherlands, Sweden, Switzerland, Brazil, and Canada.

The single greatest import item for both Azores and Madeiras was wheat, in 1974 for a dollar value of $4,911,815 and $7,125,102 respectively, that is, a little less than one-quarter the value of all imports for Azores, and considerably more than one-quarter for Madeiras. A frequent visitor to São Miguel is surprised by Ponta Delgada's and Funchal's 1974 importation of refined cane sugar, amounting to $1,959,384 and $1,994,308 respectively. He observes a thriving beet-sugar industry on São Miguel, where sugar from the other Azores islands is processed, packaged, and redistributed throughout the archipelago. The same visitor also observes the large number of private automobiles in use, purchased at unbelievably high prices. Not noticing automobiles as a significant specific item of import in the published

Straw hut (*palheiro*) on Madeira employed to house cows

statistics, he realizes that most are brought in from Continental Portugal. They are not technically imported. But Continental Portugal imports them from somewhere!

Because the port of Ponta Delgada is the largest in the Azores and the major funnel through which most goods enter from abroad, the District of Ponta Delgada showed the greatest number of imports, for instance airplanes (or one airplane) from the United Kingdom to the value of $1,471,426 in 1973. But these goods were in part subsequently distributed among the other islands by local transportation, the airplanes of the interisland airline serving Santa Maria, São Miguel, Terceira, Fayal, and Flores.

In view of the disparity in the use of ports, the figures in the column headed TOTAL AZORES in the above table are more meaningful than those for the individual districts.

Statistics, of course, must be interpreted in the light of general knowledge of local conditions. Thus, Funchal's figures on whiskey make sense only when it is realized that Madeira's tourists are a sophisticated group from the North Countries who like their scotch with few bourbon drinkers among them:

	1973	1974	1975
From United Kingdom	$116,464	$124,858	$111,386
From United States	1,277		1,565
From elsewhere	155	5,041	2,730
TOTAL	$117,896	$129,899	$115,681

One Azorean import which makes little sense to me is dried codfish: $507,371 in 1973, $638,681 in 1974, and $607,892 in 1975. Some of it was imported from the United Kingdom, most of it presumably from Iceland. In 1974, I admired the activity of a fish-canning factory on Pico, for I was told that it was preserving local tuna. In 1977, I witnessed activity at the same factory, but this time I was told that it was canning imported cod.

The list of principal export items betrays the precise nature of Insular economic activity and of the social-class structure. Lower-class male labor pulled up agar, grew fruits, vegetables, and flowers, milked cows, fished the sea, and hunted for whales, while the women—to the extent that they were gainfully employed at all—embroidered and worked in fish-canning and other small factories. Significantly, Fayal's and Pico's famed shore-based whaling netted almost one-third the total value of the District of Horta's exports in 1973 but only one-eighth in 1974. In 1975, whale oil was not even listed in the official sources I use. This industry is further discussed in the chapter on relatives in America because of the widespread use of New England whaling terms.

The Azores's main exports consisted of canned fish, agar, and embroidery. St. Michael's famed and delicious pineapples earned very little: $95,260 in 1973, $65,620 in 1974, and $84,086 in 1975. The Madeiras exported embroidery, wine, wicker work, and tapestry work, with dollar value in that order, although in 1975 wine had crept up to exceed embroidery slightly. This wine is the renowned madeira, in general an apéritif or after-dinner fortified wine which is available under four widely-known classifications based on the grapes from which the wine is made: dry *sercial*, less dry *verdelho*, sweet *bual* (a dessert wine), and *malvasia* or, in English, malmsey (the richest and heaviest of them all).

In the 1973, the value of Madeiran embroidery and delicate tapestries ($6,941,072) had been equal in value to the wine ($3,481,989) and wicker work ($3,307,216) combined. Naturally, from the value of the exported embroidery must be subtracted the value of the linen and other materials imported for the island women to exercise their handicraft on. In 1973, these imports amounted to $2,582,666 in the District of Funchal.

In order for the reader to interpret the embroidery figures in terms of individuals, I adduce the following facts. In January 1973; I spoke with a lady embroidering a table cloth in the street of her village on the north side of Madeira. It was a table cloth which would sell for about $200 retail in a Funchal shop (rather less in New York or on Miami Beach's Lincoln Road). She told me that she would work from three to four months on it and receive 1,483$00 ($57.38 at 1973's exchange rate). "They," meaning the entrepreneurs from Funchal, gave her the linen, but she had to pay for the thread, which amounted to 283$00. Result, she actually cleared only 1,200$00, that is, $46.43, for several months work.

A curious but diminishing Madeira export item was electrical apparatus "for interruption, sectioning, etc., of electric circuits": $952,602 in 1973, $728,858 in 1974, and only $346,425 in 1975, all to the United Kingdom. This item represented an effort—by the Blandy interests, I was told—to set up a British electronics factory on Madeira to take advantage of the highly skilled and capable—but cheap—local labor. In 1977, I was informed that the new political forces on the island had brought about the fledgling industry's demise.

Figures on Azorean exports become meaningful only when a knowledge of transportation among the islands as well as between the archipelagoes and abroad is brought to bear. Thus, the agar (or agar-agar, gelatinous extractive of algae) was exported almost exclusively to the United Kingdom and via Ponta Delgada, but it was harvested on islands other than São Miguel and notably on Terceira. Clearly, the ships which went to the Azores to pick it up put in at Ponta Delgada, to which the agar was moved by local transportation. Moreover, the ships may have flown the British flag and may have listed a British port as their first to stop at, but I was informed that much of the agar went to Italy and Japan. Similarly, Santa Maria's whale oil and St. George's cheese—the famed "island cheese," *queijo da ilha*, of Lisbon's restaurants—were exported via the port of Ponta Delgada and Pico's canned fish via the port of Horta.

The $2,302,381 worth of "oils for jet-propelled aircraft" exported from the District of Ponta Delgada in 1975 points up the ambiguous nature of Insular Portuguese import-export figures.

The oil obviously came from Continental Portugal, for it does not seem to be listed among imports. Here again, the oil had to come from somewhere. As for its exportation, it was not listed as going to West Germany, France, Italy, United Kingdom, or United States, but rather to "Other countries." It was probably sold to planes of "Other countries" stopping over for fuel on Santa Maria. But which other countries? Was it sold to Cubans and Russians for the famous airlift of Cuban troops to Angola, or simply to Cubana Airlines for its flights CU 476 and 477?

The income generated in the Azores by foreign military or strategic installations is not listed as an export item. The value to the Azores of the U.S. air presence at Lajes on Terceira is estimated to be of the order of $16,000,000 per year. Indirectly, the People-to-People program administered by U.S. Air Force personnel at the air base adds more, at least in kind, to the islands' economy. And then there are the French on Flores. These foreign bases have suddenly loomed large in Insular Portuguese thinking, for, as already noted, the new Constitution guarantees the participation of the autonomous regions in the negotiations concerning treaties and international agreements which involve them directly and, also, in the benefits which flow from them.

In 1975, then, the last year for which statistics are available to me by district, the dollar value of Azorean imports from the Portuguese overseas provinces and foreign countries was roughly $16,500,000, that of Madeiran imports $16,000,000. The latter imports were more than balanced by exports, but in the Azores exports amounted to less than one-half the dollar value of imports (assuming that the 1975 figures are accurate). Clearly, for two Atlantic archipelagoes roughly equal in population (their total population amounting to well over half a million inhabitants) this level of economic activity was appallingly low. A major source of additional activity was naturally the need for the islands to export to, and above all to import from, Continental Portugal. Upon an increase and change of nature of this intra-Metropolitan trade rested the hopes of vast numbers of Insular Portuguese.

☆ ☆ ☆

Serious economic planning had been in effect in Portugal since 1953, and a series of Development Plans had been worked out. At the time of the Revolution, study groups were already looking forward to the Fourth Plan. For planning purposes, Metropolitan Portugal was divided into six Planning Regions. The District of Funchal constituted the Madeira Region, and all three Azorean districts formed the single Azores Region. In each region, in the words of the *Survey of the Portuguese Economy*, a "Regional Advisory Planning Committee comprises representatives of the district authorities and the economic, social and moral interests of each area, and it co-operates with the central planning organs [in Lisbon] by drafting plans and projects of regional interest and effecting research and surveys."

In the Azores, defined in the *Survey* as "a group of thinly populated small islands, where the main activities are agriculture, livestock and fisheries," the Regional Planning Committee did not use the word "Advisory" in its title. Called Comissão de Planeamento da Região dos Açores, it had its headquarters in Angra do Heroísmo. Its planning in connection with the Third Plan (1968-1973) focused on an increase in air and sea transportation among the islands and with the outside world, an increased exploitation of the fishing potential, and the setting up in the Azores of an International Commerce Center. The results of this careful planning were already evident in the new airports just outside of Ponta Delgada and on the south side of Fayal near Castelo Branco which permitted an increase in both the interisland airline's and TAP's services.

The two Insular Portuguese planning committees were well advanced in their thinking in connection with the Fourth Plan, as was noted in Chapter 6; and the Madeira committee also omitted the word "Advisory." It is through the reports and proposals of the two committees that one can glean considerable economic information about the islands. It is upon such information that future governments of Portugal (whether of left, center, or right), of the islands themselves, and perchance of the United States must base their actions.

One chief fact emerged: the Islanders are largely agriculturalists.

Economists divide the labor force into sectors, those of the primary sector being farmers and fishermen, of the secondary sector manufacturing and construction workers, and of the tertiary sector tradesmen and clerical persons. In 1960, 60% of the economically active Azoreans were in the primary sector (mostly in agriculture, with less than 4% in fishing), 17% in the secondary

Landing tuna at Santa Cruz, Madeira, June 1964

sector, and 23% in the tertiary sector. In the Madeiras, 53% were in the primary sector (with only slightly over 3% in fishing), 22% in the secondary, with 25% in the tertiary.

"Portugal" had 43% in primary, 27% in secondary, and 28% in tertiary, showing that Continental Portugal was in advance of Insular Portugal. By "in advance" is meant more nearly like the industrialized countries, for example, Italy with 19% of the work force in the primary sector in 1971, and West Germany with 10% in the same year. The only European countries with larger primary sectors than "Portugal" were Bulgaria, Poland, Romania, and Yugoslavia.

Clearly, throughout Continental and Insular Portugal post-Revolutionary governments will have to devote maximum attention to the plight of agricultural workers, for they are poor, not to say poverty-stricken. And the Madeirans are poorer than the Continentals, the Azoreans poorer than the Madeirans. In 1970, "Portugal's" per capita gross domestic product was $631, the Madeiras's a mere $264, and the Azores's about $160 per head in the agrarian sector. In that same year, Sweden's per capita GDP estimate was $4,090, Denmark's $3,164, Norway's $2,931, et cetera.

Fortunate it is that the emigration escape hatch has existed for the Azoreans. In 1960, the population of the Azores was 327,806. Rates of natural increase (births less deaths, excluding emigration) would have increased the 1970 population to 391,072 inhabitants. Actually, the population decreased to 291,028.

Had the population increased by 63,266 and assuming that one-third of them would figure eventually among the actively employed, some 21,000 new jobs would have had to come into being. In 1960, the Azorean economy provided 33,000 nonagricultural jobs. It is inconceivable that 21,000 additional such jobs would have been created by 1970, all the more as only 4,102 had been created during the preceding decade.

The population dropped by 36,778, for 70,000 persons emigrated. Of those who departed in 1969, 70% of the economically active were from the primary sector, 11% from the secondary, and 19% from the tertiary. Rural dissatisfaction was evident.

The planning committee studies revealed a basic reason for this dissatisfaction, the inequitable distribution of economically productive land among Insular farmers.

In the Azores, whose relatively undulating and rolling area consists of 902 square miles, 378,071 acres of the total make for agriculturally useful terrain. Divided by the 38,720 farms, this acreage would provide 9.8 acres to each farm. In the Madeiras, where Madeira itself is mountainous and precipitous, the area of 307 square miles provides only 49,421 acres of potentially useful land. Divided by the 27,141 farms, each farm would amount to only 1.8 acres.

The planning committees found that 91% of the Azorean and 99% of the Madeiran farms actually engaged in cultivation consisted of less than five acres, 43% of the Azorean and 82.5% of the Madeiran less than slightly over one acre.

Additional facts are even more dismal. In general, what are listed as farms were/are composed of noncontiguous plots tilled by the same farmer. In the District of Ponta Delgada 12% of the farms with land under cultivation consisted of more than six plots, in Angra 19%, and in Horta 52%. In the District of Funchal 71% consisted of more than one plot, with 22% consisting of six or more plots.

What is more, these miniscule plots were not always owned by the farmers who worked them. In the Azores, only 40% of the farms (or amalgamations of plots) were owned in their entirety by those who cultivated them. The remaining 60% were wholly or partially rented from some outsider—some absentee owner in the district capital or Lisbon or even the Americas—or else contracted for under sharecropping arrangements. In the Madeiras, 56% of the farms were owned outright; the others were wholly or partially rented or sharecropped.

To translate these statistics into human terms, in June 1974 in the rain, I interviewed a rural laborer in Biscoitos—literally Biscuits, for the porous lava looks like biscuit dough—an area on the north side of Terceira which produces an excellent wine. He earned 50$00 per day, roughly two dollars, tending plots belonging to an absentee owner. A fair-minded man, he did not blame his boss, who in one year received only 1,000$00 ($41) each for the two barrels of wine which he obtained from the plot, and sometimes he received less. At such low wine prices, the boss could not pay his worker more.

Incidentally, the minimum monthly wage of 3,300$00 ($134) which the Revolutionary Government put into effect as of May 27, 1974, did not apply to domestic help and farm laborers. My friend in Biscoitos continued in his poverty. Those to whom it did apply continued badly off also, even in 1975, when it was increased by 20% to 4,000$00 ($146 at the new exchange rate); inflation within Portugal was 25% in 1974 and was destined to climb much higher in succeeding years.

☆ ☆ ☆

Economists working with political leaders will have to deal with the changes which the preceding data indicate are necessary and inevitable, changes in the direction of cooperativism, redistribution of land to cultivators, and reform of tenure arrangements. In the meantime, the Azorean economy is bailed out, in part at least, by intra-Metropolitan trade.

The figures on the tonnage of merchandise moved in Portuguese ships between Continental and Insular Portugal for 1969 (the last year they were included in the Government's *Statistical Annual*) reveal the same type of Island trade deficit as is evident in the foreign trade.

In 1969 the Azores sent 50,883 tons to Continental Portugal

and received 137,353 from the mainland. The Madeiran tonnage was 37,248 sent, 109,517 received. From Insular Portugal in decreasing order of tonnage went bananas, cattle, lumber, iron work, powdered milk, potatoes, chicory, finfish and shellfish, cheese, butter, pineapples, wine, and wicker and wicker work. To Azores and Madeiras went, in the same order, cement, fertilizers, clinkers, diesel oil, gasoline, corn, butane gas, salt, lime, earthenware, petroleum, animal feed, ammonium sulfate, timber, table wine, metalwork, rice, glass, and gypsum. Both Ponta Delgada and Funchal, by the way, possess breweries which produce excellent beer for archipelagic consumption.

It is of interest to compare these tonnage totals with those for the same year 1969 between Insular Portugal and Portuguese overseas provinces and with those between Insular Portugal and foreign countries. Whereas from the two archipelagoes a total of 88,131 tons were sent to the Continent, 2,172 tons were sent to overseas provinces (226 from Azores and 1,946 from Madeiras), and 179,469 tons were exported abroad (34,011 from Azores and 145,458 from Madeiras). Conversely, to the two archipelagoes came a total of 480,670 tons as follows: 246,870 from the Continent, 31,241 from overseas provinces (1,725 to Azores and 29,516 to Madeiras), and 202,559 from abroad (105,444 to Azores and 97,115 to Madeiras).

In addition to confirming a persistently unfavorable trade balance, these tonnage figures demonstrate the excessive economic dependence of the Azores on Continental Portugal. The Azores imported more from and exported more to the Portuguese mainland than from and to the overseas provinces and foreign countries combined. In effect, Continental Portugal was holding the Azores in veritable subjection, in true colonial fashion. The mainland sent out to the mid-Atlantic archipelago fertilizers, animal feed, building materials, and fuel, and it received essential foodstuffs and above all beef on the hoof and dairy products. The situation in the Madeiras was the same as far as imports were concerned, if the tonnages from Continental and Overseas Portugal are combined. On the other hand, it is clear that Madeira, at least in 1969, exported many more tons abroad than to Portuguese territory.

These tonnage figures refer only to goods loaded in Continental Portugal into Portuguese-flag ships destined for the Adjacent Islands on the one hand and, on the other hand, goods unloaded in Continental Portugal from Portuguese-flag ships coming from the Adjacent Islands. Even when foreign-flag vessels are taken into account, the problem of excess of imports over exports continued, and worsened with each passing year.

A Ponta Delgada newspaper of July 12, 1974, wished to stress how the city's port was expanding in significance. It therefore published the following headline: "The 1973 activity of the Autonomous [sic] Port Junta of the Autonomous [sic] District of Ponta Delgada: During 1973 the port of Ponta Delgada moved 309,455 tons of merchandise, 229,820 tons having been unloaded and 79,635 loaded." Revealing exactly the contrary to what the editor undoubtedly had in mind, the article went on to point out (1) that 134,429 tons were unloaded from Portuguese ships and 95,391 from foreign vessels; (2) that 75,508 tons were loaded into Portuguese ships and 4,127 into foreign vessels; and (3) that the total of 309,455 tons was higher by 62,655 than for 1972, when 51,298 fewer tons were unloaded and 1,357 fewer loaded. Simple arithmetic discloses that the real situation worsened in 1973. The 1973 situation was also bad in Vila do Porto on Santa Maria: 54,046 tons unloaded, a mere 1,004 loaded.

The same pattern obtained in 1976, according to a Ponta Delgada newspaper of July 13, 1977: Ponta Delgada unloaded 257,743 tons and loaded 91,316 tons. A total of 178,215 were unloaded from Portuguese ships and 79,528 from foreign vessels; and 85,923 were loaded into Portuguese bottoms and 5,393 into foreign ships. Similarly for Santa Maria: 33,704 unloaded, 2,988 loaded.

The Azores's largest export item to Continental Portugal in 1969, in tonnage, was cattle, that is, beef on the hoof. When combined with powdered milk, cheese, and butter, the total of 19,103 tons represented almost one-third of Azorean exports to the mainland. In 1973 a member of the Madeira Planning Committee told me that one-third of Madeira's beef was brought in from the Azores, suggesting an even more significant role for cattle-raising in the latter archipelago.

Curiously, it is thanks to the Nixon-Pompidou-Caetano meeting on Terceira in late 1971 that information on Azorean economic life suddenly became disproportionately available. Because Continental journalists went out there to cover the story and were appalled, the Continental public for the first time received a true picture of what was going on in the Atlantic. Thus, *Flama*, a popular magazine not unlike the old *Life*, in its issue of January 14, 1972, painted a picture which accorded exactly with my own observations of 1970 and 1972. It furnished figures to underline its stress on the excess of imports over exports and reported that between January 1 and September 30, 1971, the archipelago exported 20,486 head of cattle, nearly 10% to Madeira and the balance to Continental Portugal. The individual islands contributed heads as follows:

Santa Maria	218	Graciosa	591	Fayal	3,450
São Miguel	9,278	São Jorge	1,406	Flores	804
Terceira	3,258	Pico	1,351	Corvo	130

In other words, every island was getting in on this unfortunate act, even tiny Corvo. True, the suitability of Azorean soil is said to be second only—if not equal—to that of New Zealand for cattle raising. Does that mean that the soil, so badly needed for green vegetables and other products, should be devoted to bulls and cows?

Ranching has been a major Azorean activity for many years. In days past, and as recently as 1964, cattle raised on São Miguel were shipped westward to Flores to graze and fatten for several months. From Flores they were shipped eastward all the way to Lisbon, losing considerable of the Florentine weight en route. The absurdity of this mid-ocean bovine voyaging was evident from the fact that two major ships employed for these shipments were the passenger/freight vessels of the triangular service Lisbon-Madeira-Azores-Madeira-Lisbon. The São Miguel cows therefore took a veritable Cook's tour of many days duration in both directions.

More recently, with a constant increase in the level of ranching, the animals have been fattened on their island of birth, and Flores has lost its cheese and butter industry. After fattening, the cattle are led to the loading pier, where a sling is placed under their belly. With frightened and photogenic eyes, and taking a functional revenge at anyone so unfortunate as to be below and within range, they are hoisted aboard for a relatively short sail.

ITT, as was noted in the preceding chapter, has expressed an interest in moving in on the Azorean cattle business and giving it a badly needed modernization. Specifically, there was much talk of slaughtering both steers and pigs on the islands and shipping the

Loading cattle off Santa Cruz, Flores, June 1964

cut meat either in refrigerators or frozen. Meat packers would save on shipping costs and could also take advantage of by-products such as blood and bones for other commercial purposes. The Azores Planning Committee was uncertain of this step's wisdom, with São Miguel predictably opposed and Terceira in favor. Then came the Revolution.

There is no doubt that Azorean cattle-raising narrows the huge gap in the trade balance. In this noneconomist's judgment, however, ranching is the most unwise activity to which the valuable island land should be devoted. Grazing, as done in the Azores, requires extensive land. Even if the cattle do not graze, considerable land is needed to raise their fodder. And the entire industry employs few people. It makes the rich richer and keeps the poor where they were in the first place. Its future is most precisely outlined in California's San Joaquin Valley, where enterprising immigrant ranchers from the Azores and their descendants are making vast sums of money with their computerized-feeding and mechanized-milking dairy ranches. In 1975, I visited a ranch where one American lad and three Azorean immigrant boys milked eleven hundred cows twice a day. As far as I could observe, all that each boy did was wipe 2,200 udders with green paper toweling daily and open and close a door. Is that what the Azores wish? If so, there are savvy ex-Azoreans all too willing to return and show the local folk how to do it.

In the impoverished Azores, then, there has been and is a sufficiency of beef. The man in the street cannot afford to buy it, however, for it commands too high a price as an export item. A beef dinner is therefore a luxury served to the masses by the well-to-do, including returned emigrants, at Pentecost time as a result of vows previously made. Beef is often included in the famous Holy Ghost soup to be described in the chapter on the role of the parish churches in the islands.

The Traditional Church is the common man's true friend. But not necessarily the National Church, its prelates, and its solidarity with State. In July 1977, however, a bishop did break with the State's Church and came out with a statement which badly needed making.

Dom Aurélio Granada Escudeiro, Titular Bishop of Drusiliana, was born in east-central Continental Portugal on May 29, 1920. In June 1974 he arrived in the Azores as coadjutor Bishop of Angra, that is, of the Azores, in order to assist the residential bishop already there. But he did not have the right of succession, a fact whose legal significance is explained in Chapter 14.

In the Azores, Dom Aurélio naturally became quickly aware of the appallingly large dimensions of Insular emigration, as he had already known of the migration of Continental workers to Northwest Europe. In a homily delivered on August 15, 1977, at the close of the Fifth National Migrations Week held on the Continent

August 7-14, 1977, he dared say the following, widely quoted in the Portuguese-language press within the United States:

> The emigrant appears not in the role of a worthy citizen endowed with certain rights, but merely in that of a working machine and producer of foreign exchange. Woe unto a country when, instead of employment created to absorb the greatest possible number of workers, it provides facilities for emigrating. Woe unto a nation which expects and asks of its emigrants that they send money back home instead of doing everything (everything and not merely words) to render emigration duly defended, protected, and safeguarded through laws and treaties which recognize for the emigrants rights equal to those of the citizens of the target countries.

The fact is, of course, that for many years Portugal, both Continental and Insular, has been exporting workers. The official expectation has been that they would send remittances back home to their families, deposit savings in Portuguese banks, return home with savings effected abroad, and live at home in retirement with whatever pension or Social Security might be due them from abroad. And these monies amount to many escudos. Take, for instance, the monthly value of U.S. Social Security checks sent to "Portugal" (obviously Continental and Insular Portugal): $526,868 in 1971, $666,627 in 1972, $706,358 in 1973, $792,744 in 1974, $819,536 in 1975, and $877,100 in 1976. I should guess that the vast majority of these benefits go to the Azores, a little to the Madeiras, the balance to the mainland. True, a small fraction goes to Americans residing in Portugal, for example, the widowed mother of an ambassador or a consul. Even subtracting these sums, the rest is considerable. For proof, let the reader compare them with the dollar value of exported items.

Not only does the Government in Lisbon like this kind of income but so do the two Regional Governments out in the Atlantic. It is that dependency which is so detrimental to Portugal, and, as Dom Aurélio suggests, so unfair to Portuguese workers.

That the post-Revolutionary Governments are now making every effort to stabilize and increase these revenues, as well as foreign currency earned from tourists, is very understandable. Portugal faced a frightening economic crisis immediately after the

25th of April, ultimately a legacy of the economic and social policies of the preceding regimes. Tourists were afraid to go to a Portugal in turmoil, and tourism dropped to rock bottom. Emigrants and workers abroad were uneasy about the situation within their native land and became reluctant to send as much money as formerly. The countries in Western Europe to which Portuguese workers customarily repaired, as well as workers from Spain, Italy, Yugoslavia, Greece, Turkey, and even Algeria, were in a recession and required fewer outsiders in their labor force. Retirees in the New World began to wonder if, after all, it was such a good idea to return "home" with their hard-earned dollars. White Portuguese refugees from the former colonies, and especially Angola and Mozambique, began to crowd into Metropolitan Portugal in destitute condition; and the successive Governments in Lisbon were forced to house them at public expense in some of the very hotels, inns, and pensions which had formerly produced badly needed revenue from abroad. Poorly paid Portuguese workers— for instance the women who embroidered on Terceira, accustomed to a very low level of productivity with much idle chitchat between stitches—suddenly discovered that the new minimum wage which the Revolution imposed became impossible for their employers to pay, being given their output; and both employers and workers lost out.

In the Azores, the upper class, suddenly finding it difficult to hire *criadas*, note that lower-class Azoreans who emigrate to the United States work hard in their new homes beyond the seas but that those who remain behind will not work hard, even today, when more money is at hand to be earned. The observation parallels that made at the end of Chapter 3 above concerning the sudden adoption of political stances by Azoreans in America. There is clearly something in the air back home which holds Azoreans back, economically and politically.

Change, great change, must be the order of the day. Instead of wheat being the major item of importation from abroad in all four Insular districts, wheat should be grown by Azoreans in their fertile, gently rolling and therefore easily worked fields, wheat for local consumption and shipment to the Madeiras. Azoreans should not be devoting those fields to fodder for cattle, or to the cattle themselves for grazing. That cattle is traditionally for export to Madeira and the mainland. It earns vast sums for the few in the Azores while providing precious little employment for the labor force, for the common man whose era ours is in fact, whether Portugal's upper class yet realizes it or not.

I leave the solution of Greater Portugal's economic woes to others more expert in the subject than myself. I note, however, one great reason for optimism. Portugal is at long last rebecoming what it really has been all along: a nation of Europe The notion that Europe ended at the Pyrenees was a vicious one propagated by hostile opponents who wished to discriminate against the Iberian nations. It was also disseminated by imperialist apologists for Spain and Portugal. In the Middle Ages, Portugal was very much a part of Europe, undergoing every influence which radiated out of such great cultural centers as Toulouse, Paris, and the Italian city-states. During the brief period from 1415 to 1578, Portugal underwent its overseas-expansion craze, but sensible Portuguese recognized that with the overthrow of the last Spanish king in 1640 and restoration of a Portuguese ruling family—the Braganzas—to the throne of Portugal, their nation was moving back in the direction of Europe. Over the ensuing years, the hearts of most Portuguese lay in Europe. Those grand Senhoras with their chauffeur-driven Volkswagen cared not one whit for Angola, Mozambique, or Goa, or, for that matter, the remote Azores. They visited Paris, Rome, Berlin at every available opportunity. Only a handful of profiteers and exploiters prolonged the ultramarine jag, which crashed down upon them in April 1974.

Not only is Portugal seeking out Europe once again, but Europe is welcoming the new Portugal into its bosom. Specifically, the European Communities are entering into negotiations with Portugal which will better EC-Portuguese trade relations and the lot of Portuguese migrant workers in the Community and will also furnish economic and technical cooperation and financial aid.

☆ ☆ ☆

I close with the warning that the solution of Portugal's economic woes requires the collaboration of humane economists and moral theologians. The time has long since passed when affluent economists from wealthy countries like the United States can coldly survey the Portuguese scene and supply answers which may be economically sound but which consign the lower-class workers to more misery for more years. The number-one problem continues to be not the economy but the lot of those masses.

A subject ventilated in the U.S. Portuguese-language press in late 1977 serves to justify my warning. It relates to the International Commerce Center proposed by the Azores Regional Planning Committee in connection with the Third Plan. I introduce the matter by citing a statement attributed, in a totally different context, to the Chairman of the Dow Chemical Company: "I have long dreamed of buying an island owned by no nation, and of establishing World Headquarters of the Dow Company on the truly neutral ground of such an island, beholden to no nation or society." When I read the statement in 1973 in *The New York Times*, I at once penciled next to it my own reaction: "Caveant cives insularum lusitanarum!"

Back in 1945, F. D. R. and I thought of the Azores as a likely site for U.N. headquarters, and in later and more ecumenical years I would have moved the Vatican there. But United Nations and Holy See are quite different institutions from Dow Chemical and international conglomerates. The masses of the people in general have some defense against the former, for they control them in large measure. They have virtually no defense against the multinationals. The masses of the Azoreans, being given their social and political history, would be rendered absolutely defenseless if their islands became world tax-free headquarters for tax-exempt great companies, as the new proposal seems to suggest.

A report entitled "The Azorean Fight for Freedom" is said to have been in circulation in Washington and elsewhere in October 1977. Allegedly prepared and distributed by a Phoenix Foundation of Amsterdam, it apparently combines FLA ideas with those of at least one American staff member of the University-level Institute of the Azores (see Chapter 19) and those of very conservative thinkers in Europe and America. In essence, these ideas center on the use of the Azores, or of one Azorean island (presumably São Miguel), as an "International Corporate Center," that is, the headquarters of multinational corporations and international banks which are said to be searching for a base of operations as an alternate to the Bahamas, Grand Cayman, and the New Hebrides.

What is needed is a politically stable place—stable as defined by the corporations involved—which would serve as a tax haven. An independent right-wing Azores island would be ideal, located among North America, Western Europe, and Northwest Africa and served by an excellent port such as Ponta Delgada, superb international airports such as Santa Maria and Lajes, and faultless telecommunications such as might be provided by the new Ponta Delgada earth station via satellite pathways direct to the United States and Northern Europe. A formulator of these ideas is quoted as stating that the Azores "could provide the International Business World a convenient geographic location with none of the drawbacks found in existing centers, like income taxation, unpleasant living conditions, political or racial instability and undesirable criminal elements."

It is significant that this report was publicized just as news was circulating of the racial disturbances in Bermuda of early December 1977. I was told during a visit to that island in the summer of 1976 that its second-largest business is that of supplying the clerical and other needs of the many international firms incorporated there. Seven hundred or more Bermudians were so employed.

Another and parallel Azorean proposal enunciated by a member of São Miguel's nobility has recently been published in a book colored monarchical blue and white with a golden *açor* hovering above the title. His imagination soaring, its author writes:

> The Portuguese Federation would have at its disposal in the archipelagoes a sort of Atlantic Switzerlands—monetary center, tourism center, and center of industries linked to the exploitation of the sea and the land. An ideal place for headquarters of specialized agencies of the Common Market or of the United Nations. The Azorean flag would be a "flag of convenience" which would cover millions of tons of ships giving rise to fabulous consular revenues (the principal revenues of Liberia, Costa Rica, Honduras, and Panama—the Panlibhonco group—come from their port consulates, constituting the principal item of the budgets of those States). How many thousands of working posts would not be created in the offices of the shipping firms whose headquarters would be in the Azores? The Portuguese Federation would have the right to three places in the U.N. (Portugal, Madeiras, and Azores), like the U.S.S.R. with Byelorussia and the Ukraine. The importance of Portugal in world politics would be much greater. . . . The population of the Azores could rapidly triple in size, since it would then not have to emigrate, such the number of employment opportunities that would be created. It could even absorb a part of the de-

mographic surpluses of the continent. The entire national scene would without any doubt be strengthened within the framework of a Commonwealth.

Hopefully, the Azoreans after careful consideration will make up their own minds concerning the wisdom of transforming their beautiful and potentially important archipelago into a haven of the type proposed. Hopefully also, they will be guided in their consideration by sympathetic and enlightened relatives and friends in the United States, Canada, Brazil, and elsewhere and not by opportunistic, not to say unscrupulous, Overseas Azoreans interested more in a rapid escudo than in the adverse image which their islands of origin might project in the future. It is inconceivable to me that Azoreans or persons of Azorean descent, wherever located, would wish the handsome banner in blue and white, with *açor* and nine gold stars, to end up as a flag of convenience on a dirty-bottomed tanker.

Much more sensible, to my way of thinking, is the proposal envisaging the establishment of one or more "foreign trade zones" in the Azores. It was advanced by the Association for the Development of Azoreans, incorporated in Massachusetts in 1977; and it will presumably be discussed at the Congress of Azorean Communities scheduled to be held in Angra, Horta, and Ponta Delgada in the second half of August 1978.

Within such a zone various kinds of smallish factories would be set up, employing possibly several hundred workers. These factories would use local energy—for example, the geothermal energy of São Miguel and other islands which is sitting there awaiting developers—and both local raw materials and such materials imported into the zone in bulk. The imported materials or component parts would enter the zone duty free. Some of the finished products would be exported, also tax free. Only the finished products used within the Azores (or Portugal generally) would pay an import duty or other tax on crossing the line from the foreign trade zone to regular Portuguese territory.

Economic proposals concerning the Azores are thus emanating from the right (couched in a certain amount of rhetoric) and from what may be deemed the center. From the left are coming more factual analyses, but ones which are accompanied, as might be expected, by the full panoply of attacks against U.S. imperialism and the holding of Puerto Rico in feudal subjection. For the first time in many a moon, visitors to Lisbon's well-stocked bookstores can purchase these proposals in book form and evaluate them dispassionately. For the first time in decades citizens of Insular Portugal are in a position to discriminate among values. In fine, freedom is at last prevailing in Portugal.

Procession of the Infirm, Furnas (first Sunday after Easter)

13

TOURISM AND TRANSPLANTATION BY SEA AND AIR

By an extraordinary coincidence, voyages abroad in cruise ships began with the Azores. Also, sojourning in palatial residential hotels in a foreign land began with the Madeiras—and at roughly the same time.

Tourism as we know it is generally recognized as having begun with the voyage of the *Quaker City* from New York to the Mediterranean, Black Sea, and Holy Land. The ship, of eighteen hundred tons and using steam and auxiliary sails, departed New York on June 8, 1867. Its first port of call was Horta (June 21-23), whence it sailed along the coast of Pico and on to Gibraltar and farther east. It arrived back in New York on November 19, having stopped off at Bermuda on the westbound passage in true circular-sailing fashion. The stay on Fayal is only too well known because Mark Twain was aboard the ship and subsequently penned *The Innocents Abroad*. "Such a motley collection of people" was the Dabney judgment of the passengers. And here is a topic for future thesis-writing sleuths. Mark Twain mentioned the two Dabney-Webster marriages and tied them in with the Massachusetts murder, but only in the version published in the *Daily Alta California*, not in his famous book issued in Hartford in 1869.

At about the same time or slightly earlier, the British were becoming acquainted with the delights of Madeira. Old John Leacock had gone out there in the preceding century, the first Blandy at the very beginning of the nineteenth. As a result, the ground was laid for a rather massive transplantation of the Britishers who discovered that the return fare to the Portuguese island was compensated for by savings on the cost of heating their northern homes. Indeed, from this perspective, Funchal can properly be grouped with Praia da Rocha in the Algarve,

Algeciras, Gibraltar, the Balearics, and the Riviera. Of all these places, however, Madeira was probably the easiest to reach from a Channel port.

The many vessels outward bound for South Atlantic or Caribbean or even North American ports were available for the purpose of moving to the Pearl of the Atlantic. As for the voyage home, Fayal became involved very early. An English scheme for building a breakwater and stationing a collier at Horta to supply coal to steamers returning from the West Indies was discussed in 1842, the year of Horta's first hotel. Along with the collier, a small schooner would be put in regular service between Madeira and the Azores which would, in the words of Roxana Lewis Dabney, "bring passengers to Fayal to take the West India steamers to England." Regular communication between the two archipelagoes must have gone into effect immediately, for a letter from Funchal to Frances Alsop Dabney (Mrs. Charles William) of 1843 reported on conditions on Madeira. It stated that upwards of three hundred visitors were on the island, one hundred of whom were from Scotland and many from America.

It was not long thereafter that steamers were providing a more reliable service. In 1871, the Island Navigation Enterprise (Emprêsa Insulana de Navegação or E.I.N.) was formed to provide regular steamship service between Lisbon and the Azores. Eventually the E.I.N., subsidized by the Portuguese Government, added a call at Madeira between mainland and Western Islands. It even maintained an unsubsidized service Lisbon-Azores-United States between 1885 and 1910. The E.I.N's superb triangular service between Continental and Insular Portugal only ended when its last major vessels fell victim to the three colonial wars in Africa in the late 1960's. The Enterprise was then merged with the other major Portuguese shipping lines to form the Portuguese Marine Transportation Company (Companhia Portuguesa de Transportes Marítimos or C.T.M.). This company was nationalized after the 25th of April.

☆ ☆ ☆

Madeira's tourism flourished, and it continues to grow. Reid's Hotel was built many years ago. Eight-year-old John Dos Passos and his parents were guests there in 1904. The novelist with wife and daughter stayed there in 1960, his third and last visit to the island of his paternal grandfather.

Reid's, modernized, still ranks among the finest hotels in Funchal and the world. It has some very close rivals in the same flower-bedecked high section of the city, for example the stately Savoy, the ultramodern Madeira-Sheraton, and the new Casino Park (designed by renowned Brazilian architect Oscar Niemeyer and opened in 1977). A little farther out of town to the west is the Madeira-Palácio (ex-Hilton) and well to the east, beyond the airport in Santa Cruz, is the Atlantis (ex-Holiday Inn). All these hotels come replete with swimming pools, pubs, bars, boîtes, bidets, and buffets, and on occasion a shop of Brazil's H. Stern. If one allows them to, they insulate guests most effectively from Insular Portugal. If, on the other hand, one does proper background reading and gets out to see the town, the island, and even adjacent Porto Santo, one enjoys an unforgettable holiday. On the smaller island one basks on the largest and most splendid beach in Insular Portugal (if not in all Portugal).

Funchal is a year-round tourist's paradise. In recent years I have stayed there in January and July, and I have called in there

The large and splendid beach of Porto Santo, June 1978

by ship or air in May, June, and November. All seasons are equally delightful. Protected from the moisture-laden northeast trade winds which precipitate their contents on the north side of the island, Funchal is virtually humidity-free, even in summer. It offers diversions in the form of rides in a bullock cart (*carro de bois*) in the city, a bus tour up to Terreiro da Luta and back partway down to Monte, and then a slide back down to the city in a basket (*cesto*). At Monte the visitor can hire two men to transport him around the area in a hammock (*rede*) suspended from a pole reaching from a shoulder of one man to a shoulder of the other.

The shrine of Our Lady of the Mountain (Nossa Senhora do Monte) contains the beautiful tomb of the late Emperor Charles I of Austria, born in 1887. To understand who this Charles was, we must return to Dom Miguel of Braganza, who fled from Portugal to Germany in 1834.

Seventeen years after arriving in Central Europe, Michael married a lady twenty years old and therefore twenty-nine years younger than he. She presented him with a series of daughters all of whom they named Mary: Mary-of-the-Snow, Maria Teresa, Maria Ana, and Maria Antónia. And the parents married these daughters off very well indeed.

In 1873, Maria Teresa (1855-1944) became the spouse of Charles Louis (1833-1896), a younger brother of Francis Joseph I (born 1830, Emperor of Austria 1848-1916). Charles Louis, the Emperor, and another brother (Maximilian) who aspired to be Emperor of Mexico, were nephews of that Maria Leopoldina whom Crowninshield of Salem passed in the Strait of Bonifacio as she was sailing to Brazil to become the wife of Dom Miguel's brother Dom Pedro.

Emperor Francis Joseph I, or Franz Josef, lived on and on, well into World War I. His son and heir Rudolph, as the entire movie-going world knows full well, committed suicide at Mayerling outside Vienna in 1889 along with his young and beautiful lady-love Marie Vetsera. Because his brother Maximilian had been executed in Mexico in 1867, the succession passed to Charles Louis, who soon thereafter died of typhoid fever after drinking the sacred water of the River Jordan in the Holy Land. It then passed to Charles Louis's oldest son by an earlier marriage, Francis Ferdinand, but he was assassinated at Sarajevo on June 28, 1914, the event which triggered World War I. In the meantime, Francis Ferdinand's younger brother Otto (1865-1906) had died, and therefore with the shot at Sarajevo Otto's son Charles became archduke and crown prince. He succeeded his great-uncle in 1916, in the middle of the War.

From 1916 to 1918 Charles reigned as King Charles IV of Hungary and Emperor Charles I of Austria. After the end of World War I and the dissolution of the Austro-Hungarian Empire, Charles took refuge on hospitable Madeira with his wife, his heir, and other children, the last of the Habsburgs. They arrived in November 1921.

Charles's wife the Empress Zita was born in 1892. The couple were married in 1911, and as a wedding present she was informed that a new and minor planet of the solar system but recently discovered had been named "Zita." She was only twenty-nine when she took up residence on the island. Some Madeiran girls were given her name, although Zita can also be a diminutive of Luisa (via Luisita). For Portuguese girls to bear her name was most appropriate, for she was old Dom Miguel's granddaughter. Her mother was his daughter Maria Antónia (1862-1959). Charles was only indirectly descended from Miguel of the bones; his stepgrandmother Maria Teresa was Miguel's daughter.

Charles died on Madeira on April 1, 1922. The heir of Charles and Zita is Archduke Otto of Habsburg (born 1912), the pretender to the imperial throne of Austria. He now lives in Germany with his wife and several children, ever grateful to the Portuguese for their hospitality and a loyal admirer of everything Portuguese. Upon being elected to our International Academy of Portuguese Culture in 1966, he spoke the following words concerning his father: "In the midst of the first fratricidal world war in the West he had sought out peace. Banished from his country, proscribed in Europe, he found it only in the midst of your people, surrounded by the simple and generous sympathy of the inhabitants of the islands, and a few months later in the fraternal repose which God promises to the just."

Empress Zita had taken refuge in Portugal in the spring of 1940. She left Lisbon for New York via Pan American clipper on July 16, 1940, touching down at Horta, where her photograph figures among Bagatelle's treasures. She and several members of her family preferred the security of the Americas to the turmoil of Europe.

The American and Canadian tourist on Madeira, then, will wish to visit Charles's tomb replete with Cross of Christ worked into the grillwork. And they will admire the colorful flowers growing in profusion everywhere and at all seasons. Indeed, Madeira and the Azores are, like Caribbean islands, Bermuda, and Canaries, a flower-lover's heaven.

Madeira's flora is basically semitropical. A magnificently illustrated book by Rui Vieira available locally in editions in several languages including English aids the visitor in his floral identifications:

> *Plants indigenous to Madeira* such as the dragon tree; *Trees* like the delicately lavender jacarandas which line, among other streets, Funchal's Avenue of Prince Henry the Navigator leading up from town to the complex of great residential hotels, and which are threatened with extinction by the most disagreeable automobile, taxi, bus, and truck fumes mentioned in Chapter 1, and like the mixed green and deep-red metrosideros ("Christmas tree of New Zealand"); *Climbers* like the ubiquitous bougainvillea; *Herbs and shrubby plants* as, for instance, agapanthus, camellias, cannas, hibiscus, oleander, and prickly pear (the *Opuntia ficus-indica* which also decorates the Aeolian Islands and is much appreciated by Salinari in the United States), and the colorful and oddly shaped strelitzia reginae (bird of paradise) much used as gifts to beautiful ladies; and *Pot plants* such as the anthurium.

Ironically, Madeira's major tourist problem at the present time is exactly the reverse of that of the Azores. In and around Funchal there are many hotels ranging from Reid's to excellent third-class hotels and pensions, but the single runway of the single airport is incapable of accommodating the planes needed to fill the hotels rapidly with large groups such as conventioneers. In and around Angra and Ponta Delgada and up in Furnas there is a dearth of hotels, but each of the two islands is served, directly or indirectly, by a great international airport capable of receiving several Boeing 747's almost simultaneously.

Madeira's guests used to arrive by ship. And how I used to thrill to the arrival of the greatest regular caller of them all in those student weeks of 1938 and 1939! She was the *Cap Arcona* (27,500 tons and three stacks) of the Hamburg-South America Line, billed as the fastest ship to South America in the 1930's. A reproduction of a beautiful painting of her sailing on a tropical night under

South Atlantic skies is included both within and on the dust jacket of Bathe's coffee-table volume felicitously entitled *Seven Centuries of Sea Travel: From the Crusaders to the Cruises.*

In those days, hotels and transportation were roughly in balance. After World War II, the ships gradually dwindled in number virtually to zero, although some cruise ships today call at Funchal, including an increasing number of U.S.S.R. ships to fill the vacuum left by the ever fewer cruise ships of the West. But cruise ships do not fill hotels.

Immediately following World War II, a British flying-boat line, Aquila Airways, carried passengers from Southampton to Funchal and return, sometimes with stop at Lisbon. These flying boats were the only means of travel by air until 1960, when the large airport was opened on Porto Santo, still used by a weekly TAP Boeing 707 on a flight from Caracas to Lisbon. But Porto Santo is not Madeira, and a further move was necessary.

Only in 1964 was the present runway at Santa Cruz literally carved out of the side of a cliff overhanging the ocean. An arrival and landing from southwest to northeast is spectacular, for the final approach is a curve. TAP's pilots are experts with the landing, and they originally trained the pilots of the foreign charters which arrive. In spite of two crashes in late 1977, the airport's safety record is excellent. I landed there for the third time in a TAP 727 on June 18, 1978. The Captain explained the entire approach and landing procedure to me. Carefully thought out and laid down in complete detail, it requires that the cockpit crew have the runway in sight during the downwind approach, otherwise on to Las Palmas, or to Porto Santo, or back to Lisbon. I made the landing in complete confidence and would never hesitate to return to Madeira by air.

Madeira faces a major dilemma: lengthen the present runway by a monumental feat of engineering which would require fill from the bottom of the sea up to the rather considerable height of the airport, or find an alternate cloud-free and level site. The dilemma must be resolved; otherwise, the hotels will not be filled year-round. Of course this tourist problem looms as a great boon to present guests in the large hotels, for they are spared the disagreeable experience of tangling with conventions. The airport simply cannot pour into Funchal over a one- or two-day period several hundred legionnaires or foreign-language teachers or doctors or lawyers and their families.

In other words—and this point must be stressed—tourism must be carefully and responsibly controlled by the highest levels of government, or a double disaster can ensue. On the one hand, the tourists can find the local situation unsatisfactory and take their business elsewhere. On the other hand, the local population can suffer greatly from a tourist industry exploited from afar. Thus, the local folk may experience a considerable rise in prices because their products are in great demand for hotel guests, but there may not be a sufficient number of sufficiently well paying jobs generated by the hotels to compensate for the increased cost of living.

☆ ☆ ☆

Tourism does not seem to present a major problem for Madeirans, Many are employed in the hotels and ancillary industries. The money spent by visitors in residence and by tourists is making a considerable contribution to the economy, for, as already suggested, tourism is an invisible export item. For Azoreans, tourism looms as of quite a different nature.

A first problem involves the relative attractiveness of the Azores to international tourists. The climate is less semitropical than Madeira's, and it does rain in certain months. The mild temperature and the humidity, however, do lead to cultivation of a flora which in some seasons rivals that of Madeira. The rows of hydrangeas in the Azores, both the single and the doubled, delight all visitors. The mixture of hydrangeas and roses which line roads on Terceira is particularly attractive, as are the many metrosideros trees and cannas and agapanthus, the latter called "crowns of the king" on Terceira, "imperial crowns" and "St. Joseph's staffs" on São Miguel, and, on Madeira, by way of contrast, "Henry's crowns." The garden between the Terra Nostra Hotel and Yankee Hall in Furnas is incomparable.

A second problem involves transportation. It is very easy to reach the Azores by air, from Boston, Montreal, and Lisbon. Having arrived on Santa Maria or at Lajes on Terceira, one sooner or later wishes to move to another island, visits to São Miguel, Terceira, and Fayal being of the first priority. The lone interisland steamer, the C. T. M.'s *Ponta Delgada* (220 feet 2 inches in length) is too small, too uncomfortable, and too infrequent. The local surface craft are not suitable for international tourists, not even the regular launches between Horta and Madalena do Pico. Hydrofoils, so common in the Aeolian Islands, hovercraft, visible in Venetian waters, and the Boeing jetfoil, in use between Zeebrugge and London, are too expensive to operate and would result in fares which the bulk of the passengers—local persons and not tourists from abroad—could not afford to pay. Helicopters are not only too expensive but are not suitable for the peculiar swirling wind conditions of oceanic islands. These eliminations leave only the airplanes of SATA (Sociedade Açoreana de Transportes Aéreos—The Azores Airline). The SATA planes are comfortable and most competently flown, but the frequency of service, size of planes, and failure to serve Graciosa, São Jorge, Pico, and Corvo constitute major drawbacks.

These objections are at last being answered. The Regional Government of the Azores, including and especially the Regional Secretary of Transportation and Tourism, have evolved a new and very sensible air policy. It is based on three types of aircraft: commuter planes, feeder planes, and off-Azores planes. Airstrips are now being finished on Pico and Corvo and will be built on São

Elongated São Jorge from the north side of Pico

Jorge and Graciosa. Out of them, small planes will operate commuter services: Corvo-Flores, Fayal-Pico-São Jorge-Graciosa-Terceira, and Santa Maria-St. Michael's. The present SATA planes, probably increased in number, will provide the feeder services among Flores, Fayal, Terceira, St. Michael's, and Santa Maria. At the two international airports these services will connect with the off-Azores services to Continental Portugal and abroad. These feeder services will also tie in at Ponta Delgada's airport (which, like Madeira's, can accommodate Boeing 727's) with TAP's intra-Metropolitan planes direct to Funchal and direct to Lisbon. Even today, by the way, TAP's triangular air service Ponta Delgada-Funchal-Lisbon is strongly recommended to the tourist from North America, who can thus easily and comfortably visit Insular and Continental Portugal on one swing and can even add the Canaries from Funchal.

Of necessity, the Regional Government's air policy must serve Azoreans and Continental Portuguese first and foremost. For the time being, potential tourists of the future have to be considered of secondary importance. And anyway, these interisland airplanes will never provide a proper means of seeing the Azores islands. Islands, yes, even those of the Caribbean, are best appreciated from shipboard, for islands constitute a sea phenomenon.

E. I. N.'s triangular run of some twenty days' duration Lisbon-Lisbon was ideal. The ships were relatively slow. Indeed, no cruise ship should steam at over seventeen knots, the critical speed at which the ladies' hairdos blow on an open deck and force the ladies, and therefore the gentlemen, inside. On the old *Carvalho Araujo* and *Lima*, the passengers could see all the islands and go ashore for an adequate length of time on all. Moreover, all the islands are well worth seeing: Santa Maria with its magnificent view from the Pico Alto (High Peak), even to the Formigas, and with its graceful Bay of St. Lawrence; Graciosa with its Sulfur Cavern (Furna do Enxofre), an island visited in May 1791 by none other than the westbound Chateaubriand (who, eastbound, did not visit Fayal in September 1792, as has been reported); São Jorge with its rolling pasture lands and relatively sparse population; Pico with its *mistérios* and the Peak itself and the view from Areia Larga; attractive Flores with its two internal lagoons of apparently differently-hued water, the Deep Lagoon (Lagoa Funda, green) and the Lengthy Lagoon (Lagoa Comprida, black), and with its curious Rock of the Staffs (Rocha dos Bordões), vertical

The Lives of Azoreans and Madeirans

Basking in the early-morning sunshine on Corvo

sticklike formations; and Corvo, a tiny world all by itself, with less than five hundred people and with a philharmonic ensemble, that is, a band. Once the much faster *Funchal* entered service, the possibility of visiting, conveniently and comfortably, the off islands dwindled to zero.

The population density of the several islands, that is, the number of inhabitants per square mile, may constitute one measure of the relative attractiveness of the components of the Azores to visitors, as well, incidentally, as to the lower-class inhabitants. Here are the figures based on the population revealed by the 1970 Census (see beginning of Chapter 3):

Santa Maria..256	Graciosa 313	Fayal ...265
São Miguel...520	São Jorge 140	Flores .. 96
Terceira 460	Pico 108	Corvo .. 67

A wealthy and venturesome Azorean entrepreneur should consider chartering for July and August and possibly also September one of the many Caribbean cruise liners operating during the winter season out of Port Everglades, Miami, and San Juan, and putting it on the old Lisbon-Madeira-Azores cruise run. With the proper publicity, the ship might well be booked solid for each of the monthly voyages.

One way to see a single Azorean port is by international cruise ship. Some major ships are already calling at either Horta or Ponta Delgada, if not both. Those scheduled for 1977 included, at Horta, the *Canberra, Mermoz* (named after Jean Mermoz, mentioned in Chapter 10, who closed the gap between Senegal and Brazil in 1930 and was lost between Dakar and Natal six years later), *Royal Viking Sea, Royal Viking Star,* and *Sagafjord,* and at Ponta Delgada (the majority consigned to the Casa Bensaúde), the *Bellatrix, Britanis* (ex-*Lurline*), *Canberra* (three times), *Eugenio C* (twice), *Kungsholm* (three times), *Mariposa, Mermoz, Oriana,* and *Shota Rustaveli,* the latter out of Odessa and flying the flag of the Soviet Union.

The Russian vessel gives pause for reflection. Increasingly, the demands of Western maritime unions and the failure of owners to meet them are driving U.S., Italian, and other cruise ships from the oceans, the regular-run passenger ships having long since been eliminated. As a result, Russian officers and crewmen are gaining valuable knowledge and experience in the ports of Insular Portugal, just as the Russian cockpit crews of Cubana Airlines came to know Santa Maria.

A third problem confronting Azoreans desirous of realizing the tourist potential of their archipelago concerns the lack of adequately-sized hotels of a category such as to attract an international clientele. Angra has one very good hotel, the Hotel de Angra, with superb dining room overlooking the spectacular Public Garden. In addition to Ponta Delgada's Hotel de São Pedro, which is *sui generis,* that city boasts the new Hotel Avenida. And in Furnas there is the Terra Nostra. The new hotels projected for Praia do Pópulo on São Miguel's south coast east of Ponta Delgada and at the southern end of the lake in the Furnas crater have not yet materialized.

Fortunately, that Azorean city most appealing to the international set can claim the best hotel, indeed the only residential-type—or Funchal-type—hotel to which a foreigner may be transplanted. The Hotel Fayal is the former Western Union residential compound built of earthquake-proof construction by Stone &

Webster back in the 1920's at a cost of $460,093.92. In 1970, the entire ensemble was acquired by AÇORTUR (Investimentos Turísticos dos Açores), owned in considerable part by local shareholders. Sir Anthony Coningham de Waltham Denny, Bt., an English architect, designed a total conversion, and the grandiose new hotel was opened in 1973. The correspondence between the hotel units and those of Western Union follow:

Western Union designation	Hotel Fayal name
Staff house (that is, mess)	Casa A
Two-family house	Casa B
Two-family house	Casa C
Two-family house	Casa D
Two-family house	Casa E
Two-family house	Casa F
Director's house	Casa G
Chief Electrician's house	Casa H
Superintendent's house	Casa I
Recreation building	Discoteca
Infirmary	Residential cottage
Garage	Garage
Two tennis courts	Two tennis courts

(Western Union made a distinction between Director, the representative of both Western Union and Italcable, whose cable laid in 1924 the Western Union staff handled in Horta, and Superintendent, in charge of local Western Union operations.)

The major hotel addition was a large outdoor swimming pool and accompanying facilities including bathhouses. The prices of a sojourn, including all meals, are so modest that for a stay of several weeks a family's transoceanic fare is quickly absorbed. The hotel's dilemma has been until recently that of the Funchal hotels: how to fill it being given the few airplane seats daily between Santa Maria or Terceira and Fayal.

For the Fayal enthusiast who wishes a more nautical environment on the waterfront in an old fortress replete with history, the Estalagem de Santa Cruz stands available. Outstanding in every respect, it has only ten rooms, each with veranda overlooking port and Pico. The Inn's attractive little bar is an ideal spot to drink a Dramático—one-third local sour-lime juice, one-third gin, and one-third sweet vermouth—Fayal's answer to the Negroni.

A fourth problem is in my opinion peculiar to the Azores. It concerns the extremely large flow back to the islands of Azorean emigrants who have settled in the United States and Canada. These travelers return to visit and stay with relatives. They provide considerable revenue for the international airlines involved, now exclusively TAP and TWA, and for chartered planes. But they do not normally fill the best hotels or eat at the best restaurants, although some do buy the available souvenirs or are given mementoes by their relatives and friends. On occasion they deny plane seats (especially on SATA's planes) to potential tourists, who thus cannot occupy beautiful and available hotel rooms. Moreover, they tend to lower tourism in the archipelago to a common peasant denominator. After all, well-heeled tourists like to meet local residents of their own station in life and also enjoy becoming acquainted with their opposite numbers from Great Britain, France, Germany, and Scandinavia. In this respect, the contrast between Azores and Madeiras is most marked.

For the first time beginning with the summer of 1976, tourists from abroad had the opportunity of meeting, within both Azores and Madeiras, their opposite numbers from Continental Portugal. Prior to the Revolution, Continentals could hardly be bothered with Insular Portugal, especially the Azores. They had bigger fish to fry. Suddenly, after the Revolutionary euphoria subsided and Portuguese faced the stark reality that they could not spend precious escudos abroad on frivolous tourism, Continentals discovered the Western Islands. Prevented from leaving Portugal with more than seven thousand escudos, Continental tourists found that the Azores were part of Portugal and not a foreign land and were, moreover, most attractive and relatively inexpensive.

A fifth problem with respect to tourism in the Azores is the general lack of tourist development, yet the potential in this regard is tremendous. There are hardly any products of local crafts to purchase and take home, only embroidery on Terceira, with a little on São Miguel. There are no quaint and gracious tearooms in which to spend money on regional sweets based on convent recipes of old. Examples of such desserts are the puddings and cakes which Father Júlio da Rosa served us in Horta at "tea" time on July 2, 1974, in his home with beautiful china, linen, silver, and dining-room furniture—*pudim de frutas* (whipped cream, sponge cake, banana, guava, orange, pineapple, and raisins), *pudim de claras com amêndoas* (white of egg with almonds), *bolo de coco* (coconut cake), and *bolo de cacau* (chocolate cake)—hardly the ideal menu for a weight-watcher. Lastly, there are practically no books or tourist pamphlets to read, not even an illustrated booklet on the trees and flowers, much less the abundant fish in Azorean waters whose names one tries to learn at mealtime. There is one excellent book, a well-written and informative travel narrative, but it is difficult to find: *The Azores* of 1963 by Robin Bryans (that is, Robert Harbinson Bryans), whose parallel volume *Madeira: Pearl of the Atlantic* of 1959 is also worth reading. There is also a splendid Swiss book in French on Madeiras and Cape Verde Islands as well as Azores replete with excellent photographs.

Only by simultaneous attempts at solutions to all the problems outlined or hinted at above will the Azores ever come to attract non-Portuguese tourists and residents from abroad. Realistically, the numbers of these money-spenders will not be large for many years to come. Visitors to the Azores will continue to be the more discriminating and the more adventurous of travelers and not the masses. They will be Dabneys, Hicklings, and Websters, their friends, flower and bird enthusiasts, artists, cable buffs, old-time fliers, and veterans of military and naval service involving the Azores. They will be like the German U-boat commander of World War II who spent a large part of 1943 gazing at graceful Fayal through his periscope. Thirty years later, in the summer of 1973, he turned up at the Estalagem. Or like TV actor Larry Haddon, who has played in "Kojak." In the fall of 1944, when twenty-one and a deck officer on a merchant ship, he discovered that his vessel had broken down. It had to leave its convoy and put into Horta for month-long repairs. He always remembered the store on the back side of the island where he bought his father a whole cheese. In 1974, he sailed from Canada to Europe on the U.S.S.R.'s *Alexandre Pouchkine*. En route home in early July, he revisited Horta, found the store, and purchased another cheese.

☆ ☆ ☆

In the United States in recent years, the concept of the Trail has received widespread application. Examples are Boston's Freedom Trail, New Bedford's Moby Dick Trail, and Salem's Historic Trail. In a sense, these walking tours are latter-day reduced versions of the great medieval pilgrimage routes of Western Europe like the Way of St. James from France under the Milky Way across the

Pyrenees and west through Spain to Santiago de Compostela and its tomb of Apostle James (feast day July 25).

In Chapters 7 and 8, mention was made of a possible Fisher/Amory Trail on Terceira and a possible Hickling Trail on St. Michael's. Greater Horta lends itself even more to the concept, and I have taken the liberty of designing a Cable Trail. Having in mind the Horta aficionados from among the crews of the numerous transatlantic sailing yachts, the cruise passengers, and the air travelers including the large numbers of Americans of Azorean descent or birth, I envisage fifteen painted signs each containing at least a number, if not a title. I further imagine publication, possibly in inexpensive mimeographed form, of a readable pamphlet with city plan.

The pamphlet's introduction would condense information from Chapters 7-11 above and would invite the reader to visit three sites off the trail proper:

A. *Bagatelle*;

B. *Dabney Corner of the Horta Cemetery*, with the epithet "The father of the poor" on Charles William Dabney's tombstone;

C. *Meeting Room of the Municipal Chamber* (in the former Jesuit edifice just to the right or north of the Mother Church) to see Charles William Dabney's portrait bearing the inscription "An illustrious man who distinguished himself in particular during the famine of 1858-1859."

The main body of the pamphlet would describe the fifteen stops on the walking tour, which begins at the waterfront near the fortress inn. The entries would read more or less as follows, and ideally the entire text of the pamphlet would be available in French and German as well as English:

1. *Rua Consul Dabney.* The axis of the Cable Trail, it is known to marine navigators as the *Canáda* or "slot" and is useful as a reference point in mooring a vessel in Horta harbor.

2. *Trinity House.* Built in 1902 and reinforced after the earthquake of August 31, 1926, it housed the trinity of original cable companies: Europe & Azores Telegraph Co. (English), Deutsch-Atlantische Telegraphengesellschaft (German), and Commercial Cable Co. (U. S.).

3. *Joint Cable Station*. Built by Stone & Webster 1926-1928, it is in reality an addition to Trinity House, with whose southeast corner it is connected. In early 1970, Cable & Wireless, the successor company to Europe & Azores Telegraph, sold the two-building complex to private Portuguese businessmen. They in turn sold it to the Portuguese Government, which in the fall of 1973 opened the vocational high school there (Escola Industrial e Comercial da Horta). A grand opportunity was lost to create the world's greatest cable museum.

4. *Power House*. Built by Stone & Webster in conjunction with the Joint Cable Station, it contained six gasoline and two diesel generators, used in emergencies when public power failed and also on certain other occasions. It was sold in 1967 to a former C & W employee.

5. *Fredonia*. Purchased in 1835 by Consul Charles William Dabney and sold by his descendants in 1899 to Europe & Azores Telegraph. On November 11, 1969, C & W sold it to the Lar das Criancinhas da Horta. It was rebuilt as a children's home or *crèche*. This charitable institution has received extensive assistance from the U.S. People-to-People program. Fredonia was famous for its beautiful gardens which included a particularly tall Norfolk Island pine (araucaria) still standing in the western part, an identifying object on the British Admiralty chart of Horta harbor.

6. *Waldorf*. Presumably a former Dabney building, it stands just north of Fredonia. It became the residence of Europe & Azores Telegraph's station electrician. The Portuguese Government bought it together with the garden to the west up to the C & W residential cottages (No. 8) at the time it purchased Trinity House and the Joint Cable Station. Waldorf today houses the Horta branch of the official national sports organization.

7. *DAT Residential Compound*. Of the three original cable companies in Horta, only the German company provided quarters for married employees (other than top officials) before the 1926 earthquake. After that disaster, which coincided with the returning of **DAT** to Horta following World War I, the **DAT** compound was rebuilt. It came to include three apartment houses for families, a bachelors' mess at the northern end of one of the apartment houses, and superintendent's home.

The bachelors' mess is particularly noteworthy for the four beautiful stained-glass windows in its ballroom at the northeast corner. They depict symbols of various parts of Germany and constitute adequate justification for any German to make the pilgrimage to Horta:

a. *Königreich Preussen*:—Hamburg, Bremen, Lübeck, Braunschweig, Oldenburg, Lippe.
b. *Mit Gott für Kaiser und Reich!*:—Schwarzburg-Rudolstadt, Anhalt, Baden, Hessen, Waldeck, Schwarzburg-Sondershausen.
c. *Königreich Sachsen*:—Sachsen-Weimar, Mecklenburg-Schwerin, Sachsen-Meiningen, Sachsen-Coburg und Gotha, Mecklenburg-Strelitz, Sachsen-Altenburg.
d. *Königreich Bayern, Königreich Württenberg*:—Reuss I. L., Elsass, Lothringen, Schaumburg-Lippe, Reuss A. L.

When the **DAT** staff from Germany left Fayal in 1943, the company rented out its residential quarters. Early in 1974, the Portuguese Government purchased the apartment buildings and bachelor quarters and continued to rent them to local families to ease an acute housing shortage. The local government of the District of Horta acquired the superintendent's home with the idea of converting it into a residence for the civil governor. As that official departed the island following the Revolution of April 25, 1974, the plan did not materialize. Today, the superintendent's home and the bachelors' mess house the two Horta secretariats of the Regional Government of the Azores.

8. *Cable & Wireless Residential Cottages.* For married staff members, they were built after the 1926 earthquake. They are of reinforced concrete construction, of one floor, to withstand earth tremors.

9. *Commercial Cable Co. Residential Cottages.* For married staff members, they were likewise built after the 1926 earthquake. They are of wooden construction, of one floor, to withstand earth tremors. Only one is still standing. Named "Villa Houghton," it is well maintained with beautiful flower garden. The late Mr. H. N. Houghton had been an employee of Commercial Cable.

10. *The Cedars.* Built in the mid 1850's by John Pomeroy Dabney and sold by his widow Sarah Hickling Dabney in 1900 to Commercial Cable. On July 22, 1963, the cable company sold it to

Lawyer Manuel Linhares de Andrade, who lives in it, ever hospitable.

11. *Commercial Cable Co. Mess.* The three original cable companies first sent single men to Horta to initiate operations. Therefore, each company at once set up a bachelors' mess with living quarters as well as dining hall. The entrance to the Commercial Cable mess, at 21A Rua Consul Dabney, bears the date 1901. The building directly in from that entrance, adjacent to and west of The Cedars, was the portion first constructed. Subsequently, the mess was enlarged by the addition of the building to the west of the 1901 structure. The two buildings are now privately owned.

12. *Western Union Telegraph Co. Residential Compound.* Today the Hotel Fayal, described earlier in this chapter. The staff house or mess became the residential quarters of several Pan American staff members sent to Fayal at the end of 1938. During the seven years of Pan Am's flying-boat operations through Horta (1939-1945), this house often offered its hospitality to passengers delayed for one reason or another.

13. *Cable & Wireless Mess.* The first of the cable messes, it was built for the British bachelor staff before 1900. Following the earth tremors of March 1935, the Horta high school (Liceu Nacional da Horta) found itself without a satisfactory building. Arrangements were immediately made with the Eastern Telegraph Co., as it was then known locally, for the rental of the mess to house the *liceu*. The school began to function there on May 1, 1935. On July 30, 1946, the Portuguese Government purchased the building along with one tennis court and some land. The mess was later modified, and other buildings were constructed, to create the present *liceu*. These *liceu* buildings together with Trinity House and the Joint Cable Station in effect today form a large school complex at the secondary level.

14. *Cable Huts.* The three huts are located at Entre-Montes (literally "Between Hills"), between Monte Queimado and Monte da Guia. They mark the actual landing places of the second group of cables (1923-1928). From the huts the cables went underground to the Joint Cable Station.

The earlier British, German, and Commercial cables came in to huts at the Lagoa Fort below Espalamaca. These huts were later destroyed in a storm. The cables were then relaid into a new hut on the Horta side of the Ribeira dos Flamengos (Brook of the Flemings) in Conception precinct.

15. *"Prince Albert of Monaco" Meteorological Observatory.* The observatory began to function in 1901 in the south tower of the Mother Church within the ex-Jesuit complex. It was transferred to its present location atop Monte das Moças only in 1915, even though the building had been begun in 1901, in the presence of King Carlos and his queen.

A final note: The Cable Trail is extremely photogenic. Visitors should arrive equipped with camera and adequate color film.

PART II

THEIR VALUES

They also say that, when the discoverers of these islands went to the prince, he asked them about their several features and their qualities, and among other things he asked if the trees had their roots deep in the earth. And when they replied to him, "No, only on the surface of the earth," he replied, almost prophetically, by describing what we now see has come to pass, without omitting a single point: that the first inhabitants of these Azores islands would clear and work the land, and their children would sow and eat, and the grandchildren would sell, and the others, later generations and their descendants, would flee, as we see clearly today, for our inheritances are diverted to outsiders and foreigners, who come into possession of them and obtain them by dint of buying them and removing them from the hands of the natives who formerly possessed them.

Father Gaspar Frutuoso (1522-1591)

14
THE "STATE" AND THE "CHURCH"

Continental Portuguese, some Flemings, and a sprinkling of other European and African mainlanders peopled the Azores and the Madeiras, unknown and uninhabited volcanic peaks out in the Atlantic which were discovered by Portuguese mariners in the early fifteenth century. Ever closely controlled by the capital of Portugal, the new islanders and their descendants lived their lives in what was in effect midocean isolation. Sharing Continental Portugal's conceptions of social class and relationship between the sexes, they did find themselves astride the North Atlantic's main lines of communication. Those of them who were in contact with international shipping, submarine telegraphy and telephony, aviation, and telecommunication via satellite therefore were able to live a satisfying life in touch with the latest technical achievements of the modernizing world. A dream of theirs was an ever greater and profitable influx of tourists from abroad.

The vast majority of Azoreans and Madeirans, however, continued to struggle with their traditional agriculture. They remained on land, most of them not at all tempted by the abundant fish obviously swarming about their islands. Politically nonparticipatory, they did experience a moment of exhilaration in the second quarter of the nineteenth century, when the Azoreans joined the liberal side in the Portuguese political upheaval which followed the French Revolution and the Napoleonic era. This liberal stance was bolstered in part by the model before their eyes of two eminent American commercial and consular families, the Hicklings and the Dabneys. The posture curiously changed to conservatism, both in the Azores and the Madeiras, with the advent of the Portuguese Revolution, which began on April 25, 1974. The long-range effects of midocean isolation suddenly

Traditional cultivation of Terceira's land, 1974

manifested themselves in a firm bid for autonomy from Lisbon, which in the minds of some, in particular inhabitants of the Azorean island of St. Michael's, became translated into a rightist demand for separation, that is, independence. The precedent of the now-independent sister archipelago, the Cape Verde Islands, lay present for all to see.

Over the centuries, the values of Azoreans and Madeirans have been basically those of Continental Portugal, for Insular Portugal in fact was ever a part of that European nation. The islanders' attitudes toward State, Church, family, school, and doctor, the nature of their folk culture, and the extent of their sharing in the brilliant high culture of Portugal, however, can be expected to differ in varying degree from those of the mainlanders. Indeed, in some instances Azoreans will differ from Madeirans, or within an archipelago Michaelese from Fayalese, or within an island the Funchalese from the inhabitants of the north side of Madeira, or within a family one branch from another.

In any overall discussion of these values, informed generalization must be the order of the day, all the more as a sufficiency of

Their Values

detailed studies based on the methodology of modern social science is still lacking. Such studies are badly needed, however, and several are already in progress. Many will have to be written by specialists and then digested by humanistically-oriented generalists, but that day is many years away. In the meantime, humanistic synthesis of decades-long personal observations and creative writers' insights will have to serve as primary source materials.

The several institutions upon which the Insular Portuguese value system is based are here described primarily as they existed before the 1974 Revolution, for it was that period which conferred its attitudes on the majority of mature Azoreans and Madeirans living today. Some specific changes accomplished since the Revolution are mentioned, but they are necessarily tentative. They are on occasion very indicative.

☆ ☆ ☆

In the mid-1930's, Portugal issued a revealing postage stamp. Up the center runs a fasces, symbol of authority which provided the name for Italy's Fascisti of the interwar period. On the fasces, which lacks the axes, are four small shields each with five dots cruciform. Printed on a ribbon encircling the bundle of rods is the phrase "Tudo pela Nação" (Everything for the Nation). The phrase is the second part of a widely cited statement which Salazar once made: "A nação é tudo; tudo pela nação" (The nation is everything; everything for the nation).

It would be easy, but petty and misleading, to discuss the stamp, and above all the phrase, in terms merely of twentieth-century Salazar's political philosophy. Since the end of the fifteenth century, many Portuguese have conceived of their country as a unified, highly centralized, nation-state beyond and above which there is nothing, neither Emperor nor Pope nor . . . . Corollarywise, they have naturally felt that the nation-state is owed everything, even and especially gratitude, as is indicated in a rhetorical Azorean newspaper report dated December 21, 1972, of the creation in Metropolitan Portugal of three additional universities, nine higher normal schools, and other educational institutions: "The authentic Nation is grateful to the Government for this succulent Christmas cake, with which it will nourish the intelligence of thousands of Portuguese."

For an early instance of primacy of the State, take this passage from a famous Portuguese oration proferred in Latin and printed almost as soon as delivered. The day is Friday, December 9, 1485, the place a public consistory in the Sala Regia, an antechamber to the Sistine Chapel in the Vatican. The ambassador of King John II of Portugal, rendering the obedience of his monarch to Pope Innocent VIII, affirms:

> ... A most formidable king, one who is most compliant with the Roman Church and a propagator of the Christian cult, before whom the kings of the Ethiopians bow down and to whom they offer presents every year, acknowledges that Your Blessedness is in truth the vicar on earth of him concerning whom David in the 71st Psalm said: "And he shall rule from sea to sea, and from the river unto the ends of the earth. The Ethiopians shall bow down before him, and his foes shall lick the dust. The kings of Tharsis and of the island shall offer presents, the kings of the Arabians and of Saba shall bring gifts: and all kings shall adore him, and all nations shall serve him."

In other words, the Ethiopians (meaning Africans) bow down before and each year offer gifts to King John, as in fact they were doing by that time along the West African coast as far south as the Congo River and beyond. The Ethiopians also bow down before God, and certain kings offer Him gifts. John is equated with God in the oration, which specifically refers to Pope Innocent as the vicar of God on earth. The Pope operates on a lower plane than the King of Portugal.

This superior position of the State in relation to the Church was emphasized at the opening session of the Congress on the History of Discoveries, which took place in September 1960 as part of the commemorations of the fifth centenary of the death of Prince Henry the Navigator. The session itself was held in the imposing building of the National Assembly in Lisbon. Salazar presided, seated at a high table beneath which was placed the throne of His Eminence Manuel Cardinal Cerejeira, Patriarch of Lisbon. The President of the Council of Ministers remained as aloof from that notable gathering of scholars from all over the world as he did from Insular and Overseas Portugal: he uttered not a syllable but merely waved a hand for the master of ceremonies to open the meeting.

Another example was provided by the situation of the Archbishop of Goa (and Patriarch of the East Indies) vis-à-vis the Governor sent from Lisbon back in the old days before Nehru's take-over on December 18, 1961. Pico-born Archbishop José Vieira Alvernaz confided in me, when I visited with him in Goa several months after the absorption into the Indian Union, that everyone, including the masses of the people, linked him with the Governor, for in every public function he had to appear along with the Governor. Indeed, the latter even had a throne within the sanctuary of the cathedral. Apropos of this latter point, an American (non-Portuguese) priest who visited the Azores in the early 1970's told me quite spontaneously that he found the presence of the State overwhelming and oppressive. He added: "The Church kowtows excessively to representatives of the State, even to the extent of letting them sit in the sanctuary, do the readings, and participate in the Lavabo."

The relationship of bishop to governor was spelled out in the Missionary Agreement of 1940 between Church and State in the article on salaries. In colonies having a governor-general, like Angola and Mozambique, the bishops received stipends equal to those of the governors of the districts into which the colony was divided (not including the district in which the capital was located). The Archbishops of Luanda and Lourenço Marques, however, received stipends equal to those of the governors of the districts of Luanda and Lourenço Marques respectively, but not to those of the governors-general!

Exaltation of the State and acceptance of the State's domination of the Church—in chess a bishop (called a dauphin in Portuguese) is dominated by queen if not king—ran throughout the monarchy from 1140 to 1910 and throughout the New and Social States of the twentieth century until the Revolution. The fact that Portugal was theoretically Catholic altered not an iota of this political conception, which is contrary to Catholic teaching as the American Catholic knows it, especially the Irish American. As a result, Portuguese children were brought up believing in the State with a passion and trained to accept the juggling around of bishops in the several colonies as outlined in Chapter 3. In later life, they revealed themselves to be extremely and genuinely patriotic, to the point that, when abroad and engaged in serious conversation concerning grave problems of the host country and their native land, they were most reluctant to say anything bad about Portugal. They often began to do so and suddenly cut themselves off, exclaiming: "I am abroad and should not speak ill of my Patria." Outsiders, of course, should ever remember that all Portuguese are patriotic, even those normally considered internationalists such as Catholics and Communists and Socialists.

When one realizes that all forces of national life, including and especially press, educational system, and Church, inculcated the worship of the State as supreme—"a nação é tudo"—one can understand the rigidity of political conceptions in Continental Portugal and Adjacent Islands. Or the rigidity of political conceptions as openly flaunted, but not necessarily as held within one's breast and on rare occasions expressed in the privacy of one's home behind closed shutters and drawn curtains. The Insular Portuguese are not fools, and I offer a priceless piece of proof.

I was departing an adjacent island aboard the *Carvalho Araujo* in 1964. A local friend came aboard to see me off. On the dock was a local big shot seeing someone else off. I inquired of my friend concerning the identity of the prominent figure dockside. The reply: "É o maestro de toda esta música," literally, "He is the conductor of this entire orchestra." In my diary I added the comment that down deep there was widespread and profound dissatisfaction with the regime or "Situação." Situationists were those who went along with the Situation. And part of the Situation was acceptance not only of domination of Church by State but also of Azorean and Madeiran political subservience to an autocratic Lisbon, of the suffragan relationship of the Bishops of Angra (Azores) and of Funchal (Madeiras) to the Cardinal-Patriarch-Metropolitan Archbishop of Lisbon, and of the entire Insular Portuguese school system's subordination to a Ministry of National Education in the national capital.

A concordat is a formal treaty between a secular State and the Vatican State or Holy See. It is a treaty between a State and the Catholic Church only in a distorted sense of the word Church. A concordat is part of the notion, so abhorrent to faithful and practicing American Catholics, that the Catholic Church is among other things a State with a government, code of law, courts, secretariat of state, ambassadors (called nuncios when deans of local diplomatic corps and pro-nuncios when not), international treaty obligations, postage stamps, money, police force, army, and flag.

The United States does not have, and hopefully never will have, a concordat with the Holy See, nor does it exchange, and hopefully never will exchange, diplomatic representatives with the Holy See. The apostolic delegate in Washington, with residence in the beautiful building which flies the yellow and white flag on Massachusetts Avenue, is in no sense a nuncio. That he chooses to reside on embassy row is strictly coincidental and his affair. Moreover, any personal representative whom a President of the United States may choose to send to the Holy Father in the Vatican is in no sense an ambassador but merely a personal representative.

The American Catholic is opposed to these trappings of legalism because in his wisdom he knows that, when his Church tangles with his State, his State will ultimately dominate if not victimize his Church, as happened in 1834, when Peter won out over Michael. In reality, many Portuguese and many Spanish Catholics in their heart feel exactly the same way about concordats. In the two Iberian countries there is in this post-revolutionary age considerable agitation for change in if not total abolition of them.

The present Concordat between the Republic of Portugal and the Holy See is dated May 7, 1940. It represents extensive horse trading, as a result of which the Church gained support from the government of Portugal for certain institutions it deemed vital in return for concession of certain privileges to that government.

In Article XXIV, the Church seemed to gain:

> In harmony with the essential qualities of Catholic marriage, it is understood that by the very fact that they have entered into a canonical marriage [that is, married by a priest and not simply a civil official], the parties shall renounce the civil faculty of applying for a divorce, which cannot therefore be applied by civil courts to Catholic marriages.

Needless to add, that provision was abrogated within a year of the 1974 Revolution.

Earlier, in Article X, the State had definitely come out victorious:

Before proceeding to appoint a residential Archbishop or Bishop or a Coadjutor *cum jure successionis* . . . , the Holy See shall communicate the name of the person chosen to the Portuguese Government in order to know if there is any objection of a general political nature to the appointment. In the absence of any statement by the Government within thirty days from the date of the aforesaid communication, it will be understood that no objection is raised. All the measures provided for in this article will be carried out confidentially.

It goes without saying that "residential Archbishops and Bishops, their Coadjutors *cum jure successionis* and Assistants, Parish Pastors [but not Curates], Rectors of Seminaries, and, in general, Directors and Superiors of institutes or associations, endowed with personality in law and having jurisdiction in one or more Provinces of the country, must be Portuguese citizens." In the United States of 1978, aliens could be Parish Pastors and also, conceivably, in special circumstances Bishops.

Prelates can be clever manipulators, including those of Portugal. They know that there are alternate ways of skinning cats. One way involved the aforementioned Coadjutor Bishop of Angra. He was elevated to the episcopacy on March 18, 1974, before the Revolution, and consecrated on May 26, 1974, after it. When named by the Holy See to be coadjutor in the Azores, he was not given the right of succession. A loophole in the Concordat was taken advantage of, and he did not need the approval of the Government of Portugal. A Continental, he proved kind and understanding. In the long homily which he delivered immediately following his arrival in the Azores in June 1974—his plane from Lisbon was delayed as was ours from Boston by Richard M. Nixon's meeting with General Spínola in the airport of Terceira—he did not hesitate to remember with particular affection all Azoreans who had emigrated. "To all of them goes my wish that, while ever improving their lot, they remain loyal to their religion . . . ever mindful that money, essential without any doubt, is not our greatest value. Laboring for the welfare of the land which gathered them in, they will serve as an example to and will honor the land which gave them birth."

The Concordat states that, in the case of private Church-related schools, "the names of text books other than those on philosophical or theological subjects must be communicated to the

State." Continuing, Article XX adds: "The proper ecclesiastical authorities shall take steps to ensure that in the case of special subjects like History the lawful patriotic sentiments of the country shall be taken into account." As for public (State) schools, Article XXI provides that "the Catholic religion and Catholic morals will be taught in public elementary, complementary, and secondary schools to pupils whose parents or guardians have not lodged a request to the contrary."

It so happens that I live in the southeastern corner of the town of Belmont near where it borders on the cities of Cambridge and Watertown. Portions of all three civil subdivisions belong to my parish, whose church is actually in Watertown. I had long been proud of the separation of Church and State represented by this lack of coincidence between municipal and parish boundaries, and in 1963 I ventured to publish an article on the subject in the magazine of the Harvard Catholic Club. I have been told that my article was introduced as a paper for consideration by the Fathers attending Vatican Council II. If so, I feel certain that my views had no impact on Portugal, where the coincidence between civil and ecclesiastical subdivisions continued. In both Continental and Insular Portugal, *freguesia* and *paróquia* coincided in many cases. Administrative district and diocese also frequently coincided more or less, except in the Azores, where the opportunity to have three bishops instead of one was somehow overlooked. The brief final portion of the 1940 Concordat devoted to the overseas provinces contained specific provision that the boundaries of dioceses and missionary districts should be fixed so as to correspond as far as possible to administrative divisions.

This matter of jurisdictional limits has never loomed important in Insular Portugal, where the National Church personified by State-approved Bishops in reality plays a minor role in the lives of the people. It is the local parish church and its traditional *festas* which are important. In the Azores, the bishop is rarely seen except in Angra, for his see is an extensive archipelago. His authority as shepherd of his flock was made apparent over the years just before the Revolution by the presence of an episcopal vicar in each administrative district: the pastor in the town of Povoação on São Miguel for the District of Ponta Delgada, a teacher in the diocesan seminary of the see city for the District of Angra, and the pastor of the Matriz—the term is defined in the next chapter—in the city of Horta for the District of Horta. Prior to the naming of these vicars, priests on the smaller islands were literally abandoned, never seeing a bishop for years.

The Missionary Agreement between Portugal and the Holy See, also dated May 7, 1940, supplements the Concordat and makes clear that all bishops, vicars apostolic, and prefects apostolic in the overseas provinces will also be of Portuguese nationality and that all Catholic missionaries, Portuguese or foreign, secular or "regular" (that is, of a religious order) will be completely subject to them. It repeats the provisions of the Concordat concerning the manner of appointing bishops.

Concordat and Missionary Agreement notwithstanding, many Portuguese bishops were deeply spiritual and very dedicated to their flocks; and several of these came from the Atlantic islands like Archbishop Alvernaz. Another example was the late Bishop Paulo José Tavares of Macao, born in Rabo de Peixe, São Miguel. I conversed with him at length on June 11, 1962, in his palace up on Penha overlooking the Praya Grande so familiar to those who visit Salem's Peabody Museum. As we walked about his balcony, it was very moving to look across the Inner Port in the other direction into what we then called Red China. We decided that his residence was the closest to the Iron Curtain of any Catholic bishop's in the world. I quote a significant paragraph from my diary:

> We talked of the forthcoming Council. He will travel via the United States and expects to be in the Fall River-New Bedford area around the end of August. We stated we hoped to see each other there. [We did, in Harvard's Widener Library.] He thinks the Council will be over by Christmas. He said that the decisions are all being taken by the working committees and that there will not be much discussion. Here again, I hope that the bishops who converge on Rome from their dioceses will be forceful and not let a lot of intra-Vatican slick monsignori in fact run the show. I have my doubts if anything important will come out of this council!

Bishop Tavares and I were both wrong. The council lasted from October 11, 1962, to December 8, 1965. It accomplished considerable of importance.

Being given a system of political approval and ensuing tight control by the State of archbishops and bishops and their subordinates, it is understandable that the prelates from Continental,

Insular, and Overseas Portugal who attended Vatican II did not figure among the assembly's leaders pressing for the many substantial changes which resulted from the deliberations in Rome. A glance through the indexes of the four volumes which Xavier Rynne wrote covering the work of the four sessions is revealing. In Rynne's journalistic accounts, admittedly superficial and possibly premature but spontaneous and significant as rapid disseminators of important information, Portugal comes out almost always on the conservative side, the repressive side.

In the first session (October 11 to December 8, 1962), two Portuguese prelates spoke out strongly against innovation in the liturgy, and one of the pair later sided with a conservative view in the debate on unity. Meanwhile, the Cardinal-Patriarch of Lisbon used the microphone to rail against leakage of information to the press.

In the second session (September 29 to December 4, 1963), the other of the original pair, speaking in the name of thirty-eight bishops from Portugal, expressed reservations concerning restoration of the diaconate; he felt that, if restored, the law of celibacy should be imposed.

In the third session (September 14 to November 21, 1964), a Continental bishop disagreed with the proposition "that priests should have as much protection as modern employers would give to their employees." Inadvertently revealing tidbits from the history of the Church in Portugal, the bishop saw danger in going too far in this direction and said that the text under debate seemed to deprive the priest of control over certain categories of property or income which had been traditionally recognized as theirs by right, patrimonies, quasi-patrimonies, and parcimonials. He is quoted as saying: "The schema will cause anxieties and scruples for many clerics on this score."

In the fourth session (September 14 to December 8, 1965), one of the original pair of Portuguese speakers mentioned in connection with the first session was desirous of being careful not to proclaim to the world that the Catholic Church is only one among many.

But, as Brazilian playwright Ariano Suassuna has the Virgin explain in his *Auto da Compadecida* of 1955 (translated into English as *The Rogue's Trial*) apropos of an "avaricious, simoniacal, political bishop," the latter should not be blamed. At least he worked; he fulfilled his obligations. "He was on our side, and he who is not against us is for us." And here is an ironical fact: although the bishops of Portugal contributed little to Vatican II, the liturgy which I witnessed in 1964 in downtown Lisbon's Church of Santa Isabel and in suburban Carcavelos's little church was far more advanced than anything to which I was accustomed in the United States. Young priests were modern and active even then.

Modern and concerned Portuguese bishops did attend Vatican II. One was the late Sebastião Soares de Resende, Bishop of Beira in Mozambique and greatly admired by the people of his diocese, as I learned in Beira in 1967 shortly after his premature death. He had visited Canada and the United States on several occasions and knew Harvard well. He spoke up in the third session to call for the establishment in Rome of an institute to train clergy and laity in the work of Catholic Action. In the fourth session, he made a statement which caused quite a stir in Portugal: he favored condemnation of police state regimes, especially in countries under Soviet domination. There were those who took his remarks to be applicable to the New State in Portugal!

Another bishop, the personification of episcopal courage, is mentioned by Rynne as having been exiled from Portugal for supporting the right of workers to organize in political associations. António Ferreira Gomes, Bishop of Oporto, had been banished from the country by Salazar, after which event his diocese was governed by an administrator apostolic. Only with Caetano's succession to the presidency of the Council of Ministers in 1968 was the bishop permitted back in his native land. He attended the council and is mentioned as believing that collegiality is essential and the need for the cardinalate questionable.

The lack of Portuguese leadership at Vatican II was particularly striking because of a constant reminder there of Portugal's missionary vigor in the past. The reminder was supplied by the presence of a large number of active prelates from India and Pakistan with Portuguese names. The list was headed by Valerian Cardinal Gracias, Archbishop of Bombay, who became India's first cardinal in 1953. It included J. da Conceição Cordeiro, Fortunato da Veiga Coutinho, Leo D'Mello, Eugene D'Souza, Angelo Fernandes, Joseph Fernandes, and Peter B. Pereira.

☆ ☆ ☆

The cult of a Nation State backed by a National Church—not in reality an independent Church but a heavily influenced branch of the Catholic Church—was maintained via press, pulpit, and professor. It was embodied in the glorification of Portugal's Age of Maritime Discovery and therefore depicted in great works of art like the panels of the fifteenth-century painter Nuno Gonçalves (in Lisbon's Museum of Ancient Art) and the epic poem entitled *Os Lusíadas* (The Lusiads) by the sixteenth-century writer Luís de Camões (first published in Lisbon in 1572).

These examples are worthy of mention, for they are both untraditional. The panels project a sense of cooperation among State, Church, and working class, and also among Christians, Moslems, and Jews. The poem sings not of arms and a single man, like Virgil's *Aeneid* or Tasso's *Jerusalem Delivered*, but of arms and a host of matchless chiefs. In *The Lusiads*, the title signifies the sons or progeny of the god Lusus, whose name passed to Lusitania. The Lusiads are the Portuguese, and the English adjective Luso (as in Luso-American) means Portuguese.

Well-nigh all Portuguese and persons of Portuguese descent everywhere used to thrill to every repetition of the thrilling saga of the Lusiads. How they expelled the Moor from the territory predestined to be theirs. How by the middle of the thirteenth century they made of that territory Europe's oldest fully-staked-out nation. How they defended their territory from Spanish attempts to rule it. How they passed over to Morocco in 1415 and took Ceuta, the first act of overseas European expansion and one which has not yet been undone. How they advanced gradually down the west coast of Africa and out to the Atlantic archipelagoes, rounding the Cape of Good Hope in 1488. How they first sailed around Africa and on to the Malabar Coast of Southwest India in 1497 and 1498. How they revealed Brazil to Europe under the leadership of Pedro Alvares Cabral in 1500 and in the same year commenced the exploration of northeast North America (hence the Portuguese place-names Terra Nova or Newfoundland and Lavrador or Labrador). How they spread the Catholic Faith along the coasts of Africa and South and East Asia, among the islands of the East Indian archipelago, and in Japan and Brazil. How, in an amazing prelude to the scramble for bases in the Indian Ocean area at the end of the twentieth century, they established a thalassocracy in Asian waters loosely ruled from a viceregal capital in Goa and supported by naval bases at the island of Mozambique, Hormuz at the entrance to the Persian Gulf, Malacca on the Malay Peninsula, and Macao on the China coast. And how, in order to accomplish the overseas portion of these great deeds, they applied the scientific knowledge of the age and developed new and practical techniques of celestial navigation, mapmaking, ship construction, and naval gunfire.

Prince Henry the Navigator—who never navigated—was proclaimed the progenitor and generator of all the maritime activity, and the Portuguese landscape is strewn with symbols or icons which serve to remind the Portuguese of their grand national heritage. Prominent among these symbols is the portrait of Henry himself, which much later gave rise to a sculptured and highly controversial likeness in downtown Fall River, Massachusetts. The most important symbol is perhaps the angular red Cross of Christ, already fully discussed as the symbol of militant religion devoted to national purpose.

Another symbol is naturally the national escutcheon or coat of arms, personification of the Crown and therefore the State, with its five *quinas* (small shields) each with five dots or bezants, the ensemble surrounded by seven castles. Camões in his epic explains the *quinas* now as the five wounds which Christ suffered on the Cross, now as the five Moorish kings whom Dom Afonso Henriques defeated in a major battle in 1139 just before his acclamation as first king of Portugal. Camões cleverly explains the dots as the thirty pieces of silver for which Judas betrayed Christ by counting twice the five in the middle. The castles represent seven Moorish fortresses in the Algarve captured by the Christian forces in the final and successful effort to achieve territorial unity.

Yet another symbol is the armillary sphere, a magnificent modern example of which is to be found on the grounds of Phillips Academy in Andover, Massachusetts. The armillary sphere, a depiction of the celestial sphere with celestial meridians, equator, tropics, and zodiac, became the symbol of King Manuel I, surnamed the Fortunate because he was fortunate enough to have reigned during the heyday of Portuguese maritime exploration. His symbol, reminiscent of the nautical science so vigorously applied by the pilots of Vasco da Gama, Pedro Alvares Cabral, the Corte-Real brothers, and others, today appears on the national flag, where it underlies the national escutcheon.

Cross of Christ or armillary sphere or Portuguese coat of arms, or two or all three in company, may be seen carved in stone on Portuguese structures literally throughout the world: on the Tower of Belém beside the Tagus below Lisbon; in the double-level cloister of the nearby Hieronymite monastery (Jerónimos); in the monastery (called *Convento* in Portuguese) of Christ in Tomar in central Portugal; over the door of the old Church of Nazareth in Luanda; over the door of the exquisite chapel named Our Lady of the Bastion (Nossa Senhora do Baluarte) which forms an appendage to the spectacular Fortress of St. Sebastian on the Island of Mozambique; on the ruins of the sixteenth-century Jesuit seminary of Vaipicotta up the backwaters of Malabar north of Cochin; and on the façade of the Church of the Expectation atop St. Thomas Mount just outside Madras's St. Thomas Mount International Airport. An outstanding Insular Portuguese decorative use of one of these symbols, the armillary sphere, may be photographed on the wrought-iron railings of the outside balconies of the Bettencourt Palace in Angra do Heroísmo. The Palace today houses that city's splendid Public Library and District Archive.

Still another symbol to which Portuguese react very favorably is the caravel. This fore-and-aft rigged vessel, with at least one large lateen sail, was presumably responsible for the original discovery of Madeiras, Azores, and Cape de Verdes because of its ability to beat to windward. What appears to be a caravel turns up on the coat of arms of Lisbon. This caravel is transporting the body of St. Vincent (the city's patron) guarded by two ravens from the cape which bears his name to the nation's capital.

A final symbol is the *padrão*, a stone marker erected by early explorers in various places, notably along the coast of Africa. To commemorate the centenary year 1960, a mass-produced replica of these *padrões* was placed in various overseas Portuguese cities as widely separated as Praia on Santiago in the Cape Verde Islands, lovely modern Lourenço Marques on Delagoa Bay at the southern end of Mozambique, and Panjim (the capital of Goa). In delightful international Macao at the mouth of the Pearl River near Hong Kong is a different style of *padrão*, in front of the secondary school named for Prince Henry (Liceu Nacional Infante D. Henrique). The Gulbenkian Foundation recently made a gift of a beautiful *padrão* to the Commonwealth of Massachusetts for display in the Dighton Rock Museum just north of Fall River.

Although the cult of the Age of Maritime Exploration goes back a long way, even to the very years of the grand accomplishments, and was acutely developed during the Romantic era, Salazar's New State was its greatest promoter. And for good reason. By publicizing Portuguese contributions and restoring old cathedrals, monasteries, fortresses, and other buildings, the government gave the Portuguese at home and abroad—and even Americans of Portuguese descent and birth—a sense of national pride and at the same time made of Continental Portugal a most attractive country for the historically-minded tourist from abroad.

Moreover, and of immediate benefit to children of school age in the Azores and elsewhere, the New State in 1940 celebrated what became known as the Double Centenary, the eighth of the founding of the independent kingdom of Portugal in 1140 and the third of the restoration of Portugal's independence from Spain in 1640 following sixty years of the Babylonian Captivity. As part of the commemorations, the full impact of which was diminished by the advent of World War II and by Salazar's penury, the government designed a standardized, modern, and efficient elementary-school building. Schools to the new specifications were subsequently built throughout Portuguese territory in order to supplement the older school buildings and thereby expand educational opportunity. On Santa Maria I have photographed virtually all the elementary schools, those of the Old Plan and those of the Centenaries Plan. The latter, built after a delay of many years, bear a plaque proclaiming them to be a product of the Plano dos Centenários.

The cult of the Portuguese past has been of great interest to foreign scholars and to tourists from abroad. One reason was poignantly expressed by John Dos Passos in June 1961, obviously with reference to the acceptance by the Lusiads during their overseas expansion of other peoples, other races, other religions, even other than Western or Latin forms of Christianity: "The Portuguese tradition has a certain mildness about it, a lack of the racial and ideological fanaticism that has brought our civilization to the verge of destruction." But Salazar, alas, did not see the light in those fateful early months of 1961.

Unfortunately, the cult of the Portuguese past, when carried to excess, with the same details repeated ad nauseam, became very boring indeed to younger Portuguese, who referred to it as the "História Bombástica de Portugal" (Bombastic History of Portugal). These truly patriotic citizens lived in the present and looked to the future. Many felt that their nation's future lay with Europe and the North Atlantic Ocean and not with Southern Africa and the Indian Ocean. They burned with a desire to improve their beloved country, to free it from the epithet of Europe's most backward, to let fresh air in. They perceived a beginning on the 25th of April.

15

PARISH CHURCH AND *FESTAS*

The Catholic Church in Portugal has been an appendage to the State. Not surprisingly, conflicts between the Portuguese State, both Monarchy and Republic, on the one hand and the Church Universal as represented by the Holy See in Rome on the other hand have taken place at intervals since the very first years of the nation. A recent example is both interesting and amusing because of its indirect Azorean and Bostonian dimension.

On December 18, 1961, the Indian Union seized the Portuguese State of India. On October 18, 1964, the day of the canonization ceremony of the twenty-two Ugandan martyrs, the late Pope Paul VI announced to the Council Fathers present for their third session that he intended to visit Bombay briefly in early December to attend the International Eucharistic Congress. His host was to be—and in fact was—Cardinal Gracias, born in Karachi, of Goan descent, at the time anti-Portuguese, and one of the Indian nationalists in favor of Nehru's take-over of Salazar's Goa, Damão, and Diu. The Portuguese Foreign Minister promptly labeled the visit a gratuitous offense to a Catholic nation and stated that henceforth the Portuguese "must maintain the deepest silence, wounded and with dignity." The following May, Pope Paul conferred the Golden Rose on Portugal and flew to Fátima, two gestures clearly designed to smooth the ruffled feelings.

There is more. At the time of the canonization in 1964, the Holy Father made a blanket condemnation of colonialism, saying:

> ... Whereas evangelization implants the Christian religion as a new vitality that releases the spiritual powers and the latent talents of the local population and so sets people free ... colonization, based on purely utilitarian and material motives, oppresses the native populace.

Years later, in the summer of 1970, His Holiness received in the

Vatican a delegation of Blacks from Uganda. This act offended Portugal, still engaged in defending colonialism on three fronts in Africa, and Caetano's government promptly recalled its ambassador to the Holy See to Lisbon for consultations.

It was just at this point, September 9, 1970, that I flew via TAP from Lisbon to Santa Maria. Before departure that morning, I had read, on a Lisbon newspaper's front page, of a complaint from the United States to the effect that Portuguese sardine cans were so tough and the key so weak as to render very difficult their opening by hand. In a slightly less prominent presentation on that page, I had read of São Miguel-born Humberto S. Medeiros's appointment as Archbishop of Boston.

In the Boeing 707 (*Lourenço Marques*, CS-TBD, Captain Enrique Dantas Maya) I discussed with a highly-placed Portuguese government official, a fellow passenger, what to me was the most exciting news of the year. He regaled me with the explanation that the appointment was a sop on the part of the Vatican to a Portugal miffed by the reception of the Uganda delegates. When I later recounted the anecdote to Cardinal Medeiros, an American citizen trained for the priesthood in the United States who had nothing to do with the foreign policy of Portugal, he confided to me that the appointment had been settled weeks before the Africans' visit to Rome.

※ ※ ※

Fortunately, these high-level diplomatic high jinks have had little to do with the real-life role of the Church in the Azores and Madeiras. On the Atlantic islands the vast majority of priests, devout and devoted, have served as true followers of Christ. Around them has revolved not only the islanders' spiritual life but also a considerable portion of their recreational life. The very calendar by which the islanders lead their lives is the Church's, beginning with the names for the days of the week.

The Portuguese language is unique among the Romance or neo-Latin languages in several respects, in the use of *Senhora*, for example, and in the words for Monday through Friday. The other Romance languages take the names of the planets of the geocentric Ptolemaic system in the order of their increasing distance from Earth and apply them to every other day over two weeks: Moon's Day, Mercury's, Venus's, the Sun's (or the Lord's),

Mars's, Jupiter's (that is, Jove's), and Saturn's. Portuguese starts with the Lord's Day (*Domingo*) as the first day of the week and then follows the official Church calendar: Second Day (*Secunda Feria* of Church Latin, the Portuguese *Segunda-feira*) or Monday, Third (*Terça-feira*), Fourth (*Quarta-*), Fifth or Thursday (*Quinta-*), and Sixth (*Sexta-*). The seventh day is the Sabbath (*Sábado*). Would that all airlines would adopt these numerical designations, said to be Visigothic in origin! Some lines confuse Portuguese and Brazilians by using "1" as the symbol for Monday, and some manufacturers of hand-held electronic calculators do likewise.

The Insular Portuguese share with their Continental brethren and those of other Christian lands the principal Christian feasts: December 8 (Immaculate Conception) and, nine months later, September 8; March 25 (Annunciation) and, nine months later, December 25; and, among many others, January 6 or Twelfth Night, the day when the Holy Three Kings from out of the East came to Bethlehem (Belém) bearing gifts, *die Heiligen Drei Könige* whose tomb is in the Cologne Cathedral and to whom in these postconciliar days we are supposed to refer as the three "astrologers." This latter feast is particularly important to Latin children, for it is Little Christmas, a traditional day for the exchange of gifts.

Of great significance and beauty for the Islanders is the Easter cycle. Easter is the Sunday next following the full moon first occurring after March 20. It is never earlier than March 22 nor later than April 25. Forty days after Easter, the Insular Portuguese commemorate Christ's ascension **into Heaven** (a Thursday), although it is not for them, as for Americans, a holy day of obligation. Ten days later, on Pentecost Sunday or Whitsunday, they recall the descent of the Holy Ghost (*Espírito Santo*). Trinity Sunday occurs a week later, and the following Thursday is the feast of the Body of Christ (Corpus Christi or, in Portuguese, *Corpo de Deus*), also known as the feast of the Most Holy Sacrament (*Santíssimo Sacramento*), a holy day of obligation in Portugal. The Friday of the following week, that is, the day after the octave day of Corpus Christi, is the feast of the Sacred Heart of Jesus (*Sagrado Coração*), never earlier than May 29 nor later than July 2. Clearly, an interesting time to visit the Azores is between the end of Lent and Sacred Heart, all the more as Pentecost is the single greatest Azorean celebration and, in Ponta Delgada, the fifth Sunday after Easter is that city's feast par excellence.

Other important *festas* occur on January 1 and August 15, the latter the feast of the assumption of the Virgin into Heaven, celebrated as the harvests approach. Two other religious observances represent opposite ends of a spectrum: joyful Shrove Tuesday or Mardi Gras, not a farewell to meat (*carni vale*) but a taking away of the meat, as Aeolians correctly inform us with their *Carnelevara*, and, on November 2, All Souls' Day, when one thinks of the faithful departed and eats corn on the cob with anise seed.

Add to all these events—knowledge of which is indispensable for even a minimum comprehension of Insular Portuguese values—those of preferred saints, and the year is filled out. December 31, for instance, is the feast of St. Sylvester, and the New Year's Eve fireworks in and around Funchal constitute a spectacle which visitors travel from afar to behold. The feast of the nativity of St. John the Baptist (Midsummer Day, June 24) is important to all rural Christians of the northern hemisphere, and especially to those on Terceira, because it coincides approximately with the summer solstice and the beginning of the summer season. There are other more local commemorations. I recall attending a *festa* in São Mateus (literally St. Matthew) on the island of Pico in early August.

Remembrance of Christian feasts and saints represents an intimate and meaningful experience for the Insular Portuguese, who pray quite sincerely and honestly to a favorite saint and above all to the Virgin to intercede for them with God-the-Father or God-the-Son for divine intervention in connection with a physical affliction or even the loss of a simple object. Portuguese luxury liners of a few years back, *Santa Maria* and *Vera Cruz*, recalled the Virgin and the True Cross, although probably indirectly via geographical names. TAP's first two Boeing 707 jet aircraft were named *Santa Cruz* (CS-TBA) and *Santa Maria* (CS-TBB); but, as the next two were named for the capitals of Angola and Mozambique respectively (CS-TBC and CS-TBD), the conclusion is permitted that the national airline was commemorating national territorial expansion—Brazil and Azores—rather than Christianity. Yet TAP's planes are blessed by prelates, and the names illustrate the manner in which Christianity is woven into the very matrix of Portuguese culture, Continental and Insular.

Fishing boats, including many based on New Bedford, Massachusetts, receive the traditional Portuguese-Christian names. And Portuguese children of course are christened with names like

Maria, José, Joaquim, Ana, João, Manuel, Pedro, Paulo, Miguel, Jaime, and Silvestre, and also, in the case of girls, with various names of Mary: Maria da Assunção (Assumption), Maria do Carmo (Our Lady of Mount Carmel, July 16), da Conceição (Conception, "Connie" when transplanted to America), da Graça (Grace), das Neves (of-the-Snow), et cetera. A very traditional name among Portuguese as among Italians is Anthony (in Portuguese António, often pronounced Antoine in the islands, hence Antone in American English). St. Anthony of Padua was born in Lisbon, wherefore the Italians, with their richness of prepositions, refer to him as "Santo Antonio da Lisbona ma di Padova." He is not to be confused with St. Antony the Egyptian (in Portuguese Antão, as in the Cape Verdean island of Santo Antão).

The association between the Insular Portuguese and their saints is intimate and meaningful. It is also very real. In 1974, the *festa de São João* in Angra opened with a parade featuring Miss Tulare and her entourage, who had flown all the way from Tulare in California's San Joaquin Valley. Among the floats was a most realistic depiction of St. Sebastian wounded by arrows, with blood—red paint—streaming out the holes. A young and vigorous man standing in front of us promptly fainted dead away at this vision of martyrdom, amid the screams of consternation of his young wife.

The great feast of Azoreans everywhere is Pentecost, the feast of the Holy Spirit or Holy Ghost, *Espírito Santo*. The Portuguese name is almost universally pronounced *Esprito Santo*, with the accent falling on the *i* as in French and Provençal, because, to believe Harvard's late Professor Charles Hall Grandgent, the most used form in the Latin declension was *Spirítui*, the dative, which occurs in the Gloria. (How he knew the statistical relationship of the Gloria to the In-the-Name-of-the-Father he never reveals.) Pentecost is followed, eleven days later, by Corpus Christi. It is the spring season, and colorful flowers are blooming. Carpets of flowers of beautiful and intricate design are placed in the streets for the many processions which take place and which are often accompanied by outdoor Masses. These street processions over beds of flowers take place at other times as well. In Furnas on the first Sunday after Easter, the Procession of the Infirm is held, the priest going from house to house to give communion.

Next door to many churches in the Azores is a special Holy Ghost chapel building, reserved for the Pentecost ceremonies. It is known as a "theater" (*teatro*) in the Eastern Azores and as an "empire" (*império*) elsewhere. The ceremonies themselves are complicated and vary from place to place. They consist essentially of crowning an "emperor" and "empress"—or just a "queen"—chosen from among the children. Special foods are prepared and served in connection with this feast, *massa sovada*, for example. This delicacy is a rich yellow bread. When served at Easter with hard-boiled eggs baked inside, it is known as *folares*. Another specialty at Pentecost time is a flat baked cake made of corn meal and called *bolo de milho*.

My half aunt—my mother's half sister, she of Flemish descent—when in her nineties used to tell me of Esprito Santo in the olden days in New Bedford. A family in the parish would make a promise or vow. Every evening during the week preceding Pentecost Sunday, friends would gather at the family's home to recite the rosary. After Mass on the great day, they would all repair to that home for the traditional dinner. The crown would be there. The basis of the dinner was *sopas*, a hearty soup consisting of kale, potato, salt pork, linguiça (a marvelous Portuguese sausage), pieces of beef, and yellow-eyed beans. This mixture was poured over pieces of bread in the soup dish and served with sprigs of mint. And of course some wine was imbibed on the side.

The feast of the Holy Ghost has deep roots in the Continental Portugal's medieval period. In the islands it may have been reinforced by the enthusiasm of the Flemings, for the dukes of Burgundy were great promoters of the devotion. Portuguese Princess Isabel's Duke Philip endowed the Chapel of the Holy Ghost on Mount Zion and stipulated that his heart be buried there.

The tradition of crowning an emperor and empress may have been reinforced, or even in my view initiated, by the very real crowning of a real imperial pair just as the Azores were being peopled. Princess Leonor of Portugal (1434-1467) was the daughter of King Duarte and sister of King Afonso V. She was therefore the niece of Dom Pedro the Traveler, Dom Henry the Navigator, and Duchess Isabel. At a tender age she became betrothed to Holy Roman Emperor-elect Friedrich III. A proxy marriage took place in Lisbon in October 1451, accompanied by great festivities which lasted several days. Late in 1451, Leonor journeyed by sea from Lisbon to Leghorn. Aeneas Sylvius Piccolomini, later to be Pope Paul II, met her at the Italian port and escorted her to Siena to meet her spouse. In Rome on March 16, 1452, Pope Nicholas V solemnized the marriage and on March 19 crowned Friedrich and Leonor emperor and empress.

Localized on São Miguel, by way of contrast, is the special yet famous cult of the Lord Holy Christ, or, to be more exact in translation, Mister Holy Christ (Senhor Santo Cristo). This devotion is celebrated, as already noted, on the fifth Sunday following Easter Sunday, that is, on the Sunday preceding Ascension Thursday. The cult consists of veneration of a beautiful statue of Christ (the Holy Christ of the Miracles, Santo Cristo dos Milagres), which is kept in a convent of the city of Ponta Delgada. Pope Paul III (reigned 1534-1549) gave it to Azorean nuns on a visit to Rome. Pilgrims from all the Azores islands, from Continental Portugal, and from Azorean communities in Canada, the United States, and Brazil, converge on the city and witness the procession which forms an integral part of the cult. This particular devotion has even spread abroad, and one may find a Santo Cristo Club in Cambridge's Inman Square section.

The island of Madeira possesses its special cult, Our Lady of the Mountain, patroness of Funchal. The Mountain or Mount lies behind and above the capital city; tourists drive up and then return in the toboggan-like baskets. The Church of Nossa Senhora do Monte was built beginning in 1470 and entirely rebuilt in the eighteenth century. Its statue of the Virgin is the particular object of the cult, which takes place on the feast of the Assumption. It comes from the original church and is located above the main altar. Our Lady of the Mountain is venerated wherever Madeirans settle, in Honolulu, for example.

The cult of Our Lady of Fátima began in Continental Portugal in 1917. It remained relatively local for a quarter of a century. On the Continent, however, awareness of the rough official treatment accorded the children to whom the Virgin had appeared contributed greatly to public dissatisfaction with the 1910-1926 Republic and ultimately to its downfall. Only beginning with the silver jubilee in the war days of 1942 and a widely heralded discourse of Pope Pius XII did the cult attain universal proportions. It is now the source of a major part of the foreign tourism which has become a mainstay of the Portuguese economy. The cult spread very early to the island of Santa Maria, where a church on high ground, with some 165 steps leading up to it, was built in 1926. It has now spread far beyond Portugal. In the United States it has acquired politically very conservative overtones and, moreover, a "Blue Army." The overtones involve the "Secret of Fátima": pray and make reparations to halt the spread of world communism, and, if you mend your lives, Russia will be converted and an era of peace will be granted mankind. This kind of talk is just what a conservative movement in Insular Portugal, backed by rightwingers in the United States, needs for effective indoctrination of the Azorean and Madeiran masses, who will end up believing that the Virgin at Fátima in the center of Continental Portugal delivered a special message ultimately destined for executives of future international conglomerates.

The Santo Cristo and Fátima theoretically represent strictly religious devotions, although politicians have attempted to exploit both. The Holy Ghost, on the other hand, has definitely passed out of the church into the village or town square. The cult's idolization of imperial majesties, possibly strengthened by returnees to the Azores from Imperial Brazil, is in keeping with a rather widespread practice, present in New England even among Cape Verdeans, of forever crowning a queen of the ball. The practice suggests lower-class worship of the upper class manifested in the many references to *fidalgos* and *morgados*. Apparently the Insular Portuguese, like the American public of bygone years, have felt the need to adore a high society.

The secular nature of religious cults is rendered evident by the fact that several of them are actively promoted by groups of laymen rather than by the clergy. These groups are called Brotherhoods (*Irmandades*) and have remote origins in the Portuguese past. They are vaguely under the clergy but all too often, it is only fair to state, present problems to the priests. The Brotherhoods generate considerable enthusiasm in men and boys, and I relish the remembrance of a visit I paid to one outside Angra in 1964. Members were preparing meats for the festivities which were to take place the following Sunday, when an emperor was to be crowned.

In addition to meats, the Christian cycle is replete with breads, cakes, candies, and the fruit of the vine. I recall delicious fritters on Fayal (singular *filhós*, plural *filhoses*) made especially for Shrove Tuesday or, as the Portuguese call it in a shift of emphasis, *Entrudo* (entrance, beginning of Lent), and also little hard white candies with the flavor of licorish (*confeitos*). *Filhós*, by the way, parallels the English word *pea*. The original singular was *pease*, as in "Pease porridge hot," and the plural *peases*. The singular was felt as a plural, and a new singular was made. Exactly so with *filhós*, often perceived as the plural of a singular *filhó*.

The Insular Portuguese, and Latins in general, have no hangups about either bread or wine. They eat bread in quantities far in excess of what an American dietician would recommend, and they drink wine with no notion of sin or danger. Naturally so, for the essence of the Mass is the conversion, by the priest, of bread and wine into the body and blood of Christ in commemoration of the Last Supper.

☆ ☆ ☆

The cult of the Holy Ghost, with its inevitable accompaniment of foods and drinks, folk music and folk dances, manifests the intimate nature of the relationship between the traditional Catholic Church and the Insular Portuguese. There is really no rival religion. Moreover, there are very few openly professed atheists, although the population could be divided into many "practitioners" and some mere "believers." The former, more numerous than in Continental Portugal, really believe; and they discharge their religious obligations by going to confession and to Mass and receiving Holy Communion. The latter are cultural Catholics who are born, marry, and die in the Church but probably are not in regular attendance at a church during the intervals.

A typical pattern of attendance was visible during Mass on Porto Santo one Sunday early in 1939. Men and boys remained outside, with hats on, conversing at a great rate. The women were inside. During the consecration, and as an altar boy tolled the church bell in the steeple, the males uncovered and stood respectfully silent. During my many subsequent visits to Continental Portugal, I seemed to notice a change in the ratio of the sexes. Gradually, more men attended Mass than women. Men were noticing that the Situation was favoring them. Women, I thought, were moving to the left.

Being given the homogeneous and closed nature of society in the islands, the Insular Portuguese had no choice prior to the Revolution but to conform. They accepted the beliefs of the traditional Church and with them the complete moral code. Premarital sex was sinful and presumably was not indulged in. (My graduate-student field research in the islands was limited largely to phonetics.) Even if there were the desire—and of course there

"No choice but to conform"—São Sebastião, Terceira, 1964

was—little opportunity existed for its implementation. Local custom, based on Church doctrine, did not permit dating. In effect, a young couple were never, or rarely, alone together prior to the night following the religious wedding.

There was, then, little premarital sex. The population statistics suggest that there were also few abortions after marriage, although the role in this regard of "granny" midwives may have been greater, as suggested in Chapter 20, than is generally recognized. Nor was there supposed to be any artificial birth control, but that is a different matter likewise discussed in the chapter on doctors and midwives. And of course there was no divorce, for in the islands one usually married in the Church.

Brides, then, were virgins. As for the bridegrooms, all depended upon what opportunities they had to become nonvirgins. If, for military service, schooling, or business reasons, they visited the island cities, or the Continent, or the African provinces, the likelihood of their retaining their virginity was reduced. The girls with whom they made love were normally professional prostitutes, and the statement about virgin brides still holds.

Their Values

The Insular Portuguese in their archipelagoes and in America, like all Portuguese, and Brazilians, and Latins in general, were reputedly far from being cold fish. Whether as Latins the males were "lousy lovers," to use a phrase with which Helen Brown Norden Lawrenson once caused a sensation, is a point beyond the scope of the present book. The islanders were certainly human, and it is undoubtedly a good thing that traditional Catholic moral teachings imposed restraints on them. In spite of the doctrine, however, slips did occur. In this event, abortion normally being ruled out, an illegitimate child entered the world. The baby may have been placed in a convent at once by the mother or her parents, possibly discreetly with no one the wiser and only the good sisters aware of the child's existence. Or the baby may have grown up within the mother's family, possibly to be acknowledged by the father in an act of "perfiliation." Since promulgation of the new Civil Code in 1967—amended in 1977—the baby may also have been put up for adoption.

The lesson to be retained is that Catholic teachings were in general respected. Catholic teachings recognized that man, the flesh, and the devil did conspire on occasion to lead one from the paths of righteousness. In this case, provisions existed to undo the ensuing damage. What was not done was to rationalize sin and legalize sinful institutions.

The total island environment provided moral protection for growing youngsters, and also for oldsters. The temptations which existed in Lisbon, London, Paris, Amsterdam, Copenhagen, and Hamburg's Reeperbahn were nonexistent out in the Atlantic. There were no drive-ins nor art cinemas showing x-rated films, no pornographic books and magazines on sale in corner stores, no co-residential dormitories, no nothing. Even miniskirts were conspicuous by their absence, except at the air base on Terceira. That particular fashion was slow to enter Portugal, where the modest and sexually neuter pantsuits made rapid headway. Bikinis, however, did become popular very early at some Continental beaches, and I was amazed at the bikinis I observed on Santa Maria in 1970

The islanders retained their religious beliefs and Catholic morality—in fine, their Faith—as long as they did not advance in education beyond elementary school. Up to that point they faced a crucifix attached to the wall of their classroom and studied Christian doctrine as a regular school subject, the latter in accordance with the Concordat. An initial cynicism may have been engendered, however, when they saw, on the wall opposite the crucifix, a photograph of Doctor Salazar with the caption "A nação é tudo; tudo pela nação."

The islanders may have gone to one of the island cities to attend its State secondary school, in the manner to be described in a later chapter. They may even have gone on to Continental Portugal or to another country for a university education. In these cases, the ensemble of simple pious beliefs and the concomitant moral code received a rude shock, all the more as some secondary-school and many university teachers proved to be less than religious. If the individuals in question returned to their native town or village, they found themselves at odds with a large portion of their community. The cleavage lay between the relatively educated and the relatively uneducated and began to border on class distinction. In extreme cases, the returnees became very anticlerical. It was this possible transformation in both belief and morality which worried traditional parents and priests in the islands and tended to cause them to accept the forces which terminated the ongoing education of the children at an early age.

Another force operative in the islands on occasion conspired with traditional religion to hold general religious culture at a low level. This force, which theoretically stood in complete opposition to Catholic teaching, consisted of widespread superstition in general and specific beliefs such as in the evil eye in particular. They are mentioned in Chapter 22.

☆ ☆ ☆

Liturgical calendar, recreational life, and moral code all revolved around the parish church, which in the islands habitually takes its name from the civil (ex-ecclesiastical) *freguesia*. Each parish (*paróquia*) had its pastor (*pároco*). If there was need, the pastor had one or more curates (*curas* or *assistentes*). On Santa Maria in 1970 (population about 9,000), there were six priests: two in the parish of Vila do Porto (pastor and curate) and one in each of three other parishes (Almagreira, Santa Bárbara, and Santo Espírito). The parish of São Pedro adjacent to Vila do Porto had none. The sixth served the airport. There were no nuns on the island.

In constrast to the U.S. system, pastors and curates in the islands did not live together in a common rectory. Rather, each priest maintained his own residence. If his parents, or widowed mother, or spinster sister, already had a home, the priest may have lived there. Or he may have had his own establishment, with his own housekeeper, frequently an elderly lady referred to affectionately as the *velhinha* (little old lady). Among the Portuguese in America, on occasion, an apocopated version of the English word housekeeper (*'skeeper*, in Portuguese pronounced and spelled *esquipa*) was used to designate this person. Veritas requires me to add that on very rare occasions in the New World *esquipa* took on an overtone of meaning not strictly in consonance with the moral code outlined in preceding paragraphs.

Each of the four cities of Insular Portugal consists, civilly, of several *freguesias* within the *concelho* which bears the city's name. In the two cities which are the sees of the respective bishops, Angra for the Azores and Funchal for the Madeiras, the bishop's cathedral is also a parish church. Each of these *freguesias* is therefore known as the Freguesia da Sé (Precinct of the See). In the other two cities, one of the parish churches has primacy over the others. That parish, as well as the corresponding precinct, is referred to as the Mother (Matriz). Thus, in Horta are three *freguesias/paróquias*: Angústias at the southern end, Conceição at the northern end, and Matriz in the center. The Matriz church is the church of the former Jesuit secondary school. The school building itself used to house the district offices, as pointed out in Chapter 4.

The word Matriz is also used in parts of Continental Portugal to designate civil *freguesias*. In Insular Portugal, moreover, it has yet another ecclesiastical application. On a small island like Santa Maria, which forms but a single *concelho* named for the island's only town (Vila do Porto), the town itself constitutes and confers its name on one of the *freguesias*. The principal church of this chief *freguesia* of the *concelho* is called the Matriz.

Although religious orders saw their property confiscated by the government in 1834 and were virtually eliminated by the Law of Separation of 1911, they reappeared under the New State. In the islands there are some nuns, but monastic life is hardly vigorous. Clerical garb on the streets is rarely seen.

As for a relatively new Catholic institution similar to a religious order and not unknown to Cambridge, Massachusetts, the secular institute called Opus Dei gives no indication of being active in the islands. Emanating from Spain, it did allegedly penetrate high circles in Continental Portugal but on nothing like the Spanish scale.

In the islands, the architecture of the parish churches and of convent and monastery chapels is very traditional. The art contained within them is cherubic, to say the least. Insular Portuguese, like some Continentals, are very fond of their figures of saints or angels with tinted cheeks and what appears to be human hair. They also favor traditional tiles (*azulejos*) and carved wood ceilings which are often gilded. The people's taste thus does not afford the modern young priest with mid-twentieth-century artistic sensibilities much latitude in the decoration of his church.

On occasion in the Atlantic archipelagoes, the masses of the people are exposed to magnificent examples of religious art and architecture of the type so beautifully described and illustrated in the late Robert C. Smith's prize-winning book *The Art of Portugal 1500-1800*. In Angra do Heroísmo, particularly rich in this regard, the tourist visits the Church of the *Colégio*, that is, the baroque church of the former Jesuit secondary school. It dates from the mid-seventeenth century. He also visits the church of the former Franciscan monastery. Not long before his death in 1975, Robert Smith, whose last will and testament created the professorship which I hold and which he named for his mother, assured me that he intended to turn his attention to the Azorean architectural monuments.

16
COUSINS AND GODPARENTS

The Catholic Church at both national and parish levels stresses the role of the family in society. Thus, there has for long been a feast day dedicated to the Holy Family, formerly the Sunday within the octave of the Epiphany (Twelfth Night), now the Sunday within the octave of Christmas. In the old days the gospel (*Luke* 2, 42-52) told the story of the twelve-year-old Jesus being taken by His parents to Jerusalem. Unknown to them, He remained behind when they left to go back to their home. They returned to Jerusalem and found Him "in the Temple sitting in the midst of the doctors, hearing them and asking them questions." Instead of their reprimanding Him, however, and thereby keeping intact the principle of the family, He reprimanded them for interfering, as He had to be about His Father's business (today "had to be in my Father's house").

The story always seemed crystal-clear to me: it stressed the divinity of the Christ Child. Nevertheless, the folksy sermons I used to hear managed to twist it around. Stressing the phrase at the end about His being subject to Mary and Joseph after the Holy Family returned to Nazareth (today "was obedient to them"), priests played up the family angle and played down the badly needed lesson on divinity.

Having the support of Holy Scripture, it is little wonder that Portugal has stressed the role of the family in its political and administrative organization. The Political Constitution of the Portuguese Republic of pre-Revolutionary days made explicit the importance of the family to the State:

> The State ensures the formation and protection of the family as the source of the preservation and development of the Portuguese people, as the principal foundation of education, discipline, and social harmony, and as the cornerstone

of the political and administrative structure, through its grouping and representation in the precinct [*freguesia*] and in the municipality [*município*].

This statement is absent from the Constitution of the Portuguese Republic of 1976, and the omission should convey a lesson to the Church's policymakers in Rome. Just as the Church once espoused colonial imperialism only to disengage itself, as illustrated at the beginning of the preceding chapter, so the Church has stressed family. But family such as it has been traditionally known may, like Roman imperialism, feudal system, war, and male chauvinism, become modified or abandoned altogether.

The Church should not be tainted by its accommodation with particular institutions of the world. It should remain free of engagements and entanglements in order to preach its good tidings. In my opinion, a major mistake of Vatican II, one which must sooner or later be undone, is the identification of the Church and its liturgy with local and therefore varying and variable culture including language and dialect. The Church must remain above and outside the concerns of "ethnic-heritage" and "ethnic" studies. Theoretically, the Church should not enter explicitly into either this book or its companion on America. It should be presupposed as underlying them.

Protected in Portugal as a whole, then, by deep religious and national roots, the family in the Portuguese Atlantic archipelagoes is further preserved from disintegration by the lack of mobility inherent in an insular society. The individual citizen who does not emigrate is restricted to his little island if not to his city, town, or village.

☆ ☆ ☆

When Americans think of family, they conjure up a vision of the so-called nuclear family, husband, wife, and children—Jesus, Mary, and Joseph. According to a survey of real estate brokers in scattered areas of the United States, the vision embraces a single-family home standing on its own piece of land, however inefficient this type of housing may be from the point of view of space utilization. The vision places two- to four-family houses in second rank.

Regardless of type of dwelling, the American dream calls for one bedroom for the parents and at least one for each two young children. It rigorously excludes in-laws except under the most exceptional circumstances deriving from economic stress. Because the young couple want no in-laws in residence with them, they in turn do not wish to be a burden on their children later in life. They therefore take steps early to guarantee their own independence in old age. The American dream perforce excludes live-in domestic help, however desirable, because of lack of availability and/or money and also because of the ideal of being alone.

It is rapidly becoming apparent how unsatisfactory in many respects the American dream has proved to be, with its relegation of children to day-care centers by working mothers and its isolation of the elderly in homes for the aged or in specially-built and elaborate communities devoid of children and of pets, the euphemistically named leisurevilles.

In Insular Portugal, more people live together. Living together for a variety of reasons does not create some of the problems feared in the United States, although undeniably it creates others. Elderly and possibly ill parents live with the nuclear couple, and so on occasion do unmarried aunts or sisters of either husband or wife, or maybe even uncles and brothers. Because the nuclear mother can count on assistance from the other women living with her, she does not consider numerous progeny to be a burden. Moreover, her entire household is relatively easy to manage because domestic help is—or was before the Revolution—available and inexpensive. Even if she works outside the home, for example as an elementary-school teacher, she can run her home with relative facility because of all the female assistance surrounding her.

Within Continental Portugal's larger cities, the help situation has been a problem for a number of years. Maids do not wish to be referred to as *criadas*, a word which connotes decided social inferiority, but rather as *empregadas* (employees). And anyhow they prefer employment in factories. In the islands, on the other hand, a townswoman could still find a young country girl, or an older one, or even on occasion a man, willing to work in the house. Indeed, in the Azores as recently as 1970 it was cheaper to pay an elderly woman by the hour to clean the floor on her hands and knees than to pay for the electricity required to run the already purchased vacuum cleaner.

If their house is large enough, or is capable of being added to, the nuclear couple can accommodate even more people. They may allow a new brother-in-law (*cunhado*) or sister-in-law (*cunhada*) to move in. In exceptional circumstance the nuclear wife's two maiden sisters living with her may suddenly marry two males (not necessarily brothers) and bring them in. These two newcomers are *cunhados* of the wife. To the husband they are—yes, the Portuguese language has a word for it, but one rarely used in the islands—*concunhados*.

In the Portuguese islands, city, town, and even on occasion village homes tend to be built adjacent to one another and with shared walls, so-called party walls. Thus, as one walks up the principal street in Santa Maria's Vila do Porto, Rua Teófilo Braga, one has the impression of a single very long multicolored dwelling on each side of it. Occasionally, close relatives of a nuclear couple, instead of living with them, live next door, or three houses down, or across the street. Given the proximity of the dwellings, the failure to keep doors locked, and the fact that aunts, cousins, in-laws, and mothers are walking in and out at all hours of the day and evening, it is understandable how the visitor from the United States receives the impression of one huge family in one huge house.

The residence of a particular nuclear couple may be a house belonging to either the bride's or groom's family, depending upon the respective families' circumstances; or the young couple may move in with either his or her parents. Everything else being equal, there is a tendency to be close to the bride's family, for a young couple to live with or near her folks rather than his.

The very nature of family relationships and living arrangements in Insular Portugal, in a word the island gregariousness, explains the grouping of homes into villages if not larger agglomerations. Isolated living does not appeal to the islanders except as necessary on Madeira. Even the farmers live in towns or villages and make their way every day to the plots which they work.

The larger family, the extended family around the nuclear family, is known collectively in the islands as one's relatives or kin (*parentes*, which does not mean parents) or simply as "the family" (*a família*). The word *parentela*, often used in descriptions of Brazilian society, is not used in Insular Portugal.

The extended family of blood relatives may be further enlarged by inclusion of the spiritual kin—one's godparents, confirmation sponsors, marriage witnesses—if those chosen are not relatives. This enlargement may be considerable if these several functions are always fulfilled by different nonrelated persons. Often, however, the same persons serve as sponsors on more than one occasion.

Thanks to Mario Puzo's book and movie, the concept of godfather is well known to the American public, and in Italy including Sicily the Puzo productions are entitled *Il Padrino*. In Portuguese the word used for godparents (*padrinhos*, that is, *padrinho* and *madrinha*) applies not only to sponsors at the sacrament of baptism but also to those who are present at the sacrament of confirmation (*padrinhos de crisma*) and to those who stand up for the bride and groom at the sacrament of matrimony (*padrinhos de casamento*). As with so much connected with the Catholic Church, however, the concept of *padrinho* has been laicized and profaned, indeed doubly so.

The role of *padrinhos* as patrons is discussed below. Their rather more intimate role within the family as co-fathers and co-mothers with respect to the natural parents merits comment here.

The Portuguese couple often select old friends, school chums, boon companions, to be the godparents of their child. Those so chosen are the *padrinhos* of the child, and they are the *compadres* (*compadre* and *comadre*) of the parents. And the relationship between parents and co-parents is often an intimate one, on occasion with comical overtones. This is generally true throughout the Catholic world, and, depending upon the particular culture, either the intimacy or the comedy is emphasized. In Southern Italy, for example, the words for co-parents (*compare* and *comare*) have displaced *padrino* and *madrina* and have come to mean godparents. They also have the overtone of boon companion. Moreover, and perhaps for understandable reasons, *comare* implies a person's mistress, *compare* one's lover. In France, on the other hand, *compère* and *commère* connote companionship and gossip. In the Portuguese islands, the more scabrous semantic overtones seem absent, and the bosom-pal meaning predominates. Moreover, in olden times but apparently no longer, the natural parents of the bride and those of the groom thought of themselves as *compadres*.

In the islands the extended family attains such a size, with such a degree of internal familiarity, that adolescent boy and girl cousins often come to know each other well. Although an Island Portuguese girl is protected from the male of the species in general, her parents are less strict about her male first cousin living down the street because they feel certain concerning his background and sterling moral qualities. Cousin-marriages accordingly have not been uncommon. True, the Church's rule about consanguinity would seem to stand in the way, but dispensations have been easy to obtain. One applied to the bishop via one's pastor. Cousin-marriages thus have reinforced family ties and built up the family still more, to the point where family members may have few friends in the American sense simply because friends are cousins (*primos*).

Members of the younger generation in the islands do not want to marry relatives. They are rebelling, gently, against family and Church and are creating a generation gap. The marriage of a young, unrelated, and perhaps typical couple in the Azores may serve to illustrate a trend. Instead of the traditional veil, she wore a white satin cape with a hood attached. The hood was trimmed with ermine for which she had sent to Paris. The groom wore a business suit. As the rules require one witness of each sex for each partner, the groom's parents stood up for him, and the bride's uncle and his unrelated wife stood up for her.

Young couples such as this are genetically aware. They fear inbreeding and wish to avoid recreating the situation of northern communities on the island of Madeira, said to be inbred to the point of biological danger.

☆ ☆ ☆

The Portuguese family structure and living arrangements prove most advantageous to the islanders in many ways. To Americans, certain features seem unbearable. First the advantages, then a hint at some disadvantages.

Family members are mutually helpful. Unlike the modern young American couple imbued with the idea that making it on their own is a virtue, the young Portuguese couple and especially the wife have no objections whatsoever to a little assistance. This aid is particularly appreciated at the time of childbirth, an event which may take place at home with a midwife in attendance. The help and comfort of relatives is of course welcome during illnesses and at funerals.

Family is appreciated above all by the elderly, who seem to be better treated in poorer areas like Portugal's Atlantic islands than in affluent nations like the United States. A study by the World

Health Organization not only called attention to the status which the older citizens of poorer lands enjoy because of their age but also noted that the compulsory retirement which is a feature of so-called advanced countries brings with it loss of status, reduction of social contacts, and decrease in income.

In Island Portugal's multigeneration household, elderly women—grandmothers and even great-grandmothers—take considerable satisfaction in and are duly honored for preparing delicacies for the table and doing other tasks. They set the model for what in fact seems to be more common than has been suspected in the United States, particularly among ethnic groups, the "ethnic mother," rather an admirable than a derisory figure.

Because of this respectful acceptance of the elderly, the older folks join in with the youngsters and act youthful. One need only attend a wedding of Americans of Italian descent to observe the grand time which the older generation has, dancing, drinking, clowning, and dressing prettily.

In a society singularly devoid of entertainment media—little TV, poor radio broadcasts, infrequent movies, virtually no theater—the family collectively lays on family *festas* which supplement those of the parish church's annual cycle. In fact, the kinship ceremonies alone—weddings, baptisms, birthdays, and funerals—constitute a formidable and exhausting cycle of social events which substitute for other forms of amusement.

The personalized relationships resulting from the family system spill over into other areas of life. Members of the extended family may work together on common agricultural or fishing projects and may cultivate common vineyards. Accustomed to mutual assistance, those who emigrate continue their support from afar, often at considerable personal sacrifice, by sending remittances in money or in kind. Those who remain behind come to expect the remittances and possibly also passage tickets. In the case of the Azores, so close to the Greater New York area and also to New England and so accessible because of relatively inexpensive group round-trip air fares and the commercial zeal of travel agents, family members even return regularly for visits. It is reported that today, as distinguished from former days of ship or slow piston-engined air travel, members even return for services such as medical care, which prove less costly in the islands than in America.

Because members of the extended family help each other, indigent relatives tend to turn to their brethren for assistance rather than to the impersonal State. Welfare on the scale it is known in the United States does not exist, indeed has heretofore been unthinkable, in Portugal. When the Portuguese immigrate into the United States, they retain the mutual-assistance concepts of the Old Country and, at least in the past, have tended to eschew public charity. In the early days they established their own mutual-aid associations, often elaborate insurance schemes which played an important role with sickness and death benefits before the advent of Social Security. In a sense these mutual-aid societies substituted for the extended family lacking in the New World.

Personalized relationships can lead to political exploitation and even to financial corruption via illegal payments. They are naturally taken advantage of to grease bureaucratic skids. In anticipation of favors to be requested at a later date, the islander assiduously cultivates his relationships within an elaborate patronage system. Trained to politeness and meticulousness, he expands his contacts into areas which are less familial than commercial. As an example, while staying on Santa Maria I once paid a three-day two-night visit to Ponta Delgada. In effect I had one precious full day in the city to gather the materials and information I needed. During that day my host and escort, acutely aware of the patronage network within which he had perforce to function, insisted that I personally call on the publisher or editor of each of the city's five newspapers. I recall noting that the Azorean city had more newspapers than New York City.

As a frequent visitor to the islands I have built up my own network of contacts, consisting in particular of knowledgeable persons who have aided me enormously in gathering material for this book. But I pay a price. I am a *padrinho*. Some of those who have favored me in turn ask that I intervene in favor of them. And of course I am flattered and delighted to do so and am amazed that on occasion the system works.

On the negative side, the Island Portuguese family, in the American view, generates an excessive togetherness. A U.S. father, used to the intimacy of his wife and children in his own home without relatives or maids, would go quite mad in the Island Portuguese family environment.

This environment conspires with insular interpretation of Church teachings to stifle the individual, especially the female. It thereby contributes to the acceptance of political dictatorship. Indeed, stress on family holds back progress, and the English ob-

Their Values

server of the Portuguese scene quoted in Chapter 2 has written: "This absorption with family affairs may explain why the Portuguese are intensely patriotic, but not public-spirited."

The system is particularly difficult on women, of all ages but especially on adolescents. Females are constantly watched, from behind the lace curtains of the windows facing on the street and from many pews of the local church. Thus, in the fatal month of August 1939, I, at the age of twenty-four, could not walk down an Azorean town's main street with a forty-year-old spinster member of the family with whom I was living because . . . the expression used in Portugal is "Faz mal," which may be translated as "It looks bad." No one within the family saw any evil arising from our daylight promenade, but everyone recognized that the other townspeople would see evil in every step we took.

☆ ☆ ☆

Sex is a subject of universal interest. Therefore, all institutions or customs which anticipate, involve, or stem from relations be-

Doing laundry in a running Madeiran brook, January 1973

tween male and female are watched with particular relish in the narrowly circumscribed Portuguese islands.

Traditionally, young women live with their parents until marriage. If they are forced to live on another island in order to attend secondary school, the parents make arrangements with relatives, a convent, or other safe dwelling. There are no single-woman apartments. But young women from one island do meet young men from another island at such schools, and interisland marriages result.

Going steady, as Americans know it, is ruled out, although becoming acquainted within the extended family is acceptable. Engagements are customary, and they represent far more of a family affair than do the private agreements common in America. Engagements represent formal commitments to marriage, and an engaged couple thereafter may see each other, with chaperone. But the young lady cannot date any other male. To ensure that she does not, neighbors watch, ever prone to gossip. If either party breaks the agreement, especially after a period of years has

Bride from Terceira arriving off Praia, Graciosa

passed, the young lady suffers. She is suspect, for the next male will insist on being assured of virginity.

Within lower-class families the custom of the boy asking the girl's hand of the latter's father continues. This act can take place when the boy is, say, eighteen, and the girl a mere fourteen. The girl is thus tied up, possibly for the years of his military service away from her island or archipelago. The Portuguese language has an appropriate expression for her state: she is bespoke ("está pedida"). Of course he is bespoke, too, but the system permits him to wander.

The young woman wears her engagement ring on the second finger of her left hand and looks forward to adding the wedding ring to the same finger. In the Azores the engagement ring is often a cultured pearl, off center, with small diamonds around it.

An eminent social scientist writing of Portugal has pointed out that money and property are transferred at death and not marriage and that therefore there are no dowries, only trousseaus. The young woman has her hope chest, or "happiness trunk" (*baú de felicidade*), and older female relatives embroider and otherwise prepare the necessities of the future new household.

The island marriages are normally not arranged, but many result from subtle pressures exerted by one or both families. Although the marrying pair are rarely mismatched socially or economically, it is common for older men to marry much younger women. A safe generalization would hold that some marriages effected between Portuguese in the United States, even very happy ones, would never take place in the islands because of assumed mismatching, as between a city man and a country woman. On the other hand, the age discrepancy seems less in America.

As the wedding day approaches, the banns are posted on the church door for a week. I noted that those on the outside of the outer door of Ponta Delgada's Matriz include the age of both the betrothed individuals. If the banns are proclaimed from the altar—they are called *proclamas* in Portuguese—they are done so at three masses, for example, on a Saturday, a Sunday, and the following weekend.

The entire system being slow-moving and conservative, there is little reason to obtain a waiver of the banns. Moreover, as there is hardly any venereal disease in the traditional island society—to the best of my knowledge—no blood test is required by the State. What is most significant, the thought of such a test, and the possibility that the State might intervene to delay a marriage, is anathema to the Island Portuguese mind, which views U. S. premarital requirements with horror.

As noted in the preceding chapter, island couples married in the Church. Indeed, not to do so was considered shameful. In the islands as on the Continent, and as in the United States but not in Brazil, the priest effecting a marriage ceremony acted in a double capacity, religious and civil. After the marriage he reported the civil portion of the marriage to the appropriate civil registry.

In his comprehensive study of local French life entitled *Village in the Vaucluse*, Harvard's Professor Laurence Wylie points out that all young married couples of Peyrane dream of a honeymoon in Nice for two or three weeks. The equivalent couples in the Portuguese archipelagoes dream of Lisbon. Just as for most in Peyrane the Riviera is unattainable, so in Insular Portugal the best that can be hoped for is the capital city of one's district. In practice, of course, there is often no honeymoon at all, except possibly leisurely walks along cliffs overlooking the sea.

After the wedding, female members of the clan await the first baby. As a matter of fact they tend to persecute the bride on this score, as if constantly to remind her that the Church preaches no birth control.

If the marriage did not work out, there could be no divorce, for the Church had performed the ceremony. The couple simply separated. Occasionally, the husband moved to Continental Portugal. There was no formal *desquite* (legal separation), as in Brazil, and the abandoned wife was not referred to as a *desquitada*. There may have been an ecclesiastical annulment, but only under the Church's rules. Consuelo Vanderbilt could obtain an annulment of her marriage to the Duke of Marlborough back in 1926. The likelihood of Consolação Santos on the back side of São Miguel obtaining one in 1973 was rather remote.

The death of one of the marriage partners calls for a protracted period of mourning on the part of the widow. The older generation wears black, although younger widows, as in the United States, are breaking the custom down.

Mourning is an elaborate ritual with its own code. The death of one's husband calls for two years of a public display of grief, after which she may demourn gradually. The death of a parent or brother or sister or a child calls for a lesser but nonetheless substantial period of mourning, one year for a parent, six months to a year for a brother or sister. In all these circumstances, the bereaved male may wear a black armband, if he wears a coat.

As for remarriage, society permits the widower, naturally, to take the step. In accordance with the common practice of persecuting females, a practice which is hardly Catholic and conceivably owes much in Portugal to the five centuries of contact with Islam, relatives frown on the idea of the widow's remarrying. In certain merry cases, however, I am told that Island Portuguese society thinks it would be better served if she did remarry. A case in point is the sister-in-law of Ti Manel Jaquim on São Miguel: the Sunday before he died she exhausted him in the she-ass's shack, and he could not enter the Gates of Heaven as one enters the Park in Furnas but without paying. The traditional but often unvoiced objection to the remarriage of a widow stems from concern on the part of her relatives, especially her children, about the disposition of money or property she may have inherited from her husband.

The old Administrative Code named the male as the normal head of the family. He certainly thought of himself as such. He expected a submissive marriage partner, for he knew his conjugal rights. And he got one. With the 1976 Constitution, however, great changes have set in. That document affirms that "Spouses have equal rights and duties with regard to civil and political capacity and the support and education of the children."

Portuguese society is supposed to be patriarchal, but the mother seems to run the household. She is *dona de casa*, what the French call *maîtresse de maison*. She and her female relatives and, if she can afford them, her *criadas* decorate the home, select the foods to be served, direct the education of the younger children, make the important domestic decisions.

To a far greater extent, perhaps, than in the United States, the husband and wife go their own ways. An example is the cult of the glories of Portugal's maritime discoveries. Before the 25th of April, the cult had gotten well out of hand in a way which could never have happened among Americans because the Portuguese woman did not intervene and prick her husband's cultural balloons. The U.S. wife is a bombast deflator. The Portuguese wife does not, or did not, dare hazard that role.

At its most extreme, the tendency for husband and wife to go their own ways is observable only in the cities and mostly in the larger ones of Continental Portugal. In Lisbon and Oporto one has the impression that the working family head wants to postpone returning to his home until the last possible moment. From work he goes to a café and sits around for hours sipping, reading newspapers, and conversing with cronies. The cronies seem to prefer to argue about whether Miguel Corte-Real reached Narragansett Bay or perished at sea than to face wife, children, mother-in-law, sisters-in-law, and a *concunhado*, hence the traditional importance of certain cafés and restaurants in the literary history of Portugal.

When the financial means are available, the husband often takes the obvious next step, but rarely in the islands. He takes a mistress, or at least cultivates a loving female who lives alone and caters to his innermost needs. These needs are not exclusively or even necessarily sexual. Rather, they are human and involve the consolation which can be given only by one's woman more or less alone.

With seeds of family disintegration already present, one wonders what will happen when Portuguese middle- and upper-class women, in the wake of much of the rest of the world, begin working outside the home on an extensive scale. In Continental Portugal, outstanding women have long occupied important positions. In the islands, however, women have not been active in either secondary education or civil service. There was no woman civil governor, or president of a junta general, or president of a municipal chamber, much less a bishop. But, as the composition of the new Regional Assemblies of both Azores and Madeiras reveals, and also that of the original Regional Government of the Madeiras, women are pressing to the fore.

The more affluent families may have a number of maids, among whom one, older, enjoys primacy as "governess" (*governanta*). She may be older than the nuclear couple, and very likely she was a maid to either father or mother in early years. In any event, she runs the kitchen, if not the entire household. She is rarely educated in the bookish sense of the term. Normally, she knows nothing of modern dietetics. But she has her authority. Woe be to the university-trained nuclear mother who attempts to change her ways!

☆ ☆ ☆

The legal arrangements involved in marriage, especially those concerning property, are changing in Portugal. What follows may once have been true but is not necessarily so today.

When a couple married and if either or both possessed any real or personal property, they made a declaration with respect to the manner in which they would hold that property in the future, as well as the property which they would subsequently acquire. If they agreed on the system known as separation (*separação de bens*), each filed an inventory; the items so listed continued to belong to that individual after the death of the spouse and even in the event of a separation. If a bride and room agreed on the system known as communal property (*comunhão de bens*), all property was held jointly; all went to the survivor.

Property, money, social prestige, and other material considerations loom large in Island Portuguese thinking as everywhere else. The Portuguese have even been known to manipulate given and family names in such a way as to suggest affluence, distant if not immediate. They do so by prudently selecting names given to children, names of the more prominent or successful forebears.

In their simplest form, Portuguese names function in the following manner. João Almeida marries Consolação Santos. They have a son whom they christen Paulo. His complete name is therefore Paulo Santos Almeida, the Almeida being his father's family name and the Santos that of his mother. Later in life he is known as Senhor Santos Almeida. If he writes a book, American librarians will catalogue it under "A" unless they realize that their Portuguese counterparts do so under "S."

The Regional Secretary of Education and Culture in the Azores provides a real example of name-giving in the genealogy which he has published in his book on the Fishers. Secretary Reis Leite married Maria Antonieta Mendes Ferreira. Their daughter is Antonieta Ferreira Reis Leite. Secretary Reis Leite's father was João Evaristo de Sousa Leite, his mother Maria Rafael Nogueira dos Reis. Maria Rafaela's father in turn was Guilherme Reis, her mother Deolinda Ermínia Nogueira.

In the Portuguese islands, parents want the daughter to marry young and the son to marry older. Unlike so many mothers of Irish descent or birth in Massachusetts, however, the more realistic and earthier island mothers do want their sons to marry. The minimum age for marriage without parental consent used to be twenty-one for both son and daughter. Girls on occasion did marry at a younger age, even almost as children, but with consent. The minimum age for a girl was fourteen, for a boy sixteen.

According to Portuguese law, a boy or girl under twenty-one

but eighteen or over could be "emancipated" by the parents with his or her acquiescence. No parental consent was required for the emancipated child to marry. For the unemancipated child to marry, such consent was necessary, and marriage automatically carried emancipation with it regardless of the age of the child.

The combination of the rules for emancipation and the 1967 Civil Code's liberalization of the rules concerning the rights of married women made for interesting results. A fourteen-year-old married Portuguese woman could appear in Portugal's consulate general in Boston and be issued a passport for foreign travel, all of this without the consent either of her husband or her parents.

17
RELATIVES IN AMERICA

The fourteen-year-old married woman in Boston suggests another and most important influence on the value system of the Insular Portuguese. Many families in the Madeiras and virtually all in the Azores have one or more branches in the United States. Over the decades, there has been a considerable mutual impact between family members on both sides of the Atlantic, especially of those in America on those who remained behind. This impact has been effected via the mails, via visits to the home islands by the emigrants and their descendants, and via definitive returns to Insular Portugal on the part of emigrants after and even before normal retirement age.

The explanation of these transoceanic relations lies in the proximity of the Portuguese islands to the United States. Horta, Fayal, for example, is that European city closest to Boston, 181.3 n mi. nearer than Iceland's Reykjavik. Funchal, Madeira, is only 2,597.2 n mi. from Boston, that is, 170.6 nearer than Lisbon, only 94.0 farther away than Foynes on the River Shannon in Ireland. The Funchal distance, however, is rather meaningless except with respect to westbound sailing ships. It is true, on the other hand, that a Bostonian can fly to the Azores, change islands and planes, and proceed by air direct to Madeira. Madeiran emigrants presumably could do the same thing in reverse but in fact tend to make the trip via Lisbon, Portugal's exit point.

A very early and a lasting example of Madeiran-American relationships terminates in a recent transatlantic love story. In about 1830, Manuel Joaquim dos Passos (1812-1882) left his native town of Ponta do Sol on the south coast of Madeira and settled in Baltimore. He later moved to Philadelphia and there married Lucinda Ann Cattell (1814-1900). The couple had nine children, two of whom became distinguished lawyers, John Randolph Dos Passos (with a capital "D") (1844-1917) and Benjamin Franklin

Horta, Fayal, Azores—"European city closest to Boston"

Pierce dos Passos (with a small "d") (1856-1898). The two brothers practiced law together in New York.

Among other children John Randolph had the novelist John Dos Passos (1896-1970), and Benjamin Franklin Pierce had Cyril Franklin dos Passos (born 1887). Throughout his life, John Randolph, a renowned writer on legal subjects, retained an interest in his father's Madeiran and Portuguese heritage and transmitted the interest to his novelist son. Indeed, John Randolph took his son John and the latter's mother to Madeira in 1904, as has been noted. The son revisited Madeira in 1921 with poet E. E. Cummings and in 1960 with his family. The 1960 visit is commemorated by a plaque at the entrance to the ancestral Passos home in Ponta do Sol which reads: "This house was the birthplace of the ancestors of the eminent American writer John Dos Passos who visited this municipality on July 20, 1960—Homage of the Municipal Chamber."

Benjamin Franklin Pierce dos Passos also published books on the law, specifically on inheritance law. His son Cyril Franklin, to become a well-known lawyer in the Dos Passos firm, and also a famous entomologist, retained an interest in Madeira—one which grew with the years. In 1959, after the death of his first wife and when in his early seventies, he married a distant cousin from Madeira, Maria Amália Pitta Pestana dos Reis. They make their beautiful home in Mendham, New Jersey, from which they maintain contact with relatives in both Funchal and Ponta do Sol who are particularly hospitable to wandering scholars from America.

The Dos Passos example may not be typical, but it is representative. It demonstrates the continuing impact of America on Madeira. That impact, however, will inevitably diminish as the years pass, whereas U.S. influence on the Azores will equally inevitably increase, as is suggested in the following tables:

Emigration from Insular Portugal 1966-1975

Year	Total	Azores to United States	Azores to Canada	Madeiras to Venezuela
1966	14,354	6,760	3,719	2,962
1967	14,420	7,301	3,659	2,440
1968	15,738	8,124	4,373	2,277
1969	15,517	8,027	4,684	1,796
1970	12,260	5,307	4,271	1,982
1971	11,821	4,621	4,641	2,314
1972	11,117	3,867	4,669	2,226
1973	12,866	3,551	4,204	3,039
1974	16,756	4,404	7,822	1,887
1975	10,698	4,621	3,255	1,488
Total	135,547	56,583	45,297	22,411

Emigration from Continental Portugal 1966-1975

Year	Total	Canada	United States	Brazil	France	West Germany
1966	105,880	3,041	6,580	2,398	73,414	9,685
1967	78,077	2,949	4,180	2,885	59,397	2,042
1968	64,712	2,442	2,666	3,119	46,499	4,882
1969	54,648	1,805	5,064	2,315	27,231	13,274
1970	54,099	2,252	4,377	1,557	21,959	19,755
1971	38,576	2,341	4,205	1,161	10,021	16,992
1972	42,966	2,115	3,660	1,124	17,791	14,369
1973	66,636	3,044	4,440	771	20,329	31,437
1974	26,631	3,563	4,864	535	10,096	3,039
1975	14,106	2,479	4,197	1,526	2,767	1,071
Total	546,331	26,031	44,233	17,391	289,504	116,546

This table is based on official Portuguese statistics, which reflect the Portuguese habit of grouping together two quite different sets of Portuguese. The one consists of the true emigrants. The other is formed by the migrant workers (*travailleurs immigrés, Gastarbei-*

ter), those who make a temporary move with no surety whatsoever about the long-range future.

Emigration to the United States from both archipelagoes of Insular Portugal all but ceased with the American restrictions imposed in the early 1920's. With the new U.S. immigration law of 1965, the possibility was open for the old pattern to resume; but in the meantime new trends had been established.

An extensive Azorean emigration to Canada had begun in the early 1950's. By that time, Madeirans in general were not emigrating in the numbers of earlier years, for their postwar tourist boom acted as a braking force. When Madeirans did emigrate, they tended, beginning in the 40's, to move to Venezuela, taking advantage of the new air services and of the Portuguese liner *Santa Maria* during those years of the 50's and 60's when it sailed from Lisbon and Madeira to La Guaira. Continentals, meanwhile, were building up their movement, begun in the early 60's, to the industrialized countries of Northwest Europe. Perhaps because of right-wing military governments from April of 1964 on, Brazil was losing its attraction to many Portuguese. After all, no sensible emigrant wishes to jump from the frying pan into the fire.

In spite of the new trends, the United States continued to beckon both Azoreans and Continentals to its shores, above all Azoreans. It is these Azoreans who now exercise the greatest impact on Insular Portugal. They are reinforcing the influence on the native archipelago of the Azoreans who moved to the United States for over a century following the War of 1812. In the Madeiras, the English influence continues significant at upper levels of society and management. At lower levels the impact of Venezuela and its Spanish language is moving rapidly to the fore. In the summer of 1977, I heard more Spanish than ever before in and around Funchal and its airport, in part due to the direct TAP connection between Caracas and Porto Santo.

The relatives in America have informed Azoreans in Insular Portugal of liberty, the relatively low taxes, the lack of obligatory military service (except in time of war), the more open relationship between the sexes, the availability of free public education, and the possibility of rising economically and socially and even entering the professions. Above all, those in the New World have sung of job opportunities and the material goods to be had almost for the asking. To reinforce their praise of America they have sent money home—*pesos*, the dollars used to be called—and goods of

Their Values 329

all kinds, especially clothing but also even grocery-store calendars. On visits or definitive returns they have introduced U.S. institutions ranging from various types of household furniture to sash-cord windows, window screens, overshoes, and the custom of wearing black pantsuits as mourning instead of the traditional garb. In fine, as one letter writer expressed it years ago in a missive sent to his native Terceira, "Isto é uma terra santa que Deus abençoi sempre e a todos" (This is a holy land which may God bless always and for all).

As America advanced technologically, Azoreans in the Azores were apprised of the new developments, the "steam cars," telegraph, telephone, trolley cars, automobiles, and photography. In days of old, returnees introduced whaling techniques. Today, they narrate the wonders of the San Joaquin Valley's dairy-ranching techniques. Remote Azorean villagers became more sophisticated in their acquaintance with the new industrial age than Continentals distant from Lisbon and Oporto could ever imagine. I recall meeting, on Flores in 1939, an old man who had been a gardener employed by Leland Stanford Junior University and who had made the round trip between his island and California a total of seven times. He had many a tale to tell.

Success stories abound in the Azores, for example from the lips of the Ponta Delgada taxi driver whose years in New Bedford netted him the wherewithal to purchase his vehicle, or from those of the entrepreneur in Madalena do Pico who in Canada earned enough not only to purchase a taxi but also to build and furnish in excellent good taste a little café.

The contact with America even had an effect on Azorean language and literature.

With new institutions went new words to the islands: *alvachús* (overshoes), *alvacote* (overcoat), *alvarós* (overalls), and *senicas* (sneakers) for instance, and virtually the entire vocabulary of open-boat whaling including the following:

bloz!	there she blows!
clît	cleat
blequesquin	blackskin
bûme	boom
logaête	loggerhead
ampo	hump
queize	case.

As emigrants returned and their experiences became known, they provided the model for fictional characters, as in the novels of the Pico writer Dias de Melo. A perfect example of the impact of relatives in America on literature is the novel written in English by an emigrant from Flores who settled in California, *Home is an Island*, of 1951, by the late Alfred Lewis (1902-1977). A theme is the propensity of the returnee for telling tales of America, often tall tales:

> Like father, like son. It's the sea. It's the tales you hear. Why are all adventurers such liars? How many have come back rich? Must you have gold to live?

Or again:

> Oh, why must they talk when they come back? José mused, later, going home.

José's father had sailed for America in his youth. He had embarked on an American whaling schooner which took him first to the Cape Verde Islands and the African coast. After having whaled all over the seven seas, he searched for gold in California. He remained in America for fifteen years. And he came back poor, to become one of "these sad, remembering men."

As Lewis indicated in his novel, there is a decidedly negative side to emigration which in the past tended to be suppressed. Azoreans at home received the good news in their letters, saw the successful returnees like a supposed "millionaire" from New Bedford whom I encountered, replete with diamond stickpin, on the waterfront in Velas (São Jorge) in 1939. Their relatives in America were not so free in reporting the occasional lack of employment opportunities and the general hostility of the social milieu.

Trained social scientists will have to document the exact nature of the success, or lack of it, of Azorean emigrants to America. In the meantime, one must depend on a multiplicity of casual conversations. And one must be ever alert to the possibility of political propaganda.

Over the latter decades of the Salazar/Caetano years, and especially beginning with early 1961 and the seizure of the *Santa Maria*, an official hostility toward the United States was subtly and indirectly expressed in Portugal. Examples may be found even in the scholarly literature on Portuguese emigration. Non-Azorean writers glossed over Insular emigration to the United States and stressed over-all Portuguese and, in particular, Continental movement to Brazil.

An explanation of this bias lies not only in latent hostility toward the United States on the part of some Portuguese intellectuals but also in the positive desire on the part of the Portuguese government and upper class to woo Brazil. Virtually alone on the international political stage, Portugal badly needed friends. Salazar and his successor and their cohorts therefore took to referring to Brazil as Portugal's greatest creation, to Brazil as Portugal's daughter. Even Republican Portugal as early as 1922 took advantage of the centennial of Brazilian independence from Portugal not to lament a loss but to celebrate the gain of an ally. This precedent endured and reached an absurd climax when a high-level delegation from Portugal visited Brazil in 1959 aboard the liner *Vera Cruz* in order to solicit Brazilian participation in the forthcoming 1960 Henry celebrations. I know, because I was in Salvador, Bahia, at the time and witnessed the arrival of the ship and the pompous officials.

Here is an irony concerning Portuguese emigration to Brazil, even as long ago as the turn of the century and possibly earlier: some of the immigrants in Brazil decided to pack up and move once again, this time to the United States. An example is provided by the maternal grandparents of Carlton M. Viveiros, who in November 1977 was elected mayor of Fall River. They both moved from their native São Miguel to Brazil, the grandmother at age four. They met and were married in Brazil, and their first child was born in Rio de Janeiro. They then moved to Fall River, where, in 1915, the mayor's mother was born. Viveiros's paternal grandparents were also born on São Miguel and knew each other there. They moved directly to Fall River, where they were married. In that city, in 1908, the mayor's father was baptized.

Propaganda in support of both the anti-U.S. and the pro-Brazil Portuguese foreign policy trickled down within the Azores. It bore fruit in the case of the afore-mentioned Ponta Delgada taxi owner/driver, who could not say enough bad about the United States in general and my native New Bedford in particular, yet he had earned his little fortune in the Whaling City. Whether or not this particular individual had come under the influence of the Ponta Delgada-based separatist movement is difficult to say. Indeed, whether the politicking for independence will strengthen or sabotage good relations between the Azores and the United States in the future is also difficult to assess.

Americans interested in the reputation of their nation in all corners of the world including Atlantic islands must ever monitor local trends. The slight hostility which I have detected on São Miguel since the Revolution is balanced by an overt desire on the part of another Azorean group for much closer relations with the United States.

As will be seen in Chapter 21, a high degree of "culture" in the traditional social sense exists in both Azores and Madeiras. There is an educated, refined, and sophisticated upper class, and some of its members also have relatives in America. Members of this class on Fayal and other Azorean islands are rather taken aback by the constant returning of emigrants of the lower class and regret that an uneducated and unsophisticated group seems to constitute the bond linking Azores and America. They have asked me to do what I can to expand high-level cultural relations between our worlds. I in turn have passed this word to both the U.S. Department of State and the American Portuguese Society, Inc., of New York.

The strong-high-level British influence on Madeira already mentioned is due to decades-long commercial and tourist relations made possible by direct shipping and, for a few years after World War II, flying-boat links. There is also a marked British influence on the Azores, especially on São Miguel, whose extensive exportation of pastel and oranges to England in times past naturally led to visits by distinguished Englishmen, some of whom early wrote excellent books descriptive of the archipelago. A not-unexpected by-product has been a disposition in the Azores, and especially on the Green Island, for the upper class to speak English with a British accent and to wish to teach that English in the schools. British English used to be considered more genteel than its American counterpart, which was associated by the upper class with the emigrant level of society. Here was another factor which set the upper class against the lower class, one which in the final analysis represents an influence from the relatives in America.

18
ATLANTIC BRAND OF LANGUAGE

A class distinction is made among the Insular Portuguese not only by the British-English accent in current use but also and most importantly by the brand of Portuguese employed. Language is a phenomenon of which the Island Portuguese are well aware. They discuss it widely in writing, and also in conversation with the visitor from abroad. A few introductory words of general explanation concerning language may therefore be in order.

A language is the mechanism whereby members of a group communicate among themselves. It is oral, or better audiolingual, a series of sound signals from the mouth of a speaker to the ear of a listener. Thus, the Cambridge Harvard community has its language, and all members understand it, including its few peculiarities of pronunciation ("Park the car in Harvard Yard") and its special vocabulary ("Yard" and never "campus"). Harvard's language succinctly expresses the community's attitude toward the world outside the gates, as when a visitor drops by Massachusetts Hall to call on President Bok only to learn from the receptionist that "The President is in Washington today conferring with Mr. Carter."

The nuclear family is almost by definition the smallest possible community, and each such family has its own intimate language, notably a private vocabulary to express certain bodily functions. The ensemble of one's relatives, *a família*, is often the next largest community; it may share language features not used by other extended families. Then there is one's village, town, city, or entire island.

In the case of very small islands like Corvo, Porto Santo, and Graciosa, most probably the entire population constitutes a single family which speaks the same language. In the case of large and densely populated islands like Madeira with its 872 inhabitants per square mile as against Porto Santo's 245, with this population in part concentrated in a single city and several large towns, distinct communities may exist and therefore variations in language from one part of the island to another.

Over the centuries since the original peopling, the population of each of the Adjacent Islands has tended to remain on its island, except for emigrants and the well-to-do upper crust. There has been little interaction between islands, although the air base on Terceira has attracted workers from all the other Azores. In special instances, however, where two islands lie in close proximity and small craft are available to bridge the gap, there may be more interaction including intermarriage. Such pairing of islands is exemplified by Santa Maria and São Miguel, Fayal and Pico, Corvo and Flores, and Porto Santo and Madeira. As suggested in Chapter 16, the secondary schools in the cities—Horta, Angra, Ponta Delgada, and Funchal—promote interisland contact and even marriage.

Being given all the preceding facts, it is not surprising that each Portuguese Atlantic island has its own special brand of the Portuguese language and that the language of the large islands manifests regional variations.

Observable differences in the language of adjacent communities result from a fact of linguistic science: the language of a community changes with time. A case in point is Latin. Latin became the everyday language of the entire Roman Empire. In one portion of the Iberian Peninsula it evolved into Spanish and in the western portion into Portuguese, the two languages being separate and distinct descendants of the language of the Roman legionnaires. Moreover, if some of the members of a community migrate to another area and retain their language, that language from that point in time onward will change at a different rate and in different ways from that of the group left behind. Very often the language of the group which migrates is more conservative than that of their relatives and friends in the original homeland. In broadest terms, Canadian French is the seventeenth-century French of Normandy, and American English represents an earlier stage in the development of English than the language of England. In some respects Azorean and Madeiran Portuguese are more archaic than the fully evolved language of Lisbon.

As a result of the spectacular overseas expansion of Portugal in the fifteenth and sixteenth centuries, students of Island Portugal may quite properly think in terms of four general types of Portuguese today.

(1) Standard European Portuguese is the language which originally evolved from the Portuguese of the Lisbon-Coimbra area of central Continental Portugal and is now spoken by all literate and "cultivated" Portuguese. It is this language which overlies the regional speech of the masses of the people of northern and southern Continental Portugal and of the Azorean and Madeiran archipelagoes. It constitutes the language of everyday intercourse throughout not only Continental and Insular Portugal but what is left of Overseas Portugal as well. It is taught in the schools; used in pulpits, on the stage, and on radio and TV; and employed in a highly standardized written form in books and newspapers. It is what the American tourist hears in hotels, restaurants, and museums. It is the "refined" language, or, perhaps better, the language of refinement. It is the language spoken by those Portuguese persons who, to use elitist terminology, amount to something within the Portuguese world. It is what Americans and other foreigners learn when they attend special programs for foreigners run by Portuguese universities.

(2) Insular Portuguese is the language of the several islands of Insular Portugal as spoken by the masses, the very people who emigrate. This language was taken to the two groups of islands by the original peoplers, presumably in general entire nuclear families from Continental Portugal.

Insular Portuguese reflects the language of the masses essentially of southern Continental Portugal, to a lesser extent of east-central Continental Portugal. Today in the islands one never hears a *b* instead of a *v*, for example in *vinho* "wine," or a *tch* (as in English *chin*) instead of a *sh* (as in English *shin*), e.g. *chave* "key," both of which characterize northern Continental Portuguese. On the other hand, one does hear, except on Fayal, a pure vowel sound like the *é* of French *café* instead of the diphthong *ei* (as in English *lay*), e.g. *lei* "law," which rimes with *lê* "he reads," this *ê* for *ei* being a characteristic of southern Continental Portuguese.

Insular Portuguese has now been overlain by Standard European Portuguese, the language taught in the island schools, heard over radio and TV and in the mouths of civil, military, and ecclesiastical officials and of entertainers sent out from the Continent. The islanders who speak this standard language are in general, of course, those least in need of emigrating. Some do move to America, however, and in the New World it is they who can normally be expected to emerge in leadership positions.

(3) Brazilian Portuguese is the language of the many men and large number of families who migrated to Brazil from Continental and Insular Portugal down the centuries, and their descendants. True to linguistic theory, it today exhibits many features of sixteenth-century European Portuguese, for example in the unstressed vowel system. Other features are purely Brazilian, representing the natural evolution of Portuguese in the mouths of a relatively isolated community, for example the special pronunciation of t and d before the sound i (the *ee* of English *feet*) as in *ti* "thee" and *digo* "I say," in which the initial consonants sound like the *ch* of English *chin* and the *g* of English *gin*. Other features which occur almost exclusively in the vocabulary reflect the impact on the Portuguese of Brazil of American Indian (or "native American") and African languages within the South American country.

(4) Cape Verdean Creole (*Crioulo*) is the intimate everday spoken language of the masses of the people in the Cape Verde Islands. Standard European Portuguese, Insular Portuguese, and Brazilian Portuguese are all mere variations of the same relatively uniform over-all language and are all mutually comprehensible, except for a few words like "trolley car" (*carro eléctrico* in Portugal and *bonde* in Brazil). Cape Verdean Creole, by way of contrast, is most decidedly a dialect of Portuguese. As it is in general not intelligible to speakers of Portuguese, not even in its written form which is today still quite rudimentary, one might perhaps best think of it as a separate language, albeit based on Portuguese.

Cape Verdean Creole is a brand of Portuguese which arose as a tool or working language in the days when Portuguese Europeans were dominant traders and West Africans were dominated suppliers of goods and services. It is today the de facto language of the entire Cape Verdean archipelago, with variations from island to island. It is, of course, overlain by Standard European Portuguese, which is the newly independent republic's international spoken and written language. Whether *Crioulo* will prove to be the country's national language remains to be seen. It is noteworthy that the Commonwealth of Massachusetts has recognized *Crioulo* as an independent language for purposes of transitional bilingual education and that a University Extension course in that language was first offered at Harvard in the fall of 1978.

A sample of *Crioulo* is both amusing and politically significant:

Their Values 337

> Branco ta morá na sobrado,
> Mulato ta morá na lodja,
> Nego ta morá na funco,
> Sancho ta morá na rotcha.
>
> Ta bem um dia,
> Nhô Trasco Lambasco,
> Rosto frangido,
> Rabo comprido,
> Ta corrê co nego di funco,
> Nego ta corrê co mulato di lodja,
> Mulato co branco di sobrado,
> Branco ta bá rotcha, el ta tombá.

The white man dwells above the shop,
The mulatto dwells in the shop,
The black man dwells in a shack,
Sancho [the monkey] dwells on a rock.

The day will come when
Mr. Trasco Lambasco [Sancho, the monkey],
His face all wrinkled,
His tail lengthened,
Will run the black man out of the shack,
The black man will run the mulatto out of the shop,
The mulatto the white man out of his dwelling,
The white man will go to the rock, and fall off.

☆ ☆ ☆

The differences between Standard European Portuguese and the several varieties of Insular Portuguese are as nothing compared to those between Standard European Portuguese and *Crioulo*, and they vary considerably in magnitude from one Azorean or Madeiran island to another. They embrace chiefly pronunciation, including intonation. They also include items of vocabulary, but to a minor extent.

From the point of view of pronunciation, the island whose language is most different from Standard European Portuguese is São Miguel. Michaelese, as the language is called, is therefore the most difficult for a foreigner studying Standard European Portuguese to understand. But with a little effort he can manage to understand it. The next most different is the language of Madeira, Madeirese. Michaelese and Madeirese are the means of communication of the masses of the people on the two largest, most populated, most densely populated, touristically most attractive, and naturally richest islands of Insular Portugal, and apparently by the same token the two most poverty-stricken from the point of view of those masses and also, at least in the past, of the highest illiteracy rate and least cultural development. Why this is so is an intriguing problem difficult of solution.

The fact of variant pronunciation, however, should not deter the foreign student from opting to study Portuguese at either the University-level Institute of the Madeiras in Funchal or the Ponta Delgada branch of the University-level Institute of the Azores. Such a student will hear Standard European Portuguese from his teachers, the family with whom he is housed, and the circle of acquaintances of the social level in which he moves. Or, to put the matter in inverse fashion, the Institute authorities should not expose students to language teachers who do not speak Standard European Portuguese nor house them with families who do not use that form of language.

The language of Porto Santo is similar to but not as different from the norm as Madeirese, and that of Santa Maria is likewise similar to but less different than Michaelese.

The next, that is, the fifth most different, is, to judge from available and incomplete evidence, the Portuguese of Corvo. The sixth is that of Terceira. In seventh place lie Graciosa, São Jorge, and Pico on the one hand, Fayal on another, and Flores on the third hand, which is to say that the three languages differ relatively little from the standard, but they differ in different ways. A striking characteristic of Fayalese curiously renders it not only close to Standard European Portuguese but also places it in a more advanced position.

Reference has already been made to the standard pronunciation of the written diphthong *ei*, as in *lei* "law," *terceira* "third," and *madeira* "wood." An acceptable and widely heard pronunciation is roughly the diphthong of English *lay* or *they*. Standard European Portuguese, especially in the Lisbon area, renders it in a slightly exaggerated way as a diphthong midway between those of English *lay* and *lie*, or between *they* and *thy*. Whereas the Portuguese of the masses in southern Portugal and in Insular Portugal in general reduce what is written as *ei* to a pure vowel like the *é* of Spanish *Yo no sé* "I do not know," the people of Fayal move it virtually all the way to the diphthong of English *lie* and *thy*. That pronunciation instantly characterizes a native of Fayal who has not adopted Standard European Portuguese.

The most noticeable characteristic of Michaelese is the systematic shift in the pronunciation of stressed vowels. Called a *déplacement en chaîne* or *Kettenverschiebung*, that is, "chain reaction," this shift has become well known in international linguistic circles and has conferred a certain fame on the island of St. Michael's.

Essentially, the shift involves the seven basic vowels of Standard European Portuguese, which can be depicted in triangular form using as a rough equivalent the English vowel between the *b* and the *t* of the following words:

>   beet   boot
>   bait   boat
>   bet   bought
>   Bart

(To understand this triangle, *Bart* must be given the Harvard pronunciation, the *a* of *father*.)

In Michaelese, the *Bart* would be pronounced like *bought*, *bought* like *boat*, and *boat* like *boot*. The vowel of the original *boot* would become the *ü* (French *u* of *tu* "thou") already discussed in Chapter 2 in connection with the place-name Bretanha. As *Bart* shifts toward *bought*, *bet* is free to shift toward *Bart* and *bait* toward *bet*. *Beet*, however, remains stable.

These shifts are not reflected in the universally used written language, which is based on Standard European Portuguese. They can therefore greatly confuse the speaker of Standard European Portuguese, above all the foreign speaker of that language. In Portuguese, *cabra* (with the vowel of *Bart*) is "goat" and *cobra* (with the vowel of *bought*) is "snake." Imagine my surprise when I was first told that a special *cobra* cheese had been prepared for me!

By a curious coincidence, the stable *i* of Michaelese (the vowel of *beet*) is the very vowel in Madeirese whose shift constitutes that island's outstanding feature of pronunciation. The resulting sound is a diphthong very similar to the Standard European Portuguese pronunciation of the written *ei*. Because of the possibility of confusion, the visitor to Madeira is treated to a series of witticisms in order for him to understand this linguistic peculiarity. The feminine singular form of the adjective "half" is *meia*. The verb used when the cat meows is *mia*. Therefore: "Oh, Maria [pronounced Mareia], what animal has four paws and *meia*?" Or take the joke about the government official from Madeira on duty in Lisbon with chapped corners to his mouth. Asked about the physical problem, he replied: "It's because of the *freio*." (*Frio* is cold, *freio* is the bit put in a horse's mouth.)

As for vocabulary, when a speech community has an institution unique to it, its language will have a special word. Thus, the word *caldeira*, normally used for "boiler," is employed in Insular Portugal to indicate the crater of a volcano. Occasionally, an island will have its own word for a well-known institution, for example *semilha* (pronounced as if *semeilha*) on Madeira for the standard *batata* "potato."

Within the Azores, the same word may have different meanings on different islands. Thus, on Pico a *pastor* "shepherd" looks after cows; on Terceira he holds the bull by the long cord in that island's great sport of running the bulls; and on São Miguel he looks after goats. Or basically the same institution may be known by different words on different islands. Thus, the black cloak and accompanying enormous hood worn by Azorean ladies of yesteryear to the delight of nineteenth-century visitors from abroad are known on Fayal as *capote* and *capucho* and on São Miguel as *capote* and *capelo*. On Terceira the single word *manto* is used for the ensemble. It goes without saying that there are minor variations in the costume itself among the islands.

This matter of regional vocabulary, by the way, can become very tricky for the foreigner. Having learned "correct," that is, standard Portuguese in his school or university, he visits an island and encounters unfamiliar words which he concludes are used only in that locality. After further travel he realizes that they are employed by the masses of the people throughout Portuguese-speaking territory even including Brazil. There exists in effect a widespread "people's vocabulary"—if not indeed a general people's Portuguese—which is not quite acceptable to the elite but is nevertheless well-nigh universal. Examples: *outra banda* "other side (of the street or river)" for the standard *outro lado; acolá* "over there" for *lá*; and *por môr de* "because of" for *por causa de*. Very often these words or phrases are very old and once upon a time were socially quite respectable.

Their Values 341

☆ ☆ ☆

It is clear, then, that language is a most complex phenomenon; and the decision faced by, say, U.S. school administrators concerning the appointment of teachers of Portuguese in "bilingual/bicultural," "ethnic-heritage," or other programs must be made after thorough consideration of all the relevant facts of provenience and accent.

Underlying Standard European Portuguese are not only regional variations spoken by the masses in a horizontal or geographical distribution, as on the Atlantic islands. There are also social or class variations in a vertical distribution. And there can be a crossing of the two. A highly educated member of the upper class on São Miguel may speak with a Michaelese accent, using the French *u* in *escudo* and the French *eu* in *noite* "night" (approximately the *ur* of the English name *Burt*). Conversely, a humble peasant on Pico may speak with a hardly noticeable accent, although in his vocabulary using "lower-class" words like *acolá*.

More normally, however, members of the lower class give up regional pronunciations and regional vocabulary as they ascend the educational ladder and concomitantly rise economically and eventually socially. For that reason, the foreign student need not hesitate to perfect his Portuguese in the Azores or Madeiras. Indeed, doing so he will undergo a rich linguistic experience. He will learn that pronunciation and/or vocabulary can categorize a person.

Such categorization unfortunately took place, chiefly through ignorance, within the areas of Azorean settlement in America. Indeed, the natural rivalry between the two mill cities New Bedford and Fall River in Massachusetts, whose high school football teams have for long been determined antagonists, was exacerbated at the immigrant level by rival Azorean accents. In New Bedford were the Fayalese speaking their relatively standard language, and in Fall River were the Michaelese speaking their most different Portuguese.

Conclusions drawn in ignorance by some native Azoreans may prove politically significant in the future. The Azorean independence or separatist movement is today based on São Miguel, with support from neighboring Santa Maria. I have noted that, whatever their thoughts may be about being ground down by distant

Lisbon, people on the other islands seem not to favor the notion of an independent nation ruled or even dominated by São Miguel. Could Central and Western Azoreans be influenced by such a superficial criterion as language accent?

19
SCHOOLING AND BRAIN DRAIN

Down the centuries until the mid-Caetano years of the early 1970's, the Portuguese educational system functioned in elitist fashion. It kept the lower class down and the upper class up. All too often, apparent improvements in the system were designed to be mere means whereby the masses of the people would become more effective workers. Education for the larger numbers was planned as vocational training. It was not conceived as the means of imparting the four abilities to which I feel I have dedicated more than three decades of my life at Harvard, namely, "to think effectively," "to communicate thought," "to make relevant judgments," and "to discriminate among values."

Even Caetano did not quite understand world trends and the true educational needs of his country, as he made evident in a retrograde and slightly sexist speech delivered less than three months before his abrupt fall from power. The occasion was his visit on February 8, 1974, to the new building of the Ministry of National Education (today Ministry of Education and Culture) in Lisbon, and it followed four years of herculean efforts by his Minister to set things more aright. The President of the Council of Ministers said:

> And what is to be expected is not merely a multiplication of schools handing out diplomas or even spreading throughout this Country a little scientific and literary knowledge. The Ministry is called, significantly, of *Education*. And of *National Education*. It is not our mission merely to instruct: but above all to educate. Educate in order that there be men ever more perfectly molded in their moral qualities as in their intellectual and physical aptitudes, capable within the society in which they live—namely, the Portuguese Nation—of contributing to the common good as aware citizens.
>
> National education, then, cannot help having as a goal the

molding of good Portuguese—creating in them love for the Fatherland and habits of work, initiative, discipline, fulfillment of duty, and correctness of manners. National education cannot help attempting to raise the level of the dignity and morality of the Portuguese, with the certainty that it is impossible to gain the respect of another without first cultivating respect for oneself. And this is true of individuals as for nations.

Reflecting a stress on what theologians call personal salvation instead of societal good, this extract invites the outsider to translate Caetano's word *educação* by "indoctrination" rather than "education." It also causes him to wonder whether the earlier name for the Ministry of National Education—Ministry of Public Instruction—had not been a preferable one.

As a result of the failure of government, the Church, and responsible individuals in positions of power right down to Caetano to promote adequate education, Portugal was not prepared as a Western European nation to enter the post-Napoleonic era in the early nineteenth-century, nor to enter the twentieth century, nor to enter the postwar era beginning in 1945, nor really to make the most of the golden opportunities which the 1974 Revolution presented to the nation.

My personal awareness of the educational inadequacies of Portugal began, with a vengeance, during the fourteen months of my linguistic research in Continental and Insular Portugal from June 1938 to September 1939. That rich experience ranged from the 1938 summer school of the University of Lisbon—in the old Casino of Monte Estoril—to three months of intensive experimental work in Armando de Lacerda's phonetics laboratory at the University of Coimbra in the spring of 1939. It introduced me to the superjingoism of many nationalistic Portuguese professors and to the highest standards of international scholarship of a handful of truly patriotic and often unrecognized Portuguese teachers like Lacerda.

An attempt to influence Portuguese education began in 1950. In that year, Dr. Lewis Hanke was Director of the Hispanic Foundation in the Library of Congress. He organized and as its secretary-general ran the International Colloquium on Luso-Brazilian Studies held in the Library in October. I was selected to be president. Our idea in those days was, frankly, to bring into the

Their Values

international world of scholarship university professors and other publishing scholars of a Portugal still enmeshed in the throes of Salazarism and of a Brazil which five years before had rejected the dictatorship of Getúlio Vargas but which in that very year 1950 was democratically electing the same Vargas as President. The tree so planted bore fruit, and the first Colloquium was followed by five others: 1954 in São Paulo, 1957 in Lisbon, 1959 in Salvador (Bahia, Brazil), 1963 in Coimbra, and 1966 at Harvard University in Cambridge and Columbia and New York Universities in New York City.

The Sixth Colloquium proved to be the end of the line. Brazil had reverted to dictatorship two years before, and the need of dealing with two authoritarian governments and two sets of dominated universities proved to be too much for free scholars in free universities to cope with. They wished no longer to deal with any official Brazilian or Portuguese "coordinating" committees. They preferred to wait until academic colleagues in the two countries could breathe fresher air.

I have already discussed my other frustration of the 1950's, failure to involve the Universities of Coimbra and Oporto and the Classical University of Lisbon in the International Association of Universities. Had those universities participated actively in the important work of the association, some of the student and faculty energy of the ensuing years might have been diverted to more constructive channels and Mário Soares might not have felt constrained to level the strong and all-too-true attack against the Portuguese university system which he included in his autobiography.

The end-product of the neglect of education in Portugal in general and in Azores and Madeiras in particular becomes abundantly clear from the following table, based on the results of the official Portuguese censuses of the years indicated:

Percentage of Illiterates in Total Population 1911-1960

	1911		1920		1930	
	Male	Female	Male	Female	Male	Female
District of Angra	73.9	68.0	67.9	60.7	67.7	62.5
District of Horta	66.7	61.2	55.1	50.3	55.7	51.2
District of Ponta Delgada	78.8	72.7	75.9	67.5	76.1	69.1
District of Funchal	84.3	81.4	79.3	77.4	77.0	77.6
District of Lisbon	57.2	62.5	53.0	58.9	42.8	52.1
Continental Portugal	67.7	81.7	63.7	77.4	59.7	74.6

	1940		1950		1960
	Male	Female	Male	Female	Total pop.
District of Angra	57.0	50.8	47.7	41.2	37.0
District of Horta	48.7	43.2	35.6	29.9	28.9
District of Ponta Delgada	66.0	59.4	56.6	49.2	44.2
District of Funchal	69.3	71.1	55.2	58.5	45.7
District of Lisbon	35.7	44.9	28.1	37.3	28.1
Continental Portugal	51.9	65.7	41.7	54.9	40.1

A striking fact emerges: placed in order of literacy from highest to lowest, the four Insular Portuguese administrative districts lined up consistently. The most literate district was Horta, next Angra, in third place Ponta Delgada, and least literate Funchal. And with the exception of Funchal in 1930, 1940, and 1950, women were consistently more literate than men.

What is particularly noteworthy is the fact that the percentage of illiterates was always less in the district of Horta than for all eighteen districts of Continental Portugal taken as a whole. In the case of women, it was even less than for the capital district of Lisbon, which one would expect to be the most literate of all twenty-two districts of Metropolitan Portugal.

It seems clear, at least to this writer, that the table's revelations are an indirect tribute to the presence of the American Dabney family on Fayal throughout most of the nineteenth century and to the presence there of the several cable staffs from 1893 on; see Chapters 8 and 9. On the other hand, it should be stressed that illiteracy, the inability to read or write, must never be equated with ignorance. One can be totally illiterate yet very knowledgeable and well informed and very useful to society, although not necessarily successful in the mid-twentieth-century meaning of the term.

☆ ☆ ☆

The basic organization of the public or "official" educational system in Portugal as it emerged toward the end of the eighteenth century and evolved throughout the nineteenth and twentieth centuries right up to 1970 was French, and the period from 1900 to 1970 in Portuguese education has been referred to as Napoleonic-Latin. As in so much else, then and now, la belle

France provided a model and leadership for the Portuguese elitist class. France's contribution included the concept of a highly centralized national structure centered on a Ministry of Education headed by a Minister of cabinet rank in the national capital, a structure instinctively rejected by many Americans who respect their Constitution, its separation of powers, and its failure to specify education as an area of concern of the federal government, thereby reserving it to the States.

Essentially, the system consisted of four years of primary school beginning at age seven, followed by seven years of secondary school and then the university years.

Only in the 1960's did all four years of primary school become compulsory. As late as 1960, only the first three were obligatory, the fourth being voluntary. Whether the required years numbered three or four, they were all that the masses devoted to formal education. Unfortunately, not all of the masses attended school even to this extent because of the lack of schools and teachers and because of the need of child labor on the farms, hence the high percentage of illiterates throughout the country. In all fairness, however, it should be pointed out that the figures for the later censuses reflect the lack of availability of schooling of an earlier day.

The children of the upper class, never ones to suffer cultural privation, moved on to the secondary school of seven years duration. If run by the State, this school was called a *liceu* or "lyceum" (cf. French *lycée*), if by the Church or Catholic religious order or other private group, a *colégio* or "college" (cf. French *collège*).

As the system became inevitably more complex with the passing of the years, some private secondary schools continued residential with the name *colégio* but others were set up for day students with the designation *externato* or "nonresidential." An example of the latter is the five-year secondary school established at the Santa Maria airport for children of airport employees and others on the island whom parents did not choose or could not afford to send to the lyceum in Ponta Delgada.

Whether run by State, Church, or private lay group, all schools were controlled by the education ministry within the Central Government in Lisbon as far as curriculum, standards, and textbooks were concerned. True to the French formula, the Portuguese continued to attempt to keep their system unified and national even as dissident forces operated in the later 1970's. And traditionally, of course, in the past there was no managerial input from either parents or teachers. There was no PTA.

In Portugal there has never been anything comparable to the U.S. system of parochial schools. Unlike the decentralized American organization, all schools in Portugal were molded to the same pattern. In Chapter 14, the article of the 1940 Concordat was quoted which specifically gave the State power over the teaching in Church schools. The Concordat's inclusion of Catholic religion and Catholic morals in the public-school curriculum was of course the sop given the Church by the State. And State and Church were visible in classrooms to teacher and students alike. On one wall there could be pictures of the President of the Republic and of the President of the Council of Ministers. Or else, as in one public-school room I visited in 1970, on the front wall a crucifix and beneath it Our Lady of the Immaculate Conception (to whom the Feminine Portuguese Youth movement was dedicated), and on the back wall a map of Portugal with at its top "Nada contra a nação" and its bottom "Tudo pela nação." Or again, in the office of the school superintendent for the District of Funchal, in Funchal in early 1973, a picture of President Américo Tomás to the Director's right, a picture of Marcello Caetano to his left, a crucifix above the pair of presidents, and just below the crucifix a map of the island of Madeira, that of Porto Santo being on another wall.

The children of the upper class and a few other privileged youngsters, then, went on to the lyceum. Other graduates of primary school either went nowhere, as happened most often, or else attended a "technical" school at the secondary level.

In the Atlantic islands, the *escola industrial e comercial* or "industrial and commercial school" of Funchal and also that of Ponta Delgada evolved into adequate training centers offering a variety of vocational courses, all housed in most adequate buildings. The equivalent school in Angra was much more modest. That in Horta was nonexistent until the departure of the submarine telegraph cable companies provided the State with the possibility of acquiring an appropriate setting for this type of instruction.

The lyceum program led directly to a university, for parents of many lyceum students were university-minded. The seven years were grouped into three so-called cycles. The first two years were known as the preparatory cycle, an introduction as it were to sec-

Their Values 349

Funchal's Industrial and Commercial School

ondary education. The next three years formed the second cycle, which normally was terminal for those lyceum students not advancing to higher education. Thus, the diploma of the *quinto ano* or "fifth year" and the phrase "I have completed the fifth year" have considerable importance for the students who went that far in school. The last two years, that is, the third cycle, were definitely designed as final preparation for university study. Unlike the preparatory and second cycle, the third cycle offered a choice: one track for the classical university *faculdades* (literally "faculties" but better translated "schools") such as letters, law, and theology, the other for the scientific university schools such as sciences, medicine, and engineering.

The Portuguese students of days gone by were locked into a rigid system with little possibility of crossovers. Thus, if they moved from the fourth *classe* of the primary school—each year of the primary school is called a "class" and each year of the secondary school an *ano* "year"—to the industrial and commercial school, there was virtually no chance of later shifting to the preuniversity lyceum. Similarly, if after the fifth year of the lyceum they elected the classical third cycle, there was little chance of ever entering a scientific university school.

Another element of rigidity in the Portuguese educational system concerned teacher preparation. Primary-school teachers were trained in an *escola do magistério primário* or "school for primary teaching." Located near, if not an integral part of, a lyceum, the school for primary teaching provided a two-year course following the fifth year of the lyceum. In Insular Portugal these schools in fact functioned as annexes to the lyceums, the lyceum rector being the school for primary teaching's director. Moreover, some of the teachers served in both institutions, with additional remuneration.

The program of the school for primary teaching being at the level of the third cycle naturally did not attract students desirous of university training. Rather, it was the culmination of formal education for lyceum students who saw no possibility of ascending the education ladder beyond the fifth year of the lyceum yet who desired some kind of professional training. It was a laterally-located institution which locked one into a career of primary-school teaching and excluded one from virtually anything else. Being at the level of the third cycle of the lyceum, it corresponded to the tenth and eleventh years of formal schooling, to the sophomore and junior years, or tenth and eleventh grades, of the American high school.

Officials responsible for education after the Revolution naturally recognized this inadequacy. In a dispatch to *The New York Times* published on March 14, 1976, Marvine Howe discussed the problems faced by the education minister and concluded:

> Another problem carried over from the old regime, he said, is that too many people who are not teachers teach. When there was a lack of teachers, people were accepted into the profession with only the equivalent of 9th to 11th grade educations. At the same time, an increasing number of engineers, lawyers and business managers have entered the teaching profession because they cannot get jobs elsewhere as a result of the economic slump.

Lyceum teachers, on the other hand, were often and theoretically always university graduates, that is, holders of the licentiate degree granted by a Continental university after four years of classes followed by a year devoted to the writing of a thesis.

Lyceum and technical-school teachers of the humanities such as Portuguese or foreign languages and literatures received their *licenciatura* from a "faculty of letters," those of the sciences such as mathematics, physics, and chemistry received theirs from a "faculty of sciences." In fact, these two university schools—what Americans would call "colleges"—were for the most part not liberal-arts colleges in the U.S. sense at all but rather teachers' colleges. Accordingly, it made little sense for graduates of a U.S. high school to attempt to transfer to them and complete their programs.

A long distance thus separated teachers in the primary schools from those in the secondary schools because the idea that the first-grade teacher is as important to the development of the individual as the teacher of the last secondary-school year and therefore as deserving of the same salary was very foreign to Portuguese thinking. The primary-school teacher in Insular Portugal had little prestige and less remuneration. The secondary-school teacher enjoyed considerable prestige and received a much higher salary. Moreover, the latter had the great advantage of a lengthy sojourn on the European mainland, for there were no universities and therefore no programs for the preparation of secondary-school teachers in either Azores or Madeiras. Indeed, in Insular Portugal there was practically nothing labeled higher education. Not even the major seminaries in the diocesan sees (Angra and Funchal) merited that designation, even though their course of priestly formation followed the lyceum's fourth or fifth year.

Over many decades until the year in which Salazar died, the four-plus-seven system imparted schooling to the youth of Insular Portugal and by the same token was responsible for the drain of island brains to Continental Portugal and the Americas.

The primary school in particular reinforced the influence of Church, church, and family and transmitted the influence of the State. It was thus instrumental in indoctrinating island boys and girls with the values which Lisbon desired that they possess: respect for authority and admiration for Portugal and all that was Portuguese including its colonial policies.

Separation of the sexes in the early grades reinforced Christian morality as taught in church and in the home, and it continued until abolished as of October 1, 1973. The custom of having the teacher advance with his or her students through the four primary years possibly reinforced the unity of the family. In accord-

An entrance for each sex, Vila do Porto, Santa Maria, 1970

ance with this procedure a particular teacher taught the first class in say 1967-1968, second class in 1968-1969, third in 1969-1970, and fourth in 1970-1971, then to begin all over. The procedure worked except when the child was forced to remain almost interminably with the same disliked teacher or when the child became so enamored of the teacher as to substitute him or her for a parent.

The difficult hurdles over which the youngster was forced to jump, including even oral examinations with outside examiners, and the frequent failure on the part of the school authorities to promote him or her supposedly reinforced the notion of discipline and fulfillment of duty so rampant in authoritarian regimes. In fact, however, this holding back of the student resulted in lessened education, for the requirement stipulated three (and later four) years of presence in school, not the completion of the third (and later fourth) class. The examinations had what was probably their intended effect: not to uphold high quality but to keep the lower class down.

The textbooks, above all those of the history of Portugal, inculcated respect for, love of, and pride in the Patria. Take the *História de Portugal* written by Luís Reina for the third class and published in Oporto in 1965. It contains a global map with the caption "Portuguese unity in today's world." The following text is headed "Many races—a single nation" and reads:

> Observe the map up above!
> On it may be seen in black the territories which form our Portugal.
> There may be observed:
> CONTINENTAL PORTUGAL, situated in Europe;
> MADEIRAS, AZORES, CAPE VERDE ISLANDS, and SÃO TOMÉ-E-PRÍNCIPE, which are located in the Atlantic Ocean [!];
> PORTUGUESE GUINEA, ANGOLA, and MOZAMBIQUE, which are located in Africa;
> The STATE OF INDIA and MACAO, in Asia; and one half of the island of TIMOR, in Oceania.
> As may be seen, Portugal is not a little country. To the contrary, it is a great nation, formed by various territories spread throughout the World.
> In these territories, 23 millions of Portuguese live like brothers: some of the white race; others of the black or yellow race; and still others mulattoes or mestizos.
> They are persons of different races and of different habits and customs. Nevertheless, all bear in their hearts a love of the Fatherland and all stand ready to engrandize it and to defend it whenever it should be necessary.
> The fact is all are PORTUGUESE and live under the same flag, the PORTUGUESE flag.

Two observations are hardly necessary. At the time the book was published, Portugal was waging three colonial wars in Africa; and Goa, Damão, and Diu in India had ceased to be Portuguese territory on December 18, 1961.

☆ ☆ ☆

By the end of the 1960's the directions of needed educational reform in Portugal were obvious for all to see.

A first change was an increase in the number of school buildings. Overdue by at least a score of years, schools built to the Centenaries Plan mentioned in Chapter 14 began to rise. Other schools were also built, and by the mid-to-late 1960's an extraordinary reversal had taken place within the Azores, one which is illustrated by a comparison of Fayal with Santa Maria. The higher literacy rate in the District of Horta reflected the greater number of available schools in previous years. The Government therefore decided to give priority to the construction of schools on less favored islands. Visits in 1970 and 1972 revealed a physical plant on the eastern island superior to that on culturally more advanced Fayal. The new schools made possible a greater conformity of practice to the theory of a four-year compulsory education.

A second change of necessity involved an increase in the number of compulsory years to six. It was effected around 1970 in rather clever fashion. For students proceeding from the primary school's fourth class to the first year of the lyceum's preparatory cycle there was no change. For those who would never pass beyond the obligatory years a fifth and a sixth class were added to the primary school curriculum, that is, to what was known as the elementary cycle (first through fourth classes). The new years were labeled the complementary cycle and differed very little from the preparatory cycle. In addition to being located in the primary-school building rather than in the lyceum, the complementary cycle omitted the foreign language requirement.

In my "Sage Paper" entitled *Americans of Portuguese Descent: A Lesson in Differentiation* and completed on April 25, 1974, I outlined the pre-Revolutionary curriculum of the elementary and complementary cycles of primary school and the preparatory and second cycles of the lyceum as well as that of the school for primary teaching. Details are not repeated here.

With a choice between complementary cycle and preparatory cycle the student was once again locked in. By beginning the complementary cycle he was excluding himself from the lyceum and eventually the university track. On the other hand, on the assumption that he did wish to continue his studies at the secondary level it was clearly less costly for the parents to have him complete the first two years of the seven-year program locally, living at home, rather than taking up residence in the district capital in which the lyceum was located (Angra, Horta, Ponta Delgada, or Funchal). Although I was told in the fall of 1970 that it would be impossible for the student in the sixth class in say Vila do Porto,

Santa Maria, to move to the third year in say Ponta Delgada, São Miguel, I found in the spring of 1972 that that was exactly what some students were doing. They had made up their single deficiency by having private lessons in French or English, usually English. And then in October 1972 the Minister of National Education wisely made a special concession to Insular Portugal by providing for a foreign language, French or English, in the fifth and sixth classes.

It was clear in the early 1970's that the preparatory cycle would eventually be eliminated altogether in favor of the complementary cycle. Actually, events took a slightly different path. The complementary and preparatory cycles were merged to form a new two-year *escola preparatória* or "preparatory school." The new institution began to appear in towns as well as cities of Insular Portugal in the early 1970's, and I visited my first in Ponta Delgada in the spring of 1972. It was located in the old building of the industrial and commercial school, which had in the meantime moved to a splendid new building. By the time of my January 1973 visit to Madeira, although complementary cycles were still functioning in seventy-four schools on a coeducational basis, at least five preparatory schools had been established on that island.

The combination of the four years of primary school and the two of preparatory school, all obligatory, came to be known as *ensino básico* or "basic education." The way was open simply to add two more obligatory years to the preparatory school in order to begin to bring education in Portugal up somewhat nearer to prevailing international standards, an example of which was the eight-year schooling from age six to age fourteen required in Italy's Aeolian Islands when I visited them in the summer of 1972. But this could only be done once more and better-trained teachers were at hand.

The lyceum course thus became shortened to five years following preparatory school, and a new and radical change was crying out to be made. Being given the democratization of the entire world, even including Portugal, in the years following World War II, crossover had to be permitted between the formal preuniversity lyceum and the vocationally oriented industrial and commercial school. The Minister took the step, and after the school year 1972-1973 the student no longer had to make a premature career decision at age eleven, upon completion of the fourth class of primary school.

In the meantime, the inadequacies of the school of primary teaching were being recognized. There came to be talk of creating a wholly new type of institution, one, however, with a name borrowed from the French tradition: *escola normal superior* or "higher normal school." This school, at the level of higher education but apart from universities, would prepare the teachers of basic education. More importantly, its establishment in areas like the Azores and Madeiras would inevitably signal creation of a full-blown regional university.

The establishment of higher normal schools in Ponta Delgada for the Azores and in Funchal for the Madeiras was announced in 1972, although they were formally created only on July 30, 1973. On April 20, 1974, just five days before the Revolution, Ponta Delgada's planning committee initiated the carrying out of its mandate. The ceremony, with the favoring presence of the Minister of National Education who was in that city on his second visit as Minister, took place in the building which had been acquired to house the Azorean school. The building itself is a former palace, the Berquó Palace, also known in even more upper-class fashion as the Palace of the Viscounts of Porto Formoso.

The school, alluded to by the Minister at the ceremony as Europe's westernmost institution of higher education, was due to begin functioning during the ensuing academic year 1975-1976, and local personalities on São Miguel were already dreaming of a future "Azorean University," even of a "Michaelese University," located in Ponta Delgada. The Fates decreed otherwise, however.

An additional solution to the problem posed by the shortage and inadequate preparation of teachers was adopted even as the idea of higher normal schools was being floated. The first university degree, as has been noted, was the licentiate, conferred usually after five years of study. The authorities decided to revive and grant the *bacharelato* or "baccalaureate" (bachelor's degree) after the first three years and accept that training as adequate for teachers in the lyceum, at least in the lower grades of the latter's program.

☆ ☆ ☆

Behind this bewildering series of reforms of the period 1970-1974 figured the energetic and often controversial Minister of National Education, Doctor José Veiga Simão. He had received his

Ph.D. degree in nuclear physics from the University of Cambridge in England in 1957 and was very much a man of the modern world. He had then taught in the School of Sciences of the University of Coimbra. Young and dynamic, toward the end of the Salazar years he was appointed rector of the University of Lourenço Marques, at that time somewhat medievally called the University-level General Studies of Mozambique. In July 1967 he served as chairman of the organizing committee of the Second Congress of Communities of Portuguese Culture held chiefly aboard the luxury liner *Príncipe Perfeito* in Mozambican waters.

Veiga Simão's speech at the opening session of the Congress was both conservative and visionary, and full of superpatriotism, as perhaps it had to be because of the presence there of the Minister of Overseas. In it he referred several times to descendants abroad of emigrants from Portugal as "Luso-descendants," an expression which I found quite offensive. In Goa five years earlier I had discovered that the expression was one of opprobrium used to designate persons of mixed ancestry.

The speech reflected to a tee the belief that Portugal should reach out to its emigrants and descendants and continue or initiate a bond with them, as in this sentence:

> ... the essential objective of the Congress of Portuguese Communities must be one of structuring with certainty and in precise fashion the means of action which are indispensable in maintaining and expanding Portuguese culture in communities spread throughout the world.

Or again:

> ... Frequently indeed, that link with the land of their ancestors is presented to the Luso-descendants as a symbol of backwardness [retrogradismo], of which here and there Portugal is singled out as an example.
>
> The answer to such a challenge can only be given by the Portuguese University, which, with complete independence of thought and action, but always oriented by a desire to serve Portugal serving Culture, has to extend its action to those thousands of Portuguese and Luso-descendants exiled from the Patria, informing, enlightening, and opening the doors of their old house to an extensive cultural cooperation effected at university level.

Veiga Simão was and is a patriotic and dedicated Portuguese who perforce worked within the system. But the system did not let him go very far with his university in Africa. By dint of prowling around on the fringes of the Congress, I learned that that university nowhere cultivated African studies. There was no African linguistics, no African folklore. Indeed, I was hard put to find African students and never succeeded in finding out what percentage of the student body was black.

This snubbing of the Africans by the Portuguese in Mozambique was personified by Lourenço Marques's great museum. It was a natural history museum, famous for a display showing the gestation of an elephant (involving twenty months). African humans did not merit a place in the exhibits. By way of contrast, Luanda's great museum was replete with concern for the black man and his art and artifacts, as was to an even greater extent the incomparable Museum of Dundo up in northeastern Angola and the proud creation of the then Company of Diamonds of Angola. Angola I found to be a totally different country from Mozambique. After my visit I rarely if ever used the phrase Portuguese Africa, for I had learned that there was no such place.

A few years after the Congress, Veiga Simão was serving as Minister in Lisbon. A man of the future who wished to bring his beloved Portugal into the modern world, he found himself caught in a trap recently described in detail in a Portuguese publication by an American resident in Portugal:

> ... Veiga Simão was criticized by many on both the Left and the Right, but few were those who doubted his good intentions. His great drawback, in the eyes of students, teachers, and intellectuals was his being compromised by serving the Salazarist regime, no matter how well intentioned he might have been. During student protests and demonstrations for more profound educational and other social changes, especially from 1972 on, Veiga Simão followed the "hard line" recommended by the Far Right by calling in police shock units to break up meetings and otherwise harass students and faculty. Perhaps his most unpopular move was the authorization of *vigilantes* who were ostensibly responsible for keeping order and protecting students and faculty from violence, but who were suspected in fact of serving as informers of the repressive paramilitary units of the regime,

... By this move the minister alienated many in the educational system—especially in higher education—that he had intended to benefit. From this point on his reform plan for education lost much of its legitimacy in the eyes of the majority of students and many faculty.

The article just quoted makes no mention of the negative aspects of reaching out to emigrants and descendants, and the possible adverse repercussions within say Brazil, Venezuela, Canada, and the United States. Veiga Simão stayed with the idea, and in his discourse in Ponta Delgada just before the Revolution—in which he referred to Caetano as his "beloved Friend"—he expanded on a possible role for the Azorean higher normal school in this regard. Indeed, he would have had the school constructing a bridge in the middle of the Atlantic. The school would act as a meetingplace of cultures and would sponsor a dialogue between Europe and the new Continent "with the active participation of the Azoreans who, in New England and in the Santa Clara and San Joaquin Valleys, had initiated a new life in a different world."

Because of his positive contributions to the real Portugal, Veiga Simão did survive the Revolution but not as Minister of National Education. Rather, he was appointed ambassador to the United Nations in distant New York. There, in mid-1975, during the height of the power of the Left which was finally broken on November 25 of that year, he made a speech—in fact a very mild one—which was apparently a prime factor leading to his removal. For two years he remained in southern New England in a rather ambiguous situation. Then, in the fall of 1977, he returned to Portugal apparently to devote himself to problems related to his original specialty, nuclear energy. In Lisbon I recently learned that, because of his support of the Catholic University and his creation of the New University during his ministerial days, he enjoys the reputation of having initiated the proliferation of universities in the capital city. Lisbon now has five: Classical, Technical, Catholic, New, and Free.

As a kind of legacy Veiga Simão wrote an article on the problems of Portugal published in the Summer 1977 issue of *The Journal of the American Portuguese Society*. In it he asked a very good question which could be considered a mild *mea culpa*: "can any society afford to have the University at the service of transient political movements?" Then, with obvious reference to himself, he mentioned as of 1969-1973 "educational reformers present in the government who wished to dynamize the country through their attempts to bring about a more enlightened participation of the people by increasing education since they strongly believed that an educated people is a free people" and as of post-April 25, 1974, "the democratic personalities who were forced to emigrate or decided to do so because they desired to freely express their points of view in international forums which focused world attention on Portugal."

In the meantime, Veiga Simão's educational reforms were bearing fruit. As far as Insular Portugal was concerned, the truly outstanding change for the better was the transformation of the projected higher normal schools into *institutos universitários* or "university-level institutes" in both Azores and Madeiras. The Azorean institute was formally created on January 9, 1976, and began to function at once with an introductory semester beginning on March 4. A dream expressed by some of us over the radio and in print and in public talks during the preceding years was finally realized. Unfortunately the new institutions of higher education were not dignified with the name "university." Conservative opposition from vested university interests on the Continent was clearly having its effect.

In the summer of 1977, the Instituto Universitário dos Açores proved to be an expanding operation. Administrative headquarters were in Ponta Delgada, in the Berquó Palace. True to the spirit of regionalization reflected in actions of the Regional Assembly and Regional Government of the Azores, the institute attempted to confer unity on the entire archipelago by distributing its departments over the three cities instead of concentrating everything on São Miguel. These departments were the following:

 In Ponta Delgada
  Department of Teacher Preparation
  Department of Administration Sciences
 In Angra do Heroísmo
  Department of Animal Production
  Department of Agricultural Production
 In Horta
  Department of Oceanography and Fisheries.

In addition, and of greatest interest to outsiders with a general interest in the Azores, is the Center of Azorean Studies, located in Ponta Delgada.

The institute is too new for any judgment from an outsider. To conclude from observations made in June and July 1977, its rector was making every effort to render it a viable and worthy institution. He faced problems on several fronts.

First, and especially in the Center of Azorean Studies, he had to contend with local writers previously engaged in promoting Azorean "culture." Inasmuch as a large portion of the scholarship expended on the Azores in the past had been strictly at a secondary-school level, it was apparent that he had to bring in specialists from abroad for this intimate central core of research and teaching as well as for more international subjects like marine biology.

A second problem concerned "equivalency," the age-old plague attacking one's academic credentials. Some university professors at or around the older Continental universities viewed the mid-Atlantic effort at higher education with skepticism if not disdain. They refused to see that the movement of students from Insular secondary schools to Continental universities meant a pitiful brain drain, for the majority of those students would never return to contribute to the development of the archipelago. The professors refused even to be aware that parents did not wish their children to go hundreds of miles across ocean to attend an institution of higher education, even if the newly licensed university graduates did return. They refused, in fine, to understand the Insular aspiration for autonomy, even in education.

The third and perhaps greatest problem faced by the Instituto Universitário was, then, political. Enthusiastic during the first year of operation (1976-1977), some students, especially on São Miguel, faced the second year with abated enthusiasm. They cited the lack of equivalency as a basis for opposition. Some twisted that phenomenon into a reason for viewing the institute as a sop from Lisbon to the Azoreans. They seemed to want no part of it, as if it were tainted; and a few plied me with requests for information concerning admission to U.S. universities.

The Instituto Universitário da Madeira has lagged far behind that of the Azores, perhaps because the Madeiras lie closer to Lisbon, which is easier of access, and because their independence or separatist movement is more subdued, or at least less popular. Formally created on August 4, 1976, by July 1977 a planning committee was functioning, and plans were going ahead for a full-scale institute centered on Funchal.

The Government decree which established the institute specified that Madeira's previously existing Academy of Music and Academy of Fine Arts would be integrated into it. As a first step, in July 1977 the academies were transformed into *escolas superiores* or schools at the level of higher education with the names Conservatory of Music and Higher School of Plastic Arts. The arts, however, were far from being Madeira's top priority. In a speech delivered on July 14, 1977, the Regional Secretary of Education and Culture indicated that in her opinion the two most important areas to cultivate were Fisheries and Maritime Research on the one hand and Teacher Preparation on the other. No outside observer could fail to agree with her.

☆ ☆ ☆

The problems related to schooling not only in Insular Portugal but in Continental Portugal as well have been enormous. As already indicated, there has been a chronic shortage of teachers. In part, brain drain has been responsible here also, for many primary-school teachers, poorly paid, have emigrated to America, discovering that work in factories is more rewarding than teaching in their Patria.

Another form of brain drain has also been in operation, primarily on the mainland. A staggering number of Portuguese workers has migrated to industrialized countries of Northwest Europe on a temporary basis. In the fall of 1977 they and their family members totaled some 800,000 in France (half of them in the Paris area) and some 120,000 in the Federal Republic of Germany (44.8% in Nordrhein-Westfalen, the province of which Düsseldorf is the capital). The migrant parents, ever insecure concerning the future because they do not possess the permanent resident visas furnished to their brethren in the United States, wish their children to be brought up as Portuguese, in the event that they all have to return home. The Portuguese Government, anxious to receive the all-important remittances from these workers, accedes to their wishes and provides teachers of Portuguese basic education for the children. Thus, in September 1977 there were 275 such teachers in France alone, and they were teaching a total of 1,274 courses. In the Federal Republic of Germany there was a sizeable corps of teachers for the 14,000 children of school age. In order to maintain high standards in countries which themselves have such standards, a competition was held in Portugal in July 1977 to select the needed teachers and end the ad hoc selection which had prevailed before. Naturally, the children in Portugal were the losers, for, given the chaotic educational situation there after the Revolution, the posts north of the Pyrenees held immense appeal.

Along with the shortage of teachers is that of adequate school buildings. A report published in Ponta Delgada at the end of 1973 revealed that only 26 percent of the 354 primary schools had electricity: 41 of 88 in the District of Angra, 8 of 80 in the District of Horta, and 46 of 186 in the District of Ponta Delgada. At the beginning of that year I learned that on Madeira the solution of resorting to double sessions in the schools was not feasible because of the lack of lighting.

To compound the problems of the education minister came the independence of the Portuguese colonies on the African mainland and the rush of white Portuguese refugees back to the Metropolis, chiefly to Continental Portugal. The returnees numbered an estimated 400,000 in 1975, and they were dispersed in the homes of relatives and friends all over the country. "We have had to revise all our planning," exclaimed the Minister, adding that "In villages where we thought we had 1,000 students and needed 50 teachers, we now have 1,500 and need 80."

Berquó Palace, Ponta Delgada

20

DOCTORS AND MIDWIVES

In no aspect of life more than the need for medical assistance, or the fear of such need, is the isolation of mid-Atlantic islands brought home to the visitor from a mainland.

On the Fourth of July 1977, Mrs. Rogers, Natália Correia, João Afonso, and I with several others took the 12:45 P.M. launch from Horta to Madalena do Pico, a half-hour run. We wished to find and photograph the site of the Dabneys' Priory in Areia Larga, just south of Madalena. Dona Natália wished to look into the whaling museum proposed for Lajes do Pico. It was a gorgeous summer day, but the swells in the Pico Channel were at least thirteen feet high. Mrs. Rogers survived the crossing but became very ill on Pico, partly due to diesel-taxi fumes. The terror with which she continuously viewed the sea, to see if and how she would get back to Fayal, its hospital, and its generally adequate medical care, will be forever engraved in her memory. Of course there were doctors on Pico, but how many? how far away? on a visit to Horta? or Ponta Delgada? or Lisbon?

To answer the question how many, the nonmedical scholar interested in Insular Portugal logically consults the convenient compendium called the *Anuário Estatístico* (Statistical Annual) published by the Portuguese government. In its chapter on manpower he finds a table on "Personnel in service in the health establishments, according to profession." This table provides the following figures:

	M.D.'s & D.M.D.'s	Pharmacists	Nurses	Midwives	Nurse's aids
Azores					
1976	231	33	281	24	143
1975	217	30	239	19	167
1974	333	30	217	30	223

Azores	M.D.'s & D.M.D.'s	Pharmacists	Nurses	Midwives	Nurse's aids
1973	242	29	206	27	194
1972	243	30	171	31	192
1971	235	28	158	30	175
1970	229	21	133	27	169
1969	235	20	135	16	172
Madeiras					
1976	274	9	318	40	218
1975	221	8	217	19	151
1974	218	7	154	38	238
1973	245	6	148	33	228
1972	231	2	121	33	191
1971	180	4	132	35	194
1970	208	4	136	19	199
1969	194	4	136	26	166

Backtracking to the Annual for 1972, the scholar encounters a surprise. Another table, this one in the chapter on health, paints quite a different picture. It partially explains the failure to have recourse to dentists recently noted among Portuguese immigrants in Rhode Island (chiefly from the Azores), even though the number of dentists it lists appears to me to be too low:

	M.D.'s	Dentists	Pharmacists	Nurses
District of Angra	29		16	59
District of Horta	14		7	20
District of Ponta Delgada	47	1	19	127
District of Funchal	108	1	24	221

For an explanation of the discrepancy the researcher must go back to the issue for 1970. Here, in a note under the manpower table about health establishments, he learns that the individual professional is counted as many times as the number of such establishments in which he or she renders service. In other words, if a doctor on his daily rounds drops into six hospitals, clinics, and dispensaries with which he is associated, he is counted as six. This indispensable little note was omitted in later issues.

The frank table in the health chapter disappeared altogether beginning in 1973 but was restored in 1976. Its equivalent, however, was included in the annual volume entitled *Estatísticas de Saúde* (Health Statistics). The table reveals the following:

		M.D.'s	Dentists	Pharmacists	Nurses
Azores					
	1976	88	9	55	240
	1975	90	8	42	221
	1974	91		40	144
	1973	87		42	121
	1972	90	1	42	206
	1971	93	1	38	185
	1970	91	1	38	168
	1969	88	1	36	144
Madeiras					
	1976	120	4	38	492
	1975	111	4	29	453
	1974	113		27	304
	1973	107		23	262
	1972	108	1	24	221
	1971	111	1	22	254
	1970	105	1	25	271
	1969	101	1	27	246

The investigator remembers the statistics on illiteracy in Portugal, especially the confusion beginning with the 1940 census over the method of counting. Beginning with that census, statistics were given on illiteracy in persons over seven years of age. Obviously, such statistics suggest a lower rate of illiteracy, and they are acceptable only when the figures from other censuses are comparable. They were not available from the 1930 and earlier censuses. In Chapter 19 of this book, therefore, the illiteracy statistics are based on the numbers who did not know how to read within the entire population, babies presumably included. The scholar suddenly loses faith in statistics furnished by governments and concludes that all statistics must be controlled by observations in the field. Later in this chapter I report my figures garnered in the Azores in March and April 1972, on Madeira in January and February 1973, and on Porto Santo in June 1978.

☆ ☆ ☆

In general, the medical history of the Adjacent Islands parallels the educational history: most unsatisfactory in the earliest days, elitist in the nineteenth and early twentieth centuries, gradual improvement in the later Salazar days and under Caetano, rapid improvement with the Revolution. Tuberculosis was the twin of illiteracy, and U.S. officials continue to be cautious with regard to it in their screening of potential immigrants from Portugal. Indeed, the U.S. Consulate in Ponta Delgada had in 1972, and presumably still has, a panel of four Portuguese M.D.'s, two blood analysts, and two X-ray technicians, yet I was told that false X-rays were occasionally used to deceive the consul. Another continuing medical problem was the psychiatric component to many illnesses, due, knowledgeable doctors informed me, to the isolation inherent in island living. The "happy peasant" syndrome simply does not apply to Insular Portugal. If it did, why should so many of its inhabitants emigrate?

Regardless of the parallels, there are two major differences between mind care and body care.

The government in Lisbon, whether monarchical, republican, or Salazarist, presumably wishes its people to be as healthy as possible physically. An authoritarian regime, however, very much objects to mind development, or at least wishes the mind to be indoctrinated, not trained for personal judgments. One would expect that pre-1974 governments devoted more energy and money to medicine than to schools.

Physical health has another attribute. It provides fit personnel for armed forces. Soldiers at war should be healthy, but in the view of unenlightened leaders it is decidedly preferable that they not think. Portugal began its African wars in earnest in the middle of March 1961, with the uprising in Angola. The struggles in Portuguese Guinea and Mozambique followed. For a decade, the Portuguese war effort represented a major undertaking, far greater, *mutatis mutandis*, than the United States's effort in Southeast Asia over the same years. Thousands of Portuguese learned about health and received medical care who would never have been exposed to either back home on the farm. Moreover, hospitals were built back home to receive the war wounded or to care for trainees. An example was the hospital built for the Portuguese Air Force at Terra Chã, inland from Angra on Terceira. I was told that military personnel wounded in Portuguese Guinea were taken there. Its buildings now house the two Terceiran departments of the University-level Institute of the Azores.

In my opinion, the 1961-1974 war effort did more for the health of the Portuguese than for their education. It did, however, provide health education. The former fear of hospitals on the part of uneducated folk, who viewed them as places in which to die rather than get well, seems to be changing, due in part very possibly to the influence of returned armed forces personnel. Other old customs may well be changing because of this enlarged sophistication, as, for instance, rejection of sun, the night air, and sea bathing, or fear of intravenous feeding, traditionally reserved for the seriously ill. Other areas are the involvement of the whole family in the decision concerning an operation, or the excessive consumption of starchy foods, a type of diet which beautiful Italian women seem to have renounced years ago, or excessive fondness for coffee which is "black as hell, hot as the devil, and sweet as an angel."

The termination of the African wars did even more for Insular Portugal. Armed forces doctors were freed to serve "in the provinces," for example the Azores. Moreover, the practice was adopted of having interns gain experience in island hospitals after formal study in Continental medical schools. And even more, fully trained young doctors went to the Azores for a one- or two-year stint "on the periphery"; they are known as *médicos periféricos* or "peripheral doctors."

Basically, as medical care evolved in the islands under the recent totalitarianism, government-run district hospitals came to the fore, one in each district capital (Ponta Delgada, Angra do Heroísmo, Horta, and Funchal). These major institutions used to be run by a lay brotherhood under religious auspices, the Santa Casa da Misericórdia (Holy House of Mercy), originally founded in Lisbon in 1498 by John II's widow Queen Leonor. The Misericórdia in each city possessed its endowment and other income and ran its hospital, usually with an associated church still known everywhere as the Misericórdia. Gradually, as private finances failed to meet increasing needs, the government provided additional money and eventually took over.

In addition, there have been small hospitals in many towns which were the capitals of municipalities. These hospitals of course continue important on the smaller islands; but on the major islands, with improvements in the road networks, they are gradually surrendering their activities to the larger district hospitals in the district capitals. Today the outlying hospitals function principally as maternity or lying-in hospitals.

Even the *concelho* hospitals on the smaller islands are losing their importance with improvements in interisland transportation. The district hospitals will thus assume an ever greater role in Insular Portuguese health care. Already, as noted in Chapter 5, aircraft of the Portuguese Air Force and surface craft of the Portuguese Navy are lending a hand in moving patients to the Azorean cities. With implementation of the new air policy being worked out by the Regional Government of the Azores (see Chapter 13), the commuter planes will take over and greatly increase this movement.

As for the Madeiras, among TAP's so-called regional flights are those between the airport at Santa Cruz on Madeira and the island of Porto Santo in a Beechcraft King Air plane, daily except Saturday and Sunday. This very comfortable high-performance aircraft seats eight, several of the passengers on a settee which can double as a bed or hold a stretcher. TAP also flies a Boeing 727 from Madeira to Porto Santo and return early Thursday mornings and Friday and Sunday evenings, and its early Thursday A.M. flight from Lisbon to Funchal stops first at Porto Santo. (The two 727 flights on Thursday move to Madeira passengers inbound from Caracas on TAP's 707.)

I now give the results of my island-by-island survey. In the statistics on beds, I do not take cognizance of the venerable Portuguese and Brazilian custom, inevitably doomed to extinction, of providing within a private room an extra bed for husband or wife or other close relative of the patient.

SANTA MARIA. 2 M.D.'s. 2 hospitals: Vila do Porto (36 beds; 2 nurses, 2 midwives) and Airport (3 nurses). In the Vila do Porto hospital on March 30, 1972, were 3 ambulatory patients and 2 women in bed.

SÃO MIGUEL. In Ponta Delgada, the District Hospital of St. Joseph, ex-Misericórdia, formerly a Franciscan monastery (244 beds; 40 lay and 10 religious nurses). Also hospitals in Nordeste, Povoação, Ribeira Grande, and Vila Franca do Campo, chiefly for maternity cases.

In Ponta Delgada there were also private clinics, outstanding among which was the Clinic of the Good Jesus, with 60 beds and 16 nurses and with patients from as far away as Graciosa, Pico, Flores, and Corvo.

TERCEIRA. In Angra, the District Hospital of the Holy Spirit, ex-Misericórdia (51 beds in surgery, 58 in medicine, 28 in mater-

Their Values

TAP regional flight with ambulance capability, Porto Santo

nity, about 20 in pediatrics, plus 15 private rooms; 16 lay and 7 religious nurses, 4 male nurses). Also a hospital in Praia da Vitória, a *maternidade*. Two military hospitals at Lajes Air Force Base, one Portuguese and one American. Neither on Terceira, directly accessible by the largest civil and military aircraft, nor on the other major Azores islands was there a neurosurgeon. For such specialized attention, patients are flown to Lisbon.

GRACIOSA. 2 M.D.'s. Hospital in Santa Cruz.

SÃO JORGE. 2 M.D.'s, in Velas and in Calheta. Hospital in Velas.

PICO. 2 M.D.'s, in Madalena and in Cais do Pico. 2 midwives, in Madalena and in Lajes. 2 hospitals: Madalena (20 beds) and Lajes (16 beds).

FAYAL. 10 M.D.'s. In Horta, the District Hospital, of the Misericórdia (92 to 95 beds; 4 lay and 3 religious nurses, 3 male nurses). In the hospital's Infectious-Contagious Infirmary on April 3, 1972, were 24 patients, all with tuberculosis.

In Horta there was also the Lar das Criancinhas da Horta (crèche for the little children of Horta), still very active in Fredonia, the consular residence of Charles William Dabney and his son Samuel Wyllys Dabney and later the residence of the superintendent of the Europe & Azores Telegraph Co. It cares for abandoned children, children with ill mothers, and children with mothers who work during the day. It is an independent institution, with support from the Gulbenkian Foundation and Portuguese governmental agencies as well as from the People-to-People program.

FLORES. Hospital in Santa Cruz. The airstrip required for French personnel stationed on Flores brought the two westernmost Azorean islands into closer touch with the district capitals and their hospitals, and the commerical air service provided by SATA beginning in the summer of 1977 finally ended the two islands' isolation.

The French built a hospital within their compound, with a French M.D., a Portuguese M.D. partially on the French payroll, and a nurse.

CORVO. No hospital.

MADEIRA. In Funchal (on the heights behind the city en route up to Monte), the District Hospital of the Marmeleiros or "Quince Trees," ex-Misericórdia (capacity 400, with 620 patients). This hospital was being replaced, or better supplemented, by a new one within the city with a capacity of 514. Also hospitals in Calheta, Machico, and Santa Cruz, chiefly for maternity cases. There were 2 M.D.'s in São Vicente in the center of the north coast who served Porto Moniz to the west and Ponta Delgada to the east, and one M.D. in Santana.

PORTO SANTO. Small health center in a most attractive building, with 6 nurses (one a midwife). The island has one regular M.D., plus one from Funchal who stays a month and is followed by another doctor. It has one pharmacy, but the professional pharmacist lives in Funchal.

☆ ☆ ☆

Although greatly improved in recent years, medical care in Insular Portugal has been far from perfect, as the following two self-explanatory tables suggest.

Locale of Births 1970, 1973, 1975

		Total deliveries	Deliveries in hospitals	Total	Deliveries at home		
					With M.D.	With nurse or midwife	Without help
District of Angra	1970	1,705	810	894	10	407	474
	1973	1,427	944	483	5	276	200
	1975	1,397	1,064	333	4	208	121
District of Horta	1970	731	349	382	5	15	355
	1973	629	471	157	5	10	140
	1975	583	500	83	8	28	47
District of Ponta Delgada	1970	4,626	1,870	2,756	54	1,490	1,212
	1973	3,992	2,006	1,985	23	1,083	857
	1975	3,814	2,153	1,660	31	1,050	575
District of Funchal	1970	6,455	2,183	4,317	126	2,784	1,402
	1973	5,928	3,133	2,788	49	1,870	868
	1975	5,680	3,049	2,628	54	1,813	759
District of Lisbon	1970	29,988	22,566	7,376	1,521	4,257	1,577
	1973	32,591	27,226	5,318	808	3,406	1,093
	1975	36,137	31,196	4,917	1,514	2,599	798
Continental Portugal	1970	162,208	60,635	101,286	9,284	42,466	49,050
	1973	162,492	84,055	78,139	7,276	37,352	33,348
	1975	170,181	104,210	65,790	8,315	31,684	25,598

Vital Statistics 1970, 1973, 1975

		Live births	Total deaths	Deaths less than 1 year	Emigrants	Excess of births over deaths & emigration	Infant mortality per 1,000 births
District of Angra	1970	1,649	967	95	2,261	−1,579	58
	1973	1,422	914	78	2,041	−1,533	55
	1975	1,392	870	60	1,911	−1,389	43
District of Horta	1970	724	510	40	1,217	−1,003	55
	1973	621	607	35	1,003	−989	56
	1975	573	530	26	798	−755	45
District of Ponta Delgada	1970	4,569	1,787	339	6,393	−3,611	74
	1973	3,960	1,979	269	4,849	−2,868	68
	1975	3,780	1,622	180	5,238	−3,080	48
District of Funchal	1970	6,396	2,820	478	2,389	1,187	75
	1973	5,866	2,660	344	4,973	−1,767	59
	1975	5,635	2,604	219	2,751	280	39
District of Lisbon	1970	29,602	16,481	1,190	7,060	6,061	40
	1973	34,824	17,658	1,018	8,790	8,376	29
	1975	39,096	18,742	1,099	4,085	16,269	28
Continental Portugal	1970	159,417	86,770	9,074	54,099	18,548	57
	1973	160,455	89,079	6,998	66,636	4,740	44
	1975	168,268	92,124	6,500	14,106	62,038	39

Their Values 375

This last table, by the way, fails to take account of the small number of returnees, who would slightly change the excess figures. As for its last column, the infant mortality rates for selected other countries are useful as a basis of comparison. The following rates are the numbers of deaths of infants under one year of age per thousand corresponding live births:

	1970	1971	1972	1973
Sweden	11.0	11.1	10.8	9.9
Netherlands	12.7	12.1	11.7	11.5
Norway	12.7	12.8	11.8	11.8
Denmark	14.2	13.5	12.2	....
Ireland	19.5	18.0	18.0	17.8
U.S.	20.0	19.1	18.5	17.7
	1970	1971	1972	1973
Belgium	21.1	19.7	20.2	17.0
Luxembourg	24.6	20.4	13.5	14.3
Austria	25.9	26.1	25.2	23.8
Spain	27.9	18.9	16.4	15.1
Italy	29.5	28.5	27.0	25.7
Greece	29.6	26.9	27.3	24.1
Portugal	58.0	49.8	41.4	44.8

The rather low Spanish figures from 1971 on reflect exclusion of Spain's two cities in Northwest Africa, Ceuta and Melilla.

Here again, as with so much else, the districts of Insular Portugal line up in accordance with a consistent pattern: Horta and Angra best, Ponta Delgada and Funchal worst. But the pattern is inevitably changing. Terceira with its great military airport now opened to civil traffic and its expanding port of Praia da Vitória is inching ahead of Fayal, as revealed in the infant mortality statistics. Similarly, both São Miguel and Madeira are catching up with the other islands. Indeed, if we are to trust the official statistics, the District of Funchal in 1975 had the lowest infant mortality of all the island districts, the same mortality as Continental Portugal taken in the aggregate.

Or take the percentage of home deliveries. In every case it has steadily decreased, although the ranking among the island districts remains the same as of old:

	1970	1973	1975
District of Angra	52	34	24
District of Horta	52	25	14
District of Ponta Delgada	60	50	44
District of Funchal	67	47	46
District of Lisbon	25	16	14
Continental Portugal	62	48	39

Another remarkable revelation of the two tables is the constantly decreasing number of live births—or of deliveries—in all four island districts as contrasted with the District of Lisbon and with Continental Portugal as a whole. The continuing exodus of islanders on a permanent basis to greener pastures, in particular to the United States, Canada, and Venezuela as revealed by the table in Chapter 17, accounts in large measure for the decrease in island births. A role is also played by another factor, in my lay view the most significant invention in the history of mankind, the one which will account and accounts for society's greatest changes for better or for worse, the Pill.

It was in a Funchal pharmacy in early 1973 that I mustered up the courage to broach the subject of the Pill. Leaving an embarrassed wife on the sidewalk and naively believing that I was in a Catholic land which obeyed pope, bishops, and padres, I waited for the drugstore to be free of customers. I then hailed the "technical director," got him over in a corner, explained the serious nature of my North American research, and gingerly, in a low voice, asked my question. "Why of course," he replied, and with a grand sweep of his arm and what I deemed an extremely loud voice pointed to an adjacent case. "We have Portuguese Pills, and English Pills, and Dutch Pills, and German Pills. We have them for one month, and we have them for three months." Needless to say, I was amazed.

We went into another Funchal pharmacy to check our findings, then into one in the poverty-stricken fishing port of Câmara de Lobos—made famous by Winston Churchill's paintings—to see if the Pill had a sale in that type of community. It did. Same story in the Azorean cities in 1974. I even confirmed my suspicion that the farther from Ponta Delgada the higher the price. The Portuguese Monovar-D, the most widely used in the Azores, in that year in Ponta Delgada sold for 36 escudos for a one-month dosage, 90 for three months. In Angra the prices were the same, but in Horta they were respectively 36$70 and 91$80. And my vocabulary broadened even more. On those idyllic Azorean islands I heard of Anovlar, Eugynon, Anogenyl, Lyndiol, Regovar, and several additional Pills, and of the sale of condoms and vaginal cones.

And I learned more. On one island I met an American couple who were ranchers from the West Coast. They told me that the wife of one of their hands, an Azorean, did not want to go to a doctor in California for a prescription for the Pill because in that state M.D.'s insisted on a medical examination every three months. Instead, she had her mother in the Azores send her the Pill via air mail. As Portuguese pharmacists had invariably told me that they required a valid prescription for the Pill, I concluded that this mother, like Prudence, was furnishing her own.

Then there is the story about the two Portuguese immigrant women in New England which I heard in 1976. They used one prescription and divided the Pill between them.

Incidentally, I learned in the Azores that in accordance with Portuguese practice the prescription given by the doctor to the patient to be passed on to the pharmacist remains the property of the patient, not of the pharmacist. Consumer advocacy and the right to one's records may ultimately change U.S. practice.

In all my drugstore interviews concerning the Pill, I always brought up the moral issue and asked what the clergy preached on the subject. My query consistently drew a smile except once. In one Azorean city, for the first and only time, a pharmacist did express grave doubts about the morality of this widespread medical innovation. When I raised the same issue on Madeira and asked about the bishop's reaction, a lady pharmacist sighed with relief and exclaimed, "We don't have any bishop; he was transferred to Coimbra, and no new one has been named."

☆ ☆ ☆

Pharmacists, then, play a very important role in Portuguese health care, especially in remote areas. Indeed, they are literally and legally "doctors" and are so addressed.

A Portuguese university, like its French, Italian, Spanish, and Latin American counterparts, is divided into schools, among them a school of pharmacy. These are professional schools whose programs last four, five, or six years and follow the full lyceum course. The system differs markedly from that of the United States in not having a general or liberal arts program at the university level inserted between seconday school and the professional or what Americans call "graduate" school. Predictably, the European system will come to such a program, some vestibular or propaedeutical year or years within the university, leading to all professional schools and permitting a more mature career decision. The Brazilians inserted a "vestibular year" back in 1959.

The university "faculties" grant a professional degree, the licentiate, in medicine, pharmacy, or letters. The holder of this *licenciatura* is referred to officially as a "licensed one" (*licenciado* if a male, *licenciada* if female). In everyday speech the licensed one is referred to as "doctor," a title which is always spelled in Portuguese by the abbreviation *Dr*. The true Portuguese doctors hold the doctorate or *doutoramento* from a professional school. This is an advanced degree designed for university teachers, and, although pronounced the same as the other *Dr.*, is in writing always spelled out as *Doutor*. Salazar was a *Doutor*, as was Caetano, and both were once university professors. Mário Soares is a *Dr.*

The pharmacy course lasts five years, that of medicine six. In the United States, or at least in Massachusetts, pharmacy lasts five years following high school, medicine four years following college. In the United States, a wide gap separates the M.D. from the pharmacist. In Portugal, the pharmacist in his formal training is almost an M.D. He, like the physicians, is called "doctor." He enjoys prestige. He comes very close to practicing medicine and is often the only medical person available.

And he is available. In a community such as an Insular Portuguese city—and this holds for Lisbon as well—the several pharmacies take turns being open all night or on Sundays. The pharmacy on duty is said to be "on guard" (*de guarda*) or "on duty" (*de serviço*), and each pharmacy lists on its front door the duty pharmacies and when open. The duty pharmacist is entitled to a small surcharge, ten escudos in Ponta Delgada in 1972; but one morning at 6:00 A.M. he would not take it from me.

Needless to add, midwives also play a very important role in Portuguese health care, again in remote areas in particular. A professionally trained midwife (*parteira*) is in effect a specialized nurse. In the Azores she could take her three-year nursing course in Ponta Delgada, following the second cycle of the lyceum. To go on to become a midwife, however, she had to go to Continental Portugal for her specialty.

Naturally, there are "granny" midwives in the Islands. Called "curious ones" (*curiosas*), they are the knowledgeable women, mothers themselves, who with no professional training and often little formal schooling lend a helping hand at parturition. They explain in part the appalling statistics on infant mortality. They may also explain another statistic, one with which I personally have little knowledge, namely, the incidence of abortion in Insular Portugal.

In both Brazil and Continental Portugal, unscrupulous midwives are known to terminate pregnancies. In Insular Portugal, where overt defiance of Catholic teaching regarding contraception exists on all sides, presumably some *curiosas* do more business with abortions than with births. Presumably, also, the controversy which erupted on the mainland around the TV program of February 4, 1976, entitled "Abortion Is Not A Crime" would have been applicable to the islands as well. One of the program's authors summed up her reaction to the widespread criticism, according to Marvine Howe in *The New York Times* of March 13, 1976, by asserting: "The lesson is that Portugal's revolution was political but not social or cultural."

☆ ☆ ☆

It is not my intention to expatiate in this book on food (including the medical wisdom of eating onions and garlic to keep down the cholesterol level in the blood, thus avoiding heart attacks) and drink (including the excellent Michaelese and Madeiran beers), diet in general, games and sports, and play in general (including the dolls which are visibly male or female and the dogs so carefully differentiated into *cães* "male dogs" and *cadelas* "bitches" like Margarida Victória's "Pura"). In these matters, the Adjacent Islands most often follow Continental Portugal. Even mainland bullfighters and circus troops take in the Islands on their tours.

There is one topic which I deem so important, one major lesson which Portugal including its islands can so well teach Southeastern Massachusetts where many Continental and Insular Portuguese and Cape Verdeans have settled, that, before concluding with the so-called Azorean disease of the nervous system, I wish to discuss it at some length here.

I was brought up in New Bedford and lived there until I went off to Cornell University in 1932. I kept returning regularly until my mother died there in early 1975. During all those years I constantly tried to see the sea, but the stretch of coast from Rhode Island's Sakonnet along the north shore of Buzzard's Bay to the Cape Cod Canal, perhaps the most desirable recreation area in the entire United States, was peppered with signs reading "Private Property—No Trespassing." From my earliest years until the last ride on which I took my mother I resented with a passion such signs, actual or implied, at places like Westport Harbor, Smith's Neck, Salter's Point, Nonquit, Bay View, and Ricketson's Point, and others farther east including Hyannisport, and above all Colonel Green's Round Hill after M.I.T. and then the Jesuits took it over. In later years, I was very disturbed that local towns acquired stretches of beach, as at Round Hill, but excluded out-of-towners like me, or at the very least prevented me from parking so that I could attain the beach.

In Portuguese territory, the waterfront and beaches belong to all the people, as at Carcavelos, Estoril, Figueira da Foz, and other delightful places in the north. By "all the people" I mean all Portuguese and not just those of the municipality or other territorial subdivision. Since 1875, the public has had access to a zone up to fifty meters (164 feet) inland from the high-water mark. If that zone was privately owned before 1875, or if a hotel or other entity has obtained authorization to own it since, the public may not remain on it, but that public still has right of access through it to the sea. Thus, in the islands anyone can frolic on the beautiful beaches at Praia (Santa Maria), Praia do Pópulo (São Miguel), Praia da Vitória (Terceira), Praia do Almoxarife (Fayal), and Porto Santo.

An attempt in the early 1970's to have the Commonwealth of Massachusetts grant the public an "on-foot free right-of-passage along the shore, between the mean high water line and the low water line" failed of passage. The Supreme Judicial Court found it unconstitutional because appropriation of private property for public use has to be for a public purpose and reasonable compensation has to be paid.

☆ ☆ ☆

Beginning in 1968, neurologists in Boston began the slow process of identification of a hereditary noncontagious disease of the nervous system which seemed to occur only in Americans of Azorean birth and descent. A first medical report, authored by three

M.D.'s at the Peter Bent Brigham Hospital and Harvard Medical School, was published in January 1972. It discussed a Machado family most of whose members lived in Southeastern Massachusetts, many in Fall River. They were descendants of one William Machado, of Bretanha on São Miguel, the locale of the alleged French or Breton influence. Some of his children had emigrated to Massachusetts in the late nineteenth and early twentieth centuries. The report labeled the disorder "Machado disease."

Later in 1972, a second report appeared in the medical literature, this one from the Massachusetts General Hospital and Harvard Medical School. It discussed a family of Azorean descent known to the neurology service of the Mass. General since 1949. Eschewing revelation of family name and area of residence, the article conferred on the disease the breathtaking descriptive name of "Nigro-spino-dentatal Degeneration with Nuclear Ophthalmoplegia."

In the meantime, significant medical events were taking place on the West Coast. They were suddenly given wide publicity in *The New York Times* of September 30, 1975, and in *Time* of October 13, 1975.

One night, fourteen years earlier, Rose Marie Silva, of Livermore, California—in the heart of the zone of Portuguese settlement just east of San Leandro and Hayward on the eastern shore of San Francisco Bay—had suddenly realized that she might be afflicted by a crippling disease, a "family curse," the family's "shame," which had struck down members of her family over a period of nearly 200 years and about which they had maintained silence for fear it was congenital syphilis or due to incestuous marriage.

Years later, Mrs. Silva read in the *Ladies Home Journal* of September 1972 about a different nervous disorder which occurred in the Swier family of South Dakota. As reported also in *Time* of January 25, 1971, Mrs. Swier had sought help and received it from the National Genetics Foundation in New York in the persons of two San Diego medical specialists. Mrs. Silva followed the same course, and the Foundation and the same two specialists came to her help.

Publicized in the afore-mentioned issue of *The New York Times*, a gathering of Mrs. Silva's extended family took place in Oakland in late September 1975. Pieces of the puzzle were assembled, and it was revealed that the family disease had been brought to California by one Antone "Joseph," Mrs. Silva's great-great-grandfather and a native of Flores in the Azores. Obviously in possession of a more normal family name (later discovered to be António Jacinto Bastiana), he had embarked aboard a whaling ship and in the 1840's had jumped it in a Californian port. He returned to Flores for his family, and they settled in California.

The doctors who were involved labeled this disease informally as "Joseph's disease." In August 1976, they and two colleagues published their findings in a neurological journal with the title "Autosomal dominant striatonigral degeneration." This technical article, however, never named Flores, only the Azores Islands.

Like innumerable others, I first learned of this Azores-related nervous disorder in the *Times* article. Being historically minded yet knowing little of genetic diseases, I immediately began to wonder, on the assumption that it began with him, what event in Antone Joseph's life had disturbed a gene and triggered the family disease. Had something happened on that whaling voyage from Flores to San Francisco? Had he been exposed to some mysterious radiation on a remote Pacific island or shot at by a poisoned dart from some irate father's blowgun? I attached some importance to the route of the whaleship and, having recently completed a term as trustee of New Bedford's Whaling Museum, on October 10, 1975, I wrote one of the researchers involved suggesting the possibility of locating in or via the museum the very logbook of the very ship on which Joseph had embarked. Understandably, I never received a reply.

The months passed. Indeed, a year went by. In the meantime, over the past several years other medical doctors in Massachusetts had been active. One was Dr. Hilton L. Fowler, a practicing neurologist in Fall River working among Americans of Portuguese—chiefly Azorean, and among them principally Michaelese—birth and descent; he had been in Boston's Peter Bent Brigham Hospital at the time data were being worked up for the original report of January 1972. Others were researchers at the medical schools of Tufts University and Boston University. They were all supported in part by the March of Dimes Foundation.

This third Massachusetts team had been studying a third Massachusetts family of Azorean descent, descended from a man born on São Miguel around 1865. He had emigrated to Fall River with his daughter from his first marriage and with his second wife.

Children of both wives and descendants were afflicted by a disease of the nervous system similar to the three described in the medical literature. As "in this family there was considerable variability in the clinical expression of the disease in individual members," the Massachusetts doctors were led to the conclusion that the three disorders earlier described, and theirs, far from being separate diseases, were in fact variant expressions of a single disease. They published their findings in the prestigious and widely-read *New England Journal of Medicine* of June 30, 1977. Their concluding paragraph reads:

> The first family ("Machado disease"), the second family ("nigro-spino-dentatal degeneration with nuclear ophthalmoplegia"), the third family ("autosomal dominant striatonigral degeneration") and the kindred described by us are all descendants of persons born in the Portuguese Azores around the middle of the 19th century, when the population of these islands was approximately 236,000. The disease in all the families shows autosomal dominant inheritance. From all the above considerations it is tempting to advance the hypothesis that these families suffer from the same disease. The name Azorean disease is proposed since the variability in the clinical and pathological manifestations defies a more symptomatologic or pathological designation at present. As more data become available, a more specific name may be decided upon.

Clearly, the name Azorean disease is not definitive, as the Massachusetts doctors recognized. I objected to it when I first heard it used, at a meeting at the Brown University Medical School in the fall of 1976, for I knew the consternation it would cause not only among persons of Azorean descent in the Americas but also within the Azores. On the other hand, I also objected to identifying all Machados or all Josephs or all members of any one single family name as being connected with the disease. (There are 25 Machados listed in the 1978 Central Boston telephone directory and 134 in the 1978 Azores directory, 65 of the latter on São Miguel, 39 on Terceira, and none on either Flores or Corvo.) Moreover, I recognized that the disease was of variable expression and that not enough autopsies had been performed to warrant statistically significant conclusions concerning exactly what part or parts of the central nervous system were affected. I learned, also, that not enough biochemical research had been done to approach the problem of a name from that angle. Lastly, it was clear that so many medical researchers had been working on the problem that the name of no single one could be used as a label, on the model of Hodgkin's disease, named for Dr. Thomas Hodgkin (1798-1866).

The important lesson became the need to explain to the Azorean public exactly what was involved with the disease and the name. Indeed, the Massachusetts doctors had wearied of seeing the disease kept hidden in a closet, so to speak, by ashamed family members. They felt that a little shock treatment was in order and decided to use the title Azorean disease in part for that reason.

☆

The disease itself first becomes manifest by difficulty in walking. The victim finds his equilibrium disturbed, and from his gait he often seems to others to be inebriated. His vision can become double and his speech indistinct. Rigidity in his limbs may set in, and trembling and general muscular weakness.

The disease progresses. The patient manifests increasing weakness, lack of coordination, and rigidity. After many years, he is confined to bed, totally dependent on members of his family. But his mental faculties never deteriorate. He is lucid until death, which occurs after swallowing and breathing become difficult and then impossible. Often in the past the cause of death has been officially recorded, and accurately, simply as pneumonia.

The onset of the disease may take place at any time between childhood and late adulthood, and, tragically, after marriage and parenthood. The disorder does not normally shorten life, but it does render the later years extremely difficult. So far, no cure has been found, although considerable can be done to lessen the patient's difficulties. Thus, when rigidity predominates, it can be treated with the same medications used for Parkinson's disease.

What is important for all Azoreans to understand is that the disease is genetic, inherited. It is in the victim's genes. It is not "caught." It is transmitted in what is called an autosomal dominant pattern, that is, if a man or woman has it, each child regardless of sex has a fifty percent chance of inheriting it. And each child of affected children has a fifty percent chance. And so on. It does not skip a generation, and it is not like the hemophilia of Spain's royal family which is transmitted by women and affects only men and is said to have come from England's Queen Victoria.

To have the Azorean disease, a person must be Azorean or of Azorean descent—as far as is now known. Moreover, one of the parents must have or have had the illness, and it matters not that the other parent is non-Azorean. To sum up, there is only a fifty-fifty chance that an Azorean or descendant of an Azorean one of whose parents has or has had the disease will himself be afflicted. Accordingly, the medical profession must not only seek to identify victims so that they may be helped but also identify those not "at risk" and assure these nonvictims that they do not have the disease, will never have it, and will not pass it on to children.

Clearly, continued research must be conducted to discover a "genetic marker," some bodily characteristic which can be identified by a test, possibly in a child. Equally clearly, theologically-informed genetic counseling is very much in order, for young victims and also for those at risk, so that they may make rational decisions concerning marriage and also (as Mrs. Silva has asked me to make clear) career planning.

An obvious and easy solution to the problem posed, of course, is a decision not to marry, or to marry but have no children, or to marry, conceive, and then abort. Such a solution as a whole is repugnant to a Catholic society such as the Azorean. Moreover, according to one medical opinion, it is unnecessary. Persons with the disease can live long and useful lives. True, they may be physically somewhat incapacitated, and they may eventually become burdensome to the family. They may also be geniuses capable of soaring to the heights.

☆

My trip to Brown University's medical school in the autumn of 1976 had been prompted by journalistic episodes of the preceding weeks.

News of Dr. Fowler's participation in the writing of the new medical report, the one published on June 30, 1977, began to make the Fall River newspapers. Thus, the *Fall River Herald News* of September 16, 1976, carried the story beginning on its first page, with photograph, referring to the disorder as Machado's disease, the consecrated Fall River term. Then, on September 22, 1976, the Portuguese-language weekly *Jornal de Fall River* published a major article. A subscriber, I read it at once and was horrified.

Among the regions of the brain often affected by the disease are the corpus striatum (literally "striped body," in medical Portuguese *corpo estriado*) and the substantia nigra ("black substance," *substância negra*). It is for this reason that the team of researchers who studied the Joseph family described the disease as striatonigral degeneration, although one doctor who had assisted them with a pathological study disagreed with their interpretation and objected to the name as being misleading. In any event, the *Jornal de Fall River* picked up the striatonigral designation, translated the name as "enfermidade de estriado negral," and added:

> ... all of which recalls the much discussed and debatable theory of Donald R. Taft, in a book published in 1923 (*Two Portuguese Communities in New England*), according to which the high rate of infant mortality which at that time was known to exist in the community was attributed to the black blood of our ethnic heritage.

I dashed to the telephone, and on October 6, 1976, the *Jornal* took back its statement, the preposterous nature of which can be better understood after perusal of my companion volume and its discussion of the sensitivity of white Portuguese immigrants and their descendants in the United States to any suggestion that they are of part-African ancestry.

I was now involved. I recognized that the writers, both technical and lay, who were publicizing this autosomal dominant disorder knew little if anything about the Azores and seemed not to care about the archipelago of origin. Indeed, one article referred to the Azores Islands as "off Spain." I also noted that immigrants from both São Miguel and Flores had carried the disease across the Atlantic and that some at least of those from St. Michael's were from the place intriguingly known as "Brittany." I guessed that the disease must be manifest within the Azores today and concluded that American neurologists and geneticists should know about it *in situ*.

On February 11, 1977, I proposed to the Gulbenkian Foundation that it send neurologist Fowler in my company to the Azores. The foundation accepted, and in turn it proposed to us that a distinguished Portuguese geneticist of international reputation,

Dr. Jacinto de Magalhães, an M.D. of Oporto, be a member of our team. All of this came to pass; and, as we reported in *The New England Journal of Medicine* of September 29, 1977, we visited the four most populated islands (Terceira, Fayal, Pico, and São Miguel) in June and July. My medical colleagues found eight victims of the disease, two living on Terceira but of families from Flores, the remaining six of two large families in Bretanha. No victims were found on either Fayal or Pico.

An amusing fact came to light during our visit. The M.D. on São Miguel most familiar with the victims in Bretanha, a doctor whom I had met in Fall River several weeks earlier and who was most generous and helpful to us (and who passed away at 65 within a year of our visit), proved to be the father-in-law of the leader of the widespread São Miguel-based separatist movement. Little wonder that members of the Regional Government on Terceira looked askance when we explained how well we would be taken care of on St. Michael's.

Even before leaving for the islands I had begun to hear echoes of the visit to the Azores in January 1976 of a pair of Continental Portuguese neurologists, one of them a young woman M.D. They in turn had heard of the disease's U.S. existence as a result of the publicity anent the September 1975 gathering in California. They are reported to have detected forty cases in the archipelago in fifteen unrelated families.

After my departure from the Azores I learned, and rather to my surprise because I had not been previously informed of the details, that in June 1977, before our arrival, the young Continental neurologist had journeyed to the islands and there met two of the U.S. researchers concerned with the Joseph family and visited São Miguel and Flores with them. The leader of the American pair reported in a letter published in the same issue of *The New England Journal of Medicine* as ours that he had "conducted a field trip throughout the Azores Islands" and on São Miguel and Flores had found victims of what he continued to call Joseph's disease. However, the California founders of the International Joseph Diseases Foundation, incorporated in that state on November 18, 1977, with headquarters in Livermore, recognized by the plural in their title that more than one manifestation of the disease was known. And they now issue an excellent newsletter.

Medical research, like research in the humanities, is best advanced by humane competition on an open basis with prompt and full exchange of information. In the specific case of the Azorean disease of the nervous system, research must go forward both in the United States—and possibly Canada and Brazil, if victims among Azoreans should be found in them—and in Portugal including the Azores, with complete transatlantic cooperation. As the disease seems, from the present state of knowledge, to have originated in Portuguese territory, I should hope that Portugal would assume leadership.

Full Portuguese participation is all the more important as a number of nonmedical but very relevant avenues of research can best be pursued in Continental Portugal and the Azores. Thus, the geneticists are asking for documented details concerning the precise origin of the Azorean population, the order and manner in which the successively explored islands were peopled, and possible accretions to the population after the first families settled in. The fact that the disease is found in São Miguel's Bretanha causes the doctors to call for more research on the origin of that place-name.

The doctors are not unmindful of other place-names reflecting the Flemish presence. They call the attention of nonmedical scholars like myself to articles in the neurological literature which reveal that similar genetic disorders have been noted in the Low Countries. One article, published in 1955, was written by neurologists in Amsterdam and Tilburg in the Netherlands, the latter city just across the border from Belgium. Another, of 1964 and entitled "Striato-nigral Degeneration," came out of Antwerp and Ghent—both in Flanders—and was coauthored by a Belgian who at the time was at the Massachusetts General Hospital. Researchers concerned about the Azorean disease naturally wish to know details of the Azores's Flanders connection, and even about the earlier Flemish strain in Continental Portugal some of which could have gone out to the Azores. Those aware of incidence of the disease within Continental Portugal today wish to know if it is after all Mainland-European and not Azorean, or if it moved from the Azores to the Continent during the contentions of the early 1830's.

Complete archives, both civil and ecclesiastical and including parish registers, are available in very adequate housing in the Azores, with skilled archivists and competent genealogists ready to lend the doctors a helping hand. Local historians, ethnologists, and folklorists are also present. They, too, will certainly cooperate with the dedicated physicians already practicing in the Azores in a massive multidisciplinary attack, coordinated by the team of neurologists and geneticists, aimed at full understanding of the origin, or at the very least of the path to the Azores, of this hereditary genetic disorder which stands so in need of a better name.

Michaelese Theater, Ponta Delgada

21
HIGH CULTURE

The Azores and Madeiras possess archives and libraries, outstanding examples of church and domestic architecture, notable public statues like the one of the Jesuit lay brother Bento de Góis in Vila Franca do Campo, botanical gardens and other scientific-research centers, cultural institutes, historical institutes, museums, theaters, private clubs and casinos, excellent restaurants and cafés, musical conservatories, orchestras, and marching bands, in fine, all the trappings of a fully developed "high culture." Toward the end of the nineteenth century, São Miguel proudly possessed an ocarina orchestra which premiered in the Teatro Micaelense on May 24, 1883, with a first soprano, second soprano, contralto, first tenor, second tenor, baritone, and bass. As the gooselike instrument, also known as a sweet potato, was invented in Italy in 1880, São Miguel was certainly abreast of world developments then as now.

In the past, the farther up the local educational ladder one climbed, the more excellent the formal education one received. In the later years of the lyceum course, one might well have had as teachers very eminent scholars and creative writers, in some cases world-renowned figures. An Azorean example is the late Michaelese poet and playwright Armando Cortes-Rodrigues, one of the *Orpheu* group in Lisbon of early World War I days and accordingly a friend of the South African/Portuguese poet Fernando Pessoa (1888-1935). The letters which he received from Pessoa over the years 1913-1916, published in two editions, have conferred a second Azorean dimension on Pessoa, whose mother was of a Terceiran family. A Madeiran example is the novelist Horácio Bento de Gouveia (born 1902), who in 1976 had the satisfaction of knowing that one of his novels, *Águas Mansas*, of 1963, had appeared in German translation as *Stille Wasser von Madeira*.

The island world of high culture coexists with the parallel world of folk culture of the masses. High culture has traditionally belonged to the upper class, and the Michaelese who emigrated from Bretanha to Fall River around 1900 never knew the degree to which their island and their archipelago had contributed to the scientific and cultural development of Portugal. Nevertheless, there has been a slow penetration of the high culture downward in recent years; and, conversely, many able persons of humble birth have risen culturally.

Presumably, there will always be two cultural classes, in Insular Portugal as elsewhere. What is changing slowly, and must change much more rapidly in Azores and Madeiras, is the criterion for belonging to the upper class. A revitalized Church and the university-level institutes will be important factors in this metamorphosis from a basis in birth to one in ability and achievement. So also will be the dedication of farsighted island individuals who, largely unrecognized, are already making extensive contributions to the uplifting of the society in which they live.

Take Ponta Delgada's public library and the officials and librarians responsible for it. This is a great library, housing the private collections of several distinguished sons of the island like nineteenth-century poet Antero de Quental (1842-1891), prolific writer Teófilo Braga (1843-1924), and the local and wealthy Ernesto, Eugénio, and José do Canto.

Among the library's treasures is the original manuscript of the sixteenth-century priest Gaspar Frutuoso's chronicle of the Atlantic islands, *Saudades da Terra*. In July 1977, I consulted it. As I was turning its leaves, I was aware, sitting opposite us, of three young boys perhaps twelve years of age and of the lower or emerging middle class. They were filling out call slips, and one appealed to Mrs. Rogers for assistance. Curious to know what they had sent for, I was surprised to learn that it was a group of comic books. At first amused at the irony represented by the juxtaposition of the invaluable manuscript and the funny books, I came to the realization that some public-spirited individuals were using this mechanism to entice the youngsters into a library.

Another device the islands owe to the generosity and imagination of the Gulbenkian Foundation. This Lisbon-based international foundation has set up fixed public libraries in centers formerly with inadequate or no libraries—the Foundation's Fixed No. 80 is in Horta—and has also made bookmobiles available.

Their Values

And these itinerant libraries, as the Portuguese call them, are very much appreciated. After I talked with the rural laborer in Biscoitos on Terceira about his daily wage, I noted nearby, in Agualva, a Gulbenkian bookmobile. The adolescents were lined up in rain gear to turn in one book and take out another. And eighteen months earlier, I had seen a Gulbenkian Biblioteca Itinerante in São Vicente on the north side of Madeira.

Books mean public libraries, yes. They also mean bookstores. Of the four Insular cities, only Funchal can lay claim to any that are at all adequate, that is, that have a large selection of Portuguese books brought in from Continental Portugal, and foreign books in foreign languages, and locally produced books including and above all local creative literature. In one of the Madeiran stores I have even found, not surprisingly in view of his ancestry, Portuguese translations of several books by John Dos Passos, specifically of *Adventures of a Young Man*, *Most Likely to Succeed*, and *Three Soldiers*.

But Madeira is the exception. Its cultural life is concentrated in its capital city, about the size of the three Azorean cities put to-

Gulbenkian Foundation bookmobile, north side of Terceira

gether. Moreover, the many foreign tourists and residents provide a market for books, even locally produced books of general interest like Rui Vieira's on the flowers of the archipelago. Books in the Azores make for a different story.

Three small cities do not constitute a market either for booksellers or publishers. Therefore, the bookstores that do exist are modest, most often an adjunct to a stationery store or newspaper publishing firm; and it was with quite some surprise that in July 1974, after the Revolution, in the stationery store of a Horta newspaper I saw for sale a Portuguese translation of Noam Chomsky's *American Power and the New Mandarins*. A large portion of the sales in these bookstores are of primary- and secondary-school textbooks, which are not provided the students free by the State but rather must be purchased by parents. And the works of local creative literature which they also offer for sale are often printed on newspaper presses.

Whereas there does exist a modest Madeiran literature, no parallel Azorean literature can be said to exist as such. Rather, there are three Azorean literatures, one of each of the districts. Thus, the novel or volume of short stories or collection of poems by a São Miguel writer is written, printed, and sold in Ponta Delgada and is normally unavailable for purchase in either Angra or Horta. Worse still, very often—most often—locally produced, well written, beautifully illustrated, and handsomely designed examples of the bookmaker's art are unknown in Lisbon and therefore difficult for foreign librarians, scholars, and others to become familiar with, much less buy.

In all four district capitals, cultural societies or institutes, often subsidized in part by local governments, undertake the publication of major works including even creative literature. Thus, the Cultural Institute of Ponta Delgada is now terminating the publication of the six parts of Frutuoso's chronicle. In 1966, the Junta General of Funchal itself published Bento de Gouveia's collection of short prose pieces entitled *Canhenhos da Ilha* (Memoirs of the Island), with its poignant description of the island,

> ... lacking in the resources needed by the human agglomerate dispersed throughout its flatlands, ridges, valleys, and mountain slopes. And the peasant, descending from the sierra with his bundle of beech sticks for the beans and occasionally stopping to rest at the turns in the paths, casts his

Their Values 395

glance at the sea horizon and, in spite of himself, begins to feel the winged impulse to disimprison himself in a search for lands where life would be less harsh.

The author then goes on to tell of the move by many Madeirans to Hawaii and quotes an 1880 letter from Honolulu back home. He concludes the piece: "Yesterday it was Sandwich, today Venezuela."

During the long years of the Salazar/Caetano dictatorship, Madeiran creative literature tended, in my view, to flourish a little more fully than Azorean. The physical features of Madeiran living, such as the rugged, mountainous, precipitous terrain, the lack of adequate pastureland, the need for an extensive irrigation system, and the cultivation of grape vines on terraces up the sides of hills provided authors with forces to blame for the difficulty of life, as in the passage just quoted. *Still Waters* itself opens with an indication of the labor required to keep the water flowing in the *levadas* in the burning-hot month of St. John.

Cultivation of grape vines on Madeiran hillside

On the island of Madeira, then, man's great adversary was Nature, the land itself, the hand of God. In the Azores, by way of contrast, Nature or God behaved differently. Relative to Madeira, the Azorean islands are natural paradises for man, gently rolling, fertile, well-watered lands for fauna and flora. Man's adversary in the Azores, probably beginning as early as the fifteenth century, was man. Azoreans, more obviously than Madeirans but not more so in fact, have been held down by the exploitation of a ruling class. In a two-class society such as existed in Portugal, writers under the monarchy as well as in the early- and middle-twentieth century did not criticize members of their ruling class with impunity. Azorean writers chose instead to cultivate other themes, isolation and the concomitant monotony, the terrible storms, the perils of whaling, although throughout both Azorean and Madeiran literature, and Cape Verdean literature as well, the general parallelism of themes is striking.

On Madeira, where the hand of an upper class continues heavy, Bento de Gouveia has dared go beyond Nature to man. In 1975, the third edition of one of his novels was issued by a well-known publisher in Coimbra. It was entitled *Canga* (Yoke), and it was about the socioeconomic system known as the *colonia*. This word is accented on the *i* and is not the much-used word *colónia* "colony," written with an acute accent mark over the vowel which receives the main stress. A *colónia* is what Angola and Mozambique were. The *colonia* was the system of *colonos* or tenant farmers on Madeira. The *colono* worked the land owned by the *senhorio* or lord of the manor:

> Under the *colonia* system, if the lord is inhuman, the *colono* is one of the most miserable beings on earth. If the former does not permit the *caseiro* [literally the dweller in a *casa* or house, another term for *colono*] to enlarge the house in which he lives, which frequently occurs, he is responsible for the spectacle of a promiscuous life of parents and children in a single living space. It is a question of the demoralization and desegregation of the family. If perchance the *caseiro* does not please the *senhorio* under any circumstance, the latter pays him his benefices and expels him from the home. This kind of despotism leads to emigration and to misery.

In an introductory statement, of which the preceding is the last paragraph, Bento de Gouveia provided a description of the *colonia* contract between *senhorio* and *colono* as it existed in the seventeenth century. In neither the first edition of the novel (1949) nor the second edition (1960), however, did this indispensable explanatory statement appear. Moreover, the title conferred on the book in those days of national censorship was simply the patronizing *Ilhéus*.

Bento de Gouveia's three important novels—the third centering on the backbreaking labor which embroidering entailed—were all published in Coimbra on the main. Their author is therefore more than a figure of Madeiran literature. And so it goes with many other fine writers, both Madeirans and Azoreans. They belong to Portuguese literature, not a regional literature. Thus, the late Terceiran writer Vitorino Nemésio (1901-1978), who served for many years as a distinguished professor in the Faculty of Letters of the Classical University of Lisbon, has written what from one point of view is definitely an Azorean novel, *Mau Tempo no Canal* (Bad Weather in the Channel), about that very channel between Horta and Madalena do Pico whose towering waves have humbled many a noble passenger aboard local launches, yet that novel is hailed in recent literary criticism in Portugal as a major contributor to the development of the modern Portuguese novel. Thus, also, the Michaelese poet Antero de Quental figures prominently in every history of Portuguese literature, every anthology of Portuguese poetry. Translated innumerable times, he belongs to the world, not São Miguel, in part because of this sonnet, translated by the late S. Griswold Morley of the University of California:

The Palace of Delight

In dreams I deem myself an errant knight.
By dark, by dawn, o'er deserts lone and bleak,
An ardent paladin of love, I seek
The far-famed magic palace of Delight!

With armor pierced, shattered my sword in fight,
My spirit falters, wavering and weak . . .
When lo! the towers, from a distant peak,
Burst in refulgent glory on my sight!

> Eager and loud I beat the door, and cry:
> "Open! the Disinherited am I,
> The Wanderer. Open, ye gates of gold!"
>
> The gates of gold clang open, and I pass
> The long-sought portals. But within, alas!
> Are only chill, obscurity, and mould!

☆ ☆ ☆

The fact is, Insular Portugal's high culture, with the exception of certain themes and language peculiarities, is Portugal's. A potentially great writer or great artist aspires to a larger audience than can be provided him by his native archipelago, or the two groups of islands combined.

The higher one ascends that educational ladder mentioned at the beginning of this chapter, the more one becomes pan-Portuguese, the less one remains Insular; and particularly is this true of writers. High culture in the islands is most often an oceanic extension of the mainland's. All the forces of modern civilization work to strengthen that identity with Portugal: air mail, short-wave radio, cable telephone, TV, and now communication via satellite. The Continent's newspapers, magazines, books, and gramophone records circulate, frequently as a result of private arrangements. Moreover, via the Continent travel the mobile portions of the high culture of the whole of Europe.

This tie with other lands was true in olden times as well. In the nineteenth century, English visitors took high culture to Madeira and São Miguel, and Boston Brahmins took it to São Miguel and Fayal. But the foreigners also found a thriving high culture already in the islands.

As long ago as 1820 in Horta, according to the annals of the Dabney family, the theater was cultivated seriously:

> I suppose you will be quite astonished to hear we have a *Theatre* in Fayal. Mr. Terra has put himself to considerable expense to have a room fitted up as a stage, adjoining his large ball-room, which accommodates easily two hundred spectators. There have been several plays represented to the great gratification of the spectators; the scenes were painted by a *Padre*, and they produced a very pretty effect I assure

you, although the painting was none of the most beautiful. Sig. Gamboa was the principal performer, and possesses considerable talent as a comic actor; I hear he once took a character in Comedy, on the Lisbon stage, in which he succeeded very well....

In his 1867 book, Borges de Freitas Henriques of Boston describes a theater in Ponta Delgada:

> This city also boasts of a theatre, in size about equal to the Boston Howard Athenaeum, but plainly finished in the interior as well as the exterior. The circles are divided into boxes, with the numbers outside facing the stage, and are occupied mostly by ladies. The parquet is exclusively for gentlemen, many of whom, when the curtain drops, have the bad taste to get up, turn round, and scrutinize with their glasses the ladies in the boxes, talking loudly, and, upon the whole, producing an unfavorable impression on those unused to the custom, seemingly sanctioned by the public. Any one wishing to secure his seat in the parquet, while he goes out between the pieces, can do so by tying a handkerchief to the back of it. It is then considered engaged. Clapping of hands is a sign of approbation to the actors, while stamping of the feet denotes disapproval.

Sojourns in the islands by other outsiders who later achieved distinction elsewhere occasionally failed to leave a mark. A case in point is that of Adam Lindsay Gordon (1833-1870), the famous poet of Australia who perchance was born in Horta and subsequently and briefly lived on Madeira. It is difficult to find anything in his poems which echo his native Azorean city.

With the 1974 Revolution came the very logical movement for autonomy in the islands. Inevitably, regionalism in high culture will follow suit, assisted by the university-level institutes. Already, a new anthology of Azorean poetry has appeared, edited by a distinguished native of Flores, Pedro da Silveira. Equally inevitably, the new cult of regionalism will cause reactions in distant Lisbon. Already, the well-known Continental critic of the erroneous sexological pedagogy has had his say concerning the Silveira anthology, and, in accordance with a Portuguese literary tradition, he has said it in a leading newspaper, Lisbon's *Diário de Notícias*

(News Daily). His patronizing references to the *ilhéus*, his repetitious references to literary regionalism (and one to provincialism), his realization that some Azoreans may feel in 1977 that Lisbon is not Portugal, and his amusing employment of Silveira's own verb *autonomizar* "to render autonomous" (not in any of my dictionaries) in a statement to the effect that he sees virtually nothing in Azorean poetry "which would autonomize it vis-à-vis poetry in the Portuguese language in general whether Brazilian or African"—all of this suggests a strong political preoccupation on the part of the reviewer, not in the party-politics sense but rather in that of national-destiny politics.

I first knew of the anthology from a review in the pages of the *Jornal de Fall River*. If Insular autonomy carries with it a continuing genuine interest in the high culture of the islands on the part of island emigrants abroad who are literate in the Portuguese language, then, of course, the products of that high culture will enjoy wider markets and become more viable. Moreover and conversely, those productions may have an impact on Continental Portugal. At long last, Continentals may be attracted to Atlantic regionalism, as Brazilians in Rio and São Paulo are captivated by the novels of Jorge Amado and other writers of Brazil's famed Northeast.

Autonomy is now the reality in Insular Portugal, and independence is not an impossibility. This separation from Portugal could take the form of a two-archipelago Atlantic republic not unlike the Trinidad/Jamaica combination dreamed of in the Caribbean in the late 1950's. Or, as seems more likely, there could be two republics, one Azorean, the other Madeiran, with the two Madeira islands resembling the modern Trinidad and Tobago. Or, as seems most likely, if there is to be any independence at all there will be three republics, with the Eastern Azores split off from the remaining islands in a manner recalling Grenada separate from Barbados. Regardless of the exact nature of the political future, the language of both the Azores and the Madeiras will continue Standard European Portuguese, as English continues to serve in all the West Indian lands just listed.

Azorean and Madeiran literature, being written in Portuguese, will partake of the projection of that language, which for four and one-half centuries has numbered among the world's most important from a high-culture point of view. Thus, in a recent discussion of the Henry David Thoreau of 1836 and his university education, it was stated that he "did well in languages (Harvard has some broad offerings here, including even Portuguese)."

Whether viewed as a part of Portuguese literature or accepted purely on its own merits, Azorean and Madeiran literature has already made a great contribution by depicting the plight of islanders living in oceanic isolation. It is an experiential literature which reflects the experience of islanders, narrating to the world what it means to be an islander, an *ilhéu*, an oceanic hick. Indeed, if a wide-ranging anthology of this Portuguese archipelagic literature were available in English, there would be little need of large segments of the present book.

The old saw affirms that truth is stranger than fiction. Today's students of literature might well reverse the aphorism's thrust and state that fiction is more truthful than scholarly studies. The traditional scholar is hampered by the obvious bias contained in documents, including armed-forces "action reports" and the handouts of private companies. Above all is he inhibited by the natural desire not to offend friends and acquaintances. The novelist or playwright or poet knows none of these bounds.

He can present a clear, even a critical, picture of the lives and values of Azoreans and Madeirans. The example has already been cited of a novel of Azorean literature written in English, Alfred Lewis's *Home is an Island*. Examples abound in the genuine Atlantic literature written in the islands in Portuguese.

A 1973 Michaelese novel entitled *The Black Shawls* concerns gossipy women forever clothed in that traditional garment, which is still widely used in the islands in conjunction with black skirt, stockings, shoes, and just about everything else. The book portrays how Azorean young men view Azorean young women as mere sex objects. It is this thingification of women to which the opponents of the Miss Portugal 1972 contest objected. It is exactly this which forms the true theme of the famous poem replete with three-, four-, and five-letter words which, published in *Male and Female Under 18*, ran into trouble in the Chelsea (Massachusetts) High School in 1977 and caused a nationwide flap.

Here is what may be read in the novel by José de Almeida Pavão, on the faculty of the University-level Institute of the Azores. Ermelinda is going by bus into the city to deliver the clothes which she had laundered in her village:

> Her companions pleased her not at all, as she sat down in

back, in the last row. Among the passengers she made out some women in black shawls which covered their heads and shoulders and practically hid from view the features of their faces, whence emerged scrutinizing eyes, like lighthouses in a dense fog.

Their tongues wagged:

> What is she going to do in the city? Fool around is what she wants, in a place where nobody will know her, without eyes which will spy on her. Like mother, like daughter. Shameless bitches!

As if this were not bad enough, this identification of black shawls as custodians of morality, more befalls her when she reaches the city:

> Upon stepping down, Ermelinda's ears resounded to the canaille-like madrigals of a young man who, from his post at the door of a shop, exposed her svelte lines to his gaze with daring glances. She answered him with a gesture of contempt and felt herself on an equal with the she-dogs in the street.

In order to translate passages such as these, one must be familiar with colloquial and even intimate meanings of Standard European Portuguese as well as with Insular Portuguese including the vocabulary of each archipelago and even that of each island. What I translated above as "bitches" is literally, in the Portuguese, "she-goats" (*cabras*). And what I rendered as "she-dogs" is literally "bitches" (*cadelas*), as in the title of Margarida Victória's book.

In another novel, *Black Rocks*, by the Pico writer Dias de Melo, the outsider learns of the precise nature of midocean living:

> "... Do you see these paths? To be living on an island is to live in a prison. On ours, from the town to here via the southern route and from Prainha de Cima via the northern route, no one dares to go by land to any place whatsoever, except out of absolute necessity, for all of us are appalled by those horrible paths. Thus, every precinct [*freguesia*] is a cage, within the larger cage which is the Island. We have the sea. But if the sea is running high ... How many people

have not already died because we could not get them to the doctor in time? And the problem of water? Where are the fountains that might bring it to the villages? Thanks be to God, it has rained these last years. But, when the drought comes, and the cyclones . . ."

"We die there like dogs." And with grave mien the men wrapped themselves up in the smoke of their cigarettes.

In a volume of poems by Pedro da Silveira one learns of the importance to an Insular Portuguese community of the arrival of the monthly steamer from Lisbon:

When the steamer arrives, it is as if it were a holy day on the island, St. Steamer's day. The high-muck-a-mucks of the Treasury, the president of the Chamber, the conservator of the Registry of Deeds, the commissioner and the judge, and those gentlemen who are the cream of the crop in the town, butter and whaleoil merchants, put on their Sunday suits and their topcoats and go aboard to drink beer and smoke foreign-brand cigarettes in the first class bar.

Or take this sonnet by one of the greatest Azorean poets, Roberto de Mesquita of Flores:

Exiled

When the evening light becomes dim in the west,
Laying nostalgic tones o'er a velvet afternoon,
And the mystical emotion which appears all too soon
Receives a vibrant echo from a prayer full of zest,

For him in a strange land who evokes the absent nest
Exile becomes at once a far from favorable boon,
And in his deep-sunk heart, as if a piercing tune,
Nostalgia worms its way, by now a pungent pest.

But none exists, like I, who does his exile hold
In his own land, and hears that alien longing bold
Which in my deep-sunk heart morbidly multiplies

At times, when after noon the glance distantly I lean:
Longing for a country much vaguer than a dream
And which I'll never see, I know not where it lies . . .

Even telecommunications, so dwelt upon in the first part of this book, turn up in literary form. In his collection of tales published posthumously in 1958, Manuel Greaves of Horta tells how he came to know Marconi, not the CPRM but Guglielmo himself, on July 17, 1922. Greaves, writing years later, takes advantage of the occasion to add a commentary concerning the role of radio stations in the Azores:

> Around that time, and later, all the islands used such stations for their communications, until Lisbon let a contract with the Marconi Company, set up on São Miguel, for service outside the archipelago, giving it exclusive rights. The commercial interests of the five islands of the central group, the tourist and marine interests, which used to take advantage of the foreign submarine cables of Horta, accessible, and causing no harm to the State, ceased doing so, with a diminution in convenience and general facilities and an increase in the resultant losses.
>
> Because, people out there in the broader world often think that Azores is "a single island," when they are constituted by nine. It is "the Island." Not even the radios of the Navy, in possession of powerful stations on the islands of Graciosa, Fayal, and Flores, are available to those interests.

Ponta Delgada has a superb museum heavily concentrated in painting, including the incomparable canvas by the late Domingos Rebelo (1891-1975) entitled "Emigrants" which dramatically depicts the leavetaking of Michaelese emigrants bound for America and carrying with them even a print of the Santo Cristo. Angra has a complete general museum replete with almost everything from Picasso to artillery, including even the very Vickers-Armstrong 3.7-inch antiaircraft guns which so concerned us as we planned that takeover back in 1941. To my lasting regret, Horta does not have its comparable museum, the world's cable museum par excellence. Located among Dabney souvenirs, it would stand as a tribute to the contributions of that family and to Greaves's courage in bucking a trend emanating from distant Lisbon. It would exemplify once again the diversity of Insular Portuguese high culture.

22

FOLK CULTURE

In a rigorously constituted two-class society, such as Continental and Insular Portugal has traditionally been, the upper class had its high culture and the lower class its folk culture. Formal schooling, the resultant literacy, and the use of Standard European Portuguese were privileges of the upper class, as was internationally-based medicine including the tropical medicine in which the Portuguese pioneered. The sophisticated Christian CHURCH with its complicated theology and its hierarchy likewise belonged to the upper class, but over the centuries a traditional Church based not on episcopal palaces but on the residence of parish pastors came to be the possession of the lower class.

The parish church and its *festas* exemplify the trend in all other sources of the Insular Portuguese value system. The lower class is sharing more and more of what used to be the upper class's, and we can apply the term "middle class" to those who have one foot in each camp. In other words, in the twentieth century it is difficult to find folk culture as such, in its pure state, in the Azores or Madeiras.

Even back in 1938-1939, I had difficulty in finding, on São Miguel or Madeira, individuals who spoke what I considered to be pure Michaelese or pure Madeirese. Thus, on Madeira I ran afoul of the two words *leite* "milk" and *leito* "bed." Both were widely pronounced by the masses throughout Portuguese-speaking territory as *leit'* without a final vowel, so that they sounded alike. In pure Madeirese, however, the initial *l* was palatized, that is, pronounced like the *lli* of English *million*. Out in the country near a stream—*leito* is used for the bed of a river—I struck up a conversation with two boys. I tried to get them to tell me what the cow gave. "*Leito*," they insisted, with a well-sounded final vowel. I realized at once that their primary-school teacher had been endeavoring to have pupils pronounce final vowels. In this case, although they pronounced the kind of *l* I wished to hear, the boys attached the *o* to the wrong word. A crossing of cultures had taken place.

Because the lower class is slowly giving up its folk culture in all its elements, even its traditional foods, it has become fashionable among scholars both at home and abroad to study the various manifestations of that culture before their disappearance. Indeed, Ph.D.-seeking and grants-conscious Americans have begun to invade Insular Portugal, areas whose isolation has led to the preservation of archaic texts of folk literature as well as the ancient linguistic features noted in Chapter 18. As a result, there are already becoming available some sophisticated and detailed studies of Azoreans and Madeirans, strictly upper-class looks at lower-class phenomena. And these studies, like my own Ph.D. thesis on regional pronunciation, invariably go beyond what is under the researcher's nose on his Atlantic island and ask questions about ultimate origins.

There are linguistic features which are pure Michaelese and others pure Madeirese. There are also pronunciations and items of vocabulary heard among the lower class in Insular Portugal which occur literally everywhere else, the dropping of the final *e* and *o*, for instance, or the use of *a gente* "the people" for *nós* "we," as in "a gente não gosta de tomar banho no mar" ("we the people don't like to go swimming in the sea"). Just so, there are items of folk culture, a proverb, for example, or a ballad or dance, which belong to the masses on a single island, others which belong to the entire archipelago or to Insular Portugal as a whole, still others which belong to the masses throughout Portuguese territory, yet others which are pan-Iberian or pan-European or universal.

It is very difficult for the outside observer to isolate pure Fayalese or pure Azorean or pure Insular Portuguese items, for they are in fact genetically connected. The folk culture of Azores and Madeiras went out into the Atlantic in the fifteenth century from Continental Portugal, with possibly a few items such as the design of windmills on Fayal taken there by Flemings out of Flanders. And whence did the Continental Portuguese, or for that matter the Flemings, inherit their respective folk cultures? The researcher is led ever farther back in time along a path which is bestrewn with difficulties for him.

My Harvard colleague Dr. David E. Bynum, a distinguished student of folklore, once drove home a point which made a lasting impression on me as he lectured in my course entitled "The Language and Literature of the Cape Verde Islands." He narrated a typical folktale heard in those islands. He next recited a very similar one which came from Senegal on the West African mainland. He read on his audience's faces the quick conclusion which they were drawing, namely, that Cape Verdean folk culture was of course largely African. He explained the extent of the overland commerce between West Africa and the Mediterranean in the Middle Ages and suggested that folktales could have moved along that route to Europe, trickled over to Portugal, and then gone out to the Cape Verde Islands by sea with the Portuguese in the fifteenth century.

Whatever their ultimate source, the several elements of Insular Portuguese folk culture are rich and interesting. From a scholarly point of view they merit preservation, and scholars in their applications to foundations, governments, and other sources of support are fond of stressing the urgency of their missions. Hopefully, the traditional sources of funds will be as solicitous of sending young Azorean and Madeiran linguists, folklorists, and others abroad to acquire up-to-date methodologies to be applied on their return home as of sending to the Atlantic archipelagoes young scholars equipped with the latest in methodology, tape recorders, and other trappings of modern scholarship. Unfortunately, the latter are all too often deficient in the language and general cultural background of the geographical area proposed for study.

From the point of view of the folk, alas, the folkloric elements are appendages to be given up as one ascends the educational/social ladder. Indeed, the folk often wish to have nothing to do with visiting scholars and occasionally deny any knowledge of the object of the research. They probably feel that any money spent on them might more wisely be invested in their betterment than in the preservation of something in which they themselves have no interest. As I wandered from village to village on foot in those pre-World War II days, I not only received no cooperation in many instances but was on occasion branded a spy of either Salazar or a foreign power. Little did I realize then that in two years' time I would be involved in another kind of preservation, an attempt to preserve the Insular Portuguese—and Cape Verdeans—from a Nazi takeover.

☆ ☆ ☆

The folk culture of the Azores and Madeiras can be divided, for the convenience of the layman if not of the professional folklorist, into six important categories. This classification inevitably omits many topics of great interest to students, for example games, toys, play in general, domestic architecture, and the techniques and dancing, drinking, eating, and singing associated with harvest time and with *matanças* or pig slaughterings, the latter around Christmas or after Twelfth Night.

(1) Folk literature consists of prose tales (*contos*), most often told by men without accompaniment, and narratives in verse in ballad form (*romances*) or in series of quatrains (*quadras*), usually sung by women. The Portuguese Atlantic islands do not have the professional tellers of tales so famous in the Balkans. Nevertheless, communities have individuals well known for their prodigious memories and store of texts, for example a man on Flores who over a period of five days spun thirty-seven tales in thirty-four hours of interview time to an American graduate student recording oral literature.

Folktales and folk songs, like proverbs and even U. S. jokes about Pat and Mike, were each and every one created originally by an individual. What makes them subjects for the present chapter is the fact that they were created orally and not on parchment or paper and that they were transmitted orally from one generation to another and not via books or gramophone records or, as today, tapes and cassettes. At some point in time, of course, a particular tale or song might be recorded, in book form in the early days, on records more recently. From that point on, it belonged not to folk culture but to high culture, even though not in itself sophisticated or even particularly artistic.

Thus, many of the tales enumerated by researchers as belonging to the oral tradition of the Atlantic islands were printed long ago in Iberia in chapbooks. In Portugal these productions were referred to as *literatura de cordel* "string literature" and in Spain as *pliegos sueltos* "loose sheets." The sheets of which they consisted were printed and then hung up to dry on strings in the printshop. The chapbooks were sold by the sheet, the sheets often being numbered sequentially in addition to or in place of the normal foliation or pagination. Chapbooks circulated widely among those of the masses who could read, and a reader often read aloud to others and so restored the text to the oral tradition. Or else, as often happened, a folktale or song would be lifted from the oral tradition by an eager textbook writer and included in a reader designed for the Third Class of Primary School. The pupil would read and remember it and years later recite it as if inherited by ear and not be eye.

An example of a traditional Portuguese ballad is the "Nau Catrineta" (Ship Named Kathie), long ago disseminated in print. Replete with typical Portuguese nautical themes, terminology, and superstitions, it appears in *The Oxford Book of Portuguese Verse* and is depicted on murals painted on the inside walls of Lisbon's large marine passenger terminal. It has even suffered adaptation in Hawaii, where a version in quatrains begins:

> Uma história sucedida
> Aqui vou participar,
> A uma fez perder a vida
> E a outra fez pasmar.
>
> A story that truly happened
> Here I intend to relate.
> It cost the life of one girl;
> Another it caused to faint.

Insular Portuguese ballads and other similar compositions often treat of animals. On occasion, by means of animals Azoreans and Madeirans make known their true sentiments concerning a wide variety of subjects, including even going to Mass. Thus, out of São Miguel comes a witty and antireligious poem in quatrains in which prim and proper women and the pious priest are distracted by a flea and a louse who went to Mass in the place known as Fenais (Fields of Hay), the flea going on ahead, the louse holding back:

> A pulga mais o piolho
> Foram à missa aos Fenais,
> A pulga foi adiante,
> O piolho ficou atrás.
>
> The flea along with the louse
> To Mass at Fenais did go,
> The flea was always in front,
> The louse in his pace was slow.

(As in quatrains the second and fourth lines of each stanza must rime—more or less—it is convenient to remember that a final stressed -*ais* in Michaelese is usually pronounced as if written -*ás*.)

Insular Portuguese storytelling also involves considerable boasting, a trait which seems to be the folk equivalent of the upper-class proclivity toward writing Portuguese history in a pompous manner, the so-called Bombastic History of Portugal. Ingredients of the latter history have even become entwined with portions of folk literature, and the scholar must be particularly careful to make judicious differentiations. Thus, the legend of Robert Machin and Anne d'Arfet and their early sojourn on Madeira, and the legend of the Seven Cities in the Azores, both mentioned in Chapter 1, are legends, true, but not today folk legends. They have erudite origins and have entered popular literature, which I distinguish from folk literature. One writer on Madeiran folklore, however, opens his book with a recounting of the Machin legend, yet his first paragraph outlines the literary uses of the tale in sixteenth- and seventeenth-century Portuguese high culture.

(2) Folk sayings and proverbs abound, it almost goes without saying, in Insular Portugal. Some are very traditional, expressing sentiments held internationally: "Aguas passadas não movem moínhos" (Water that has already passed does not turn any mills) or "Agua mole em pedra dura tanto dá até que fura" (Soft water hitting a hard rock is eventually sufficient to drill a hole in it). Some reflect more closely certain civilizational traits of the sayers: "Mais vale pão duro que figo maduro" (Hard bread is more valuable than ripe figs, suggesting the propensity for an unbalanced diet which overemphasizes starch). And here is one from Terceira which explains succinctly the local view on landholding: "Casa quanta moras, terra quanta a vista alcança" (A house sufficient for your dwelling needs, land as far as you can see).

(3) Superstitions and witchcraft have been widespread in Insular Portugal, the latter in particular on São Miguel. Thus, after you go to a funeral, you may not visit anyone on the way home (or else that person may also die). Or, the first time you visit someone's house you must leave by the same door through which you entered (otherwise you remove the good luck already present in the house). Or, if a girl is particularly anxious that a certain boy be attracted to her, she solicits the aid of a witch, who in turn puts items in the boy's food or drink such as to cause him to fall in love and marry the girl.

The evil eye is well-nigh universal, and folk healers and spell-removers are omnipresent. An example stems from Cambridge, Massachusetts. A local teacher had a brilliant Azorean boy in her class. All was going well, and he was receiving excellent marks. Suddenly, his performance dropped off noticeably. The teacher sent for his mother, who did not seem alarmed at all: "Don't worry; I'll take care of the problem." She then sent fifty dollars to the Azores; the spell or evil eye or whatever was responsible for the problem was removed by the recipient of the sum; and within six weeks the boy's marks came back.

I leave to other and younger scholars the identification of the *benzedeiras* and *curandeiros*, as they are called (literally female blessers and male curers), and said still to exist on São Miguel, and the discovery of the source of their powers, a type of research which involves more overhearing than direct asking. I add only the fact that the English word "fetish" seems to come from the Portuguese *feitiço*, literally something artificial or false, that is, factitious. I should also like to suggest that superstitions and witchcraft seem to me to be the lower-class equivalent of the upper class's astrology. Proper interpretation of the position of the planets relative to the sun and earth was a highly developed and thoroughly respectable practice in court circles as Portugal began to move overseas at the end of the fifteenth century. King John II had his astronomer-astrologer, Abraham ben Samuel Zacut. Decades earlier, astrologers had served in the fleet which took Princess Leonor of Portugal from Lisbon to Leghorn at the end of 1451 so that she could marry an emperor and become an empress, these "master astrologers" participating in the navigation.

(4) Folk medicine is so widespread that all of us have our private remedies and treatments such as mustard plaster and horse linament. I am told that there is a herbalist on São Miguel to whom the Azorean immigrants in Cambridge on occasion appeal for help.

Folk medicine on São Miguel is now the object of the research of several young Americans, and more and accurate information should soon become available. In a preliminary report which he kindly furnished me, one researcher who has been in the Azores cites the remedy for a dog bite: "a poultice of some of the dog's hair cooked in olive oil, cooled, and placed on the bite." He also states that in the community with which he is familiar, more than thirty-five herbs and flower tops, both cultivated and wild, are used for making medicinal teas.

(5) Folk music, instruments, dances, and costumes are the most obvious manifestations of folk culture in Insular Portugal. The explanation lies in the political and commercial exploitation of recent years. This use or abuse occurs in performances laid on by the government during international congresses, in establishments such as Lisbon's Restaurante Folklore which did not survive the Revolution by long, in the gramophone industry, and in the downtown Funchal sale of flowers to tourists by women dressed in the colorful costume of Camacha.

The folklore troupes which entertain the *grand public* combine the costumes with the dances, and the dances depend on the music and on the words to the music, and the music in turn on the instruments. In the Azores, however, one rarely sees beautiful costumes comparable to those of Madeira.

Among the better-known dances are the Madeiran *bailinho*, a winding snakelike dance, and the Azorean *chamarrita*, a musical/poetic art form put to a square dance and particularly popular on Fayal.

Fortunately, a Fayal collector active since 1912 has put together an invaluable book, published in 1960 with the aid of a subsidy from the District of Horta, in which he presents the music, words, and choreography of folk dances from his district. He includes a diagram of the much-used *viola* (Americans would say "guitar"), a twelve-string instrument with two heart-shaped openings. Its wire strings are grouped into five sets (two, two, two, three, and three). These sets are tuned respectively to E (both strings), B (both), G (bass string, with the second or wire string an octave higher), D (bass, with the other two strings an octave higher), and A (bass, with the other two strings an octave higher). (The Portuguese scale is pronounced the same as the American, except that our *ti* is their *si*, that is, B.)

The collector has a lengthy discussion of the *chamarrita*. He leaves open, however, the origin of its name, which many believe is a combination of the imperative of the verb *chamar* "call" and the girl's name *Rita*.

This compiler alludes to the extensive Azorean emigration to Brazil in the seventeenth and eighteenth centuries, which preceded the exodus to North America, and tells of dances which returnees brought back in those days. He brings his book up to date in a later chapter where he discusses a dance much used at carnival time. Here he presents a variant noted in a precinct on the south side of Fayal in 1953, near where the airport is now located. The words concern emigration to Canada, which began only in 1952. These words even mention, on two occasions, the X-ray examination required for a visa; they serve as a document for historians of Canadian immigration, for they suggest that Fayalese were emigrating to the north country in the early 1950's.

Portugal's fado also came from Brazil. It is now known throughout the world, due largely to the ability of the greatest fado singer of them all, Amália Rodrigues. In places like New Bedford, Cambridge, and Montreal it is sung in what are known as *restaurantes típicos*, a phrase which means not "typical restaurants" but rather restaurants which serve foods typical of a particular region.

The fado does not belong to folklore. It does not derive from the Moorish presence in Iberia but can be pinpointed to the Lisbon of 1833, when it was brought in by sailors from Brazil. It was based in part on the *lundum* carried by slaves from the Congo to Brazil in the eighteenth century and possibly also in part on another song, the *modinha*, very popular in eighteenth-century Brazil. A famous fado singer of around 1840 was Maria Severa, well known for her love affair with the Count of Vimioso. Because of that romance the fado entered high Continental society. It became an urban folk song and soon spread throughout Portugal, but not too extensively in the Adjacent Islands.

(6) Folk cooking is the most durable component of folk culture, the one which brings classes and nations together, which unites and does not divide. The lower classes of Insular Portugal are unashamedly proud of their culinary accomplishments and delight in acquainting visitors from abroad with them. They take their recipes with them when they emigrate, introduce their delicacies to the new society, and even improve on them in the new environment. As a result, one may obtain better linguiça in New Bedford, in my opinion, than anywhere else in the Portuguese-speaking world. Linguiça is an important ingredient of the islanders' kale soup. In New Bedford and elsewhere in America both linguiça and this soup are entering the mainstream of American life. They represent very real contributions made by the Portuguese. They bid fair to become as American as croissants, pizza, chow mein, and tacos.

Island foods, like so much else of folk culture, have their origins, and today their equivalents, on the Continent. The spicy meats like linguiça, *chouriço*, and *salpicão* (also called *paio*) are pan-Portuguese. Indeed, *chorizo* is an important ingredient in Spanish cuisine, and linguiça has close affinity with the Polish kielbasa.

But there are also typically Azorean and typically Madeiran dishes, and, within the archipelagoes, dishes which are typical of specific islands. Thus, Eastern Azoreans use hot red pepper to enliven the taste of meats and other items, whereas the Azoreans of islands farther west use the milder paprika.

Members of the Regional Government of the Azores based in Angra on July 1, 1977, in a *restaurante típico* of that city kindly played hosts to a magnificent and typically Terceiran dinner at which Dr. and Mrs. Fowler, Dr. Jacinto de Magalhães, Mrs. Rogers, and I were the guests of honor. The menu:

> Pumpkin soup; Squid, a very Azorean delicacy; *Morcela*, a kind of *chouriço* whose principal ingredient is pig's blood, in other words, blood pudding;
> *Alcatra*, a very Terceiran dish, a special piece of beef cooked slowly in wine;
> Madeiran sugar-and-water candy (too sweet for one of the guests!); The famous pan-Portuguese *arroz doce*, or sweet rice, with cinnamon liberally sprinkled over it;
> Wines galore.

At a second dinner in Angra we were treated to another Terceiran specialty, *pudim de requeijão* (curd cheese pudding), which reminds one of the *requesones* placed by Sancho Panza in the visor of Don Quixote's helmet.

In Madeira that same summer, visitors were able to eat the famed *espetada*, skewered meat prepared with rock salt and served at table hanging from a hook in such a way that the fat dripped into a cup placed beneath.

In Chapter 15 mention was made of the special dishes associated in the islands with carnival, Easter, and Pentecost. Folk cooking is in many respects an appendage to the liturgical ceremonies of the traditional Church. In fact, the entire ensemble of Insular Portuguese folk culture including even superstitions and witchcraft and cooking are inextricably intertwined with Catholicism as practiced by the masses of the people. The Church is sustained in the islands by the several elements of the folk culture.

Their Values

Easter bread with hard-boiled eggs, Angra do Heroísmo, 1972

The more the masses of the people are weaned away from that culture and the higher they rise educationally and socially, the greater the challenge will be to the Church.

In order to convey its message to the emerging middle class, the Church must be reinforced by another and appealing cultural ensemble. The postconciliar Church experimented with folk culture once again. While that strategy may be satisfactory and necessary in some areas of the globe, it no longer makes sense in societies like that of Insular Portugal, much less Harvard Square, where guitar Masses replete with bottles of wine on a table carried no meaning to many members of the Catholic community. Azoreans and Madeirans seem to this observer to be crying out for a renovated or "adjourned" Church recognizing their new aspirations, which happen to be those of the isolated of the entire world: desire to belong and to participate in the new global society as it is shaping up at the end of the twentieth century.

☆ ☆ ☆

The folk culture of the Insular Portuguese is diversified and, to the outsider looking in, fascinating. But that outsider must always remember that an element of embarrassment, almost of shame, attaches to many of its elements. This overtone is due, of course, to the natural desire of the individual in modern times to wish to rise above his origins. In the peculiar case of Portugal, however, it is quite possibly due to a supplementary factor.

The gulf which separates upper from lower class is particularly wide in Continental and Insular Portugal; and, at least until April 25, 1974, the upper class intended to keep it that way. One device which the upper class possessed for keeping the lower class in its place was a demonstrated interest in folk culture, in the curious and interesting ways of "nosso povo" ("our wonderful little lower class"), as if lower-class people liked nothing more than to hear themselves described as picturesque.

During the Third International Colloquium on Luso-Brazilian Studies (Lisbon, 1957), participants were treated one evening to a magnificent folkloric *festa* on the grounds of the government-run hotel in the Seteais Palace next to Sintra. Folk-dance troupes in costume and with their musical instruments were brought in at government expense from all corners of Continental Portugal to entertain us. The affair was ruined for me because I sat among members of the upper crust. I was forced to suffer through their patronizing remarks about "nosso povo." My heart bled for the performers, with whom I identified far more than with my hosts.

That evening I recognized that I had done the right thing during my graduate-student days in seeking out and studying the everyday language of the people. I resolved then and there that henceforth I would supplement my research in and teaching of the "high" language and "high" literature of Portugal by simultaneously introducing my students to the reality of the folk civilization, including, as objectively as possible, a folk language and folk literature.

I went farther. On May 12, 1970, during the height of the wave of so-called student rebellions and just before I was to initiate my third cycle of visits to Portugal's Atlantic islands, I introduced, and my colleagues passed by unanimous vote, the following resolution:

WHEREAS, from the events on university campuses throughout the world over the past several years, it is evident that faculty members and their students increasingly recognize the full range of personal and environmental problems confronting humanity as coming within their purview,

and WHEREAS, by its very nature, a university department of foreign languages and literatures is specially qualified to contribute to the identification, understanding, and possible solution of many such problems, and above all to communicate effectively with persons confronted by them,

BE IT THEREFORE RESOLVED that the Department of Romance Languages and Literatures of Harvard University, while continuing its central concern with the standard languages and linguistics and the main literary currents of the several Romance-speaking countries,

(1) expand its academic commitment to embrace the culture of the underprivileged, the oppressed, and the poor of those countries and of "Third World" territories which employ Romance languages as regular means of communication,

(2) direct its attention in particular to groups of the peoples in question who are immigrating to the United States in ever larger numbers and often live in close proximity to the University, viz. (a) the French Canadians, (b) the Italians of Boston's North End and elsewhere, (c) the Portuguese-speaking immigrants from Continental Portugal, Azores, Madeiras, and Cape Verde Islands who have settled in southern New England, and (d) Americans from Puerto Rico and immigrants from other emerging Spanish-speaking areas, and

(3) formalize this new responsibility by making every effort to offer additional relevant *courses* at both the undergraduate and graduate levels and also in University Extension and Summer School, and by expressing its interest in directing relevant baccalaureate and doctoral *theses*, the courses and theses to treat the literature, folklore, dialectology, and other cultural manifestations of those peoples whether resident in the Continental United States or in their native lands.

THE HERITAGE OF ISLANDERS

> The Madeiras and the Azores will have the duty of constituting reserves of democratic legality if in Continental Portugal there is a hardening of positions on the part of radical parties of either left or right.
>
> *Alberto João Jardim, 1978*

During the 1970's in U.S. schools and universities, a new interest emerged, a long overdue recognition that many different groups have contributed to the making of America. These included the racial or so-called minority groups, namely, Native Americans, Blacks, East Asians, and "Spanish-surnamed Americans" (originally a euphemism for nonwhite Puerto Ricans and Chicanos), all of whom had been badly discriminated against in U.S. society. They also came to include the white Central-, South-, and East-European so-called ethnic groups like the Greeks, Italians, and Poles, and of course the Portuguese, of whom the majority were Azoreans and Madeirans.

As a result, U.S. scholars, in the wake of earlier and distinguished historians of immigration, began to cultivate minority or ethnic studies, that is, the phenomenon ethnicity and its several manifestations in the United States. They also talked of ethnic-heritage studies, and in 1972 the Congress established the Ethnic Heritage Program, the purpose of which was "to provide assistance designed to afford to students opportunities to learn about the nature of their own cultural heritage, and to study the contributions of the cultural heritages of the other ethnic groups of the Nation."

Ethnic studies are one thing, ethnic-heritage studies quite another. The former can, theoretically, be pursued by political scientists, sociologists, and others working within the United States. In my view, however, they are best cultivated by those who know the civilization and above all the language of the country of origin, in other words, the ethnic heritage of the U.S. ethnic group.

A group's heritage is the ensemble of society's impact on the group and on the individuals within the group. It is what they emigrated with. Indeed, it is the ensemble of the forces which caused them to emigrate. It is what they introduced into the United States, to be transformed into something else within a day of arrival, even the linguiça made in America being different, of inevitably different ingredients under different hygienic conditions and in accordance with a different philosophy of the use of additives including preservatives.

In the broadest sense, heritage embraces the entire civilization, including history and high and folk culture, of the country of origin, Portugal in the case of emigrants from Azores and Madeiras. But emigrants leaving with only the third class of the primary school hardly knew anything of their own rich culture, of Camões's poem, Mendes Pinto's prose epic, the novels of Júlio Diniz and Eça de Queiroz, the sophisticated poetry of Quental and Pessoa, the painting of the fifteenth-century Nuno Gonçalves and the twentieth-century Vieira da Silva, and the details of Portuguese maritime discovery, overseas expansion, and colonial imperialism including acquaintance with celestial navigation, cartography, naval architecture, and naval ordnance. All of this was their heritage, of course, and a purpose of the 1972 Act was precisely to give Portuguese immigrants within the United States the opportunity to learn in America of what they missed in their own country.

Emigrants from Azores and Madeiras did leave home with a heritage, however, basically what is outlined in this book. It might prove useful to summarize what appear to me to be some of the salient features of that heritage as it existed up to April 25, 1974, what an ethnic-heritage museum in its exhibits might wish to display or at least suggest. The museum of course would have to include an appended wing outlining changes in the heritage after the full effects of the Revolution have been felt.

(1) A sense of isolation which stemmed from living on oceanic islands hundreds of miles from the main. This isolation led to a feeling of abandonment, of being overlooked and neglected by the rest of the world. It also led to boredom and to dissatisfaction with one's milieu, especially with the smallness and the resultant pettiness of the milieu, its eyes ever watching and tongues ever wagging.

(2) A certain fatalism inherent in indefensible people who in-

The Heritage of Islanders

habited small islands ever subject to unpredictable volcanic eruptions and earthquakes. This fatalism often led to an acceptance of one's lot in life and occasionally to a lack of ambition.

(3) A feeling of being manipulated from a distance by a donatary or the captain-of-the-donatary, of not being in direct control of one's destiny. This feeling, combined with the tendency to accept, resulted in bowing and scraping, in adherence to hierarchy, in being dominated from above and wishing in turn, once having risen, to dominate anyone underneath, in respecting authority and desiring to be authoritarian, in resenting, in fine, a peer who rises. In other words, Azoreans and Madeirans became dependent peoples; they never maintained an independent self-sufficient life.

(4) A failure to cooperate which stemmed from living on separate islands in oceanic archipelagoes. In order to rule them from a distance, Lisbon separated the eleven inhabited islands of Insular Portugal into four administrative districts. Lisbon never created a sense of archipelagic identity or of community responsibility, and therefore the islanders never perceived a reason for mutual cooperation. Even their military defense was provided by the distant capital.

Noon sight—12:54 GMT, June 9, 1964, course 045°: 35° 18′ N

(5) A two-sex social system in which men were fully and carefully differentiated and in general separated from women. In this system, the men were accepted as dominant. Some men in turn viewed women as objects, a few even as mere sexual playthings, the latter propensity being well demonstrated in cartoons and pictures of Queens and Miss This-or-That occasionally published in the Portuguese-language press of the United States.

(6) A two-class social system in which God created the land and the sea and their richnesses for the use of the upper class and created the lower class to serve, and indeed to pay the expenses of, the upper class.

(7) A recurring vision of what the world was like out there beyond. A counterpoise to the oceanic isolation was provided by the strategically important location of the Azores and Madeiras, which brought to them ships and planes, cable and wireless personnel, and enlightened businessmen and consular officials.

(8) A wanderlust, engendered by the foreign presence and by the sea horizon. This in its turn created a reaction to fatalism and helped promote the inevitable emigration to which the Insular Portuguese were led by isolation, abandonment, pettiness, and boredom.

(9) An agricultural tradition and a virtually total neglect of the fruits of the sea except on a very local basis. In the islanders' hierarchy of values, fishing, in spite of St. Peter, ranked very low. In the days of emigration by sea, many feared and came to live in horror of the voyage. Having emigrated, not only did they never set foot on ship again—not even on the steamer to go from New Bedford to Oak Bluffs—but many eschewed beaches and swimming. Farmers, the islanders emigrated to continue in their farming. If, once abroad, they turned to fishing, it was because they perceived this activity in a new light not part of their heritage.

(10) Economic frustration, if not outright poverty; a feeling of financial inadequacy vis-à-vis the rich man down the street. An envy of the rich, a desire to become rich, a dream of making money, owning a home, paying off the mortgage. A materialism which was caused by the local upper class and which added to and increased the materialism of the lands to which Azoreans and Madeirans emigrated, the very materialism which the homeland's upper class in its hauteur was most fond of criticizing.

(11) A certain reserve, not really inhospitality but rather a

quietness, a shyness, which stemmed from lying off the beaten track. Although ships and later planes touched at the islands, they did so only for revictualing and refueling, not, as in the case of the medieval pilgrims en route along the Way of St. James across France and Northern Spain, to linger awhile and intermingle and partake of food and drink and bed. In the two places where visitors did congregate in the past, Funchal on Madeira and Furnas on St. Michael's, they took advantage of commercially available hospitality.

(12) A highly-developed sense of patriotism, of *étatisme*, of acceptance of the State or Nation as everything and deserving of everything. This sense, of course, was an implantation from above and beyond, probably having its origin in the reign of John II, coincidental with or just following the peopling of the islands. The patriotism felt by Azoreans and Madeirans, however, was not perceived as entailing rights flowing down from the State concomitant with the responsibilities owed by the individuals. Rather, it was a one-way street, an upflowing string of obligations and duties. When in a society which guaranteed them rights, immigrants from the islands often waived them, being quite unsophisticated as regards constitutional law.

(13) A deeply-felt and folksy Catholicism which ever presented an inbuilt contradiction and was therefore viewed ambivalently. On the one hand, there was complete identification of the Church with the total folk culture including *festas* and the associated processions, dances, foods, and drink, and therefore Catholicism was accepted. On the other hand, there was ever the presence of the ruling upper class including the Church's hierarchy, this class ostentatiously Catholic but, from the lower class's point of view, hardly Christian. This religious amibivalence, not unlike that of Italians, in the New World contrasted markedly with the Catholicism of the Irish and French Canadians, for whom religion was an important ingredient in their defense against an outside oppressor or enemy or at least opponent of a different religion.

(14) A strong sense of family derived from pronouncements of both State, for which the family was basilar, and Church, for which the family was the center of the divine ordering of things. Combined with respect for authority, this sense of family resulted in parents dominating children, making decisions for them, even arranging their marriages. Moreover, marriage being perceived

as a sacrament, marital relations, and by extension family relations, were the province of the Church including the priest in confession, and the concept of outside quasi-medical family counseling was excluded. Family on occasion, however, was viewed as something more than a divine creation for the mutual comfort of man and woman. It was an institution ready at hand to provide needed help, a godfather, a friend in court.

(15) An awareness of family members ever beckoning to them from abroad, from Brazil in the early centuries of the island living, from the United States, Venezuela, and Canada in later years. Thus, the New World attracted, just as the Old World after an initial repelling from the Continent continued to repell from midocean bases.

(16) A geographical and a social differentiation in speech which reinforced the sense of isolation and the spirit of uncooperation. Indeed, when once aware of the geographical differentiation, as upon arrival with fellow-archipelagians in the Americas, the Insular Portuguese were led to partial rejection of one another, to antagonisms which projected those existent within the upper class in the islands.

(17) An inadequate educational system within Insular Portugal which perpetuated illiteracy and locked the masses within the lower class. One aspect of the system's inadequacy was the requirement, for all but the residents of the four island cities, to move in order to progress from primary to secondary school, not only to the lyceum but even to vocational school. This requirement presented educational advancement as linked to an impossible movement and often resulted, in the New World, in wishing only the education available close at hand. Another aspect of the system's inadequacy was excessive emphasis on acquisition of facts, with little if any critical thinking, for the upper class had no interest in providing the lower class with the ability "to think effectively," etc.

(18) Inadequate medical care within Insular Portugal and the resultant perpetuation of disease, the effects of injury, and a high rate of infant mortality. Combined with sense of family and traditional perceptions of the Church's teachings, Insular Portuguese medicine often engendered taboos, among them reluctance if not refusal to permit the autopsies necessary for a greater understanding of the so-called Azorean disease of the nervous system.

(19) A visible set of appurtenances of the upper class such as lyceums, theaters, private clubs, and casinos which reinforced the class separation and served as reminders to the masses of what they were missing.

(20) A highly developed folk culture which embraced all aspects of living from design of utensils, tools, dwellings, garden, clothes, and vehicles to the full range of amusements including culinary delights.

(21) Finally, and combining with the wanderlust engendered by the foreign presence and the sea horizon and with the awareness of family members ever beckoning from abroad, the guts—inherited from fifteenth-century ancestors—required to pick up and move out, to establish oneself anew beyond the seas, to seek elsewhere "uma vida melhor" (a better life).

When society does not provide the individual with the opportunity of developing as he feels he should, that person emigrates. Continental Portugal at the end of the Middle Ages was just such a society, and lower-class Portuguese beginning in 1415 with the seizure of Ceuta moved to many different destinations south and west. Some peopled the Madeiras and, slightly later, the Azores. But, from the viewpoint of the centuries, this oceanic peopling proved temporary. Soon Insular Portuguese were moving to South America. Then, with the birth of the United States, many moved to it. Finally, Madeirans moved to Venezuela and Azoreans to Canada.

The oceanic migration of European Portuguese was thus effected in two stages, from mainland to Atlantic archipelagoes, and from the islands to America. With the single exception of the Norwegians who moved to Iceland in 874 and in the nineteenth century moved on to North America, the Portuguese were the first European emigrant group to begin the trek to that New World revealed to Europe by Columbus in 1492. In other words, the phenomenon labeled by historians the expansion of Europe led directly to the nineteenth- and twentieth-century immigration of Portuguese into the United States, above all of Azoreans and Madeirans who carried a specific heritage with them to be modified or substituted.

A SELECTION OF SOURCES

The following references give sources of quotations or otherwise acknowledge my debts for particular facts and ideas. In drawing up this selection I was greatly aided by the efficient and ever patient reference librarians and other staff members within the Harvard University Library. Indeed, without that magnificent library in all its ramifications I could not have written this book.

INTRODUCTION. Annexation—Roxana Lewis Dabney, comp., *Annals of the Dabney Family in Fayal*, 3 vols. paged continuously (Boston: Press of Alfred Mudge & Son, for private circulation, ca. 1899), p. 1363. Immigration—U.S. Department of Justice, Immigration and Naturalization Service, *1976 Annual Report*, Tables 14 & 12A; Portugal, Instituto Nacional de Estatística, *Anuário Estatístico, Continente e Ilhas Adjacentes*, 1975, Chap. II, Table 18. William F. Buckley, Jr., *Airborne* (New York: Macmillan, 1976), p. 226. Mário Soares, *Portugal Amordaçado* (Lisbon: Arcádia, 1974), pp. 18 & 31. Paternal grandfather—*Representative Men and Old Families of Southeastern Massachusetts*, Vol. III (Chicago: J. H. Beers, 1912), pp. 1652-1653 (s.v. Capt. John Rogers); Manoel da Silveira Cardozo, comp., *The Portuguese in America 590 B.C.-1974: A Chronology & Fact Book* (Dobbs Ferry, N.Y.: Oceana Publications, 1976), pp. 112-113; Pat Amaral, *They Ploughed the Seas: Profiles of Azorean Master Mariners* (St. Petersburg, Florida: Valkyrie Press, 1978), pp. 109-112.

CHAPTER 1. 1884 Conference—*International Conference Held at Washington for the Purpose of Fixing a Prime Meridian and a Universal Day, October, 1884: Protocols of the Proceedings* (Washington, D.C.: Gibson Bros., 1884). Selvagens—U.S. Defense Mapping Agency Hydrographic Center, *Sailing Directions for the West Coasts of Spain, Portugal, and Northwest Africa and Off-Lying Islands*, 6th ed. (Washington, D.C.: Government Printing Office, 1952), that is, H.O. 51, sections 6-48 through 6-57. New England traveler—

R. L. Dabney, 1899, p. 834. Funcho–Gabriel Grisley, *Viridarium Lusitanum* (Lisbon: António Craesbeeck, 1661), p. B2^v, a reference I owe to a former student, Duane A. Kolterman, Harvard, '75. 590 B.C.—Cardozo, 1976, p. 1. Monk—José de Santa Rita Durão, *Caramurú* (Lisbon: Regia Officina Typografica, 1781). Currach-Tim Severin, *The Brendan Voyage* (New York: McGraw-Hill, 1978). Barry Fell, *America B.C.* (New York: Quadrangle/The New York Times Book Co., 1976). David Armitage Bannerman & W. Mary Bannerman, *Birds of the Atlantic Islands*, Vol. III, Azores (Edinburgh: Oliver & Boyd, 1966), p. 251. Raca—Egerton Sykes, *The Azores and the Early Exploration of the Atlantic*, 2nd ed. (London: Markham House Press, 1968, mimeographed), p. 7. Horta governor—Miguel Torga, *Diário XI* (Coimbra: Gráfica de Coimbra, 1973), p. 80, a reference I owe to a graduate student, Ms. Lisa Godinho. Frederico Machado & Victor Hugo Forjaz, *Actividade Vulcânica da Ilha do Faial (1957-67)* (Horta: Comissão Regional de Turismo da Horta, 1968). 1926 earthquake—Stone & Webster collection, Manuscripts Division, Baker Library, Harvard Graduate School of Business Administration; L. H. Matthews, "The Fayal Earthquake," *Stone & Webster Journal*, XXXIX (July-December 1926), 432-441; also same journal, XXXVIII, 648, XXXIX, 292, 293, 295-302, and XL, 509. Lists of eruptions & earthquakes—Porfirio Bessone, *Dicionário Cronológico dos Açôres* (Cambridge, Mass.: author's edition, 1932), pp. 128-130 & 322-339. FAMOUS—*National Geographic*, CXLVII (1975), 586-615.

CHAPTER 2. Recently written history—Francisco Carreiro da Costa, *História da Sociedade e Cultura Açorianas* (Ponta Delgada, 1977, mimeographed), sheet 90; published in book form as *Esboço Histórico dos Açores* (Braga: Livraria Editora Pax, 1978), p. 115. 1433 grant—Bailey W. Diffie & George D. Winius, *Foundations of the Portuguese Empire* (Minneapolis: University of Minnesota Press, 1977), p. 65. Donataries—Manuel Monteiro Velho Arruda, ed., *Colecção de documentos relativos ao descobrimento e povoamento dos Açôres* (Ponta Delgada: Oficina de Artes Gráficas, 1932), pp. lxxxiii-cxiv. Henry's chronicler—Gomes Eanes de Zurara, *Chronica do descobrimento e conquista de Guiné*, ed. Visconde da Carreira & Visconde de Santarém (Paris: J. P. Aillaud, 1841), Chap. 7. Foreign strain—Elizabeth Nicholas, *Madeira and the Canaries* (London: Hamish, 1953), p. 25; Robin Bryans, *Madeira: Pearl of the Atlantic* (London: Robert Hale, 1959), p. 32. 1943 appeal—

A Selection of Sources 429

Portugal, Ministério dos Negócios Estrangeiros, *Documentos Relativos aos Acordos entre Portugal, Inglaterra e Estados Unidos da América para a Concessão de Facilidades nos Açores durante a Guerra de 1939-1945* (Lisbon: Imprensa Nacional, 1946), pp. 4, 8. Flemings—Francis M. Rogers, "Insular Portuguese Pronunciation: Alleged Flemish Influence," pp. 209-221 in Urban T. Holmes, Jr., & Alex. J. Denomy, eds., *Mediaeval Studies in Honor of Jeremiah Denis Matthias Ford* (Cambridge: Harvard University Press, 1948); Martim Afonso Jardim Cunha da Silveira, "Do Contributo Flamengo nos Açores," *Boletim do Instituto Histórico da Ilha Terceira*, XXI/XXII (1963-1964), 5-144; Lilliane Wouters, "Les Açores, îles flamandes?" *Septentrion: Revue de la culture néerlandaise*, IV (1975), 85-89, and a luncheon conversation with her in Brussels on October 9, 1977. Beguines—Gualter Pereira Cordeiro, " A Reconstrução do secular recolhimento de Santa Maria Madalena," *Correio dos Açores, Suplemento "SANTA MARIA,"* February 25, 1972, pp. 1, 4. Jennets—R. L. Dabney, 1899, p. 198. French or Celtic theory—Francis M. Rogers, "Insular Portuguese Pronunciation: Alleged Breton Influence," *Romance Philology*, II (1949), 305-314; Marcello Caetano, *Welcome to the Azores* (Lisbon: Secretaria de Estado da Informação e Turismo, 1971), p. 6; Claude Dervenn, "Les Bretons aux Açores," pp. 149-151 in *La Bretagne, le Portugal, le Brésil: Échanges et rapports* (Paris: Presses du Palais Royal, 1973); *Portuguese Times*, New Bedford, Mass., November 21 & December 5, 1974. Levadas—António H. de Oliveira Marques, *History of Portugal*, 2 vols. (New York: Columbia University Press, 1972), I, 153-154; Käte Brüdt, "Madeira: Estudo lingüístico-etnográfico," *Boletim de Filologia*, Lisbon, V (1937-1938), 59-91, 289-349, at p. 64. Minority groups—"The Importance of Ethnic-Religious Minorities and European Immigrants for the Colonization of Madeira and the Azores in the Fifteenth and Sixteenth Centuries," a paper which I treasure from my course Portuguese 200 in 1949-1950, written by the late Professor Edward Glaser of the University of Michigan who on August 29, 1972, suffered a most tragic premature death. Bensaúdes—Alfredo Bensaúde, *Vida de José Bensaúde* (Oporto: Litografia Nacional, 1936). Samuel Eliot Morison, *The European Discovery of America: The Northern Voyages* (New York: Oxford University Press, 1971), p. 211. Poem—Otília Frayão, "Poema," *Açoria: Fascículos de Cultura e Arte*, Ponta Delgada, II (1959), 19; I have already published my translation in *Americans of Portuguese Descent* (Beverly Hills: Sage Publications,

1974), p. 20. Human geography—Orlando Ribeiro, *Portugal, o Mediterrâneo e o Atlântico*, 2nd ed. (Lisbon: Sá da Costa, 1963), pp. 19, 40, 43. English lady—Sarah Bradford, *Portugal* (New York: Walker, 1973), p. 21.

CHAPTER 3. U.N. General Assembly Resolution 1542— Dusan Jovan Djonovich, *United Nations Resolutions. Series I. Resolutions Adopted by the General Assembly*, Vol. VIII, 1960-1962 (Dobbs Ferry, N.Y.: Oceana Publications, 1974), pp. 154-155. Salazaristic deception—Soares, 1974, p. 290. Anomaly—*Providence Journal*, October 25, 1969: *New Bedford Standard-Times*, October 26 & 31, 1969; *Bristol Phoenix*, October 31, 1969. *Unknown Islands*—Raúl Brandão, *As Ilhas Desconhecidas* (Lisbon: Aillaud e Bertrand, 1926); see also José Leite de Vasconcellos, *Mês de Sonho* (Lisbon: Museu Comercial de Lisboa, 1926), especially pp. 279-283. Distribution of bishops—*Annuario Pontificio per l'Anno 1966* (Vatican City: Tipografia Poliglotta Vaticana, 1966). Francis M. Rogers, "Os Açores: Plataforma no Atlântico," *Boletim da Academia Internacional da Cultura Portuguesa*, II (1966), 193-209. Precincts on Madeira—*Luso-Americano*, Newark, New Jersey, December 30, 1976/January 5, 1977, p. 1. Scholar-priest—Father Júlio da Rosa, *A Consciência da Comunidade na Vida e História do Povo Açoriano* (Ponta Delgada, 1965), p. 6, reprinted from *III Semana de Estudos dos Açores, realizada na cidade da Horta, Faial, no mês Março do ano de 1964*. President and administrator—José Cutileiro, *A Portuguese Rural Society* (Oxford: Clarendon Press, 1971), p. 167. British writer—Hugh Kay, *Salazar and Modern Portugal* (New York: Hawthorn Books, 1970), p. 66.

CHAPTER 4. Travelers to Asia—The Italian was Ludovico de Varthema, the Dutchman Jan Huygen van Linschoten. Angra Jesuit church—João Miguel dos Santos Simões, *Azulejaria Portuguesa nos Açores e na Madeira* (Lisbon: Fundação Calouste Gulbenkian, 1963), p. 44. Separate establishments—Pedro Calmon, *O Rei do Brasil: Vida de D. João VI*, 2nd ed. (São Paulo: Companhia Editora Nacional, 1943), p. 140. C. W. D.'s niece—William Henry Dabney, *Sketch of the Dabneys of Virginia, with some of their Family Records* (Chicago: S. D. Childs, 1888), p. 8 (in "Life of William H. Dabney" written by his daughter Olivia Frederica Dabney). Dom Pedro in Cambridge—Samuel Longfellow, ed., *Final Memorials of Henry Wadsworth Longfellow* (Boston: Ticknor,

1887), p. 247. Ladies working—R. L. Dabney, 1899, pp. 702-703. Barons—Vitorino Magalhães Godinho, *A Estrutura da Antiga Sociedade Portuguesa* (Lisbon: Arcádia, 1971), p. 127, quoting Almeida Garrett; Almeida Garrett, *Viagens na Minha Terra*, 5th ed., 2 vols. (Lisbon: Imprensa Nacional, 1870), I, 122-124. More recent writer—Bradford, 1973, p. 67. Numbers of religious—T. Bentley Duncan, *Atlantic Islands: Madeira, the Azores, and the Cape Verdes in Seventeenth-Century Commerce and Navigation* (Chicago: University of Chicago Press, 1972), p. 82. 1972 stamps—*Catálogo Eladio de Santos de Selos de Portugal Continental, Insular, Ultramarino e Novos Países de Expressão Portuguesa*, 39th ed. (Lisbon: Eladio de Santos, 1978), p. 71. Azorean discontent—R. L. Dabney, 1899, pp. 107, 817, 818, 1028, 1029, 1197, 1409, 1428. Well-known historian—Fortunato de Almeida, *História de Portugal*, Vol. VI, 1816-1910 (Coimbra: Fortunato de Almeida, 1929), p. 479; Oliveira Marques, 1972, II, 74. Apologist—Oscar Paxeco, that is, Fausto Fontes, *El-Rei D. Carlos o Grande Caluniado* (Lisbon: Neogravura, 1964), pp. 179-185. Anti-Kennedyism—Bradford, 1973, p. 127. *Boston Post*—Jeremiah Digges, *In Great Waters: The Story of the Portuguese Fishermen* (New York: Macmillan, 1941), p. 263. Role of aircraft in Azores—Carlos Manuel Ramos da Silveira, "O Faial na História da Aviação," *Arquivo Açoriano*, XVI (1972), 477-545, at pp. 541-542. Braganzas in America—Caetano Beirão, *El-Rei Dom Miguel I e a sua Descendência* (Lisbon: Portugália, 1943), pp. 55, 62, 124, 137-138.

CHAPTER 5. Adjacent Islands—António de Spínola, *Portugal e o Futuro* (Lisbon: Arcádia, 1974), p. 209. True Cabinet Minister—*2.° Governo Constitucional: Estrutura e Composição* (printed & distributed by Divisão de Relações Públicas, Secretaria de Estado da Comunicação Social, Lisbon), p. 1. 1859 statement—R. L. Dabney, 1899, p. 920. Carlos and Brazil—Douglas L. Wheeler, *Republican Portugal* (Madison: University of Wisconsin Press, 1978), pp. 43-44. Reactionary nature—Soares, 1974, p. 292. Move of capitals—José Oswaldo de Meira Penna, *Quando Mudam as Capitais* (Rio de Janeiro: IBGE, 1958). CWS news release—December 21, 1977.

CHAPTER 6. 1977 word list—José de Almeida Pavão, *Aspectos Populares Micaelenses no Povoamento e na Linguagem* (Ponta Delgada: Oficinas Tipográficas do *Diário dos Açores*, 1977), p. 104.

Medieval verses—António de Oliveira Marques, *Daily Life in Portugal in the Late Middle Ages*, tr. Sharon S. Wyatt (Madison: University of Wisconsin Press, 1971), p. 160; Francis M. Rogers's review of preceding in *Speculum*, XLIX (1974), 130-135, at p. 132. Women as flight attendants and in the government—*The legal situation of the Portuguese woman* (Lisbon: Secretaria de Estado da Informação e Turismo, 1971), pp. 11, 14. Working women—*Parade*, November 23, 1975. Noteworthy speech—R. L. Dabney, 1899, p. 1367. Maria Isabel Barreno, Maria Teresa Horta, & Maria Velho da Costa, *The Three Marias: New Portuguese Letters*, tr. Helen R. Lane (Garden City, N.Y.: Doubleday, 1975), pp. 339-340 & 150-152. Natália Correia, *Descobri Que Era Europeia: Impressões duma Viagem à América* (Lisbon: Portugália, 1951), p. 69. Margarida Victória, *Amores da Cadela "Pura": Confissões* (Amadora: Livraria Bertrand, 1976), p. 52; João Gaspar Simões's review, *Suplemento Cultural do Diário de Notícias*, Lisbon, No. 18 (May 6, 1976). Rogerio Perez, comp., *Servidor de Reis e de Presidentes* (Lisbon: Editora Marítimo-Colonial, 1945). Sodomy—Oliveira Marques, 1971, p. 180. Title of Grand Master—Diffie & Winius, 1977, p. 26. Different mentality—*Survey of the Portuguese Economy* (Lisbon: Secretaria de Estado da Informação e Turismo, 1971), p. 5. José de Almeida—*Jornal Português*, San Pablo, California, August 7, 1975, pp. 1 & 5. Rose Dabney Forbes, *Fayal Dabneys* (Arlington, Vermont, & New York, N.Y.: Vida Lindo Guiterman, 1932), p. 43; Emily Hahn (distinguished wife of the distinguished historian Charles R. Boxer), "The Azores. I—Timelessness in Mid-Atlantic," *The New Yorker*, November 14, 1959, pp. 131-168, at p. 160 (the first of three excellent articles in three successive issues).

CHAPTER 7. Figure 8—Manuel Luciano da Silva, M.D., *Portuguese Pilgrims and Dighton Rock* (Bristol, Rhode Island: Nelson D. Martins, 1971), pp. 18, 20. Tracks of latter-day whaling ships—Dorothy Cottle Poole, "Antone Fortes, Whaleman," *Dukes County Intelligencer*, Edgartown, Mass.: Dukes County Historical Society, XI (1970), 129-152, especially p. 148. Note and dollar bill—*Boston Sunday Globe*, August 14, 1977, p. 13. Plastic float cards—*Boston Globe*, February 26, 1978, p. 4. Grenville and Portuguese poet—Américo da Costa Ramalho, *Estudos Sobre a Época do Renascimento* (Coimbra: Centro de Estudos Clássicos e Humanísticos, 1969), Chap. 17. Crown regulations—Duncan, 1972, p. 126. Harriet Low—Katharine Hillard, ed., *My Mother's Journal* (Boston: George

H. Ellis, 1900); Elma Loines, ed., *The China Trade Post-Bag of the Seth Low Family of Salem and New York 1829-1873* (Manchester, Maine: Falmouth Publishing House, 1953). Francis B. Crowninshield, comp., *The Story of George Crowninshield's Yacht* Cleopatra's Barge *on a Voyage of Pleasure to the Western Islands and the Mediterranean 1816-1817* (Boston: privately printed, 1913), pp. 55, 224; David L. Ferguson, *Cleopatra's Barge: The Crowninshield Story* (Boston: Little, Brown, 1976), p. 101 (complete omission of Fayal!). Mark Twain, *The Innocents Abroad, or The New Pilgrims' Progress* (Hartford: American Publishing Company, 1869), pp. 55-56; Daniel Morley McKeithan, ed., *Traveling With the Innocents Abroad: Mark Twain's Original Reports from Europe and the Holy Land* (Norman, Oklahoma: University of Oklahoma Press, 1958), pp. 16-17. Spray–Walter Magnes Teller, ed., *The Voyages of Joshua Slocum* (New Brunswick, New Jersey: Rutgers University Press, 1958), pp. 241-242. Samuel Eliot Morison, *Introduction to* Whaler Out of New Bedford, *A Film Based on the Purrington-Russell Panorama of a Whaling Voyage Round the World 1841-1845* (New Bedford: Old Dartmouth Historical Society, 1962), p. 12. Ray's journal—Edouard Stackpole, "Dear Anna, Now Farewell. . . .'," *Cape Cod Compass*, XXVIII (1976), 38-43. Authority on wines—H. Warner Allen, *The Wines of Portugal* (New York: McGraw-Hill, 1963), p. 101. Boston report—Manuel Borges de Freitas Henriques, "The Azores," *North End Mission Magazine*, Boston, II (1973), 73-75, at p. 73. F. D. R. 1918—Ernest K. Lindley, *Franklin D. Roosevelt: A Career in Progressive Democracy* (New York: Blue Ribbon Books, 1931), pp. 165-169. Devalued dollar—June Goodwin, "Portuguese Elegance," *Christian Science Monitor*, May 16, 1972. F. D. R. 1940—Clarence K. Streit, "When FDR Proposed The Azores as Atlantic Union Capital," *Freedom & Union*, XXV, 1/2 (January-February 1970), 2-6, at p. 3. F. D. R. 1945—Donald Day, ed., *Franklin D. Roosevelt's Own Story: Told in His Own Words From His Private and Public Papers* (Boston: Little, Brown, 1951), p. 435. Location universal—Rogers, 1966, p. 198. Benjamin Franklin—Duncan, 1972, p. 250. Fayal's port charges—Poole, 1970, p. 147. Madeira Protestants—George Rawlings Poage, "The Coming of the Portuguese," *Illinois State Historical Society Journal*, XVIII (1925), 101-135; Jordan D. Fiore, "Mr. Lincoln's Portuguese Neighbors," *Lincoln Herald*, LXXIII (1971), 150-155; Irving Stone, *Love Is Eternal* (Garden City, N.Y.: Doubleday, 1954), p. 301. Madeirans on Bermuda—James Purves, "Portuguese in

Bermuda," *Bermuda Historical Quarterly*, III (1946), 133-142, at p. 135. José Guilherme Reis Leite, *Os Fisher* (Angra: "Separata da Revista 'Atlântida'," 1977), p. 6. Thomas Amory—William Babcock Weeden, *Economic and Social History of New England 1620-1789*, 2 vols. paged continuously (New York: Hilary House, 1963), pp. 565-573, a reference kindly given me by João Afonso of Angra. Baron Henri de Rothschild, *S. M. D. Carlos, Rei de Portugal, do Livro, em Preparação*, "Cinquante ans de souvenirs" (Oporto: Tip. Costa Carregal, 1944). Albert in the Azores—Jules Richard, *Les campagnes scientifiques de S. A. S. le Prince Albert Ier de Monaco* (Monaco: Imprimerie de Monaco, 1900); Raymond Damien, *Albert Ier Prince souverain de Monaco* (Villemomble: Institut de Valois, 1964). Prince Albert I of Monaco, "Sur un Cachalot des Açores: Note," Académie des Sciences, Paris, *Comptes Rendus*, Vol. CVII (July-December 1888), pp. 923-926. Princess Alice Bank—H. O. 51, section 5-16. 1893 cablegram—Frank Stanley Weston, "Os Cabos Submarinos no Faial," *Boletim do Núcleo Cultural da Horta*, III (1963), 215-230, at p. 219. Azores High—For his expert assistance I am deeply indebted to José Pinto Peixoto, Professor of the Classical University of Lisbon & Director of its Institute of Geophysics. Afonso Chaves—H. Amorim Ferreira, *Afonso Chaves, primeiro director do serviço meteorológico dos Açores* (Lisbon: Publicações do Serviço Meteorológico Nacional, 1959); d.°, "Observatório Magnético de S. Miguel," pp. 229-236 in *Geomagnética: Publicação commemorativa do 50.° aniversário do Observatório Magnético de S. Miguel, Açores* (Lisbon: Serviço Meteorológico Nacional, 1962); both studies provided me by Professor Pinto Peixoto. Paris meridian—Lloyd A. Brown, *The Story of Maps* (Boston: Little, Brown, 1949), p. 261. Azores meridian—*International Conference Held at Washington*, 1884, pp. 50, 57, 60, 61, 63, 66, & 67. James Cook, *The Voyage of the* Resolution *and* Adventure *1772-1775*, ed. J. C. Beaglehole (Cambridge, England: University Press, for the Hakluyt Society, 1969), pp. 673-677.

CHAPTER 8. Hickling family—João Hickling Anglin, "Tomás Hickling," *Correio dos Açores*, Ponta Delgada, September 21, 1947; d.°, "Tomás Hickling," *Insulana*, Ponta Delgada, V (1949), 108-115. Jarvis—Mrs. Mary Pepperrell Sparhawk Cutts [Jarvis's daughter], *The Life and Times of Hon. William Jarvis, of Weathersfield, Vermont* (New York: Hurd and Houghton, 1869), pp. 63-69, 128 ff. Prescott's biographer—C. Harvey Gardiner, *William Hickling Prescott: A Biography* (Austin, Texas: University of Texas Press, 1969), p. 30. Well-known letter—C. Harvey Gardiner, ed., *The Papers of William Hickling Prescott* (Urbana, Illinois: University of Illinois Press, 1964), pp. 5-12. Amelia H. Nye Papers, 1847-1854, in Massachusetts Historical Society, the gift made in April 1973 of Mrs. Raymond Emerson, that is, Amelia Forbes Emerson. Jefferson—Alice Forbes Howland, *The Descendants of John Bass Dabney and Roxa Lewis Dabney 1766-1966* (Milton, Mass., 1966, mimeographed), p. i; James H. Guill, *A History of the Azores Islands* (Menlo Park, California: author's edition, 1972), p. 126, a book filled with fine descriptions of the islands. Statement of J. B. D.'s granddaughter—W. H. Dabney, 1888, pp. 5, 8 (in "Life" by Olivia Frederica Dabney). Dabney vessels—"Ships that plied between Boston and Fayal," pp. 41-45 in *Old Shipping Days in Boston* (New Bedford: Reynolds-DeWalt, 1969), first printed in Boston in 1918 for the State Street Trust Company. Swain's letter—R. L. Dabney, 1899, p. 736. Offshore whaling—Bernard Venables, *Baleia! Baleia!: Whale Hunters of the Azores* (New York: Knopf, 1969); Trevor Housby, *The Hand of God: Whaling in the Azores* (London: Abelard-Schuman, 1971). 1817 visit—F. B. Crowninshield, 1913, p. 54. Continuation of quotation in Chapter 4—W. H. Dabney, 1888, p. 8. Interisland rivalry—R. L. Dabney, 1899, p. 881. View of Pico—R. L. Dabney, 1899, p. 839. Roxa's letter of 1829—R. L. Dabney, 1899, p. 241. Of Mrs. Webster—R. L. Dabney, 1899, p. 547. Dr. Webster's borrowing—Robert Sullivan, *The Disappearance of Dr. Parkman* (Boston: Little, Brown, 1971), p. 105. About the entire affair—R. Sullivan, 1971, pp. vii-viii. Gravest scandal—Samuel Eliot Morison, *Three Centuries of Harvard 1636-1936* (Cambridge: Harvard University Press, 1946), p. 282. Trinity Church—Trinity Church Papers Collection in the New England Historic Genealogical Society, for knowledge of which I am indebted to Bettina A. Norton, Archivist and Historian of Trinity Church in the City of Boston; among them is a letter dated Newport, March 4, [1872], from a Cunningham to "My dear Cousin" (presumably George Minot Dexter) which states: "... I have written to Sarah and advised her to call upon you and consult with you upon the best course for us to pursue. Perhaps you can tell her where we can purchase—and we shall be very much obliged if you will give her your advice upon the removal of the bodies ...", it being very tempting to suppose that a descendant of Roxalina

Dabney is writing about Mrs. John Pomeroy Dabney, the oldest of the four Webster daughters. Cleveland Amory, *The Proper Bostonians* (New York: E. P. Dutton, 1947), p. 213. Street renamed— *Testimonial from the Senate of Horta and Other Gentlemen of Fayal, to Charles W. Dabney, Esq., U. S. Consul at Fayal* (Boston? 1863?), p. 11, translated from *O Fayalense* of November 15, 1863). Description of Pico—C. Alice Baker, *A Summer in the Azores with a Glimpse of Madeira* (Boston: Lothrop, Lee & Shepard, 1882), pp. 85-86. Prescott's letter in the Amelia H. Nye Papers. Photographs of local Azorean costumes—João Afonso, "O Trajo nos Açores: Subsidios de Estudos de Vestiária Antiga, *Boletim do Instituto Histórico da Ilha Terceira*, XXXV (1977) (contains photographs from the 1880 album). Longfellow letter—R. L. Dabney, 1899, p. 644. Helen Thomson, *Murder at Harvard* (Boston: Houghton Mifflin, 1971). King of the colony—Robert H. Lord, John E. Sexton, & Edward T. Harrington, *History of the Archdiocese of Boston*, 3 vols.(New York: Sheed & Ward, 1944), III, 218. Freitas Henriques's death—Roberto de Mesquita, *Almas Cativas e Poemas Dispersas*, ed. Pedro da Silveira (Lisbon: Ática, 1973), p. 228. Thomas Wentworth Higginson, "A Trip to the Azores," *Nation*, September 19, 1867, p. 231; R. L. Dabney, 1899, p. 1314; Higginson, "Fayal and the Portuguese," *Atlantic Monthly*, VI (1860), 526-544, included as pp. 225-268 in his *Atlantic Essays* (Boston: J. R. Osgood, 1871).

CHAPTER 9. Cables in general—Charles Bright, *Submarine Telegraphs: Their History, Construction, and Working* (London: C. Lockwood, 1898); K. C. Baglehole, *A Century of Service: A Brief History of Cable and Wireless Ltd. 1868-1968*, 2nd impression (London: Cable & Wireless, 1970); K. R. Haigh, *Cableships and Submarine Cables* (London: Adlard Coles, 1968); Weston, 1963; I am further greatly indebted to Mr. Field Curry of Pittsburgh, Pennsylvania, for assistance with the history of the cables. I am indebted to Mr. K. C. Baglehole of C & W in London for the transatlantic loan of the complete run of *The Monthly Correspondent*. 1895 cablegram—Digges, 1941, p. 132, and also pp. 81, 179, 252, & 268-269. Whales and cables—Bruce C. Heezen, "Whales entangled in deep sea cables," *Deep Sea Research*, IV (1956-1957), 105-115. Transit tax, subsidy, and rates—*The Commercial Cable Company 1883-1918* (n.p., n.d., booklet of 54 pp.), p. 25. Local Azores-North America traffic—*The Commercial Cable*

A Selection of Sources 437

Company, p. 27. Alleged ITT dealings—Anthony Sampson, *The Sovereign State of ITT* (New York: Stein and Day, 1973), pp. 9, 27-47, 57-58. Characterization of Horta—Pedro da Silveira, "O conto açoriano e os seus caminhos," *Estrada Larga*, Oporto, I (1959), 544-547, at p. 545, a reference I owe to Ms. Lisa Godinho. 1921 statement—Clarence H. Mackay, *International Cable Communication: Statement. . . before the Senate Committee on Interstate Commerce* (Washington; D.C., January 10, 1921), p. 11 & *passim*. B.O.P.—Kay, 1970, pp. 108-109, 114. For many unpublished details concerning Horta and the cables, especially his Commercial Cable Company, I am indebted to Mr. Frank Stanley Weston of Horta. Three projects—Stone & Webster collection, Job Order Numbers 4616, 4576, & 4764. Italian cables—Letter of July 2, 1973, from Dr. Ing. O. Oddone, L'Ispettore Generale Tecnico, Ispettorato Generale delle Telecomunicazioni, Ministero delle Poste e delle Telecomunicazioni, Rome.

CHAPTER 10. Marconi in Horta—Manuel Greaves, *Outras Histórias que Ouvi* (Horta: author's family's edition, 1958), pp. 119-123. Early transoceanic flights—Francis M. Rogers, *Precision Astrolabe: Portuguese Navigators and Transoceanic Aviation* (Lisbon: Academia Internacional da Cultura Portuguesa, 1971, distributed in North America by Wm. S. Sullwold, Taunton, Mass.); d.°, "The Plath-Coutinho Sextant and the Night Flight of the ARGOS," *Revista Militar*, Lisbon, XXIX (1977), 105-136. *The History of Lufthansa German Airlines* (New York: Lufthansa, 1963); "German Airlines: Seventeen years old but forty-six years long," *Esso Air World*, XXIV (1972). Aurelio Liotta, *La "L. A. T. I." nei suoi primi quattro anni di vita* (Rome: Linee Aeree Transcontinentali Italiane, 1943); R. E. G. Davies, *A History of the World's Airlines* (London: Oxford University Press, 1964), pp. 222-223; Cesare Falessi, "Dagli SM-83 al DC-8: Trent'anni di ali italiane sull'Atlantico del Sud," *Freccia Alata: Settimanale di Informazioni Alitalia*, X (1970), 4; Paolo Corsini, "Commercial Aviation in Italy: The flying boat era," pp. 16-20 in *Transpo 72 Review* (1972); dinner conversation with Cesare Falessi and his assistant Aldo Pittoni in Rome-Eur on July 25, 1972. Details on the Azores—Silveira, 1972, *passim*. Catapulting—John Malcolm Brinnin, *The Sway of the Grand Saloon* (New York: Delacorte, 1971), p. 466; John Maxtone-Graham, *The Only Way to Cross* (New York: Macmillan, 1972), p. 253; Basil W. Bathe, *Seven Centuries of Sea Travel* (New York: Tudor, 1973), p. 222; Tom Hughes, *The*

Blue Riband of the Atlantic (New York: Charles Scribner's Sons, 1973), p. 147. Pan Am statistics—Silveira, 1972, p. 540, supplemented by information he kindly gave me in person in July 1974. *Horta Swell*–Silveira, 1972, p. 538. Vernon A. Walters, *Silent Missions* (Garden City, N.Y.: Doubleday, 1978), pp. 76-77; Roland Eugene Vintras, *The Portuguese Connection: The Secret History of the Azores Base* (London: Bachman & Turner, 1974), p. 42; *Jornal de Fall River*, Fall River, Mass., April 5, 1978, p. 16. *Ares*– "Pararescuers Aid ARES Man," *AMVER Bulletin*, 4/5 (1972), p. 7. For information on the role of U.S. service personnel on Terceira, I am indebted to then Captain Angelo J. Cerchione, USAF, who in 1973 sent me considerable material, including "People-to-People Program Is Unique Feature of Azores Tour for USAF Veterinary Service Chief," *Journal of the American Veterinary Medical Association*, CLXII, 1 (January 1, 1973), 11-13. Louis Castex, *Mon tour du monde en avion* (Paris: Plon, 1945), p. 209 (copy given at the end of 1953 by Castex to Armando Monteiro of Santa Maria with the following handwritten dedication: "A M. le Chef de la Camara Municipal de Santa Maria en souvenir de ma visite le 21 décembre 1935 à Santa Maria au cours de laquelle j'ai eu la chance de trouver la surface plaine qui est actuellement la plaque tournante de l'Atlantique-Nord. Cordial hommage de Louis Castex 2.12.53."). Iberia—César Gómez Lucia, *Diagonal Histórica del Tráfico Aéreo Español* (Madrid: Iberia, Airlines of Spain, 1964), pp. 102, 105, 107-110, 135-136, a book kindly sent me, with references marked, by Félix Izquierdo Pérez, Subdirector de Medios de Comunicación, Iberia, in Madrid. 1973 airlift—Dana Adams Schmidt, "C-5—America's secret weapon?" *Christian Science Monitor*, December 28, 1973, p. B1; Drew Middleton, "Importance of U.S. Munitions to Israel Assayed," *New York Times*, December 2, 1974, p. 3. Cuban division—William F. Buckley, Jr., in *Boston Globe*, April 29, 1978, p. 7. Range of Ilyushins—*Jane's All the World's Aircraft*, 1972-1973, pp. 456 & 458. Marcello Caetano, "The Strategic Significance of the Cape Verde Islands," pp. 11-12 in *Portugal's Reasons for Remaining in the Overseas Provinces* (Lisbon: Secretaria de Estado da Informação e Turismo, ca. 1971). Unsinkable aircraft carrier—John Biggs-Davison, "The Cape Verde Islands and Western Defense," *African World*, November 1969, p. 4. Zaire—*Portuguese Times*, May 25, 1978, p. 3A.

CHAPTER 11. Telephone cables in general—H. H. Schenck, comp., *The World's Submarine Telephone Cable Systems* (Washington, D.C.: Government Printing Office, 1975); *Via Portucale: Revista Ilustrada das Actividades da Companhia Portuguesa Rádio Marconi*, 1966-1973; for courtesy and information during my two visits to Green Hill, I am indebted to Mr. Garnet Haley, Station Manager. Windmills—*Via Portucale*, No. 44 (September 1970), pp. 16-21, supplemented by information kindly given me on June 14, 1978, by Engineer Fernando José Pereira Galhardo, Chefe do Departamento de Estudos Técnicos, Direcção de Sistemas de Telecomunicações, CPRM. St. Gabriel—*Via Portucale*, No. 55 (June 1973), pp. 2-5, 9-11. "Deep down there . . .": *South Africa-Portugal Submarine Telephone Cable System* (January 1970), *BRACAN-1 Submarine Cable System* (April 1973), & *Columbus 1977 Transatlantic Submarine Telecommunication System* (1977), three beautifully illustrated brochures issued by Standard Telephones and Cables Limited. CAM-1—*Via Portucale*, No. 53 (December 1972). ITT experiments—Haigh, 1968, p. 237. Information as of October 1977—Kindly provided via telephone November 9, 1977, by Mr. Allan Galfund, Senior Information Officer, COMSAT. Uniqueness—*Via Portucale*, No. 55 (June 1973), p. 19. Cacuaco & Boane—Thoughtful letter of December 9, 1977, from the Director de Sistemas de Telecomunicações, CPRM. Eavesdropping—*Boston Globe*, December 23, 1977, p. 37, & December 24, 1977, p. 2. Three L's—*Via Portucale*, No. 56 (September 1973), pp. 33 & 34. Cautionary note—*New York Times*, May 31 & June 1, 1974. Coalition—*New York Times*, November 3, 1974. Ponta Delgada—*Estação Terrena de Ponta Delgada, S. Miguel–Açores*, brochure issued by the CPRM, December 1977. Direct dialing—*The Whole World Will Be Talking* . . . , leaflet no. L76213, 2/78, issued by the Bell System; supplemental information by telephone from the Bell System. *Diário de Notícias*, Funchal, January 29, February 1, & February 2, 1973; *ibid.*, June 20, 1975. Cristiano Frazão Pacheco, *As Cinco Desgraças do Arquipélago dos Açores: Em defesa do Arquipélago e dos seus habitantes* (Ponta Delgada: author's edition, 1961). Rate per word—*The Commercial Cable Company 1883-1918*, p. 28. 1974 landing fees—Letter of March 18, 1974, from Ms. Ann Wood, Staff Vice President, International Airport Charges, Pan American World Airways. Henrique Galvão, *Santa Maria: My Crusade for Portugal*, tr. William Longfellow (Cleveland & New York: World,

1961), p. 129. TAT-4 order—In July 1973 Mr. David H. Hindman, Overseas Staff Supervisor (Results), AT&T Long Lines, kindly sent me a copy. AFAR—See also Vintras, 1974, p. 95. Satellite-triangulation sites—*New York Times*, August 12, 1973, p. 36. Seizure of fishing boat—*Luso-Americano*, August 26/ September 1, 1976, p. 1. New agreement—*As Flores*, June 23, 1977; *Jornal de Fall River*, May 10, 1978, p. 17.

CHAPTER 12. Dollar value of foreign trade—Portugal, Instituto Nacional de Estatística, *Estatísticas do Comércio Externo* or *Anuário Estatístico*; for exchange rates I use those given in *International Financial Statistics*, XXXI, 5 (May 1978), 321, namely, in 1970 $1 was 28$750, 1971 27$560, 1972 27$000, 1973 25$845, 1974 24$596, 1975 27$472, 1976 31$549, 1977 39$855. Value of U.S. presence at Lajes—*Portuguese Times*, September 16, 1976, p. 4. *Survey*, 1971, pp. 10 & 9. Planning committee reports—Comissão de Planeamento da Região Açores, *Trabalhos Preparatórios do IV Plano de Fomento: Relatório de Propostas, 2? Volume, I-Análise e Diagnóstico da Situação Regional* (March 1972), which I brought back in the spring of 1972, and Comissão de Planeamento da Região Madeira, *Relatório de Propostas* (2 vols. in 3, March 1972), which my student Gregory F. Rocha, Jr., brought back in the summer of 1973; *The Case for Agrarian Relief in Portugal's Adjacent Islands,* unpublished Independent Work Project by my undergraduate student Howard Kailes, Harvard College, '74, Harvard Law School, '77, a concentrator in Economics who used the *Relatórios de Propostas*. Ponta Delgada newspapers—*Correio dos Açores*, July 12, 1974, pp. 1 & 2; *Açores*, July 13, 1977, p. 2. Meeting on Terceira—Rui Camacho & Carlos Gil, "Açores: Entre Dois Mundos e Dois Tempos," *Flama*, Lisbon, January 14, 1972, pp. 23-47. Bishop Escudeiro—*Jornal de Fall River*, August 24, 1977, p. 27. S.S. benefits—Annual report issued by the Social Security Administration entitled *Beneficiaries Residing Abroad*. Dow Chemical—Leonard Woodcock, "Force Social Responsibility on International Companies!" *New York Times*, January 7, 1973. 1977 report—*Jornal de Fall River*, December 7, 1977, pp. 1, 24, 31, & December 21, 1977, pp. 1, 32, 42. Formulator—*Jornal de Fall River*, December 7, 1977, p. 31. Bermuda—*Jornal de Fall River*, December 7, 1977, pp. 1 & 22. São Miguel's nobility—José Honorato Gago da Câmara de Medeiros (Visconde do Botelho), *Um Açoriano no Mundo (Memórias Políticas)*, 2 vols. boxed (Ponta Del-

A Selection of Sources 441

gada: Livraria Mondis, 1977), I, 29-30. For information on foreign trade zones I am indebted to Mr. Rino Moriconi, Project Manager, Foreign Trade Zone, Massport, Boston. Factual analyses from the left—*Açores: Do 25 de Abril até aos nossos dias* (Lisbon: Cooperativa Arma Crítica, 1977), proclaimedly by "Um Grupo de Estudantes Açoreanos Alunos do Instituto Superior de Economia de Lisboa"; A. Borges Coutinho, A. Soares de Melo, Carlos Enes, José Bettencourt, & Victor Avila, *Que Futuro para os Açores?* (Lisbon: Editorial Caminho, 1978).

CHAPTER 13. Motley collection—R. L. Dabney, 1899, p. 1292. Fayal's involvement—R. L. Dabney, 1899, pp. 439, 441, 440, 463. Planet "Zita"—*Jahrbuch der Astronomie und Geophysik*, XXIII (1912), 14; Gordon Brook-Shepherd, *The Last Habsburg* (London: Weidenfeld and Nicolson, 1968), p. 22. Archduke Otto of Habsburg, "L'idée impériale portugaise," *Boletim da Academia Internacional da Cultura Portuguesa*, I (1966), 161-176, at p. 163. Rui Vieira, *Flowers of Madeira*, tr. G. E. Maul (Funchal: n.p., 1974). Bathe, 1973, p. 221. Aquila Airways—Sacheverell Sitwell, *Portugal and Madeira* (London: B. T. Batsford, 1954). François Auguste René, Vicomte de Chateaubriand, *Mémoires d'outre-tombe*, Édition du Centenaire, ed. Laurice Levaillant, 2nd ed., 4 vols. (Paris: Flammarion, 1949-1950), I, 262-265 ("Les Açores.—Île Graciosa"); George D. Painter, *Chateaubriand: A Biography, Volume One (1768-93), The Longed-for Tempests* (London: Chatto & Windus, 1977), pp. 164-165; Osório Goulart, "Chateaubriand na Ilha do Faial," pp. 169-170 in *Livro do Primeiro Congresso Açoreano, que se reüniu em Lisboa de 8 a 15 de Maio de 1938* (Lisbon: Casa dos Açores, 1940); *Jornal de Fall River*, February 8, 1978, p. 32; *Luso-Americano*, February 16-22, 1978, pp. 20, 23. Ex-cable official Frank Stanley Weston introduced me to the Dramático. Robin Bryans, *The Azores* (London: Faber and Faber, 1963); Catherine Gygax, *Îles atlantiques* (Berne: Kümmerly & Frey, 1971). Slot— Manuel Maria Sarmento Rodrigues, *Ancoradouros das Ilhas dos Açores*, 3rd ed. (Lisbon: Instituto Hidrográfico, 1967), p. 179.

CHAPTER 14. Salazar's phrase—Oliveira Marques, 1972, II, 180, 211. Newspaper report—*Diário dos Açores*, December 21, 1972. Famous oration—Francis M. Rogers, *The Obedience of a King of Portugal* (Minneapolis: University of Minnesota Press, 1958), p. 52. Abrogation—*The Pilot*, Boston, February 28, 1975, p. 2.

Homily—*União*, Angra, June 20, 1974. Francis M. Rogers, "Spatial Organization of the Church," *The Current: A Review of Catholicism and Contemporary Culture*, Cambridge, Mass., IV (1963), 221-226. Xavier Rynne, *Letters from Vatican City: Vatican Council II (First Session)* (New York: Farrar, Straus & Company, 1963); d.°, *The Second Session* (New York: Farrar, Straus & Company, 1964); d.°, *The Third Session* (New York: Farrar, Straus & Giroux, 1965); d.°, *The Fourth Session* (New York: Farrar, Straus & Giroux, 1966). Dos Passos—*Standard-Times*, New Bedford, Mass., June 18, 1961; Francis M. Rogers, *The Portuguese Heritage of John Dos Passos* (Boston: Portuguese Continental Union of the United States of America, 1976), p. 35.

CHAPTER 15. Condemnation—Xavier Rynne, *Vatican Council* (New York: Farrar, Straus & Giroux, 1968), p. 433; *Acta Apostolicae Sedis*, LVI (Ser. III, v. vi), no. 15, p. 908 (speech of October 18, 1964). Corn on the cob—Deolinda Maria Avila, *Foods of the Azores Islands* (Palo Alto, California: author's edition, 1977), p. 12. Charles Hall Grandgent, *An Outline of the Phonology and Morphology of Old Provençal*, revised ed. (Boston: D.C. Heath, 1905), p. 12. Imperial crowning—Francis M. Rogers, review of Oliveira Marques's *Daily Life* of 1971, pp. 134-135; d.°, "Celestial Navigation: From Local Systems to a Global Conception," pp. 687-704 in Fredi Chiappelli, ed., *First Images of America: The Impact of the New World on the Old*, 2 vols. paged continuously & boxed (Berkeley: University of California Press, 1976), at pp. 688 & 702. Secret of Fátima—*Fort Lauderdale News and Sun-Sentinel*, January 28, 1978, p. 5B. Practitioners vs. believers—*Portuguese Times*, February 9, 1978, p. 5. Helen Brown Norden Lawrenson, "Latins Are Lousy Lovers," *Esquire*, VI, 4 (October 1936), 36-37, 198; d.°, *The Hussy's Handbook, including Latins Are Lousy Lovers* (New York: Farrar & Rinehart, 1937); d.°, *Latins Are Still Lousy Lovers* (New York: Hawthorn Books, 1968). Robert C. Smith, *The Art of Portugal 1500-1800* (New York: Meredith Press, 1968).

CHAPTER 16. Real estate brokers—*Fort Lauderdale News and Sun-Sentinel*, January 19, 1974. Parentela—Charles Wagley, *An Introduction to Brazil* (New York: Columbia University Press, 1963), Chap. 5. "Biological danger"—Duncan, 1972, p. 28. W.H.O. study—*New York Times*, July 21, 1974. Ethnic mother—*Boston Globe*, December 2, 1973. English observer—Bradford, 1973, p.

A Selection of Sources 443

142. Eminent social scientist—Cutileiro, 1971, p. 95. Laurence Wylie, *Village in the Vaucluse* (Cambridge: Harvard University Press, 1960), p. 133. Ti Manel—Cristóvão de Aguiar, *Raiz Comovida: A Semente e a Seiva, Romance* (Coimbra: Centelha, 1978), pp. 18-19. Regional Secretary—Reis Leite, 1977, pp. 181, 182. 179.

CHAPTER 17. Emigration to Canada—Grace M. Anderson & David Higgs, *A Future to Inherit: Portuguese Communities in Canada* (Toronto: McClelland and Stewart, 1976); Domingos Marques & João Medeiros, *Imigrantes Portugueses 25 Anos no Canadá* (Toronto: Movimento Comunitário Português e Festival Português, 1978), p. 7. Madeirans in Venezuela—Miguel Acosta Saignes, *Historia de los portugueses en Venezuela* (Caracas: Publicaciones de la Dirección de Cultura de la Universidad Central, 1959). Letter writer—Luís da Silva Ribeiro, "Cartas da América," *Boletim do Instituto Histórico da Ilha Terceira*, V (1947), 231-246, at p. 239. New words—Manuel de Avila Coelho, "Pequeno Subsidio para o Vocabulário Regional, das Ilhas do Faial e Pico," *Beletim do Núcleo Cultural da Horta*, II (1959), 35-45; Pavão, 1977, p. 90; Venables, 1969, p. 39. Dias de Melo, *Mar Rubro: Baleeiros dos Açores* (Lisbon: Orion, 1958), *& Pedras Negras; Narrativia Açoriana* (Lisbon: Portugália, 1964). Alfred Lewis, *Home is an Island* (New York: Random House, 1951), pp. 7, 213, 108; Francis M. Rogers, "The Contribution by Americans of Portuguese Descent to the U.S. Literary Scene," pp. 409-432 in Wolodymyr T. Zyla & Wendell M. Aycock, eds., *Ethnic Literatures Since 1776: The Many Voices of America*, 2 vols. paged continuously (Lubbock, Texas: Texas Tech Press, 1978), at pp. 414-416; Maria Margarida Cymbron de Bettencourt Barbosa, "Viagem aos Estados Unidos para recolha de elementos sobre o escritor Alfred Lewis (1970)," *Insulana*, Ponta Delgada, XXIX/XXX (1973/1974).

CHAPTER 18. Special brand of language—Francis M. Rogers, "Insular Portuguese Pronunciation," *Hispanic Review*, XIV (1946), 235-253, XVI (1948), 1-32, & XVII (1949), 47-70. Variations in Creole—Mary Louise Nunes, "The Phonologies of Cape Verdean Dialects of Portuguese," *Boletim de Filologia*, Lisbon, XXI (1962/1963), 1-56 (a senior honors thesis at Radcliffe College). International linguistic circles—A. G. Haudricourt & A. G. Juilland, *Essai pour une histoire structurale du phonétisme français* (Paris: C. Klincksieck, 1949), p. 109; 2nd ed., revised (The Hague: Mouton, 1970), p. 116; A. Martinet, "Function, Structure, and Sound

Change," *Word*, VIII (1952), 1-32, at pp. 7 & 11. General people's Portuguese—Francis M. Rogers, review of Göran Hammarström, *Etude de phonétique auditive sur les parlers de l'Algarve* (Uppsala & Stockholm: Almqvist & Wiksells Boktryckeri, 1953), in *Romance Philology*, VIII (1955), 284-299, at p. 297.

CHAPTER 19. The four abilities—Paul H. Buck et al., *General Education in a Free Society: Report of the Harvard Committee* (Cambridge: Harvard University Press, 1945), p. 65. Marcello Caetano, *As Escolas Estão ao Serviço da Educação Nacional* (Lisbon: Secretaria de Estado da Informação e Turismo, 1974), p. 5. Portuguese university system—Soares, 1974, pp. 36-37. Napoleonic-Latin—José Veiga Simão, "The University of Today: The Portuguese Experience," *Journal of the American Portuguese Society*, XI (1977), 32-40, at p. 34. Changes in the 1960's—Oliveira Marques, 1972, II, 204 (see also p. 30). Abolition of separation of sexes—*Diário dos Açores*, November 21, 1972. Special concession—*Diário dos Açores*, October 25, 1972. Minister's step—*Açores*, August 14, 1973. "Michaelese University"—Augusto da Silva Branco Camacho, "Universidade Micaelense," *Correio dos Açores*, November 9, 1973, p. 1. José Veiga Simão, "Fortalecimento dos Laços Lusíadas no Mundo," pp. 55-63 in *II Congresso das Comunidades de Cultura Portuguesa*, Vol. I (Lisbon, 1970), at pp. 58 & 60. Caught in trap— Henry H. Keith, "Point, Counterpoint in Two Centuries of Reforming Portuguese Education (1750-1974)," *Studia*, XXXIX (1974), 79-104, at p. 98. A meetingplace of cultures—*Açores*, April 21, 1974. A kind of legacy—Veiga Simão, 1977, pp. 32, 34, 35. Creation of Instituto Universitário dos Açores—Decreto-Lei n.° 5/76, January 9, 1976. A dream expressed—João Afonso, "As Multi-Situação Insulares estão a ser analisadas por um Professor de Harvard," *Diário Insular*, Angra, April 8, 1972, pp. 1, 4. Creation of Instituto Universitário da Madeira—Decreto-Lei n.° 664/ 76, August 4, 1976; *Jornal Português*, September 2, 1976. Speech of Regional Secretary—*Diário de Notícias*, Funchal, July 17, 1977, pp. 1, 4. Northwest Europe—Personal observations in Paris region, Luxembourg, & Bonn-Mönchengladbach region, September/October 1977. Shortage of school buildings—*Correio dos Açores*, December 25, 1973; *Diário dos Açores*, January 1, 1974. Minister's exclamation—Marvine Howe in *New York Times*, March 14, 1976.

CHAPTER 20. Rhode Island—Lois A. Monteiro, "Immigrants and the Medical Care System: The Example of the Portuguese," paper presented at the Smithsonian Institute Bicentennial Conference, "The New Immigration: Inplications for the United States and the International Community" (Washington, D.C., November 16, 1976, xeroxed); d.°, "Immigrants without Care," *Society*, XIV, 6 (September/October 1977). Old customs—Victor M. Pereira da Rosa, "Überlieferte Werte und der Unwille zu Veränderungen auf den Azoren," *Die Dritte Welt*, V (1977), 468-477, at pp. 474-475. Peripheral doctors—*Jornal de Fall River*, March 8, 1978, p. 14. Infant mortality in selected countries—*U.N. Demographic Yearbook 1974*, Table 20, that is, pp. 342-363. TV program on abortion—Loretta Porto Slover, "The Three Marias: Literary Portrayals of the Situation of Women in Portugal," unpublished Ph.D. thesis (Harvard University, 1977), pp. 8-10. Onions and garlic—Manuel Luciano da Silva, M.D., "A Cebola e o Alho Evitam os Ataques do Coração!" *Bristol* [Rhode Island] *Phoenix*, November 4, 1976, p. 20. Right-of-passage bill—Massachusetts Senate 804 & 1924, 1973; *Belmont Citizen*, Supplement, August 22, 1974. Kenneth K. Nakano, David M. Dawson, & Alexander Spence, "Machado disease: A hereditary ataxia in Portuguese emigrants to Massachusetts," *Neurology*, XXII (1972), 49-55. Bryan T. Woods & Herbert H. Schaumburg, "Nigrospino-dentatal Degeneration with Nuclear Ophthalmoplegia: A Unique and Partially Treatable Clinico-pathological Entity," *Journal of the neurological Sciences*, XVII (1972), 149-166. Roger N. Rosenberg, William L. Nyhan, Carolyn Bay, & Parkhurst Shore, "Autosomal dominant striatonigral degeneration," *Neurology*, XXVI (1976), 703-714; Edwin Kiester, Jr., "Six Generations Of One Family—Linked Together By A Deadly Gene," *Today's Health*, LIV, 3 (March 1976), pp. 32-35, 50-51; William L. Nyhan, *The Heredity Factor: Genes, Chromosomes, and You* (New York: Grosset & Dunlap, 1976), pp. 59-64. Flaviu C. A. Romanul, Hilton L. Fowler, João Radvany, Robert G. Feldman, & Murray Feingold, "Azorean Disease of the Nervous System," *New England Journal of Medicine*, CCXCVI (1977), 1505-1508; June Goodfield, *Playing God: Genetic Engineering and the Manipulation of Life* (New York: Random House, 1977), pp. 46-49, 54. Queen Victoria—Theo Aronson, *Royal Vendetta: The Crown of Spain 1829-1965* (Indianapolis: Bobbs-Merrill, 1966), pp. 182-183; Nyhan, 1976, pp. 141-143, 155. Disagreement—Surl L. Nielsen, "Striatonigral degeneration disputed in familial disorder [Letter to the Editor]," *Neurology,* XXVII (1977), 306, with Dr. Rosenberg's reply. Donald R. Taft, *Two Portuguese Communities in New England* [Portsmouth, Rhode Island, & Fall River, Mass.] (New York: Columbia University, 1923, reprinted New York: AMS Press, 1967, & New York: Arno Press and The New York Times, 1969). Sensitivity of white Portuguese immigrants—Francis M. Rogers, "The Portuguese Experience in the United States: Double Melt or Minority Group?" *Journal of the American Portuguese Society,* X (1976), 1-16. Neurologists in Amsterdam and Tilburg—A. Biemond & J. L. M. Sinnege, "Tabes of Friedreich with Degeneration of the Substantia Nigra, a Special Type of Hereditary Parkinsonism," *Confinia Neurologica,* XV (1955), 129-142. Article out of Flanders— Raymond D. Adams, Ludo van Bogaert, & Henry Vander Eecken, "Striato-Nigral Degeneration," *Journal of Neuropathology and Experimental Neurology,* XXIII (1964), 584-608. Flemings in Continental Portugal—Diffie & Winius, 1977, p. 15. Moved from the Azores—Conversation with Pedro da Silveira in Lisbon June 16, 1978.

CHAPTER 21. Ocarina orchestra—Bessone, 1932, p. 135. Horácio Bento de Gouveia, *Canhenhos da Ilha* (Funchal: Junta Geral do Funchal, 1966), pp. 101, 103. *Still Waters*–Horácio Bento de Gouveia, *Aguas Mansas*; *Romance* (Coimbra: Coimbra Editora, 1963), p. 17. Horácio Bento de Gouveia, *Canga: Romance* (Coimbra: Coimbra Editora, 1975), p. 12. Third novel—Horácio Bento de Gouveia, *Lágrimas Correndo Mundo: Romance* (Coimbra: Coimbra Editora, 1959). Figure of Madeiran literature—His fourth novel, *Torna-viagem* (Returnee) is scheduled to be published by Coimbra Editora in September 1978. Antero de Quental, *Sonnets and Poems*, tr. S. Griswold Morley (Berkeley: University of California Press, 1922), p. 33. Theater in Horta in 1820—R. L. Dabney, 1899, p. 94. Boston's Old Howard—Manuel Borges de Freitas Henriques, 1867, p. 101. Adam Lindsay Gordon, *Poems*, ed. Frank Maldon Robb (Oxford: Humphrey Milford, Oxford University Press, 1913). Pedro da Silveira, ed., *Antologia de Poesia Açoriana (do Século XVIII a 1975)* (Lisbon: Sá da Costa, 1977); João Gaspar Simões, "O símbolismo entre os ilhéus," *Diário de Notícias,* Lisbon, September 8, 1977, pp. 15-16; d.°, "Existirá uma literatura açoriana?" *ibid.,* June 15, 1978 (issue devoted to the Azores), pp.

13-14; Pedro da Silveira, "Geraldo Vieira e Alfred Lewis (passando por Nemésio)," *ibid., ibid.* Henry David Thoreau, *The Correspondence*, ed. Walter Harding & Carl Bode (New York: New York University Press, 1958), p. 3. Nancy Larrick & Eve Merriam, eds., *Male and Female Under 18* (New York: Avon Books, 1973), p. 95. Black shawls—José de Almeida Pavão, *Os Xailes Negros* (Ponta Delgada: Oficinas Tipográficas do *Diário dos Açores*, 1973), pp. 13, 14. Black rocks—Dias de Melo, 1964, p. 140. Monthly steamer—Pedro da Silveira, *A Ilha e o Mundo: Poemas* (Lisbon: Centro Bibliográfico, 1952), p. 18. Sonnet—Roberto de Mesquita, 1973, p. 172, translation mine. Radio stations—Greaves, 1958, pp. 120-121. Painting entitled "Emigrants"—Joaquim do Espírito Santo Mota de Vasconcelos, *Epopeia do Emigrante Insular* (Lisbon: author's edition, 1959), p. 160; Museu Carlos Machado, *Homenagem a Mestre Domingos Rebelo* (Ponta Delgada, 1975).

CHAPTER 22. Preservation of folk literature—Manuel da Costa Fontes, *A New Portuguese Ballad Collection from California* (Los Angeles: Dept. of Spanish & Portuguese, UCLA, 1975, mimeographed), pp. 3, 9. Urgency of preserving folk culture—Joanne B. Purcell, "A riqueza do romanceiro e outras tradições orais nas Ilhas dos Açores," *Atlântida*, Angra, XIV (1970), 223-252, at p. 223. *Matanças*–Avila, 1977, p. 12. Tales on Flores—Purcell, 1970, p. 228. *Literatura de cordel*–Francis M. Rogers, "Printed Quire and Sheet Numbers, II: Spanish Examples," *Harvard Library Bulletin*, VIII (1954), 364-367; d.°, *The Travels of the Infante Dom Pedro of Portugal* (Cambridge: Harvard University Press, 1961), pp. 269-273. Adaptation in Hawaii—José Tavares de Teves, "Only God Does Not Err!" tr. Edgar Knowlton, Jr., *Portuguese Journal, Hawaii Edition*, April-May 1974, pp. 2, 7, 8. Flea and louse—Mary-Anne Lee (Mrs. William T. Vetterling), "Animals in Insular Portugal's Oral Literature," paper for my course Portuguese 219r (1977), pp. 98-99, which she took from Francisco Carreiro da Costa, "Versos dos animais," *Insulana*, I (1945), 531-540, at pp. 533-534; Purcell, 1970, p. 242. Boasting—Cutileiro, 1971, p. 243. Writer on Madeiran folklore—Alfredo de Freitas Branco, Visconde do Porto da Cruz, *Folclore Madeirense* (Funchal: Câmara Municipal, 1955), p. 13. Proverbs and superstitions—My examples were kindly given me by my graduate student Ms. Ana Maria Rocha, a native of Terceira. Master astrologers—Rogers,

"Celestial Navigation," 1976, p. 688. Dog bite—R. Bruce Clymer, *Traditional Health Practices and Beliefs in the Azores: A Preliminary Report* (Chapel Hill, North Carolina, 1977, typed), pp. 6, 7. Fayal collector—Júlio Andrade, *Bailhos, Rodas e Cantorias: Subsídios para o registo do folclore das ilhas do Faial, Pico, Flores e Corvo* (Lisbon: Comissão de Recolha e Divulgação do Folclore do Distrito da Horta, 1960). X-rays—Andrade, 1960, pp. 209 & 217. Fado—Asta-Rose Alcaide, "Fado," *What's On in Lisbon* (July 1977), p. 27. *Alcatra*–[João Afonso], "A alcatra é uma especialidade terceirense que honra Portugal inteiro," *Banquete: Revista Portuguesa de Culinária*, No. 158 (April 1973), pp. 12, 13, 14, 29, an article repeated in part in *Jornal de Fall River*, March 15, 1978, p. 11. *Don Quijote*, Part II, Chap. 17. *Espetada*–Porto da Cruz, 1955, p. 129.

THE HERITAGE OF ISLANDERS. Jardim's statement—*Jornal da Madeira*, June 18, 1978, pp. 1, 3. Ethnic Heritage Program—PL 92-318 (June 23, 1972), Title V, Section 504, which became Title IX of the Elementary and Secondary Education Act of 1965 (PL 89-10). Cartoons—*Luso-Americano*, December 29, 1977/January 4, 1978, p. 27. *Etatisme*–Rogers, 1958, p. 91.

SUGGESTED ADDITIONAL READING. Roger N. Rosenberg, William L. Nyhan, Paula Coutinho, & Carolyn Bay, "Joseph's Disease: An Autosomal Dominant Neurological Disease in the Portuguese of the United States and the Azores Islands," *Advances in Neurology*, eds. R. A. P. Kark, R. N. Rosenberg, & L. J. Schut (New York: Raven Press, 1978), Vol. XXI, pp. 33-57. Paula Coutinho & Corino Andrade, "Autosomal dominant system degeneration in Portuguese families of the Azores Islands," *Neurology*, XXVIII (1978), 703-709. Richard Henderson, *East to the Azores: A Guide to Offshore Passage-Making* (Camden, Maine: International Marine Publishing Company, 1978). Caetano Valadão Serpa, *A Gente dos Açores: Identificação, emigração e religiosidade, Séculos XVI-XX* (Lisbon: Prelo Editora, 1978). Fred Strasser and Brian McTigue, "The Fall River Conspiracy," *Boston* (November 1978), pp. 121-122, 124, 175-180, 182-184. "Ligações automáticas entre América e Açores," *Azorean Times*, December 20, 1978, p. 3.

INDEX

Places, persons, and subjects which recur throughout the book are not indexed: inhabited islands of the Azores and Madeiras, the Insular Portuguese cities, Cape Verde Islands (or Hesperides), Canary Islands (or Fortunate Islands), Brazil, Canada, France, United States, Boston, Cambridge, Harvard University, Caetano, Henry the Navigator, Salazar, autonomy, emigration, independence, separatism.

Abortion, 304, 305, 379, 385
Academia Internacional da Cultura Portuguesa, 261
Açor, 14, 29, 102, 253, 254
AÇORTUR, 269
Açorianidade, 34
Adelheid von Löwenstein-Wertheim-Rosenberg, 79, 260
Adoption, 305
Aeolian Islands, 52, 56, 149, 262, 265, 298, 355
Aeroflot, 207
AFAR. *See* Azores Fixed Acoustic Range
Affonsa, Frances, 135
Afonso V, King of Portugal, 39, 40, 300
Afonso VI, King of Portugal, 78
Afonso Henriques, King of Portugal, 292
Afonso, João Dias, 365, 434
African Direct Telegraph Co., 180, 181
Agar, 49, 237, 238
Agualva, Terceira, 393
Agüimes, Gran Canaria, 211, 216
Air France, 196
Alabama (ship), 153
Albert, Prince of Monaco, 138, 140, 141, 276
Alcatra, 414
Algiers: Battle of the Villas, 181
Almagreira, Santa Maria, 306
Almeida, Fortunato de, 84

Almeida, José de (19th century), 175
Almeida, José de (20th century), 102, 121, 387
Almeida Garrett, João Baptista da Silva Leitão, Visconde de, 80
Alsop family, 161
Alvernaz, Archbishop José Vieira, 283, 288
Amado, Jorge, 400
Amalie von Leuchtenberg, 153
Amaral, João Bosco Mota, 96
American Portuguese Society, 332, 359
American Telephone and Telegraph Co., 210, 215, 225, 226. *See also* AT&T Long Lines
Ames family, 18
Amory, Cleveland, 162
Amory, Thomas, 137
Amphibious Corps, U.S. Atlantic Fleet, 199, 200
Amzalak, Mosés Bensabat, 50
Andover, Maine, 215, 219, 221, 222
Andrade, Corino, M.D., 387
Andrade, Júlio, 412
Andrade, Manuel Linhares de, 275
Angústias, Horta, 65, 68, 307
Annals. *See* Dabney, Roxana Lewis
Annexation, 13, 82, 83, 85, 88
Annulment, 320
Antilia, 23
Anuário Estatístico, 243, 327, 365
Anzio, Italy, 187

Aquila Airways, 200, 263, 332
Araucaria. *See* Norfolk Island pine
Areia Larga, Pico, 156, 168, 169, 266, 365
Ares (ship), 201
Arfet, Anne d', 29, 410
Argo Merchant (ship), 127
Arriaga, Manuel de, 13, 84
Ascension (island), 73, 142, 177, 184, 203, 207, 216, 230
Association for the Development of Azoreans, 254
Astrology, 41, 297, 411
Atlantic Union, 133
Atlantis, Lost Continent of, 28
AT&T. *See* American Telephone and Telegraph Co.
AT&T Long Lines, 209, 218
Australia, 101, 399
Azevedo, Father Inácio de, 172
Azor (ship), 151, 153, 165, 166; renamed *Fredonia*, 152
Azorean (ship), 152, 168
Azorean disease of the nervous system, 51, 53, 379, 380-389, 424
Azores Fixed Acoustic Range, 46, 102, 229
Azores High, 126, 139
Azulejo, 54, 75, 308

Babylonian Captivity, 52, 53, 56, 294
"Bagatelle," Horta, 154-157, 164, 166, 167, 173, 197, 198, 261, 272
Baglehole, K. D., 436
Balbo, Italo, 195
Balzac, Honoré de, 184
Bands, Marching, 267, 391
Bannerman, David Armitage, 29
Barbados, 127, 206, 207, 400
Bartolomeu Dias (ship), 156
Bastiana, António Jacinto, 382
Bathe, Basil W., 263
Bathurst, Gambia, 180, 192, 193
Bay Roberts, Newfoundland, 177, 188, 209
Beaches, 380, 422
Beatrice, Duchess of Viseu, 40
Beauty contests, 59, 111, 401
Beechcraft King Air, 370
Beer, 244, 379, 403
Beevor, Mrs. John. *See* Dabney, Susan Heard Oliver

Beguines, 44
Belém do Pará, Brazil, 199
Belmont, Massachusetts, 287
Bensaúde family, 50, 135, 136, 145, 167, 180, 184, 224, 268
Bermuda, 30, 127, 135, 180, 196, 203, 224, 253, 257, 262
Berquó Palace, Ponta Delgada, 356, 360, 364
Bettencourt Palace, Angra do Heroísmo, 293
Bilingual education, 121, 336, 341
Birth control, 220, 304, 320, 376, 377, 379, 385
Biscoitos, Terceira, 243, 393
Blacks, 48-50, 61, 153, 225. *See also* Slaves
Blandy family, 136, 238, 257
Blue Army, 302
Boane, Mozambique, 218
Boeing jetfoil, 265
Boer War, 184
Bombay, India, 175
B.O.P. *See* British Observers in Portugal
Borges, Maria Isabel do Canto de Barcelos Coelho, 51
Borges de Freitas Henriques, Manuel, 171, 172, 399
Borkum, Germany, 140, 183-185, 187, 196
Boston, Massachusetts: Franklin Park, 165; Great Fire, 17, 162, 166; Howard Athenaeum, 399
Boxer, Charles R., 432
Botelho, José Honorato Gago da Câmara de Medeiros, Visconde do, 253
BRACAN-1, 211, 216, 221, 227
Braga, Teófilo, 13, 84, 104, 312, 392
Braganza family, 79, 86, 251
Brasília, Brazil, 101
Brava, Cape Verde Islands, 27
Brazil (island), 23, 78
Brazilian Submarine Telegraph Co., 178, 179
Bremen (ship), 195
Brest, France, 180, 183
Bretanha, São Miguel, 44, 45, 121, 339, 381, 386-388, 392
Bretons. *See* Brittany
Brighton, Massachusetts, 155
British Observers in Portugal, 186

Index

Brittany, France, 44-46, 48, 51, 56, 101, 381
Brooke family, 172, 173
Brotero, Frederico Dabney de Avelar, 108, 152
Brotero, José Maria de Avelar, 153
Bruges, Belgium, 43, 44, 52, 77
Brum, Mrs. Francisca Paula Terra, 166
Bryans, Robin, 271
Buckley, William F., Jr., 14
Bullfights, 52, 113, 340, 379
Bynum, David E., 406

C-5A (plane), 204
C & W. *See* Cable & Wireless
Cable & Wireless, 177, 179-181, 185, 189, 190, 211, 216, 273-275
Cabo Girão, Madeira, 36
Cabral, Amílcar, 206
Cabral, Gonçalo Velho, 40
Cabral, Pedro Álvares, 291, 292
Cabral, Sacadura. *See* Sacadura . . .
Cacuaco, Angola, 218, 219
Cais do Pico, Pico, 74, 76, 81, 371
Caldeira, 32, 340
Calheta, Madeira, 372
Calheta, São Jorge, 371
CAM-1, 211, 212, 227
Camacha, Madeira, 42, 412
Camacho, Jaime de Ornelas, 96
Câmara de Lobos, Madeira, 376
Cambridge, Massachusetts: Mt. Auburn Cemetery, 162
Camões, Luís de, 291, 292, 420
Camuri, Venezuela, 211
Canberra, Australia, 101
Canso, Nova Scotia, 140, 182, 183, 186
CANTAT-2, 221
Canto family, 132, 392
Cap Arcona (ship), 262
Cape Canaveral, Florida, 216
Capelinhos Islets, Fayal, 30, 31
Capelo, Fayal, 30, 156
Capet, Hugues, 30, 45
Capitão-do-donatário, 40, 421
Captain general, 74, 75, 77, 78, 82, 97, 101
Caracas, Venezuela, 203, 208, 211, 263, 328, 370. *See also* Venezuela

Carcavelos, Portugal, 138, 139, 175, 177-180, 184, 186, 190, 290, 380
Carlos, King of Portugal, 12, 78, 83, 84, 100, 116, 134, 136, 138-140, 183, 276
Carlota Joaquina, Queen of Portugal, 76, 77
Carob, 54
Carthaginians, 28, 29
Carvalho, Bishop Manuel Afonso de, 248
Carvalho Araujo (ship), 59, 74, 118, 134, 224, 246, 266, 284, 421
Casablanca, Morocco, 134, 142
Castelo Branco, Fayal, 82, 240
Castex, Louis, 202
Castro, Dom João de, 137
Cattell, Lucinda Ann, 325
"The Cedars," Horta, 163, 167, 173, 174, 182, 274
Cedros, Fayal, 50
Celts, 29, 44, 45
Cemeteries, 65
Censorship, 198, 397
Cerchione, Angelo J., 438
Cerejeira, Manuel Cardinal, 282, 288
Chamarrita, 412
Chambers, Emma (Mrs. Edward C. Jones), 149, 150
Chambers, Hugh, 149
Charco da Madeira, São Miguel, 221
Charlemagne, 30
Charles I, Emperor, 77, 260, 261
Charles the Bold, Duke of Burgundy, 52
Charlestown, Massachusetts, 153
Chateaubriand, Vicomte François René de, 266
Chaves, Afonso, 141
Chelsea, Massachusetts, 401
Cherbourg, France, 189, 195
Chomsky, Noam, 394
Christ, Military Order of, 40, 117, 118, 261, 292
Churchill, Winston, 376
Cidade de Luanda (plane), 298
City of Paris I (ship), 179
Clemens, Samuel Langhorne, 130, 257
Cleopatra's Barge (ship), 129, 154
Clymer, R. Bruce, 411
Code, Administrative, 67, 68, 321

Code, Civil, 112
Code, New Civil, 108, 109, 305, 324
Colón, Diego, 40
Colonia, 396, 397
Columbus, Christopher, 40, 126, 211, 212, 425
"Columbus" (cable), 211, 212, 216, 227
Commercial Cable Co., 173, 177, 181-188, 197, 224, 272, 274, 275
Common Market. *See* European Communities
Communications Satellite Corporation, 215, 216, 218
Compagnia Italiana dei Cavi Telegrafici Sottomarini, 187, 188, 210, 269
Compagnie Française des Câbles Télégraphiques, 182, 185
Companhia de Diamantes de Angola, 358
Companhia Portuguesa Rádio Marconi, 191, 210-212, 216, 218, 219, 221, 223, 404
Companhia Portuguesa de Transportes Marítimos, 258, 264
Compañía Telefónica Nacional de España, 210
COMSAT. *See* Communications Satellite Corporation
Conceição, Horta, 33, 276, 307
Concordat of 1940, 285-288, 306, 348
Coney Island, New York, 140
Conglomerates, International. *See* Multinationals
Congress of Azorean Communities, 254
Congress of Communities of Portuguese Culture, 2nd, 357, 358
Congress on the History of Discoveries, 282, 331
Conil, Spain, 209-211, 221
Conscription, 12, 81, 328
Constitution of 1971, 309
Constitution of 1976, 15, 65, 88, 89, 91, 95, 98, 101, 105, 310, 321
Contraception. *See* Birth control
Cook, Captain James, 142, 143
Cordeiro, Joseph Cardinal, 290

Correia, Margarida Victória Jácome, 112, 379, 402
Correia, Natália, 112, 365
Corsica, 61, 129
Corte-Real, Miguel, 292, 322
Cortes-Rodrigues, Armando, 391
Corvi Marini, 23, 27
Costumes, Regional, 118, 412
Council of the Revolution, 89-91
Cousteau, Jacques, 42
Coutinho, Carlos Viegas Gago, 192
Coutinho, Bishop Fortunato da Veiga, 290
Coutinho, Paula, M.D., 387
CPRM. *See* Companhia Portuguesa Rádio Marconi
Criada, 114, 115, 250, 311, 321
Crimean War, 137
Crioulo, Cape Verdean, 336, 337
Crivo, 19, 152
Cross of Christ. *See* Christ, Military Order of
Crowninshield, George, Jr., 129, 154, 260
C.T.M. *See* Companhia Portuguesa de Transportes Marítimos
Cuba, 183, 204, 219, 229, 239
Cubana Airlines, 204, 206, 207, 239, 268
Cummings, Edwin Estlin, 326
Cunha, Paulo, 62
Cunningham, Charles, 156, 157, 160
Cunningham, Frederic, 157, 160
Curral das Freiras, Madeira, 53, 66
Curry, Field, 436
Cutileiro, José, 319

Dabney family, 122, 132, 136, 137, 146, 172, 184, 271, 279, 346, 365, 404
Dabney, Alfred Stackpole, 164
Dabney, Alfred Stackpole, Jr., 164
Dabney, Alice, 168
Dabney, Carl, 158, 159, 167
Dabney, Catherine Prescott, 161, 166
Dabney, Charles William (1794-1871), 13, 78, 150, 152, 154-158, 160, 163-167, 169, 170, 172, 173, 180, 272, 273, 372
Dabney, Charles William, Jr. (1823-1870), 157, 159, 160, 165, 169

Index 453

Dabney, Charles William (1867-1936), 168
Dabney, Clara (1820-1904), 168
Dabney, Edith, 167
Dabney, Ellen, 168, 170
Dabney, Emmeline (Mrs. Adam Paterson, later Mrs. John Ward Gurley Stackpole), 154, 155
Dabney, Frances Alsop ("Fan," Mrs. George Stewart Johonnot Oliver), 158, 165-167
Dabney, Frances Susan, 168-170
Dabney, Francis Oliver ("Frank"), 163, 165
Dabney, Frederick, 154-156, 164-167
Dabney, Frederick, Jr. ("Fritz"), 164, 165
Dabney, Frederick Lewis, 164
Dabney, Frederick Lewis, Jr., 164
Dabney, George Bigelow, 164
Dabney, George Stackpole, 164
Dabney, Herbert, 168
Dabney, John Bass, 108, 150, 151, 153, 154, 156, 166, 167
Dabney, John Lewis, 167
Dabney, John Pomeroy, 157-161, 163, 166-168, 170, 174, 274
Dabney, Lewis Stackpole, 164
Dabney, Mary Oliver Alsop ("May," Mrs. Walter Boreham), 169
Dabney, Nancy (Mrs. João Maria de Avelar Brotero), 109, 153
Dabney, Olivia, 154, 155, 161
Dabney, Olivia Frederica, 78, 151, 155, 159, 168
Dabney, Ralph Pomeroy, 169
Dabney, Rose (2nd Mrs. John Malcolm Forbes), 122, 168, 169
Dabney, Roxalina (Mrs. Charles Cunningham), 156, 157, 435
Dabney, Roxana Lewis, 13, 80, 82, 151, 156-159, 161, 165, 166, 168-172, 257, 398
Dabney, Samuel Wyllys, 138, 150, 159, 162, 163, 166-168, 170, 172, 372
Dabney, Sarah Hickling ("Sally," 1861-1930), 168, 170
Dabney, Susan Heard Oliver ("Zay," Mrs. John Beevor), 166, 169
Dabney, Walter, 164
Dabney, William Henry, 153, 154, 156, 159, 167, 168

Dana, Edward, 172
DAT. *See* Deutsch-Atlantische . . .
Davis, Captain Jacob Samuel, 168
Delgado, General Humberto, 67
Denny, Sir Anthony Coningham de Waltham, 269
Density, Population, 267, 333
Dentists, 365-367
Déolen, France, 183, 185
Desertas, Madeiras, 26, 36
Desquite, 320
Deutsch-Atlantische Telegraphengesellschaft, 181-184, 187, 196, 272-274
Development Plans, 62, 120, 239, 240, 245, 247, 252
Dexter, Franklin, 157
Dexter, George Minot, 435
Diário da República, 95, 112
Diário do Governo, 95
Dias de Melo, 330, 402
Dighton Rock, 293, 322
Dillenz, Lilli, 195
Dinis, King of Portugal, 117
Diniz, Júlio, 169, 420
Diogo, Duke of Viseu, 40
Discover (verb), 26
Divorce, 285, 304, 320
Dixie Clipper (plane), 196
D'Mello, Bishop Leo, 290
Dominica, 127
Donatário, 39, 40, 43, 421
dos Passos, Benjamin Franklin Pierce, 325
dos Passos, Cyril Franklin, 326
Dos Passos, John Randolph, 325, 326
Dos Passos, John Roderigo, 258, 294, 326, 393
dos Passos, Manuel Joaquim, 258, 325
Double Centenary, 294
Dow Chemical Company, 252
DO-X (plane), 195
D'Souza, Archbishop Eugene, 290
Duarte, King of Portugal, 25, 39, 43, 300
Duarte Nuno, Duke of Braganza, 84
Dunbar, Anna Lowell, 168
Dunn, Admiral, 131
Dutra, Jorge, 43
Dyer, U.S.S. (ship), 9, 132

Eanes, General António Ramalho, 15, 16, 93, 94, 98

Eastern and Associated Telegraph Companies, 177, 179
Eastern Telegraph Co., 177, 179, 181, 184-186, 188, 275
Eça de Queiroz, José Maria de, 420
Edward VII, King of England, 84
Edward Cary (ship), 130
E.I.N. *See* Emprêsa Insulana...
Elections. *See* Voting
Elizabeth Islands, Massachusetts, 28. 150
Emancipation, 324
Emden, Germany, 140
Emerson, Amelia Forbes. *See* Forbes, Amelia
Emprêsa Insulana de Navegação, 258, 266
Escudeiro, Bishop Aurélio Granada, 248, 249
Espírito Santo. *See* Holy Ghost
Esquipa, 307
Estepona, Spain, 209
Etam, West Virginia, 215, 216, 219
Étatisme, 117, 423
Ethnic studies, 310, 419
Ethnic-heritage studies, 310, 341, 419, 420
Europa (ship), 195
Europe & Azores Telegraph Co., 172, 181, 184, 185, 272, 273, 372
European Communities, 52, 251, 253

Fado, 55, 116, 413
Faeroe Islands, 23
Faia, 27, 154
Fajã de Cima, São Miguel, 221
Falder, Sarah (2nd Mrs. Thomas Hickling), 145, 146
Falessi, Cesare, 437
Fall River, Massachusetts, 165, 221, 222, 288, 292, 293, 331, 341, 382, 385, 392, 400
Family planning. *See* Birth control
FAMOUS. *See* French-American Mid-Ocean...
Far Rockaway, New York, 183-185
Fátima, Portugal, 295, 301, 302
Fayal Ranch, California, 151
Fayal wine, 143, 151
Federal Communications Commission, 225, 226
Fell, Howard Barraclough, 29
Fenais, São Miguel, 409

Fernandes, Archbishop Angelo Innocent, 290
Fernandes, Bishop Joseph, 290
Fernando, Duke of Viseu, 39, 40
Fernando de Noronha, 142, 187, 189, 193
Ferreira, José Manuel de Medeiros, 113
Ferro. *See* Hierro
Fidalgo, 114, 169, 302
Figueiredo, General Galvão de, 94
Fisher family, 136, 137, 323
FLA. *See* Frente de Libertação dos Açores
FLAMA. *See* Frente de Libertação do Arquipélago da Madeira
Flama (magazine), 245
Flamengos, Fayal, 17, 43, 44
Flanders, 17, 40, 43, 44, 48, 50, 51, 53, 101, 279, 300, 388, 406
Flemings. *See* Flanders
Fogo, Cape Verde Islands, 27, 30
Folares, 300, 415
Fontes, Vital Ferreira, 113-115, 123
Forbes, Amelia (Mrs. Raymond Emerson), 173, 435
Forbes, John Malcolm, 149, 168, 173
Forbes, John Murray, 149, 150, 154
Forbes, Captain Robert Bennet, 150
Forbes, Rose Dabney. *See* Dabney, Rose
Foreign trade zone, 238, 254
Formigas, Azores, 26, 266
Fort Ninigret, Rhode Island, 211
Fowler, Hilton L., M.D., 382, 385, 386, 414
France: French on Flores, 46, 102, 226, 228, 230, 239, 372
Francis I, Emperor, 76
Franco, Francisco, 214
Franklin, Benjamin, 134
Frayão, Otília, 53
"Fredonia," Horta, 155-158, 163, 166, 167, 170, 172, 181, 182, 273, 371
Fredonia (ship), 152, 166, 172. *See also Azor*
Freedom House, 98
Freitas Henriques, Manuel Borges de. *See* Borges...
French-American Mid-Ocean Underseas Study, 35, 46
Frente de Libertação do Arquipélago da Madeira, 14, 91
Frente de Libertação dos Açores, 14,

Index 455

91, 92, 101, 102, 252, 387
Friedrich III, Emperor, 300, 301, 411
Friesenland (ship), 196
Frutuoso, Father Gaspar, 45, 277, 392, 394
Funchal (ship), 82, 267
Furnas, São Miguel, 32, 146, 147, 256, 262, 264, 268, 299, 321, 423

Galápagos Islands, 220
Galfund, Allan, 439
Galhardo, Fernando José Pereira, 439
Galvão, Henrique, 225
Gama, Paulo da, 73
Gama, Vasco da, 73, 126, 292
General Armstrong (ship), 132, 153
"General Education," 255, 343, 368, 424
Generation of 1870, 177
Genetics, 314, 380ff.
Geothermal energy, 254
Ginêtes, São Miguel, 45
Glaser, Edward, 429
Gloucester, Massachusetts, 125
Godinho, Lisa M., 428, 437
Góis, Bento de, S. J., 391
Góis, José Graciano Mendes de, 221
Gomera, Canary Islands, 126
Gomes, Bishop António Ferreira, 290
Gonçalves, Nuno, 291, 420
Goonhilly Downs, England, 211
Gordon, Adam Lindsay, 399
Goulart de Medeiros family, 173
Gouveia, Horácio Bento de, 391, 394-397
Gracias, Valerian Cardinal, 290, 295
Graf Spee (ship), 193
Graf Zeppelin (airship), 193
Graffiti, 35, 92, 102
Gran Canaria, Canary Islands, 23, 24, 134, 193, 211, 214, 216
Grandgent, Charles Hall, 299
Greaves, Manuel, 404
Green, Sarah (1st Mrs. Thomas Hickling), 145
Green Hill, Rhode Island, 209-211, 215, 221
Greenhorn, 115
Greenland, 23
Grenville, Sir Richard, 128
Guaçu, 28
Guadeloupe, 46
Guanches, 24, 101

Guiterman, Vida Lindo, 169
Gulbenkian Foundation, 19, 293, 372, 386, 392, 393
Gulf Stream, 127
Gygax, Catherine, 271
Gypsies, 48

Habsburg Family, 260, 261
Haddon Larry, 271
Haiti, 180, 183
Haley, Garnet, 439
Halifax, Nova Scotia, 185, 222
Hammels, New York, 186, 187, 190, 192
Hanke, Lewis, 344
Harbinger (ship), 151, 157
Hartford, Connecticut, 130, 257
Hathaway, Charles, 168
Hathaway, Emma B., 168
Hawaii, 13, 88, 90, 91, 179, 301, 395, 409
Hayward, California, 381
Healy, George Peter Alexander, 165
Helicopter, 99, 265
Henri Poincaré (ship), 46, 229
Henriques, Manuel Borges de Freitas. *See* Borges . . .
Hewitson, William Hepburn, 135
Hickling family, 136, 137, 153, 156, 157, 172, 271, 279
Hickling, Amelia Clementina (Mrs. Hugh Chambers, later Mrs. Thomas Nye, Jr.), 146, 147, 149, 150, 160-162, 168, 435
Hickling, Catherine Green (Mrs. William Prescott), 145, 160, 161
Hickling, Elisabeth Flora (1st Mrs. William Ivens), 146
Hickling, Frances (Mrs. Joaquim António de Paula Medeiros), 146
Hickling, Harriet Frederica (Mrs. John White Webster), 146-149, 157-164
Hickling, Mary Ann (2nd Mrs. William Ivens), 146, 150, 160-162
Hickling, Thomas, 145, 146, 150, 173
Hickling, Thomas, Jr., 150, 164
Hierro, Canary Islands, 24
Higginson, Thomas Wentworth, 172, 173
Hindman, David H., 440
Hodgkin, Thomas, M.D., 384
Holy Ghost, 248, 297, 299, 300, 302, 303, 414

Homosexuals, 106
Hoppin, Martha Jay, 165
Hoppin, Thomas Frederick, 165
Horta Swell (newspaper), 198
Hotel de São Pedro, Ponta Delgada, 118, 124, 131, 146, 159, 162, 268
Houghton, H. N., 274
Hovercraft, 265
Howe, Marvine, 229, 350, 379
Howitt, Mary Botham, 169
Hunt, Leavitt, 165
Hunt, William Morris, 165, 166
Hurtere, Josse van. *See* Dutra, Jorge
Hydrangeas, 27, 35, 264
Hydrofoil, 264

Iberia Air Lines of Spain, 203, 206
Iceland, 23, 199, 200, 203, 224, 237, 325, 425
al-Idrisi, Muhammad ibn Muhammad, 24, 29
Île de France (ship), 195
Illegitimacy, 305
Illiteracy, 345-347, 354, 367, 424
Imperial and International Communications, 177, 181, 185
Infant mortality, 374, 375, 379, 424
Innocent VIII, Pope, 282
Inquisition, 50
Instituto Superior Técnico. *See* University of Lisbon, Technical
INTELSAT. *See* International Telecommunications Satellite Organization
International Association of Universities, 50, 345
International Colloquia on Luso-Brazilian Studies, 344, 345, 416
International Commerce Center, 240, 252
International Joseph Diseases Foundation, 387
International Meridian Conference, 24, 142
International Telecommunications Satellite Organization, 216, 218, 219, 223
International Telephone and Telegraph Corp., 183, 212, 214, 218, 226, 227, 246
Io (ship), 151, 162

Ireland, 18, 55, 137, 183, 188, 323, 325, 423; Home Rule for, 179
Irmandade, 302
Isabel of Portugal, Duchess of Burgundy, 43, 52, 300
Italcable. *See* Compagnia Italiana . . .
ITT. *See* International Telephone and Telegraph Corp.
ITT World Communications, 210, 215, 218
Ivens, William, 146

Jacksonville, Illinois, 135, 153
Jácome de Bruges, 43
Jardim, Alberto João, 96, 419
Jarvis, William, 147, 159, 165
Jews, 49, 50, 106, 291. *See also* New Christians
John I, King of Portugal, 25, 43
John II, King of Portugal, 40, 282, 369, 411, 423
John VI, King of Portugal, 76, 77, 81, 129
John, Duke of Beja, 40
John of Gaunt, 43
Johnson, Lyndon Baines, 225
Joint Cable Station, Horta, 33, 38, 188, 273, 275
Joinville, Prince de, 155
Jones, Edward C., 149
Jones, Sarah (1st Mrs. John Malcolm Forbes), 149, 173
Joseph's disease. *See* Azorean disease

Kailes, Howard, 440
Kale soup, 248, 300, 413
Kalley, Robert Reid, 134
Kennedy, John. Fitzgerald, 84, 215, 225
Kolterman, Duane A., 428

Lacerda, Armando de, 344
Lagoa, São Miguel, 67
Lajes, Pico, 365, 371
Lajes, Terceira, 35, 46, 70, 78, 136, 189, 197, 200-204, 223, 226, 227, 230, 231, 239, 253, 264, 305, 334, 371, 375
Las Palmas, Gran Canaria, 24, 134, 187, 203, 224, 263
L.A.T.I. *See* Linee Aeree Transcontinentali Italiane
Lauri Anna, 170

Index

Lawrenson, Helen Brown Norden, 305
Leacock family, 136, 257
Legname, 23, 27
Leonor, Queen of Portugal, 369
Leonor of Portugal, Empress, 300, 301, 411
Leste, 36
Levada, 46, 47, 395
Lewis, Alfred, 330, 401
Lewis, Roxa (Mrs. John Bass Dabney), 150, 155, 156, 166, 167
Liceu, 68, 75, 112, 182, 201, 275, 347
Lieutenant de Vaisseau de Paris (plane), 196
Lima (ship), 246, 266
Lincoln, Abraham, 135
Lindbergh, Anne Morrow, 195
Lindbergh, Charles Augustus, 161, 195
Linee Aeree Transcontinentali Italiane, 193, 195
Linguiça, 300, 413, 414, 420
Linschoten, Jan Huygen van, 73
Lipari, Aeolian Islands, 149
Literatura de cordel, 408
Livermore, California, 381, 387
Livramento, São Miguel, 146
Longfellow, Henry Wadsworth, 79, 153, 184
Longfellow, Samuel, 153, 170
Loose, Fritz, 195
Lopes, Manuel, 179
Loran, 227, 228
Lothrop, Harriet Eleanor, 168
Lothrop, Thomas Jackson, 164, 165
Louis XIV, King of France, 90
Louis XVII, King of France, 45
Louis-Philippe, King of France, 155
Lourenço Marques (plane), 296, 298
Low, Harriet, 129
Lowell, Amy, 171
Lufthansa German Airlines, 193, 196
Luís, Infante Dom (16th century), 137
Luís, King of Portugal, 17, 113, 134, 156, 175, 178
Lusitania, 29, 87, 291
Lusitania (ship), 87
Lusus, 291

Macao, 41, 42, 60, 87, 94, 99, 112, 129, 288, 291, 293
Machado, General, 132
Machado disease. *See* Azorean disease
Machico, Madeira, 29, 40, 372
Machin, Robert, 29, 410
Mackay, Clarence H., 185, 186
Mackay, John W., 185
Madalena, Pico, 156, 264, 329, 365, 371, 397
Madeira wine, 42, 136, 148, 178, 237
Madison, Wisconsin, 202
Magalhães, Jacinto de, M.D., 387, 414
Málaga, Spain, 187-189, 209
Manhattan Beach, New York, 140, 182, 183, 185, 188, 190
Manuel I, King of Portugal, 40, 292
MAPA. *See* Movimento ...
March of Dimes Foundation, 382
Marconi, Guglielmo, 191, 404
Maria I, Queen of Portugal, 76
Maria II, Queen of Portugal, 78, 79, 156
Maria Amélia, Queen of Portugal, 12, 83, 134, 136, 140, 276
Maria Ana of Braganza (1861-1942), 260
Maria Antónia of Braganza (1862-1959), 260, 261
Maria das Neves of Braganza (1852-1941), 260, 299
Maria Leopoldina, Queen and Empress, 76, 77, 129, 260
Maria Pia, Queen of Portugal, 17
Maria Teresa of Braganza (1855-1944), 260, 261
Marichal, Juan (Professor), 211
Marie of Burgundy, 53
Martha's Vineyard, Massachusetts, 28, 150, 232
Martinique, 31, 199, 200, 220
Mary and Susan (ship), 18
Mary Celeste (ship), 126
Maspalomas, Gran Canaria, 216
Massachusetts Historical Society, 150, 435
MAT-1, 209
Matanças, 408
Matos, José Maria Caetano de, M.D., 387
Matriz, Igreja, 74, 272, 276, 287, 307, 319

Maya, Captain Enrique Dantas, 296
Mediros, Humberto Cardinal, 80, 100, 296
Medeiros, Joaquim António de Paula, 146, 148
Melville, Herman, 30, 130
Mendes Pinto, Fernão, 420
Mermoz, Jean, 192, 268
Mesquita, Roberto de, 403
Michaëlis, Carolina (Mrs. Joaquim de Vasconcellos), 107
Middle class, 121, 122, 322, 405, 415
Middletown, Connecticut, 165
Midsummer Day. *See* St. John the Baptist
Midwives, 304, 314, 373, 378, 379
Migrant workers, 92, 231, 248, 251, 327, 362
Miguel of Braganza, Dom (1802-1866), 76-82, 85, 86, 260, 261, 285
Miguel, Duke of Viseu, 86
Miguel, Colonel Lino, 94
Military service. *See* Conscription
Mindelo, São Vicente, 178-180, 184, 186, 187, 189, 190
Minister of the Republic, 39, 90, 91, 94, 96, 97, 99
Miscegenation, 46, 49
Misericórdia, Santa Casa da, 74, 369-372
Missionary Agreement of 1940, 283, 288
Mistério, 30, 266
Monjardino, Álvaro, 95
Monte, Madeira, 260, 301, 372
Monte Christo (ship), 159
Monteiro, Armando, 438
Montreal, Quebec, 264, 413
Moors, 28, 48-50, 54, 56, 291, 292, 413
Morgado, 114, 115, 302
Moriconi, Rino, 441
Moriscos, 49
Morison, Samuel Eliot, 51, 130, 161
Morize, André, 198
Morley, S. Griswold, 397
Morris, Mrs. Lewis G. *See* Stewart, Anita
Movimento de Autodeterminação do Povo dos Açores, 91
Mowrer, Edgar Ansell, 198

Multinationals, 102, 227, 252, 253, 302
Mutual-aid associations, 316. *See also* Misericórdia

Nantucket, Massachusetts, 28, 127, 130, 151, 183, 232, 233
Napoleon I, 42, 53, 63, 76, 77, 118, 279, 344, 346
NASA. *See* National Aeronautics and Space Administration
Natal, Brazil, 192, 193, 199, 203, 268
National Aeronautics and Space Administration, 214, 216, 220
National Genetics Foundation, 381
National Geographic Society, 30
NATO. *See* North Atlantic Treaty Organization
Naushon, Elizabeth Islands, 150, 152
Nautical mile: defined, 11
Nazis, 86, 177, 183, 188, 193, 199, 200, 407
NC-4 (plane), 192, 195
Nemésio, Vitorino, 397
New Bedford, Massachusetts, 17-19, 121, 130, 133, 134, 149, 151, 156, 165, 168, 178, 222, 224, 271, 288, 298, 300, 330, 331, 341, 379, 382, 413, 422
New Christians, 49, 50. *See also* Jews
New England Historic Genealogical Society, 435
New England Journal of Medicine, 383, 387
Newport, Rhode Island, 86, 127, 151, 165
Nicholas V, Pope, 300
Nicknames, 114
Niemeyer, Oscar, 259
Nixon, Richard Milhous, 45, 132, 226, 227, 245, 286
Nordeste, São Miguel, 67, 370
Norfolk Island pine, 163, 273
Norsemen, 23
North Atlantic Treaty Organization, 11, 46, 102, 131, 132, 208, 223, 224, 229
North Easton, Massachusetts, 18
Norton, Bettina A., 435
Nuncio, 284, 285

Index

Nurses, 373, 378
Nye, Amelia H. *See* Hickling, Amelia Clementina
Nye, Eliza Williams (Mrs. Charles Hathaway, later Mrs. Edward Dana), 149, 150, 168, 172
Nye, Thomas, Jr., 149, 160
Nyhan, William L., M.D., 381, 382, 387

Oak Bluffs, Martha's Vineyard, 422
Oakland, California, 381
Obsidian, 149
Ocarina, 391
Oddone, O., 437
Oidium, 131, 136, 167
Oliver, Francis Johonnot, 158
Oliver, George Stewart Johonnot, 158, 159, 166, 167
Oliver, Susan Heard (Mrs. Charles William Dabney, Jr.), 158, 159, 166
Opus Dei, 307, 344
Orleans, Massachusetts, 183
Otto of Habsburg, Archduke, 77, 261

Pacheco, Cristiano Frazão, 224
Padrão, 293
Palheiro, 36, 236
Palo, Italy, 209
Pan American World Airways, 29, 68, 86, 173, 195-198, 224, 261, 275
Parade (magazine), 229, 432
Parker, Mary Anne Dabney (Mrs. William Henry Dabney), 159
Parkman, Rev. Francis (1788-1852), 158, 159
Parkman, Francis (1823-1893), 158, 161
Parkman, George, M.D., 160, 161, 170, 171
Patronage, 70, 313, 316
Paul II, Pope, 300
Paul III, Pope, 301
Paul VI, Pope, 295
Pavão, José de Almeida, 401
Paxeco, Oscar, 84
Pedro the Traveler, Prince, 25, 39, 43, 300
Pedro IV, King of Portugal, 76-82, 85, 86, 153, 155, 260, 285

Pedro V, King of Portugal, 134
Pedro I, Emperor of Brazil. *See* Pedro IV, King of Portugal
Pedro II, Emperor of Brazil, 78, 79
Peixoto, José Pinto, 434
PENCAN-1, 227
PENCAN-2, 211, 221, 227
PENCAN-3, 211, 227
Pentecost. *See* Holy Ghost
Penzance, England, 184, 185
People-to-People program, 202, 239, 273, 372
Pepperell, Massachusetts, 164
Pereira, Bishop Peter B., 290
Perestrelo, Bartolomeu, 40
Pérez, Félix Izquierdo, 438
Perfiliation, 305
Peripheral doctors, 369
Perkins, Louisa Dumeresq (Mrs. William Morris Hunt), 165, 166
Pessoa, Fernando, 391, 420
Pharmacists, 376-378
Philip I, II, and III, Kings of Portugal, 52, 83
Philip the Good, Duke of Burgundy, 43, 300
Philippa of Lancaster, 43
Philippines, 83, 84
Phoenicians, 28
Phoenix Foundation, 252
Phylloxera, 131, 136, 167
Picasso, Pablo, 404
PIDE. *See* Polícia Internacional e de Defesa do Estado
Pill, the. *See* Birth control
Pilot, The, 19
Pinedo, Francesco de, 195
Pirates, 53
Pittoni, Aldo, 437
Pius XII, Pope, 301
Plato, 28
Pliny the Elder, 24
Plymouth, England, 127, 192
Polícia Internacional e de Defesa do Estado, 59
Polígono, 229
Pomeroy, Frances Alsop (1797-1862, Mrs. Charles William Dabney), 155, 158, 163, 165-167, 170, 258
Pompidou, Georges, 46, 132, 226, 245
Ponta Comprida, Fayal, 30

Ponta Delgada, Madeira, 372
Ponta Delgada, São Miguel: earth station, 219, 221-223, 253
Ponta Delgada (ship), 264
Ponta do Castelo, Santa Maria, 88
Ponta do Sol, Madeira, 325-327
Porthcurno, England, 175, 178, 184, 185, 192
Port of Spain, Trinidad, 135, 203
Porto Judeu, Terceira, 49
Porto Moniz, Madeira, 372
Porto Novo, Madeira, 211, 227
Porto Pim, Horta, 65, 138, 156
Porto Santo: airport, 102, 208, 263, 328, 370, 371
Portuguese-language press in U.S., 46, 100, 207, 249, 252, 422
Postage stamps, 36, 58, 61, 82, 281, 285
Povoação, São Miguel, 67, 287, 370
Praia, Graciosa, 318
Praia, Santa Maria, 380
Praia, Santiago, 61, 179, 180, 293
Praia da Vitória, Terceira, 35, 77, 78, 101, 371, 375, 380
Praia do Almoxarife, Fayal, 380
Praia do Norte, Fayal, 30
Praia do Pópulo, São Miguel, 268, 380
Prainha de Cima, Pico, 402
Prescott, Catherine Elizabeth (Mrs. Franklin Dexter), 157
Prescott, Edward Goldsborough, 157
Prescott, William, 145
Prescott, William Hickling, 145, 147, 157, 160, 163
Prevailing westerlies, 26, 28, 126
Prime meridian, 24, 141, 142
Princess Alice Bank, 138
Príncipe Perfeito (ship), 357
Prostitutes, 304
Proverbs, 410
Provincetown, Massachusetts, 125
Ptolemy, Claudius, 24, 141, 296
Puerto de la Cruz, Tenerife, 24, 119
Puerto Rico, 48, 203, 254, 417, 419
Pumice, 149
Purcell, Joanne B., 408
Purrington-Russell panorama, 130
Puzo, Mario, 313

Quaker City (ship), 130, 257

Quental, Antero de, 177, 392, 397, 420

Rabo de Peixe, São Miguel, 288
Raca, 29, 30
Racism, 123, 253
Raleigh, Sir Walter, 53
Ray, Joseph Edward, 130
RCA Global Communications, 210, 215, 218
Rebelo, Domingos, 404
Recife, Brazil, 138, 178, 179, 189, 190, 192, 199, 211
Reina, Luís, 353
Reis, Maria Amália Pitta Pestana dos (Mrs. Cyril Franklin dos Passos), 327
Reis Leite, José Guilherme, 136, 323
Rennes, France, 46
Resende, Bishop Sebastião Soares de, 290
Restaurante típico, 413, 414
Revolt, 14, 82, 85, 179, 225
Ribeira dos Flamengos, Fayal, 43, 276
Ribeira dos Flamengos, Terceira, 43
Ribeira Grande, São Miguel, 30, 67, 370
Ribeirinha, Fayal, 116, 195
Richardson, Henry Hobson, 18
Rocha, Ana Maria, 447
Rocha, Gregory F., Jr., 440
Rockaway, New York, 192
Rockaway Beach, New York, 186
Rodrigues, Amália, 413
Rodrigues, Emanuel do Nascimento dos Santos, 95
Rogers, Captain John, 18, 125
Roosevelt, Franklin Delano, 9, 132, 133, 136, 199, 201, 252
Rosa, João da. *See* Rogers, Captain John
Rosa, Father Júlio da, 68, 270
Rosenberg, Roger N., M.D., 381, 382, 387
Rosto de Cão, São Miguel, 144, 146, 159
Rothschild, Baron Henri de, 138
Roxbury, Massachusetts, 159, 166
Russia. *See* Soviet Union
Ryan, George E., 19
Rynne, Xavier, 289, 290

Sabrina, Azores, 53

Index 461

Sacadura Freire Cabral, Artur de, 192
Sagres (ship), 117
St. Anthony of Padua, 299
St. Antony the Egyptian, 299
St. Brendan, 23, 28, 29
Saint-Exupéry, Antoine de, 192
St. Helena (island), 73, 142, 177, 184, 211
St. Hilaire de Riez, France, 210, 225
St. John the Baptist, 52, 78, 298, 395
St. Julian's School, Carcavelos, 177, 179
St. Paul, 109
St. Peter, 422
St. Sebastian, 299
St. Sylvester, 298
St. Thomas the Apostle, 293
St. Vincent, 293
Sal, Cape Verde Islands, 193, 203, 204, 206, 207, 212, 229
Salem, Massachusetts, 129, 260, 271, 288
Salina, Aeolian Islands, 262
Salvages. *See* Selvagens
San Fernando, Spain, 211
San Joaquin Valley, California, 248, 299, 329, 359
San Leandro, California, 381
San Zorzi, 23, 27
Sandwich Islands. *See* Hawaii
Santa Bárbara, Santa Maria, 306
Santa Clara Valley, California, 359
Santa Cruz, Flores, 46, 228, 247, 372
Santa Cruz, Graciosa, 371
Santa Cruz, Madeira, 227, 241, 259, 263, 370, 372
Santa Cruz, Tenerife, 119, 211
Santa Cruz (plane), 298
Santa Maria: airport, 67, 136, 140, 197, 200, 202-204, 206, 224, 253, 264, 306, 347, 370
Santa Maria (ship), 225, 298, 328, 330
Santa Maria (plane), 298
Santana, Madeira, 372
Santiago, Cape Verde Islands, 60, 61, 180, 293
Santo Antão, Cape Verde Islands, 179, 299
Santo Cristo, 297, 301, 302, 404

Santo da Serra, Madeira, 42
Santo Espírito, Santa Maria, 306
São Miguel Arcanjo, Pico, 83
São Pedro, Santa Maria, 306
São Roque, Pico, 74
São Sebastião, Terceira, 304
São Vicente, Cape Verde Islands, 138, 177-179
São Vicente, Madeira, 372, 393
SAT–1, 207, 211, 212, 216, 222, 227
SATA. *See* Sociedade Açoreana...
Saudade, 44, 115, 169, 171
Schlesien (ship), 188
Schwabenland (ship), 193, 196
Scramble for Africa, 142, 180
Sebastianism, 116
Selandia (ship), 133
Selvagens, Madeiras, 26, 30, 57
Seminary, Catholic, 287, 351
Sepoy Rebellion, 175
Sesimbra, Portugal, 209-212, 216, 221, 222
Sete Cidades, São Miguel, 28, 32, 146, 410
Sicily, 24, 29, 42, 52, 55, 56, 154, 313
Silva, Rose Marie, 381, 385
Silveira, Carlos Manuel Ramos da, 438
Silveira, Guilherme da, 43
Silveira, Pedro da, 184, 399, 400, 403, 446
Silveira, Edwards & Company, Horta, 180
Simão, José Veiga. *See* Veiga Simão, José
Simões, João Gaspar, 113, 399
Sintra, Portugal, 218, 219, 221, 222
Sirène (ship), 155
Sister cities: Angra/Tulare, 299
"Situation," 284, 303
Slaves, 46, 49, 50, 155. *See also* Blacks
Slocum, Joshua, 130
Smith, Nancy Clark, 19, 308
Smith, Robert Chester, Jr., 308
Soares, Mário, 15, 16, 59, 89, 94, 97, 100, 112, 113, 345, 378
Social Security, U.S., 249, 316
Sociedade Açoreana de Transportes Aéreos, 236, 240, 265, 266, 270, 372
South African Airways, 207, 229

Soviet Union, 11, 46, 58, 102, 214, 219, 239, 253, 263, 268, 290, 302
Spanish Civil War, 186
Spínola, General António Sebastião de, 81, 87, 286
Spray (ship), 130
Springfield, Illinois, 135, 153
Stackpole, Roxana (Mrs. Frederick Dabney), 155, 164, 165
Standard Telephones and Cables, 227, 439
Starke, Rolf, 195
Statute for the Autonomous Districts of the Adjacent Islands, 63, 65, 67, 68, 87, 88, 90
Stern, H., 259
Stewart, Anita (Duchess of Viseu, later Mrs. Lewis G. Morris), 86
Stone, Irving, 135
Stone & Webster, 33, 188, 268, 273
Stonington, Connecticut, 18
Streit, Clarence K. *See* Atlantic Union
Stuart, Gilbert, 170
Suassuna, Ariano, 289
Sullivan, Judge Robert, 161, 171
Superstition, 306, 410
Survey of the Portuguese Economy, 120, 240
Swain, W. W., 150, 152

Taft, Donald Reed, 386
TAP. *See* Transportes Aéreos ...
TAT–1, 225
TAT–2, 225
TAT–3, 225, 226
TAT–4, 225, 226
TAT–5, 209-212, 221
TAT–6, 210, 211
Taunton, Massachusetts, 18, 164
Tavares, Bishop Paulo José, 288
Taxation, 12, 42, 81, 82, 231, 252-254, 328
Technical University of Lisbon. *See* University of Lisbon, Technical
Teixeira, Tristão Vaz, 40
O Telégrafo (newspaper), 85, 180, 198
Telegraph Construction and Maintenance Co., 180
Television, 215, 216, 220, 221, 223, 271, 315, 335, 398
Tenerife, Canary Islands, 23, 119, 127, 154, 167, 193, 207, 211
Tennyson, Alfred, 128
Terra Cha, Terceira, 368
Terra family, 43, 166, 398
Terreiro da Luta, Madeira, 260
Teyde, Pico de, Tenerife, 23, 30
Thomson, Helen, 171
Thoreau, Henry David, 400
Three Kings, Feast of the. *See* Twelfth Night
Three Marias, 110, 111
Toledo, Ohio, 166
Tomás, Admiral Américo Dias Rodrigues, 67, 75, 81, 82, 348
Trade winds, 11, 25, 126, 134, 260
Trails: Cable, 189, 272, 276; Fisher/Amory, 137, 272; Hickling, 146, 272
Transportes Aéreos Portugueses, 99, 107, 203, 207, 240, 263, 266, 270, 296, 298, 328, 370, 371
Trans World Airlines, 203, 224, 270
Trinidad, 135, 212, 400
Trinity Church in the City of Boston, 162
Trinity House, Horta, 38, 184, 188, 272, 273, 275
Tuberculosis, 268, 371
Tuckerton, New Jersey, 225
Tulare, California, 299
TWA. *See* Trans World Airlines
Twain, Mark. *See* Samuel Langhorne Clemens
Twelfth Night, 119, 297, 408

Union Now. *See* Atlantic Union
United Nations, 41, 42, 58, 85, 132, 133, 216, 219, 221, 252, 253, 359
United States (ship), 18
University of Coimbra, 50, 107, 345, 357
University of La Laguna, Tenerife,
University of Lisbon, Catholic, 359
University of Lisbon, Classical, 107, 122, 344, 345, 359, 397
University of Lisbon, Free, 359
University of Lisbon, New, 359
University of Lisbon, Technical, 50, 359
University of Oporto, 345
University-level Institute of the Azores, 102, 121, 227, 252, 338, 360, 361, 368, 392, 399, 401

Index

University-level Institute of the Madeiras, 102, 121, 338, 360, 361, 392, 399
U.S. Department of State, 151, 332
U.S. National Ocean Survey, 229
U.S. National Oceanic and Atmospheric Administration, 127
U.S.S.R. *See* Soviet Union

Vale Formoso, Fayal, 31
Van der Haghe, Willem. *See* Silveira, Guilherme da
Vanderbilt, Consuelo, 320
Vargas, Getúlio, 90, 345
Variation, Compass, 137, 141
Varthema, Ludovico de, 73
Vasconcellos, Joaquim de, 107
Vatican Council II, 287-290, 295, 297, 310, 415
Veiga Simão, José, 356-360
Velas, São Jorge, 33, 34, 330, 371
Venereal disease, 319
Venezuela, 92, 203, 211, 212, 327, 328, 359, 376, 395, 424, 425. *See also* Caracas
Vera Cruz (ship), 298, 331
Versailles, Treaty of, 184
Veterinarians, 201
Vetterling, Mary-Anne (Lee), 447
Vickers-Armstrong antiaircraft guns, 404
Victória, Margarida. *See* Correia, Margarida Victória Jácome
Vieira, Rui, 262, 394
Vieira da Silva, Maria Helena, 420
Vienna, Austria, 77, 260
Vila do Porto, Santa Maria, 67, 68, 104, 245, 306, 307, 312, 352, 354, 370
Vila Franca do Campo, São Miguel, 33, 67, 370, 391
Ville de Saint Pierre (plane), 196
Vintras, Roland Eugene, 201
Viseu, Duchess of. *See* Stewart, Anita
Vitória, Graciosa, 127
Viveiros, Carlton M., 331
Vocational education, 103, 273, 343, 348, 349, 355, 424
Voting, 67, 70, 71, 89, 95, 98, 107

Walters, Vernon A., 200
Washington, D.C., 24, 90, 101, 202, 216, 229, 252
Watertown, Massachusetts: Sacred Heart Parish, 287
Waterville, Ireland, 140, 183, 186
Webster family, 157, 172, 271
Webster, Catherine Prescott ("Kate," Mrs. Thomas Jackson Lothrop), 149, 158, 160-164, 168
Webster, Harriet Wainwright (Mrs. Samuel Wyllys Dabney), 149, 158, 159, 161-163, 167, 168, 170, 172
Webster, John White, M.D., 148, 157, 160, 161, 170-172
Webster, Marianne ("Mollie"), 149, 157, 158, 161-166
Webster, Sarah Hickling (1821-1909, Mrs. John Pomeroy Dabney), 149, 157-160, 163, 166-168, 170, 173, 274, 436
Welfare, 316
Western Telegraph Co., 179
Western Union International, 210, 215, 218
Western Union Telegraph Co., 33, 177, 186-190, 197, 218, 268, 269, 275
Westfalen (ship), 193
Weston, Frank Stanley, 437, 441
Whaling, 25, 65, 118, 127, 130, 133, 134, 138, 151-153, 171, 178, 180, 224, 237, 238, 329, 330, 365, 382, 396, 403
Whitman, Walt, 184
Widemouth, England, 222, 225
Widows, 67, 108, 320, 321
Wilcox, Captain Thomas, 18
Windmills, 44, 210, 406
Windsor, Treaty of, 43, 177
Winston, Captain William A., 173, 196
Wood, Ann, 439
Wood's Hole, Martha's Vineyard, and Nantucket Steamship Authority, 232, 422
Woodcock, Leonard, 252
World Health Organization, 314
Wouters, Lilliane, 429
Wylie, Laurence, 320

X-rays, 368, 413

Yachts, Transatlantic, 127-129, 272
Yankee Clipper (plane), 196

Yankee Hall, Furnas, 146, 147, 159, 264

Zacut, Abraham ben Samuel, 411

Zarco, João Gonçalves, 40
Zita, Empress, 261
Zurara, Gomes Eanes de, 41

Set in 11 point Baskerville (VIP) by New Hampshire Composition. Printed on 55 pound Gladfelter Offset (B-30) by Alpine Press. Bound in Holliston Roxite A50444 cloth by Alpine Press. Three-color jacket printed on 80 pound Mead Offset Enamel by Webster Print.

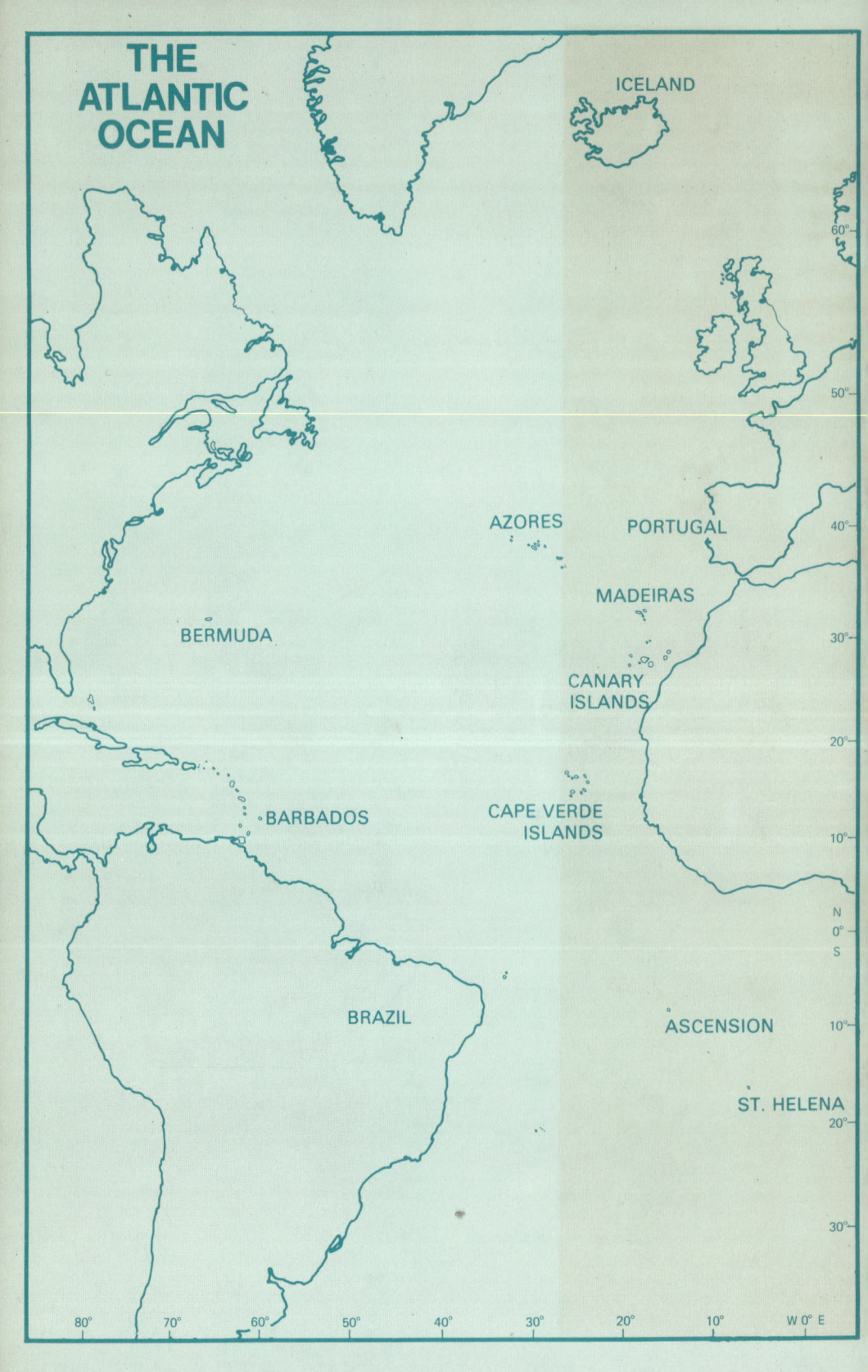